Colonial America

DISCOVER
HISTORIC
AMERICA
SERIES

Colonial America

A TRAVELER'S GUIDE

by

PATRICIA AND ROBERT FOULKE

A VOYAGER BOOK

The Globe Pequot Press

OLD SAYBROOK, CONNECTICUT

Photo credits: p. 2: Antiquarian & Landmarks Society, Hartford, Conn.; p. 34: Connecticut State Department of Economic Development; p. 68: copyright © Plimoth Plantation; p. 155: photo by John W. Corbett, courtesy The Preservation Society of Newport County; p. 345: photo by Clay Nolen, courtesy North Carolina Travel and Tourism Division. All others by the authors.

Cover and book design by Nancy Freeborn

Library of Congress Cataloging-in-Publication Data

Foulke, Patricia.
    Colonial America : a traveler's guide / by Patricia and Roubert Foulke. — 1st ed.
        p. cm. — (Discover historic America series)
    Includes bibliographical references and index.
    ISBN 1-56440-520-6 : $15.95
    1. United States—Guidebooks. 2. Historic sites—United States-Guidebooks.
3. United States—History—Colonial period, ca. 1600-1775.
I. Foulke, Robert, 1930- . II. Title. III. Series.
E158.F63 1994
917.404'2—dc20   94-36727
                                                CIP

Manufactured in the United States of America
First Edition/First Printing

Contents

Introduction *1*

New England

CONNECTICUT 9
   The Connecticut River Valley *13*
   Eastern Connecticut *21*
   The Long Island Sound Shore *31*
   Western Connecticut *36*

MAINE. 41
   Down East 46

MASSACHUSETTS 61
   Plymouth and the South Shore. 67
   Boston 83
   Salem and other North Shore Ports 93
   Central Massachusetts and the Berkshires. 103
   Cape Cod and the Islands. 107

NEW HAMPSHIRE. 115
   The New Hampshire Shore 119
   The Merrimack River Valley 126
   Western New Hampshire. 127

RHODE ISLAND. 131
   Providence Area 135
   East Bay 142
   Newport County. 147
   South County 157

VERMONT 163
   Lake Champlain 168
   Southern Vermont. 173

The Middle Atlantic

DELAWARE 181
    Delaware Bay Area 183
    The Delaware River Valley 187

MARYLAND 193
    St. Marys County 197
    Annapolis 200
    The Eastern Shore 206

NEW JERSEY 211
    Delaware River and Bay Settlements. 215
    The Pine Barrens. 217
    Revolutionary War Sites in Central New Jersey. . . 218

NEW YORK 225
    New York City. 230
    Long Island 234
    The Hudson River Valley 239
    Forts in the Adirondacks 246
    The Mohawk River Valley 257

PENNSYLVANIA. 263
    Philadelphia. 269
    Southeastern Pennsylvania 273
    The Susquehanna River Valley. 280
    Western Pennsylvania 285

Contents

The South

VIRGINIA 293
    Tidewater Virginia. 297
    Along the Potomac 306
    Jefferson's Charlottesville 314

GEORGIA 321
    Fort King George 324
    Savannah. 324
    Fort Frederica on St. Simons Island. 327
    Jekyll Island. 330

NORTH CAROLINA 331
    The Outer Banks. 335
    The Great Sounds 336
    The Piedmont. 342

SOUTH CAROLINA. 347
    Charles Towne 352
    Charleston. 352
    Beaufort 358
    Georgetown 361

FLORIDA. 363
    St. Augustine. 366

For Further Reading 371
Index 373

Acknowledgments

We are particularly grateful for the help of Tadahisa Kuroda, professor of history and associate dean of the faculty at Skidmore College. An old friend and colleague who specializes in the colonial period, Professor Kuroda provided extensive bibliographic aid and historic counsel for this book. He is not responsible for any errors and omissions, but he is an important source for whatever virtues it may contain.

Introduction

People who travel, walk through history, whether they are conscious of it or not. In this book we hope to enhance the pleasure of your travel along the Eastern seaboard by developing and refining a sense of place. Heightened awareness of what happened where we walk now and whose footsteps preceded ours satisfies not only curiosity but also a natural longing to be connected with our surroundings. Those who claim to live only in the present—a persistent myth in American popular culture—forget how disturbed they are when revisiting childhood sites that have changed almost beyond recognition. Constructing the past, and often idealizing it in the process, creates an orientation in time that is inseparable from the sense of place that defines who we are, both individually and collectively. Just as we rewrite our own internal autobiographies year by year, each generation recasts the past in its own molds.

Colonial history is a kaleidoscope of movement and change, but it is clearly tied to many places that remain. Rediscovering those places and expanding their meaning is the aim of this book. It is not designed for committed antiquarians or for those who reduce the past to a prologue of the present. It is designed for travelers with a persistent curiosity, people who like to build contexts around what they see. The book explores colonial sites, forts, government buildings, churches, inns, houses, historic districts, museums, and living history museums, as well as reenactments and festivals throughout the original thirteen British colonies and surrounding French and Spanish settlements. The area covered stretches from Machias, Maine, to St. Augustine, Florida, and the time span begins with the first colonies in Florida, North Carolina, and Virginia and ends with the Constitutional Convention of 1788.

Colonial America combines the features of travel guides and historical narratives to recreate the conditions and ambience of colonial life for travelers and armchair travelers alike. As avid armchair travelers ourselves, we hope to bring you a vivid sense of place, time, and character. You may enjoy reliving trips already taken, or you may be considering a new venture and want specific information on potential activities and sites within various regions.

1

Liberty Bell Pavilion in Philadelphia

Each chapter begins with a brief account of the founding and development of the colony. The focus then shifts to places that can still be seen by visitors who want to walk into their heritage to understand it better. That focus remains on specific places, linking each town and building or site with the events that occurred there, but the emphasis is less on memorializing important political and military events than on understanding the context in which they occurred, so the book includes much material on the social and cultural history of everyday life—architecture, clothing, food, transportation, occupations, religious practices, customs, folklore, and the like.

The idea of a quintessential colonial America is itself more a convenience for historians than a reality; in fact there were many disparate settlements that gradually and often reluctantly banded together for limited common purposes. Since the thirteen British colonies were quite diverse in topography and economic activity, with peoples drawn from different ethnic, regional, and religious traditions in Europe, the story has to be retold for each within the larger framework of American expansion. The process of their amalgamation lasted through the Revolution and beyond, eliciting much controversy and sometimes bumptious behavior. Regionalism, by no means dead today, persisted throughout the colonial era and blocked many attempts at cooperation among the colonies.

Also, many early European attempts to establish colonies in America were dismal failures, often because the entrepreneurs and adventurers who came were bent on exploiting the new land. Those with money to invest in shares were not used to hard work and often ill equipped for the rigors of living in the wilderness. Many of these failed ventures became footnotes in the history of colonization but a few, like the "Lost Colony" on Roanoke Island, are still widely remembered. Among the settlements that survived and prospered, some, like St. Mary's City in Maryland, were later abandoned as economic or political conditions changed. Permanence, order, and stability were envisioned in royal charters but seldom realized in the early history of colonies.

One of the destabilizing forces was the constant flow in and out of colonies. People uprooted from their European homelands to escape religious persecution, political suppression, or the devastation of wars continued to migrate within and between the colonies searching for better land or other opportunities. Many moved on simply to find a new place with topography reminiscent of their home regions, whether flatland, rolling hills, mountains, or river valleys. The cultural diversity that we prize today also fragmented American experience. Succeeding waves of immigrants— English Puritans, French Huguenots, Welsh Quakers, German Mennonites, Moravians, Lutherans, and Scotch-Irish Presbyterians—clung together in enclaves united by religious principles, ethnic origins, language, and folk traditions. They maintained their identity through forms of worship and customs from home—precious objects from the past, Christmas or festival decorations, and clothing worn on special occasions.

Colonial America, then, is no single fabric but a patchwork quilt of many pieces, each with its own distinctive character and design. As you explore its many wonderful places, keep an eye out for change, instability, transience, variety, and anomaly, and be prepared for surprises. During our research for this book, most of the generalizations we had harbored from American history courses were shattered, to be replaced by sharper images and a keener sense of the many stories that are never fully or conclusively told. When you discard preconceptions and look closely at the places you visit, you, too, will begin rewriting colonial history in your own mind.

First Settlements

1565 St. Augustine, Florida

1587 The "Lost Colony" on Roanoke Island, North Carolina

1607 Jamestown, Virginia

1620 Plymouth, Massachusetts

1623 Odiorne Point, New Hampshire

1625 Manhattan, New Amsterdam

1630 The Massachusetts Bay Colony

1634 St. Mary's City, Maryland

1635 Hartford, Connecticut

1636 Providence, Rhode Island

1638 New Sweden on the Delaware River

1653 Albemarle colony in North Carolina

1669 Charles Towne, South Carolina

1682 Philadelphia, Pennsylvania

1690 Chimney Point, Vermont, settled briefly

1720 Fort Dummer, near Brattleboro, Vermont

1733 Savannah, Georgia

TRIP PLANNING

We have grouped places you may want to visit geographically rather than chronologically, since you will be traveling in literal space and imaginative time. Each colony has its unique character, and we have tried to emulate that in order of presentation. Sometimes we chose to begin with the earliest settlement, branching out in various directions to follow people as they moved to new locations; in other cases we were more strictly geographical, according to patterns of migration.

In colonial times the sea was the primary means of migration, followed by long navigable rivers such as the Hudson and the Delaware and shorter ones like the Penobscot, Kennebec, Merrimack, Connecticut, Susquehanna, and Potomac. Settlement clung to these waterways throughout most of the seventeenth century and slowly moved to other inland areas with the development of roads during the eighteenth century. Even so, only small portions of the fifteen states established from thirteen British colonies had been settled before 1760.

Although the colonial settlements of particular interest are listed within their current states and grouped geographically, we cannot pretend to establish travel patterns that will match each reader's interests and timetable. We do not suggest stock itineraries that "cover" the colonial high points in any region, though any reader so inclined could construct one from this book. Most people will want to browse through a region without a rigid schedule, pausing to enjoy unexpected glimpses of daily life two or three centuries ago.

Your local library is a good source of information as you begin to plan a trip. For the latest updates contact the state tourist offices or local convention and visitors' bureaus that offer detailed maps of towns and regions, guides to historic sites, locations for outdoor recreation, and lists of accommodations and restaurants. For your convenience, we list addresses and telephones of state tourist offices, and they usually can provide full information on any region that interests you. Because many historic sites are manned by volunteer staff, their hours and seasons change frequently; the best source of current information is a state or local tourism office. Such offices also have calendars of festivals and special events that you may want to work into your travel plans. We list some of the traditional festivals, but their dates change and some are not held every year; it is always wise to write or call before you go.

ACCOMMODATIONS AND RESTAURANTS

In a country where plentiful wood was the primary building material, restricting suggestions for lodging and food to authentic colonial inns, B&Bs, and restaurants makes little sense because most of them have burned down; you would be out in the cold and hungry in many regions of historic interest. But you can find wonderful accommodations from former eras for an overnight stay if you are not too fussy about the date the structure was first built. This policy makes sense for another reason: Many inns and houses, especially in New England, grew with the trade or the family as addition by addition formed an elongated T at the back of the original square or rectangular structure. Restorers of such buildings have to decide which era will set the pattern. Architectural purists may reject the additions that keep the house alive and full of people, but social historians understand such processes of growth and adaptation. Discriminating travelers usually find Colonial, Federal, or Victorian lodgings preferable to larger but less interesting modern hotel and motel rooms, so we list the former, but never the latter unless there is a special reason to do so.

Restaurants present another problem not so easily resolved. Only a handful of inns have survived from the colonial era, and most of them serve a melange of contemporary cuisines with a few colonial specialties. Others listed are located in authentic historic buildings or have succeeded in recreating the ambience of former eras. Although we have at some time enjoyed a meal in the restaurants we list, in no case can we guarantee the current quality of the food: menus change by the season and the year, and good chefs are notoriously peripatetic. As the old saw says, "you take your chances when you walk through the door."

We do not pretend to be comprehensive in our suggestions for a pleasant place to spend the night or eat a good meal. We like the establishments we list but know there are many others of equal quality that we have not yet discovered. For your convenience, we list the phone and fax numbers of recommended inns, B&Bs, and restaurants so you can make reservations and get current information.

The hours listed in this guidebook were confirmed at press time.
We recommend, however, that you call establishments before traveling
to obtain current information.

New England

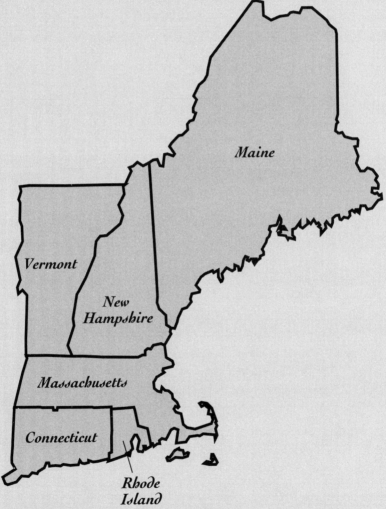

Maine

Vermont

New
Hampshire

Massachusetts

Connecticut

Rhode
Island

Connecticut

Historical Introduction to the
CONNECTICUT COLONY

*T*he Dutch were the first settlers to arrive in the Connecticut River Valley, where they built a trading post in 1623. Ten years later Pilgrims settled and built a trading post at Windsor. An exodus of settlers from Massachusetts "squatted" in rural areas of eastern Connecticut. Reports of rich farmland beguiled many of them, and religious persecution drove others to seek less regulated territory.

Democracy in the River Towns

Thomas Hooker, who had settled in New Town (Cambridge), left Massachusetts in May 1636, with a hundred people, and they struggled through the country for 120 miles to Hartford. Because the emigrants were traveling with all their possessions and cattle, they made only about 10 miles a day. Within a few months others came to settle nearby in Windsor and Wethersfield. Hooker believed that a "general council, chosen by all, to transact business which concerns all, I conceive most suitable to rule and most safe for the relief of the whole people." His views led to the adoption of the Fundamental Orders of Connecticut in January 1639.

Indian Problems

At the time Hooker settled in Hartford, sixteen Indian tribes in Connecticut were all under the Algonquian Confederation. These Indians were fearful of the Mohawks and thus wished to live harmoniously with the newcomers. They sold land and helped the settlers learn more about hunting, fishing, and farming in the region, but when the Pequots arrived from the Hudson River Valley, the short-lived equilibrium of peaceful coexistence was upset. There was no doubt that the Pequots were intent on getting rid of white communities in Connecticut. They killed a number of traders and isolated settlers, then attacked Saybrook and Wethersfield.

Puritan Capt. John Mason and his soldiers planned an offensive to decimate the Pequots in 1637. During a surprise night raid on the Pequot compound at Mystic, the Puritans killed and burned all the Indians they could find, then followed the rest into a swamp in Fairfield and killed them there; the few Pequots that remained alive were taken as slaves.

Puritans Come to New Haven

John Davenport reached Boston in 1637 with a group of Puritans, spent the winter there, then journeyed to the mouth of the Quinnipiac River and settled in New Haven. Although the area was thought to belong to the Dutch of New Netherlands, the Earl of Warwick had granted the same land to friends of Davenport and Theophilus Eaton.

In 1638 they proceeded to write formal "articles of agreement between the English planters at Quinopiocke and Momaugin, the Indian sachem of Quinopiocke," which gave them the right to the land. In return the Indians received "Twelve Coates of english trucking cloat[h], Twelve Alcumy spoones, Twelve Hatchetts, twelve hoes, two dozen of knives, twelve porengers and four[e] Cases of french knives and sizers." In addition, another Indian, Mantowese of Mattabezeck, offered a larger piece of land for "Eleven coates made of Trucking cloth, and one Coate for himselfe of English cloth, made up after the English maner."

The members of the group established this colony on theocratic principles. They believed that "the word of God shall be the only rule" and allowed only church members to vote. Theophilus Eaton, a London merchant, became the first governor, and he gave primacy to the laws of Moses as the model for the colony. New Haven did not allow trials by jury because this concept is not mentioned in the Bible.

Other towns grew around New Haven—Milford, Guilford, Stamford, Fairfield, Medford, Greenwich, and Branford. They were all part of the colony of New Haven and opposed to the politics of the river towns clustered around Hartford; in fact, New Haven tried to go its own way and become a separate colony.

Charter Disputes

John Winthrop, Jr., arrived to found New London in 1646. As a well respected and educated governor, he was sent to London in 1661 to try to get a charter for Connecticut from the newly restored Crown. The charter was ready on May 10, 1662, and the colony was authorized to govern itself. By 1687 Hartford was known as a town unwilling to give in to English control. When Sir Edmund Andros, the English Governor, declared all charters void and asked Hartford to return the one it had kept for twenty-five years, patriots took matters into their own hands. Mysteriously the charter disappeared into a hole in the trunk of a large oak.

Revolutionary War Attacks

During the Revolutionary War Connecticut was struck by four British attacks. Danbury was the first in 1777, when Major General William Tryon, the royal governor of New York, burned the Continental Army's tents and food. In 1779 Tryon arrived in Greenwich to destroy the saltworks, and in July of that year the British ravaged New Haven, Fairfield, and Norwalk.

The last assault was led by Benedict Arnold, who invaded New London and Groton in 1781. First Arnold attacked Fort Trumbull and then moved on to Fort Griswold. The British continued to kill soldiers after they had surrendered, including those who were wounded, and they torched New London. Earlier Benedict Arnold had tried to give the fort at West Point to the British, but Connecticut patriots found this brutal attack by a native son particularly repugnant. The sentiment was shared in other colonies. John Brown of Pittsfield, Massachusetts, wrote that "money is this man's god, and to get enough of it he would sacrifice his country."

From the British point of view, the attack was not unwarranted. By 1779 New London had become a major privateering center. Merchant-shipowners applied for commissions from Governor Trumbull to legalize their operations. These privateers continually harassed British ships and also captured a number as prizes of war.

Regions to Explore

T he narrative begins with a region that includes the three towns that were established in the Connecticut River Valley between 1633 and 1636: Hartford, Wethersfield, and Windsor. The second region focuses on New London and other parts of eastern Connecticut, both inland and along the shore. The third region deals with New Haven and other towns on the shore of Long Island Sound, and the fourth region with parts of western Connecticut.

Connecticut

THE CONNECTICUT RIVER VALLEY

The story of the **Charter Oak** in **Hartford** may be more legend than fact, but it does incorporate some real political events that took place where the Traveler's Tower stands today. On October 31, 1687, the Zachary Sanford Tavern stood there. Sir Edmund Andros, the Governor appointed by King James II, arrived in town and demanded the return of the liberal charter that had been given to the Hartford Colony in 1662 by King Charles II. During a discussion of the charter, the sun set and candles were lit, which then mysteriously blew out. The charter disappeared—one of the colonists had hidden it in the trunk of an old oak tree, thereafter known as the Charter Oak Tree. The charter did not reappear until 1715. Visitors can see the original charter in the **Raymond E. Baldwin Museum of Connecticut History** in the State Library at 231 Capitol Avenue. Call (203) 566–3056 for information.

Hartford's growth has obliterated all but traces of the seventeenth-century settlement in the center, but there are remnants from the eighteenth century. The oldest house in Hartford is the **Butler-McCook Homestead** at 396 Main Street (203–522–1806), home to four generations of the same family. The part that dates from 1782 was built as a blacksmith shop and a butcher shop. Original furnishings, silver, bronze, and children's toys, which belong to the family, are on display. Open Tuesday, Thursday, and Saturday from noon to 4:00 P.M., mid-May to mid-October. Closed holidays.

Not far away the **Wadsworth Atheneum** stands at 600 Main Street. The Nutting Collection includes two restored colonial-period rooms that

The Prolific Charter Oak

Although the tree blew down during a hurricane in 1856, many objects were said to have been made from its wood. Mark Twain—never one to be reverential—listed some of them: "A walking stick, dog collar, needle case, three-legged stool, bootjack, dinner table, tenpin alley, toothpick, and enough Charter Oak to build a plank road from Hartford to Salt Lake City."

were taken out of their original homes and authentic seventeenth-century furniture. The Atheneum contains a fine collection of artworks from a number of centuries. When it's time for lunch, try the Atheneum cafe. The museum is open from 11:00 A.M. to 5:00 P.M. except on Mondays and holidays. Call (203) 278–2670 for more information.

Just across the corner, at Main and Gold streets, you'll find **Center Church,** where Thomas Hooker preached 350 years ago. The present church, which dates from 1807, has Tiffany windows for you to enjoy. Many of the first settlers in Hartford lie in the adjacent Ancient Burying Ground. If you can't pass by old cemeteries, plan to spend some time searching for stones that date from the 1640s.

Most of us are fascinated by the folderol associated with cannon ceremonies. If you'd like to see a cannon fired, be on hand for the Yankee Doodle Cannon Salute from the **Old State House** at 800 Main Street. A corps in Continental uniforms does the honors. (This is a seasonal event; for more details call (203) 522–6766.) A portrait of George Washington by Gilbert Stuart hangs in the building.

If you're interested in genealogy, visit the **Connecticut Historical Society** at One Elizabeth Street (203–236–5621). There are more than 2 million manuscripts on Connecticut history and genealogy plus nine galleries of permanent and changing exhibits. You'll also find colonial furniture from the seventeenth century. The society is open Tuesday through Sunday, noon to 5 P.M. from Labor Day to Memorial Day. For the rest of the year, it is open Tuesday through Friday and Sunday, 9:00 A.M.–5:00 P.M.

Noah Webster wrote the *Blue Backed Speller* of 1783 in the **Noah Webster House,** 227 South Main Street in **West Hartford** (203–521–5362). Webster had been born in the house in 1758. Some of his possessions, including his desk, are in this eighteenth-century farmhouse. Open weekdays except Wednesday, 10:00 A.M.–4:00 P.M., and Saturday and Sunday 1:00 P.M.–4:00 P.M. June 15 through September 30; Thursday through Tuesday 1:00 P.M.–4:00 P.M. the rest of the year.

After Ethan Allen burst into Fort Ticonderoga and captured a number of sleeping British officers, some of them were held in the **Sarah Whitman Hooker House** at 1237 New Britain Avenue. Built in 1720 as a saltbox, the house was remodeled into a Federal structure in 1807. Visitors can see the porcelain collection as well as original wallpapers, and the garden blooms with plants of the period. Open Monday and Wednesday, 1:30–3:30 P.M.; call (203) 523–5887 for more information.

When it's time for a meal or a rest overnight, head west over the mountain to **Avon Old Farms Inn** on Route 44 in Avon. This country inn, in operation since 1757, is furnished with antiques to maintain the atmosphere of older days. Call (203) 677–1651 for reservations.

Across the river from Hartford, a colonial saddlemaker built the **Huguenot House** at 307 Burnside Avenue (Route 44) in **East Hartford**. This gambrel-roofed house has vaulted dormer windows. Call (203) 528–0716 or 568–6178 for more information, and don't forget to ask about the ghost!

During the Revolution General Rochambeau's soldiers set up their tents on Lawrence Street and Silver Lane in East Hartford. A marker identifies the spot; there's a sack of silver coins depicted on it because the men were paid in silver, and local people did not often see such a treasure.

Just downstream from Hartford, on the west side of the Connecticut River, you will find some remarkable colonial houses. Like parts of Providence and Salem, Old Wethersfield survived over the years because it was not subjected to industrial development. As a smaller town it was even luckier and lost fewer buildings. The **Wethersfield Historical Society,** at 150 Main Street (203–529–7656), houses local historical pieces, and there is a library with research archives in the building.

Look for the house with small casement windows that seem almost medieval and you've found the **Buttolph-Williams House,** at Broad and Marsh Streets. Dating from the early 1700s, it is the oldest restored house in Wethersfield. The house is furnished with antique pieces of the period; you'll see seventeenth-century chairs and tables, pewter and delft, a curved settee, and authentic implements in Ye Greate Kitchin. Open daily except Monday, noon to 4:00 P.M., mid-May to mid-October. Call (203) 529–0460 or 247–8996 for details.

Sitting Straight

Colonial furniture included a settle, or sette, which was designed with a high back to ward off drafts. Wainscot chairs look very stiff and square, and they pulled up to oak trestle tables. A combination bench-table could be converted easily with a flick of the wrist.

Three eighteenth-century houses are grouped together as the **Webb-Deane-Stevens Museum** at 211 Main Street. These houses were used during the 1781 strategy conference between George Washington and Rochambeau that resulted in the British defeat at Yorktown. Visitors today will see the different life-styles of the owners of the three houses—a merchant, a diplomat, and a tradesman. The **Webb House** (1752) was built by a West Indies merchant, Joseph Webb. Mrs. Webb redecorated in a flurry, with French red-flocked wallpaper, just before Washington arrived; you can still see the paper on the walls of the room where he slept. A china closet glows with bright red, blue, and mustard paint and has a scallop-shell dome at the top; bright colors were often used to enliven rooms that depended on candlelight.

After Webb's death in 1761, his wife married Silas Deane, a diplomat and lawyer; they lived in the **Deane House**. A number of Deanes had tuberculosis and one of the bedrooms contains a mahogany medicine chest. In one of the drawers, you'll find copper wires, which were used to produce a chemical reaction when dipped in vinegar. The resulting fluid was called verdigris, and it was said to minimize chest pains, although no one knows if it really helped tuberculosis. The **Stevens House** was built by a leather worker, Isaac Stevens. Furniture and household pieces date from 1690 and later. Open daily except Tuesday, 10:00 A.M.–4:00 P.M., May through October; Saturday and Sunday 10:00 A.M.–4:00 P.M. the rest of the year. For more information on all three houses, call (203) 529–0612.

A Greek Revival home, the **Chester Bulkley House B&B** at 184 Main Street, in Wethersfield has the original beehive oven still in the house. It's located in the center of historic Old Wethersfield. Call (203) 563–4236 for reservations.

If you drive due west from Wethersfield, you will reach **Farmington**, now another satellite of Hartford but then a separate town. You may wonder why the **Stanley-Whitman House,** at 37 High Street, has such an enormous overhang, making the second floor far larger than the first. Some say it may have been to avoid high taxes, which were traditionally levied on the first floor of a home. This 1720 house has diamond window panes that are handsome indeed. An eighteenth-century garden is a bonus. To find out more information, call (203) 677–9222.

If you have a passion for Indian lore, head for the **Day-Lewis Museum** at 158 Main Street. This archaeology museum displays artifacts that were found locally, the last home of the Tunxis Indians. Call (203) 678–1645 for more information.

If you head east from Old Wethersfield and cross the river, you will reach another town full of fine colonial houses, most of them still private homes. In **Glastonbury** you can visit the **Welles-Shipman-Ward House** (1755) at 972 Main Street (203–633–6890). Captain Thomas Welles built it as a wedding present for his son. The U.S. Department of the Interior describes this house as having "exceptional architectural interest." The ornate wood-work is certainly worth a visit. Open Sundays, 2:00 P.M.–4:00 P.M., mid-May through June and mid-August through October.

The **Museum on the Green,** at Main and Hubbard Street (203–633–6890), is the home of the Historical Society of Glastonbury. Visitors will see exhibits on local Indians, early farming artifacts, and folk-art portraits.

Butternut Farm, at 1654 Main Street, in Glastonbury is a bed and breakfast in an eighteenth-century jewel of a colonial home. It is furnished with antiques. Call (203) 633–7197 for reservations.

North of Hartford the most significant early settlement was **Windsor.** One of the oldest frame houses in Connecticut is the **Walter Fyler House** (1640) at 96 Palisado Avenue. Fyler arrived in America aboard the *Mary and John* in 1630 and received land because of his devotion to the cause of fighting the Pequots. His house is the last surviving building within the Pallizado, which was a stockade fort designed to protect the settlers from Indians and wolves. Captain Nathaniel Howard, a sea captain in the West Indies and coastal trade, bought the property in 1772 and started a general store and post office. It is now the home of the Windsor Historical Society. The **Hezekia Chaffee House** dates from 1765 and adjoins the Fyler House. Dr. Chaffee practiced medicine there until his death in 1819. The house has been furnished with period pieces from the Windsor Historical Society collection. The **Wilson Museum,** on the same property, is a fine place to see colonial furnishings. Open Tuesday through Saturday, 10:00 A.M.–4:00 P.M., April through November and by appointment the rest of the year. Closed holidays. Call (203) 688–3813 for more details on all three properties.

The Old Burying Ground nearby was also inside the Pallizado; the cemetery was expanded to the west, where visitors can look for graves of Roger Wolcott, a Connecticut governor, and Oliver Ellsworth, the third Chief Justice of the United States. **The Founder's Monument,** on Pallizado Green, stands on the site of the 1639 Meeting House. The monument was dedicated in honor of the early founding families of Windsor and the First Congregational Church, which had been founded in Plymouth, England, before they left for America.

The Windsor Colony continued to have trouble with the Indians, as this 1706 letter, written by William Pitkins, attests:

Since I cam home I am informed that Sollomon Andross having had his house broaken up by the Indians, and three Indians breaking in again this morning a little before day—hath killed one of them and the other two fled up this way, he pursued but they were too light of foot for him . . . probably they swam over the River, where they left the horse they tooke. . . .

A famous Revolutionary patriot, Oliver Ellsworth, built his home here in 1781. The **Oliver Ellsworth Homestead,** on Palisado Avenue (203–688–8717), remained home to Abigail and Oliver Ellsworth until his death in 1807. Besides being one of the framers of the United States Constitution, Ellsworth was Connecticut's first senator and the author of the Judiciary Act, now the key to our federal judicial system. Visitors will see Ellsworth possessions and documents, including a letter to him from George Washington, who visited in 1789. The Ellsworth Homestead is open Tuesday through Saturday, 1:00 P.M.–5:00 P.M., April through October.

A historic farmhouse, now a bed and breakfast, the **Charles R. Hart House,** at 1046 Windsor Avenue, in Windsor features a handsome Palladian window and ceramic-tiled fireplaces. Call (203) 688–5555 for reservations.

The first mention of a Christmas tree in the colonies dates from the story of a Hessian soldier, Hendrick Roddemore. After deserting the British forces and arriving in Windsor to work as a farmhand, he put up a Christmas tree in his cabin in **Windsor Locks.** On that site Henry Denslow built a house. At one point the family fled to the Windsor palisade; Henry went back to his house on April 6, 1676, and was killed by Indians. An engraved memorial boulder to Denslow was errected on South Main Street. Later the

Game Aplenty

Windsor account books indicate the abundance of game that was available to the colonists. In *Transit of Civilization* Edward Eggleston wrote, "Between 1691 and 1702, 1,636 lbs. of venison, 50 lbs moose, 60 lbs of bear, besides numberous Blak Duks, Rakoons, piegones, dear skins are charged and credited." The venison was prepared for family use by salting, and the business of dressing the skins of the wild animals entered largely into the occupations of the period.

Noden-Reed House was built on the site of his home at 58 West Street. Visitors today will see period rooms, displays of Indian artifacts, and colonial furniture, which includes Seth Dexter's high chest (ca. 1770). The barn houses sleighs, surreys, and old farm equipment. Open Sunday and Wednesday 1:00 P.M.–5:00 P.M., May through October and December. For further information call (203) 627–9212.

There's also an interesting house to visit in **Enfield,** north of Windsor on the other side of the river. Land was set aside for the use of future "parsons" in Enfield, and John Meacham built the **Parsons House** at 1387 Enfield Street, Route 5, in 1782. It was called Sycamore Hall because a row of sycamore trees at one time stood there. By coincidence the last family to live in the house was named "Parsons." John Ingraham, who was a retired sea captain from Saybrook, bought the house for his family in 1800; his granddaughter married Simeon Parsons, hence the name. The furniture in the house belonged to the families who lived there. The George Washington Memorial Wallpaper was advertised, "It is hoped that all true-born Americans will so encourage the Manufactories of their Country, that Manufactories of all kinds may flourish, and importation stop." Indeed, there's a point! The house is open Sundays in May through September, 2:00 P.M.–4:30 P.M. Call (203) 745–6064 for more information.

Although the Connecticut River remained the lifeblood of the region, eventually more settlers moved farther from it, seeking land. Northwest of Hartford lies the town of **Bloomfield**, where early settlers arrived in 1661 to buy land from the Indians. The oldest house, the **Fuss House**, at 4 Park Avenue, was built by the Goodwin family. It is privately owned and not open to the public.

St. Andrew's Church, in North Bloomfield, dates from the early 1740s. It is the oldest Episcopal church in northern Connecticut. The parish was called Wintonbury, using parts of the names of the three towns the people came from—Windsor, Farmington, and Simsbury. Roger Viets, an early rector, was responsible for the establishment of many other Episcopal parishes in Connecticut and Massachusetts.

Beyond Bloomfield in the same northwesterly direction is **Simsbury,** located in the Farmington River Valley. **Massacoh Plantation,** at 800 Hopmeadow Street, is a complex of buildings centering on an eighteenth-century house that contains period furnishings and a collection of costumes. Don't miss the vaulted ceiling in the ballroom. Phelps House (1771) was a tavern when the canal trade was thriving in Simsbury. A one-room schoolhouse dates from 1741. Weavers will be interested in the loom in the Hendricks Cottage. Call (203) 658–2500 for more information.

A historic country inn, the **Simsbury 1820 House,** is located at 731 Hopmeadow Street. The inn is furnished with antiques, and meals are also served. For reservations, call (203) 658–7658.

A number of Simsbury residents moved out of town and settled farther north on Salmon Brook Street in **Granby**; by 1709 eleven families lived there, in what is known as the Salmon Brook Settlement, but they were always concerned about Indian attacks. Daniel Hayes was out looking for his horse one day when he was spotted and captured by Indians, who then took him to Canada. During the thirty-day trip he was tied up at night, beaten, and starved. When they reached a large Indian settlement he was forced to "run the gauntlet" between two rows of Indians with clubs. He ran into a wigwam where an old woman lived; she told the Indians that her house was "sacred" and thus saved his life. He lived with her until she died; then he was sold to a Frenchman who taught him to weave, sharing profits between them. After seven years of captivity, he bought his freedom and returned to his home in Granby.

The oldest building left in the Salmon Brook Settlement is the **Abijah Rowe House,** at 208 Salmon Brook Street. Rowe, a blacksmith and a farmer, built the house sometime around 1753. The paneling and corner cupboard in the south parlor are original. Look for the unusual front door with its carved trim, a frieze with triglyphs, and a cornice. The furniture comes from early Granby homes; two rare Connecticut spinning wheels stand in the house. To find out more information, call (203) 653–3965.

In the same region north of Hartford stands a notorious prison, **Old New-Gate Prison and Copper Mine,** on Newgate Road in **East Granby**. In 1703 English settlers, upon discovering a green rock, surmised that copper was present. The mine was developed, but, unfortunately, the miners were required to send the ore to England to be smelted, which cut their profits considerably. Other illegal mines sprang up, sponsored by Dutch or New York companies. Doctor Samuel Higley even minted his own coins—with which (if the story can be believed) he paid his bar bills!

When the mine faltered, the Colonial Government of Connecticut bought it and turned it into a prison. Thus began one of the darker chapters in Revolutionary history. Officials thought that prisoners would not be able to escape from the deep pit, but actually they turned their spare time to profit, using mining tools to dig tunnels to the outside. Then they were brought above ground to work—making nails, shoes, or wagons—but were forced to return into the damp, crowded, rheumatic mine to sleep at night. Besides murderers, horse thieves, and counterfeiters, Tories or Loyalists were placed in the prison if they were considered too dangerous to the Revolution to be left free.

In 1781 the wife of one of the imprisoned Tories arrived to see her husband. After her visit with her husband, the sergeant on duty escorted her to the entrance, then changed his colors to become British instead of American. The Tories were freed, two guards were killed, and the mass escape succeeded.

Visitors to the mine will see the room where the prisoners slept as well as the solitary-confinement room, where there is a bench dug out of the rock, some initials, and a link of chain. Above ground, there is the chapel, the remains of some workshops, and a cell block. The notoriety of the prison was not entirely deserved. Surprisingly, the men were in better health than the general population; insects were the principal carriers of disease, and they could not live so far below ground. The food was plentiful, with each prisoner receiving one pound of meat every day, two pounds of potatoes, and a dry measure of beans. (Sailors on board the fighting ships of either navy would have been delighted with those rations!) Three half-pints of hard cider were standard, plus a shot of rum for good behavior. Call (203) 566–3005 for more information. The prison is open 10:00 A.M.–4:30 P.M. Wednesdays through Sundays and holidays, mid-May through October 31.

First In, First Out

John Hinson was the first prisoner in New Gate in 1773. Hinson spent eighteen days in the prison until his girlfriend tossed a rope down into a shaft near the entrance. He climbed up, and they escaped and fled.

EASTERN CONNECTICUT

Leaving the Connecticut River towns of Hartford, Wethersfield, and Windsor does not mean leaving rivers as we explore the colonial history of Connecticut. The Thames River (pronounced "thaymez" not "temz") gives **New London** one of the best deep-water ports in New England. In the seventeenth century farmers used the river to ship their produce; a hundred years later whalers sailed home with fortunes to be made from the oil in their holds. Although we are no longer largely dependent on rivers and ports for transportation, as our colonial ancestors were, it is no accident that New London remains important in the twentieth century as the home of the Coast Guard Academy and submarines.

The New London Colony was founded by John Winthrop, Jr. in 1646. He became a major figure in the political history of Connecticut, and his statue stands where Masonic Street and Eugene O'Neill Drive meet (names themselves that are suggestive of the varied history of this corner of the New England seaboard). Luckily the coastal area, which includes Groton, Mystic, and Stonington, has long been concerned with preserving its colonial heritage, so there is much for a visitor to see.

The **Joshua Hempstead House,** at 11 Hempstead Street in New London, dates from 1678. It is one of the few intact seventeenth-century houses in Connecticut still standing. And there is an added attraction here. The diary of Joshua Hempstead, describing the daily life of his family, provides a window into the colonial mind and experience.

Another home to visit on the same grounds is the **Nathaniel Hempstead House,** built in 1759 for a rope-maker grandson of Joshua. It is one of two houses in the state that represent the cut-stone architecture of the mid-eighteenth century, and it also has a beehive oven. Both Hempstead houses contain a number of original pieces of furniture. They are open 1:00 P.M.–5:00 P.M. daily except Monday, May 15–October 15. For further information call (203) 443–7949 or 247–8996.

During the Revolutionary War the **Shaw–Perkins Mansion** (1756), at 305 Bank Street, was used as Connecticut's naval office; George Washington really did sleep here. Captain Nathaniel Shaw, Jr., was a shipowner, part of a community heavily involved in breaking the blockade of the coast. The house contains family portraits and collections of silver and china. Call (203) 443–1209 for more information.

The New London effort to harass the British fleet was too successful for the town's good. A number of New London vessels, acting as privateers, raided and captured hundreds of British ships. The devastating attack on the town near the end of the war, on September 6, 1781, was retribution: Thirty-two British ships with 1,700 men on board, led by turncoat Benedict Arnold, destroyed the city. As a native of Norwich, he knew the territory, and, according to some reports, he watched New London burn from the Burial Ground on Hempstead Street.

Joshua Hempsted's "kitchin," complete with early wrought iron, woodenware, and pewter

The **Nathan Hale Schoolhouse** is located on Captain's Walk; Hale taught before he enlisted in the army. After the battle at Lexington, Hale felt inspired to join the patriots and gave a speech declaring his feelings.

If you've a yen to explore more Indian lore, visit the **Tantaquidgeon Indian Museum,** at 1819 Norwich–New London Turnpike. The Tantaquidgeons were direct descendants of Chief Uncas of the Mohegans. After your visit you may want to find **Cochegan Rock,** where Chief Uncas and his councillors used to meet in secret. The rock is located west of Mohegan Hill, off Raymond Hill Road. The museum (203–848–9145) has collections of stone, bone, and wooden objects, mostly from Eastern Woodlands Indians. It is open 10:00 A.M.–4:00 P.M. Tuesday through Sunday, May through October.

If you want to spend the night in the area, try the **Lighthouse Inn,** at 6 Guthrie Place in New London. It has four-poster beds and antique furnishings.

Don't miss the elegant spiral staircase. Call (203) 443–8411 for reservations.

Fort Griswold Battlefield State Park, at Monument Street and Park Avenue in **Groton**, stands on Groton Bank, where it was crucial to the defense of New London harbor as well as coastal shipping. Groton men had been active in the Revolutionary war, many of them on privateers, so, for both reasons, it was no accident that the British attacked Fort Griswold in the retaliatory raid against New London on September 6, 1781, a massacre of American patriots by the British. The Groton monument was dedicated to those who died, and their names are inscribed on it. Reenactments of the Battle at Fort Griswold are held every year, drawing large crowds. Monument House contains mementos of the massacre, period furniture, and displays on whaling. It is open daily 10:00 A.M.–5:00 P.M. from Memorial Day to Labor Day and 10:00 A.M.–5:00 P.M. on Saturday and Sunday from the day after Labor Day to October 12. For details call (203) 445-1729.

East of Groton, **Mystic** was also once the site of a bloody retaliatory raid. First settled in 1654, the town's name derived from the Pequot Indians' Mistuket. Earlier, in 1637, after much harassment from the Pequots, settlers from surrounding areas surprised them on Pequot Hill; the **John Mason Monument,** named after their leader, marks the spot. The settlers set fire to the Indian encampment and shot or burned most of the Pequots. Luckily the later history of Mystic has been much more tranquil and prosperous, both as a seaport and shipbuilding center, and that prosperity produced many fine old houses, which you can see by walking through Old Mystic and along the Mystic River.

The **Denison Homestead** (203–536–9248), on Pequotsepos Road, was built in 1717. Eleven generations of the Denison family lived here, and some personal possessions are still in the house. Visitors take delight in the wooden Indian doll, period costumes, spinning wheels, silver, glass, and even George Denison's will from 1693. Captain George Denison brought his wife and children to build the first house here. His grandson, George Denison III, built the house that stands today. Look for the rare "trimmer arch" over the kitchen fireplace; it holds up a hearthstone in the room above. The house is open daily except Tuesday, 1:00 P.M.–5:00 P.M., mid-May to Labor Day and 1:00 P.M.–4:00 P.M. from then until mid-October. By appointment the rest of the year.

There's another trimmer arch to see in the **Whitehall Mansion** (1774), located just off exit 90N of Interstate 95 (203–535–1131). This Revolutionary War home has been furnished and restored. It was built by Dr. Dudley

Woodbridge, a local physician. The house contains "twelve over twelve" windows on the first and second stories. Open 1:00 P.M.–4:00 P.M. Wednesday to Sunday, May to October, and by appointment the rest of the year.

Mystic has been a major tourist destination for decades, largely because it is the site of the first and most extensive living-history museum dedicated to preserving New England's maritime heritage. At **Mystic Seaport Museum** you will find boats and ships galore, in all sizes and from many eras, including a classic whale ship, a Grand Banks schooner, and a sail-training square-rigger, all from later times. Alas, there are no ships from the colonial era: Wooden vessels don't last that long unless they are buried in sand or mud; nevertheless, the Seaport is the best place to go if you want to sense what seafaring under sail or oar was like—the only power available to colonial seamen. Interpreters row classic craft on the river and set and furl sails on square-rigged ships; shipwrights repair the Seaport's vessels, using traditional techniques, and boatbuilders produce authentic replicas of older types.

The Seaport also offers seventeen acres of homes and buildings collected within a village setting, and some of these do represent ways of life that go back to the colonial era. It really is a living village: Craftspersons ply their trades here and are more than willing to talk with visitors. Many of the displays and centers relate to maritime activities and trades, whereas others demonstrate weaving, printing, and open-hearth cooking. **Buckingham House** (1695) is the place to be when they're cooking; the smells are wonderful. The Seaport is open daily 9:00 A.M.–8:00 P.M. in June through August; 9:00 A.M.–5:00 P.M. in April, May, September, and October; 9:00 A.M.–4:00 P.M. in November and December; and 10:00 A.M.–4:00 P.M. in January through March. Closed December 25. For further information call (203) 572–5315.

Since there are other attractions in Mystic, including cruises and an aquarium, you may want to stay the night. When it's time to do so, try the **Old Mystic Inn,** at 58 Main Street, Old Mystic, which dates from the early 1800s (203–572–9422) or **Red Brook Inn** (203–572–0349), also in Old Mystic, which is actually two houses—Haley Tavern and Crary Homestead. During summer be sure to call for reservations in advance.

East of Mystic near the Rhode Island border, **Stonington** has both a sheltered deep-water harbor and a fine collection of captain's houses, both suggesting its primary activity in earlier eras, which has not changed much. The harbor is now full of yachts, and the houses have been elegantly restored. Most of them are privately owned, but you can enjoy their facades

and gardens by wandering around the quiet streets near the end of the peninsula. Some of the houses have cannonballs embedded in them, prized remnants not of the Revolution (although it was attacked then) but the War of
1812, when Stonington successfully withstood three days of heavy bom-
bardment from a British fleet and wreaked enough damage from its own
cannons to drive the fleet away.

The town was not settled until after 1662, when the competing territorial claims of Massachusetts and Connecticut were resolved. As the name
suggests, the land around Stonington was rocky, and settlers had a difficult
time producing food. They also found it hard to keep wolves away from nec-
essarily shallow graves. Eventually the townspeople began to top each grave
with a heavy stone slab. These "wolf stones" can still be seen in the cemetery near Wequetequock, off Greenheaven Road, south of Route 1.

If you're ready for an authentic colonial meal, where the dishes are
cooked on an open hearth, stop at **Randall's Ordinary** on Route 2 in
North Stonington. This 1685 farmhouse is the setting for wonderful meals
and also has rooms for overnight stays. In addition visitors can sign up for
hearthside cooking lessons. Call (203) 599–4540 for reservations.

North of New London on the Thames River, **Norwich** is the site of the
Leffingwell Inn (203–889–9440), at 348 Washington Street. It is actually
two small saltbox houses joined together with an addition at the back. The
older section dates from 1675, when it was owned by William Backus, one
of the original settlers of Norwich. In 1701 owner Thomas Leffingwell
received a license to "keep a publique house for the entertainment of
strangers." As his family grew, more additions were built. His descendant
Christopher Leffingwell was an adventurous entrepreneur and patriot, who
became one of the chief financial backers of the Revolution. The Tavern
Room was the site of many Revolutionary War meetings that included major
figures like George Washington, Governor Jonathan Trumbull, and Silas
Deane. Open 10:00 A.M.–noon and 2:00 P.M.–4:00 P.M. Tuesday through
Sunday, mid-May to mid-October; by appointment the rest of the year.

The **John Baldwin House,** at 210 West Town Street, dates from 1660. It
started life as a 1½-story saltbox and was expanded to two stories during the
mid-eighteenth century. The center fireplace is still in use for heating and for
cooking. The house contains genealogical collections and a children's bookstore. It is still a private residence, but guided tours are available. It is open
10:00 A.M.–5:00 P.M. Tuesday through Sunday, mid-May to Labor Day; by
appointment the rest of the year. For more information call (203) 889–5990.

Norwich is also known as the burial site of Chief Uncas in 1683. He was the greatest chieftain of the Mohegan Indians, and his monument stands in the **Royal Mohegan Burial Ground** on Sachem Street.

Indian Leap, located off Yantic Street at Yantic Falls, was a watering hole of the Mohegans. Its name derives from a story that as Narragansetts ran from the Mohegans during the Battle of the Great Plains, they suddenly came to the falls and had to leap into the chasm below. After the Narragansetts were defeated, the colonists who were allied with the Mohegans decided to kill the captured leader, Miantonomo. Chief Uncas believed that he would receive strength if he cut a bit from the dead Indian's shoulder and ate it—he did. The Miantonomo Monument stands on Elijah Street, where he was captured. One more marker, that of the **Battle of Great Plains,** stands on the New London Turnpike in Norwich.

Heading northwest from Norwich will take you to **Lebanon,** a small town with major historical sites from the Revolution. When it was first settled in the late 1600s by people who left Norwich, they were heading for real wilderness. Later it was the home of the Trumbull family, prominent in the West Indies trade; the **Jonathan Trumbull House,** on West Town Street, dates from 1735. The house is open 1:00 P.M.–5:00 P.M. Tuesday through Saturday, mid-May to mid-October. Trumbull was known as a "colonial war governor" because of his staunch support for the Revolution. He was involved in the transfer of equipment from Connecticut to the army. George Washington wrote, "but for Jonathan Trumbull, the war could not have been carried to a successful conclusion."

After a price was set on his head, Trumbull retired to a second-floor room without windows, except for a 27-inch-square shuttered opening located above the head of anyone seated in the room. Trumbull furnishings

Mirror, Mirror . . .

Because fathers had the right to decide which young men would call on their daughters, the men made "courting mirrors" to give to girls. If a girl looked into the mirror, the man was allowed to continue courting, but watch out if she turned the mirror face down—this meant she had turned him down and he would have to leave.

in the house include a Queen Anne chair used by the governor at church; a Duxbury chair brought by his bride, Faith; a Chinese lacquer dispatch box used by Trumbull; and a spectacular set of red china, with the medallion of a bull, which indicates the family name. The **Wadsworth Stable** was moved from Hartford to the Trumbull property in 1954. George Washington kept his favorite horse, Nelson, here when he visited Hartford. The stable is open during the same hours as the Trumbull House. Call (203) 642–7558 for more details.

Trumbull's son, John, created paintings to portray the major events of the Revolution. He also painted scenes in the state Capitol rotunda, including the well-known *The Signing of the Declaration of Independence.* The **Jonathan Trumbull, Jr., House,** on South Street, dates from 1769. This center-chimney farmhouse has eight corner fireplaces—count them. Open 1:00 P.M.–5:00 P.M. Tuesday through Saturday, May 15 to October 15. To find out more call (203) 642–6040.

The **Revolutionary War Office,** on West Town Street, was built as the Trumbull family store in 1727. Goods were sent from this store to Washington's army. Ox sleds of supplies, including arms, tents, food, and clothing, were loaded from his store. Call (203) 642–7558 for more information.

The "Father of Physiology of Digestion" lived in the **Dr. William Beaumont House,** on West Town Street, also part of the Trumbull complex. Displays include Beaumont's trunk and surgical instruments of the period. At a later time Beaumont lived at Fort Mackinac, on the island off northern Michigan. There he attended a man whose stomach wound never did heal; thus Beaumont was able to observe gastric secretion over an eleven-year period. One of the displays in the Fort has two models of the stomach in graphic detail. For details call (203) 642–7558.

North of Lebanon is the town of **Coventry**, remembered in Revolutionary history as the birthplace of Nathan Hale. The **Nathan Hale Homestead** (203–742–6917) is located on South Street. This is open to the public from 1:00 P.M. to 5:00 P.M. daily, mid-May to mid-October. Unfortunately he never lived in the house because he was captured and executed by the British before it was finished. A schoolteacher, he would perhaps be pleased to know that his final words, "I only regret that I have but one life to lose for my country," have been taught to students ever since. Many Hale family pieces are in the house.

Nearby the **Strong-Porter House Museum** stands at 2382 South Street. The eastern part of the house dates from 1730. It was built by Aaron

Strong, a maternal great-uncle of Nathan Hale. Call (203) 742–7847 for more information.

The Nathan Hale Ancient Fifes and Drums and Knowlton's Rangers take part in Revolutionary War battles and musters in July. Also in July Coventry Colonial Days are held for students who want to immerse themselves in the era. These programs are sponsored by the Antiquarian and Landmarks Society. To find out more information, call (203) 247–8996.

Caprilands Herb Farm, at 534 Silver Street, is a great place to tour period gardens. Owner Adelma Simmons' eighteenth-century farmhouse is surrounded by thirty herb gardens. She conducts the tours and lectures on herbs. All this is followed by a delicious lunch that features herbs from the farm. Call (203) 742–7244 in advance for reservations.

Back on the shore west of New London, the broad reaches of the lower Connecticut River invited maritime activity. At its mouth **Old Saybrook** was first settled by Dutch traders during the early decades of the seventeenth century, but they were displaced in 1635 by John Winthrop, Jr., who brought Puritans from England and founded a colony.

The **General William Hart House** (1767), at 350 Main Street, was the home of a colonial merchant who was proud to put in beautiful paneling. Count the eight fireplaces inside. An especially interesting one has Sadler & Green transfer-print tiles that depict Aesop's *Fables.* There's also a colonial garden to explore and sniff. Call (203) 388–2622 for more information.

A local inventor, David Bushnell, was far ahead of his time when, in 1775, he designed a submarine that could theoretically submerge long enough to travel to an enemy vessel and attach a mine to it. The *American Turtle* was greatly admired, even though its pilot couldn't make the mine adhere to a ship. Benjamin Franklin was on hand to watch the sea trials of the *American Turtle* off Ayer's Point in the Connecticut River. While at Yale, David Bushnell was successful in designing and exploding the first of his underwater mines. Later he made a "drift" mine that worked; the crew of an enemy frigate pulled the drifting object onto the deck and it exploded, killing three British soldiers. (For information on the *American Turtle* replica, see the write-up on the Connecticut River Foundation, page 30.)

Across the river **Old Lyme** is filled with eighteenth- and nineteenth-century captain's houses spread along Lyme Steet. In more recent times the town has become a noted art colony associated with American Impressionism. Most of the houses are still private homes, but there are two fine inns to try here. The **Bee and Thistle Inn,** at 100 Lyme Street, dates from 1756. The house contains many fireplaces, four-poster beds, quilts, and Early American furnishings. Call (800) 622–4946 or (203) 434–1667 for reservations. **Old Lyme Inn,** at 85 Lyme Street, was built in 1850 as a working farm on 300 acres. For reservations call (203) 434–2600. Both inns have noted restaurants in elegant and historic surroundings, so dinner reservations are advised.

Half a dozen miles upriver from Old Saybrook and Old Lyme stands lovely **Essex,** which has preserved the romance of its maritime and architectural past. Its sheltered riverside setting, now filled with yacht yards and yachts, first became a major shipbuilding center in the 1720s. The town gave the *Oliver Cromwell,* a twenty-four-gun vessel built in 1776, to the patriots during the Revolutionary War.

A replica of the *American Turtle,* described above (see Old Saybrook), can be seen at the **Connecticut River Foundation** (203–767–8269), which tells David Bushnell's story and much more related to the rich maritime history of the area. Archaeological exploration has produced artifacts from the foundation's home at Lay's Wharf, a site that has been in use since prehistoric times. Other exhibits include a display on shipbuilding, a collection of traditional boats from the region, models, and paintings. Open 10:00 A.M.–5:00 P.M. Tuesday through Sunday; closed Labor Day, Thanksgiving, and Christmas.

Like the other towns in this region, Essex has many fine old houses. The **William Pratt House** (203–767–2470), at 20 West Avenue, dates from 1725, when the house began life as one room, then expanded to four rooms with a gambrel roof. The house is filled with early period furniture and is open Saturday and Sunday 1:00 P.M.–4:00 P.M., June through September.

Battle of the Kegs

The Battle of the Kegs was set off by David Bushnell, who produced forty buoyant wooden kegs to house his mines. He set them adrift to float down the Delaware River and into the British fleet; however, the British fired on the mines before they reached their ships. There's a song that mentions the fears of the British, especially their idea that the kegs contained rebels "packed up like pickled herring."

If you would like to see more of the lower Connecticut valley and the river by land and water, you can take a combined steam-train ride and river cruise. Start out on the **Valley Railroad,** Railroad Avenue, and connect with a boat, or finish the round-trip on the train. Call (203) 767–0103 for the train schedule.

For sleeping and eating **The Griswold Inn,** on Main Street, is a popular 1776 inn that has the charm of the past with modern conveniences. Dinners are memorable in this authentic colonial setting. For reservations call (203) 767–1776. In nearby Ivoryton you can try the **Copper Beech Inn** (203–767–0330), at 46 Main Street. An ivory importer lived here at one time. The Copper Beech also serves dinners. A little farther north, **Bishopsgate Inn** (203–873–1677), Goodspeed Landing in East Haddam, offers lodging in an 1818 shipbuilder's home. The inn has family antiques and lots of fireplaces.

THE LONG ISLAND SOUND SHORE

The **New Haven Colony,** one of the most powerful colonies in Connecticut, began with a strong Puritan bias. In 1638 Reverend John Davenport and Theophilus Eaton came from England to New Haven after a brief stay in Boston, which they felt was too liberal. The two men established harsh laws to govern the settlement through the church. They interpreted the Bible strictly and enforced its edicts rigidly. With good financial backing and a fine deep-water harbor at the mouth of the Quinnipiac River, the colony prospered and soon spread out to additional settlements along the coast of Long Island Sound.

Yale University was founded in 1701 in Branford; classes were held in Old Saybrook in 1707 and finally moved to New Haven in 1716. Two years later the school was renamed for Elihu Yale, in appreciation for his gift to the college of £562. The oldest building is the 1752 Connecticut Hall. Tours of the University are available from Phelps Gateway off College Street, at the Green. The Yale Information Office (203–432–2300) located there provides maps and schedules.

The campus, with its separate enclosed colleges sealed off from busy streets, is very much like that of Oxford University. A carillon in Gothic-style Harkness Tower fills the air with melody throughout the day. Inside in the Memorial Room, you can follow the history of the college through a series of wood carvings.

The **New Haven Green,** one of nine squares laid out by the founders of the colony, is like a European square, filled with people doing business, relaxing, or talking with friends. It's also the site of a local celebration. In late April or early May, there's a historical reenactment of Powder House Day, the day Captain Benedict Arnold asked for the keys to the Powder House before he took his troops off to Boston to join the rebellion. The ceremony is complete in detail, with the Governor's Footguard wearing Revolutionary War uniforms.

Another relic of the Revolutionary era is the **Pardee-Morris House** (1780), at 325 Lighthouse Road (203–562–4183). Amos Morris had built a house on this site prior to 1780, but it was burned when the British invaded New Haven in July of 1779, so he rebuilt it in 1780 with the help of his son. The house contains furnishings from the seventeenth century through the nineteenth century. The house is open 11:00 A.M.–4:00 P.M. on Saturday and Sunday from Memorial Day to Labor Day; other times by appointment.

West Rock Park is a place many visitors want to explore. There's a trail along the ridge that offers views of cliffs and harbors, tracks of prehistoric animals, and marks of glacial movement in the sedimentary rocks. Along the trail visitors will come to **Judges' Cave,** which was home for three months to two British regicides.

Black Rock Fort and **Fort Nathan Hale,** both on Woodward Avenue, are reconstructed forts from the Revolutionary War and the Civil War respectively. British General Tryon's troops captured and burned Black Rock Fort during the invasion of 1779, but it was later rebuilt. Both forts are currently being restored; they also offer views of the harbor. They are open from Memorial Day to Labor Day. Call (203) 787–8790 for further details.

The **New Haven Colony Historical Society,** at 114 Whitney Avenue, has historical and industrial exhibits, a research library, and a permanent decorative arts gallery that displays tablewares of New Haven. It offers both permanent and changing exhibits of maritime artifacts, furniture, and paintings. It is open 10:00 A.M.–5:00 P.M. Tuesday through Friday and 2:00 P.M.–5:00 P.M. Saturday and Sunday. For more information on current exhibits, call (203) 562–4183.

A bed and breakfast worth trying is the **Inn at Chapel West,** at 1201 Chapel Street. Some bedrooms have fireplaces. Call (203) 777–1201 for reservations.

Off with His Head

In 1661 Edward Whalley and William Goffe, who had signed a warrant for the arrest and execution of King Charles I fourteen years earlier, fled for their lives when Charles II, the son of the beheaded king, offered a £100 reward for their capture. A plaque bolted to a nearby boulder tells the story:

Here, May 15th 1661, and for some weeks thereafter, Edward Whalley and his son-in-law William Goffe, Members of Parliament, General Officers in the Army of the Commonwealth and signers of the death warrant of King Charles I, found shelter and concealment from the officers of the Crown after the Restoration. Opposition to tyrants is Obedience to God!

In 1639, a year after the New Haven Colony was established, Henry Whitfield led another Puritan congregation from England to Connecticut. They settled just east of New Haven in **Guilford,** probably named after Guildford in Surrey. The town has not suffered the industrial development of its neighboring city and thus has been able to preserve a remarkable number of houses from the colonial era. The **Henry Whitfield State Historical Museum,** on Old Whitfield Street, is the oldest house in Connecticut, dating from 1639, as well as the oldest stone house in New England.

Henry Whitfield—who had been rector of St. Margaret's Church in Ockley, Surrey, beginning in 1618—and his wife, Dorothy, left England for the New World. During the voyage the men on board ship signed the Guilford Covenant, an agreement of mutual support. They landed in New Haven to a warm welcome from the settlers who had come there two years earlier, since the new arrivals had brought news of friends and relatives. The new settlers agreed to buy land from the Menuncatuck Indians and paid "12 coates, 12 fathom of Wompom, 12 glasses, 12 payer of shooes, 12 Hatchetts, 12 paire of stockings, 12 hooes, 4 kettles, 12 knives, 12 hatts, 12 porringers, 12 spoons and 2 English coates." Henry Whitfield signed the Indian Deed.

Whitfield's stone house—also intended as a secure fortress for the colony, if needed—rose with a large north chimney stack; the original masonry has held up remarkably well over the years. Diamond-paned leaded casement windows give charm to the front of the house. Inside, the Great Hall is 33

The Henry Whitfield House is said to be the oldest stone house in New England.

feet long, with a fireplace at each end. Henry and Dorothy Whitfield and seven of their nine children lived in the house, along with servants. Today the house contains a collection of seventeenth- and eighteenth-century furnishings, including the Governor William Leete wainscot chair, a 1685 Phinney chest with carved front and sides, a Jacobean press cupboard, and a large seventeenth-century loom. The Whitfields owned pieces still in the house—a bedstead, a table and chairs, and books. Outside visitors may stroll in the formal herb garden. For further information call (203) 453–2457 or 566–3005.

More houses to see? Scores of them from the seventeeth and eighteenth centuries are very much alive today as private homes, but visitors can get inside two more. The **Hyland House** (1660), at 84 Boston Street, is a colonial saltbox with striking woodwork inside. Three fireplaces, big enough to walk into, display seventeenth-century cookware. Open 10:00 A.M.–4:30 P.M. daily except Monday, June through Labor Day, and Saturday and Sunday from Labor Day to Columbus Day. Call (203) 453–9477 for information. Another saltbox in town is the **Thomas Griswold House Museum,** at 171 Boston Street, dating from 1774. Displays detail local history, and there is a collection of costumes and furniture. Open 11:00 A.M.–4:00 P.M. daily except Monday, mid-June through Labor Day, and Saturday and Sunday from Labor Day to Columbus Day. Call (203) 453–3176 or 453–5517 for more details.

At the western edge of the New Haven Colony's influence is **Greenwich,** first settled in 1640, when the Indians sold the land for twenty-five coats. (Try that for a down payment on property here today!) Buried in the modern fashionable suburb are two colonial houses. You can't miss seeing the scalloped-shingled house known as the **Putnam Cottage** (203–869–9697), at 243 Putnam Avenue, which dates from 1690. During the Revolution it was called Knapp's Tavern, and General Israel Putnam entertained leaders here. When the British arrived to destroy the saltworks in February 1799, Putnam reputedly escaped by riding his horse over a cliff. The house has handsome fieldstone fireplaces. It is open 1:00 P.M.–4:00 P.M. Wednesday, Friday, and Sunday. The **Bush-Holley House** (1732), at 39 Strickland Road, was the home of David Bush, a mill owner and farmer. The house contains interesting collections of eighteenth-century Connecticut furniture, as well as paintings, sculpture, and pottery. Open noon –4:00

P.M. Tuesday through Friday and 1:00 P.M.–4:00 P.M. on Sunday; closed holidays. For more information call (203) 869–6899.

Visitors who would like to stay overnight in Greenwich should try **The Homestead,** at 420 Field Point Road. This attractive inn, which dates from 1799, has individually decorated rooms and offers a fine gourmet restaurant. Call (203) 869–7500 for reservations. If you're heading east, try the **Silvermine Tavern,** at 194 Perry Avenue in Norwalk, for a meal or an overnight stay. The Coach House, the Old Mill, the Gatehouse, and the Tavern are all within earshot of a waterfall. Call (203) 847–4558 or fax (203) 847–9171 for reservations.

WESTERN CONNECTICUT

The landscape of northwestern Connecticut, where the Taconic Range tails off into hills, is somewhat reminiscent of the Cotswolds in England, and it has the same kind of charm today. Because the region is remote from navigable water, which was so essential in the colonial era, it was settled relatively late and only then for its industrial potential. Like much of rural Connecticut in the eighteenth century, it was largely deforested for farms, and its factories built the towns that are now so attractive to residents and visitors. Gone now are the noise, stench, and confusion that produced the affluence so evident in the beautiful colonial houses that remain.

If you'd like to visit a living museum of eighteenth-century life, head for **Litchfield**, one of the earliest restoration projects in America. Its residents, through amazing foresight, began preparing for the twentieth century in the nineteenth, by restoring older buildings to their original state and converting newer ones to colonial styles—and there were plenty of buildings to work on. Early settlers, led by John Marsh and John Buell in 1719, built churches, gristmills, houses, and a school on the rolling hills of the town. During the Revolution the town was active as a communication and supply link for the patriots.

The **Litchfield Historical Society** (203–567–4501) offers an eighteen-page booklet for a walking tour; it includes information on the date, style, and original owners of the houses on North and South Streets. Although most of the homes are private, some of them welcome visitors on each Open House Day in July. The museum houses a fine collection of early American

Melting Down a King

According to local legend a lead statue of King George III was lifted from its base on Bowling Green in New York and taken to the woodshed behind Oliver Wolcott's house in Litchfield. The women and girls in town melted it down and made the lead into bullets.

paintings, furniture, decorative arts, galleries of special exhibits, and a research library. Open 11:00 A.M.–5:00 P.M. Tuesday through Saturday and 1:00 P.M.–5:00 P.M. Sunday, April through October.

South Street takes you by the **Tapping Reeve House** and **Law School.** In the house you'll find hand-stenciled walls in the front hall, a lovely paneled dining room, and fine period furnishings, many of which belong to the Reeve family. Tapping Reeve graduated first in his class from Princeton University in 1763. While working as a tutor, he taught Sally and Aaron Burr, the children of the late president of the college. He and Sally fell in love but were not allowed to marry because she was too young. Finally in 1773 Tapping and Sally were married, and set up housekeeping in Litchfield. The school, about 100 feet from the house, is the one-room building where legal education in this country began in 1784. Among its graduates were Aaron Burr, John C. Calhoun, Horace Mann, and many members of Congress. Open 11:00 A.M.–5:00 P.M. Tuesday through Saturday and 1:00 P.M.–5:00 P.M. on Sundays, May through October; closed holidays. Call (203) 567–4501 to find out more.

When you're ready for a meal or a place to spend the night, head for the **Toll Gate Hill Inn,** on Route 202, formerly a way station on the stage-coach line between Litchfield and Hartford in the late eighteenth and early nineteenth centuries. Dating from 1745, the building is also called the Captain William Bull Tavern. For reservations call (203) 482–6116.

Apart from Litchfield, most of the prosperous eighteenth-century industrial towns of northwestern Connecticut—like those of the Brandywine Valley in Delaware—were located on or near the Upper Housatonic River, hardly navigable in the deep-water sense (it's now good for canoeing) but nevertheless a source of water power. **Salisbury** defied this economic logic through its very rich high-quality ore beds, and it soon became an early ore-producing center. It was first settled in the 1720s by Dutch families from New York. The earliest forge, which was located in the Lime Rock area on Salmon Creek, dates from 1734.

The nearby village of **Lakeville** was the site of the most important blast furnace in the colony. In the Salisbury area three blast furnaces were in full swing during the Revolution: Lakeville Blast Furnace, Mount Riga Blast Furnace, and the Lime Rock Blast Furnace. Ethan Allen was one of three partners in the Lakeville furnace. During the war this furnace produced both heavy and light cannon, cannonballs, grapeshot, huge cast-iron kettles (which were used for making stews and soups for the army), and other products. Today visitors can see the remains of a furnace on Mount Riga.

Salisbury has a bed and breakfast that contains once-hidden paneling— the lumber was supposed to be turned over to the king of England but instead was hidden under the attic floorboards! **Under Mountain Inn,** on Route 41, was built during the 1700s and has more than enough history to intrigue visitors. The paneling now lines the English Pub. Call (203) 435–0242 for reservations.

On the upper Housatonic **Kent** was a busy industrial center by 1758, with three iron furnaces roaring in the area. Just downstream Bull's Bridge was built during the Revolution so that iron ore could be brought to a forge. Bull's Bridge achieved a bit of notoriety in 1781 when a horse, perhaps a favorite of George Washington, fell into the tumultuous Housatonic River. His travel expense account detailed: "Getting a horse out of Bull's Falls, $215.00." From the size of the bill, the rescue must have been difficult, and Washington, as always, was under time pressure to get on his way—perhaps to the next place that might claim he slept there.

Just north of Kent on Route 7 stands the **Sloane–Stanley Museum** (203–927–3849), located in a rustic barn. There is a replica of artist and author Eric Sloane's studio, exhibits of his work, and an extensive collection of wooden tools, some dating back to the seventeenth century. The ruins of a Kent blast-iron furnace on the grounds help to complete the picture of work in early Kent. Open 10:00 A.M.–4:00 P.M. Wednesday through Sunday and holidays mid-May through end of October.

The **Fife and Drum** on Main Street is a handy place for lunch after touring the Sloane-Stanley Museum. Eric Sloane prints hang on the walls of the Tap Room. For reservations call (203) 927–3509 or just stop by.

The **Institute for American Indian Studies,** in **Washington,** is a wonderful place to learn about Native Americans—not only of the colonial period but all the way back to prehistory. Visitors can explore a simulated archaeological site, a reconstructed Algonquian village that contains a long-house, which is furnished with sapling-supported bunks covered with skins, and then walk along the Quinnetukut habitat trail through the woods. Open 10:00 A.M.–5:00 P.M. Monday through Saturday and noon–5:00 P.M. Sunday; closed holidays. Call (203) 868–0518 for more details.

The **Gunn Historical Museum** (203–868–7756) is located in a 1781 house on Wykeham Road. The house originally had a gambrel roof and two chimneys instead of the one that remains. Today visitors will see dolls, doll-houses, period furnishings, needlework, and spinning wheels. Open noon–4:00 P.M. Thursday through Sunday, April to December; closed holidays.

South of Litchfield is a town that is famous for its special **Bethlehem** Christmas postmark and Christmas Festival. For a very unusual and moving experience, visit **Regina Laudis Abbey,** on Flanders Road. An eigh-teenth-century Neapolitan nativity scene is on display here. It's the sort of exhibit you can look at for a long time and still not see every figure. To find out more call (203) 266–5702.

Chief Pomperaug of the Pootatuck Indians sold land for "ancient Woodbury" in 1659. A marker for him stands in the middle of **Woodbury**. The first settlers raised sheep, and by the time of the Revolutionary War, they were exporting woolen products, including shipments to the army.

Glebe House (203–263–2855), on Hollow Road, was built as a minis-ter's farm in 1771. Woodbury's first Episcopal priest, John Rutgers Marshall, lived in the house with his wife, Sarah, and their children. A very important meeting was held in the house just after the declara-tion of American independence. Samuel Seabury was elected by a group of Episcopalians as the first bishop in America. This group proclaimed both the separation of church and state and religious tolerance in the newly independent colonies. Open 1:00 P.M.–4:00 P.M. Wednesday through Sunday, April to November; other times by appointment.

Colonial Perks

A *glebe house* is named for the glebe, a plot of land that was given to a cler-gyman as part of his salary.

The oldest house in town is the **Hurd House,** which dates from about 1680. This house is actually two houses joined together; visitors can see the joint in the upstairs hall, to the left of the window. John Hurd built the first gristmill in Woodbury 300 yards away from his house, on the Pomperaug

River. Period furniture embellishes the house, as well as colonial gardens.

When you're ready for lunch or a place to spend the night, head for the **Curtis House,** on Route 6, which is Main Street in Woodbury. First opened as the Orenaug Inn in 1754, it was later called Kelly's Tavern. Call (203) 263–2101 for overnight reservations or stop in for a meal.

FOR MORE INFORMATION

State of Connecticut Department of Economic Development
865 Brook Street
Rocky Hill, CT 06067–3405
(800) 282–6863

Maine

Historical Introduction to
MAINE

*T*he arrival of European ships in the coves and reaches of the Maine coast is a mere blip in the record of human habitation there. Centuries before, Algonquians had migrated eastward to the sea and remained, becoming a group of tribes referred to as the Abnaki, meaning people of the dawn. Later, feisty Europeans first settled along the coast, where they could move about by water to fish and farm while trying to survive the rugged winters in a rockbound landscape.

Sporadic Settlement

The early colonial history of Maine is fraught with uncertainty and confusion of many kinds—a tale of grandiose schemes, abandoned settlements, political maneuvering for access to its bounty of forests and fish, and almost incessant involvement in wars of European origin. Initial settlements in the first two decades of the seventeenth century were ephemeral at best and were often evacuated after a rigorous winter or an attack by opposing British and French forces.

Unlike the neighboring Massachusetts Bay Colony, which eventually absorbed it, Maine was the object of many entrepreneurial projects early in the seventeenth century. Many of them originated in Plymouth, England, where Sir Fernando Gorges organized a joint stock company for the colonization of all New England in 1620 and took advantage of the politics before the English Civil War to get a grant from Charles I for the whole Province of Maine in 1635. Earlier two experienced ship captains visited the coast, John Smith of Virginia, who had charted it in 1614, and Christopher Levett of the Royal Navy. Both had argued that its unlimited resources of fish and timber could be more efficiently exploited through permanent British settlements, and both wrote books to spread their views. The outcome of their case for solid, permanent colonization, however, remained ephemeral—a handful of trading and fishing outposts in competition with those sponsored by the Massachusetts Bay Company, most of which had to be abandoned during the ravages of King Philip's War in the last quarter of the century.

Abnaki Indians and English Fishermen

When white settlers arrived during the early seventeenth century, a number of Indian tribes lived in the area, including the surviving Penobscots and Passamaquoddies. The Abnaki once included a multitude of tribes spread through Maine, New Hampshire, and northern Massachusetts. At first these Indians were friendly and helpful to the settlers, who needed their expertise in growing food to survive. Corn was a staple because it could be used for both animals and humans, and by 1635 several water-powered corn-grinding mills had been built along the Piscataqua River and in Berwick.

Early settlers made their living by fishing, fur trading, and lumbering. John Smith was so impressed with the great variety of fish that he built a fishery on Monhegan in 1614. The Banks of Maine were fished by men from southern England, especially Cornwall, Devon, Dorset, and Somerset.

The King's Broad Arrow

The first sawmill in the United States was created in York in 1623. The Waldo Patent of 1630, earlier known as the Muscongus Grant, became the first timberland grant. Forests on the Androscoggin, Kennebec, and Penobscot were cut for all purposes, but the tall, straight pines were especially valuable to an expanding Royal Navy that was running out of good timber at home. Lumbermen cut "mast ways," which were roads in the wilderness designed to bring out the giants without damage. Special ships were built to carry five hundred masts back to England on each voyage.

George Tate, of Portland, was in charge of selecting trees and sailing them to England. He marked trees that were taller than 74 feet and more than 24 inches in circumference around the trunk with three slashes, the "King's Broad Arrow," which meant that they belonged to the king and not the colonists. Of course the colonists bridled at this restriction on rights to cut their own timber, but the Crown was not negotiable.

Steadfast Royal Trees

There still may be a very few giant pines left in the forests blazed with the "King's Broad Arrow" designating royal ownership. Of course it would be extraordinary to find such an ancient pine: Any tree that was large enough before 1775 must be 300 years old by now. And how could such a tree still stand after centuries of logging and battering by frequent gales and some hurricanes? Yet foresters have identified one that may have survived. They won't know for sure until it topples on its own and they can then check under the bark for the telltale blaze.

Shipbuilding

The combination of extensive coastline, sheltered harbors, deep rivers, and abundant timber favored shipbuilding in Maine. It began early in the brief Popham settlement with the *Virginia* (1607), the first ship built in America. The Popham colonists were parolees from an English jail who left after their first winter, but before long John Winter started another shipyard on Richmond Island in 1632. Soon more shipyards developed on the coast and along the rivers and became a major occupation for many of the inhabitants. Some boats were built in unlikely places far inland because the timber stood there. By 1762 William Swanton had created contract shipbuilding in Bath, where yards built ships for Spain, France, and the West Indies.

Wars

Along with trying to make a living, the inhabitants had to contend with one war after another as England and France harassed each other. Both sides used the Indians, who were struggling for survival and no longer on friendly terms with the settlers. From the beginning of King Philip's War in 1675, when Casco and Scarborough were destroyed in the first raids and many other settlements during the following year, people emigrated to safer places for the next forty years. The eighteenth century was not much kinder to Maine. Although permanent settlements had been established along the coast from Kittery to Casco Bay and beyond, a series of wars throughout the century made them constantly vulnerable.

Mostly fueled by British-French rivalry for the domination of New England and Acadia, one war succeeded another: Queen Anne's War (1703–13), which left only Kittery, Wells, and York intact; Lovewell's War (1722–25) against raiding Indians in the southwest; King George's War (1744–48), during which many settlers retreated again to other colonies, and the French and Indian War (1754–60). At the same time colonists in Maine were fighting political battles for independence from the Massachusetts Bay Colony, which had formally claimed the territory in 1661 and began administering it as a province the next year. The Continental Congress reaffirmed that arrangement, and Maine remained a part of Massachusetts until 1820.

Apart from a British naval attack that obliterated Falmouth (later renamed Portland) in 1775, Maine was not a significant battleground during the Revolution, but it was the scene of two disastrous military adventures: In 1775 Col. Benedict Arnold led more than a thousand men up the Kennebec into the wilderness to lay siege on Quebec, a six-week trek that destroyed the effectiveness of his demoralized force; and in 1779 Commodore Richard Saltonstall brought an amphibious force of the same size against Castine in Penobscot Bay but failed to dislodge the British and had to destroy much of his own fleet when the Royal Navy arrived.

Regions to Explore

Maine's long rocky peninsulas and heavy forestation made road travel very difficult, and settlers usually went no farther inland than about 20 miles, apart from riverbanks. Why should they bother, when they could easily reach good lumbering territory along rivers and move between sections of saltwater farms by boat? Right from the beginning, going Down East from Massachusetts has been a nautical affair, sailing downwind on the prevailing sou'westerlies to reach your destination in a fjordlike mixture of land and water. So even today a road trip through colonial Maine is likely to begin at the border with New Hampshire and head east along the coast, with occasional forays to the interior up major rivers like the Kennebec and Penobscot.

DOWN EAST

The approaches to the Piscataqua River were protected by the first fort on the site, begun in 1690 and developed in the early eighteenth century in **Kittery. Fort McClary State Historic Site** (207–429–2845), Kittery Point Road (Route l03), provided protection against the French and Indians as well as pirates. It was named Fort William after Sir William Pepperell, a Kittery native knighted by the British for his leadership of the Louisbourg expedition in 1745, then renamed during the Revolution, when commemoration of a victory of combined British and colonial forces over the French seemed inappropriate. The hexagonal blockhouse, brick magazine, and barracks were built some years later. Photographers may want to stand below the blockhouse and look up for an unusual shot. It is open daily from 9:00 A.M. to dusk, Memorial Day to September 30.

The **Isles of Shoals** are part of New Hampshire but located just offshore from Kittery. Mainlanders accused the islanders of housing the pirates that harassed their shipping, and also of seducing ships onto the treacherous shoals by changing the location of navigation lights. Then the wreckers, aptly named "mooncussers," could remove valuable goods from the stranded ships.

Maritime aficionados will want to visit the **Kittery Historical and Naval Museum,** on Rogers Road (207–439–3080), which records the history of seafaring in Kittery as well as along the coast. Models of ships, including a 13-foot replica of John Paul Jones's *Ranger,* dioramas, a collection of shipbuilding tools, navigation instruments, and photographs portray this heritage. Shipbuilding is a major focus in the museum. The museum is open 10:00 A.M.–4:00 P.M. Monday through Friday, from Memorial Day to October 3; by appointment the rest of the year.

The U.S.S. *Ranger* was built in a Kittery shipyard in 1777, and most of the crew was composed of Kittery men. All gentlemen seamen and able-bodied landsmen who have a mind to distinguish themselves in the glorious cause of their Country, and make their Fortunes were urged to join ship, and the recruiting poster offered other enticements too: "Any gentlemen volunteers who have a mind to take an agreable voyage in this pleasant Season of the Year, may . . . meet with every Civility they can possibly expect."

John Paul Jones breezed out of nearby Portsmouth, New Hampshire, and made his way to France with the news that Burgoyne had surrendered. His ship received the first salute given to a ship under the American flag. Then she harassed British vessels in European waters until finally captured by the British in 1780, when she became part of the Royal Navy. A monument of John Paul Jones stands on Route 1 in Kittery.

A 1736 colonial house nearby could be where you will choose to spend the night. **High Meadows Bed & Breakfast,** on Route 101 in Eliot, is about 5 miles from Kittery. The house was built by Elliott Frost, a merchant shipbuilder and captain. For reservations call (207) 439–0590.

The **Old York Historical Society** maintains a living-history village of seven historic buildings in **York. Jefferds Tavern,** on Lindsay Road, is the place to get information and begin tours. Visitors begin touring at the Tavern, a mid-eighteenth-century saltbox tavern that started its life in Wells. Interpreters engage in a variety of craft and living-history demonstrations there. The buildings in York are open 10:00 A.M.–5 P.M. Tuesday to Saturday, mid-June to September 3. Call (207) 363–4974 for more details.

Old York village has most of the buildings that were considered essential for a settlement in the colonial era. Like to pretend you're a child in an eighteenth century school? The **Old Schoolhouse,** one of the oldest schools in Maine, dates from 1745 and is furnished with typical school desks and benches of that era. There's a church, too, although churches were extremely scarce in the beleaguered settlements of Maine until Cotton Mather cajoled young Harvard graduates to go there as missionaries in the middle of the seventeenth century. One of these, Samuel Moody, arrived home after the siege of Louisbourg and devoted himself to supervising the building of York's **First Parish Congregational Church** in 1747; he served as its pastor for forty-seven years. Parson Moody's son, Joseph Moody, was the subject of one of Hawthorne's most famous short stories, "The Minister's Black Veil."

Water, Anyone?

Beverages were served during colonial times in pewter mugs, wooden noggins, or boiled-leather mugs called "black jacks." In them you would find ale, beer, wine, or rum, and sometimes hard cider. Americans today, who consume more water than any other nationality and expect to find it available in public places, may be surprised to learn that their colonial forebears hardly ever drank it.

Moody accidentally killed a friend while they were out hunting. He felt so guilty that he wore a handkerchief over his face for the rest of his life.

The John Hancock Wharf at Old York Village

Around the bend stands the **Emerson-Wilcox House** of 1724, which was a general store, tailor shop, tavern, and home for Edward Emerson. The Emerson Tavern entertained Presidents John Quincy Adams and James Monroe, as well as the Marquis de Lafayette, and then served as a private home. It is now a museum, which displays the Mary Bulman collection of American eighteenth-century crewelwork bed hangings. Visitors will find twelve rooms to explore.

Dungeons and cells are grim reminders of what it must have been like to linger in the **Old Gaol,** but at least it was an improvement on the older Maine practice of confining prisoners in small chambers dug into the earth. Built in 1719, this gaol was once the King's Prison for Maine; both hardened criminals and debtors were held there. The gaoler's family quarters are also open.

The **John Hancock Warehouse** offers displays on maritime traffic, industry, and life on the York River. The house was built by Thomas Donnell, then owned by John Hancock, one of the signers of the Declaration of Independence and also a Governor of Massachusetts.

Lucky indeed is a house that has been lived in by the same family for generations. The **Elizabeth Perkins House,** built in 1730, is a Colonial Revival House with original Perkins family pieces. Both Elizabeth Perkins

The Candlemas Massacre

One of the most infamous raids of the incessant Indian wars that plagued Maine was the Candlemas Massacre during the French and Indian sweep of Maine settlements. On the night of February 2, 1692, 500 Abnaki killed 80 York inhabitants and burned many of the buildings. The site is known as Snowshoe Rock because the Abnaki abandoned their snowshoes just before attacking. About 5 miles north of town on Chases Pond Road, you'll find an identifying marker set into "Snowshoe Rock."

and her mother, Mrs. Newton Perkins, gathered antiques from other countries, and their collections are on display.

Another old family home nearby is the **Sayward-Wheeler House,** at 79 Barrell Lane Extension in York Harbor, located right on the water. Owned by Jonathan Sayward, who was involved in the attack on the French fortress at Louisbourg, Nova Scotia, in 1745, the house has been maintained with its original family portraits and furnishings. To find out more call (207) 363–2709.

Gravestone aficionados will find the **Old York Cemetery** a treasure. Some of the headstones are decorated with a winged death's-head and inscriptions in Old English. Don't miss the "witch's grave," covered on top by a large stone so that the "witch" buried there in 1744 could never escape.

If you're in York the weekend after Columbus Day, attend the Harvest Fest, which offers a variety of colonial activities. Call (207) 363–4422 for information.

When it's time to rest for the night, consider stopping at the **Cliff House,** a few miles north of York in Ogunquit. The house dates from a later era, 1872, but there are advantages to that: The rooms have balconies with an ocean view from Bald Head Cliff. It was built by the wife of a sea captain with wood milled in the family sawmill in Ogunquit. Call (207) 361–1000 or fax (207) 361–2122 for reservations. Just a little farther on, you'll find the **Kennebunk Inn,** at 45 Main Street, Kennebunk. The building dates from 1799, with additions. Local folklore says that the Marquis de Lafayette visited the inn in 1825. For reservations call (800) 743–1799 or (207) 985–3351.

The town of **South Berwick** was settled in 1623 on the Salmon Falls River, and a sawmill was built there in 1634. According to local legend a vessel appropriately named the *Pied Cow* brought the first cows to Maine in 1634, landing on the east bank of the Salmon River in Vaughan Woods, off Route 236.

If you've read *The Tory Lover* by Sarah Orne Jewett, you'll recognize the setting for this historical romance. **Hamilton House,** on Vaughan's Lane, off Route 236, was built in 1785 by shipbuilder Jonathan Hamilton. This substantial hipped-roof house has four large chimneys. Admiral John Paul Jones visited the house a number of times. Call (603) 436–3205 for details.

South Berwick has a claim to fame as the home of Maine's best-known writer of fiction. Sarah Orne Jewett (1849–1909), often labeled a "local colorist" by literary historians, nevertheless has a fictional voice that rings true Down East. She gained national recognition for *A Country Doctor* (1884), remembered alongside other notable publications of that year and the next, Mark Twain's *Huckleberry Finn* and a New England classic, William Dean Howells's *The Rise of Silas Lapham.*

Now you can see where she lived. The **Sarah Orne Jewett House,** at 5 Portland Street, built about 1774, was bought a few years later by Capt. Theodore Jewett. This hipped-roof, dormer-windowed house has a Doric portico with fluted columns. Inside, a floral window brightens the landing. Jewett's grandfather and father filled the house with furniture from abroad, tapestries, engravings, silver, and willowware. There is a hidden stairway that leads from the guest room to the cellar and attic. To find out more call (603) 436–3205.

Following traders and explorers, **Portland** (then called Casco) was first settled in 1623 by Christopher Levett, a captain in the Royal Navy whose *Voyage into New England* argued strenuously for permanent colonization in Maine. He built a stone house in Casco and wintered there before returning to England, leaving ten men behind in his house. The story stops because he never returned, dying at sea seven years later on a voyage from the Massachusetts Bay Colony to England. The early history of the settlement is marked by another frontier incident. By 1628 Walter Bagnall, or "Big Walt," had moved into a hut on Spurwink River and proceeded to trade junk trinkets and liquor with the Indians for furs. As he built a fortune, the Indians began to suspect his motives, and an Indian chief, Squidraset, killed him a few years later.

George Cleeve arrived with his family around 1631 and connived to be named deputy governor of the province until it was discovered that he had lied by creating trumped-up charges against earlier deputies. He went to England and managed to find a patron who bought the patent of the Plough (a patent of land, at Sagadahoc, that was named after the ship *Plough*) and named Cleeve deputy president of the patent of the Plough. Cleeve and Sir Ferdinando Gorges, the proprietor of Maine, fought back and forth in the courts in Boston and in England over the Casco Bay Colony until the Maine Colonies became part of Massachusetts in 1661.

By 1675 Casco had been renamed Falmouth, and the settlement numbered about 400 residents. King Philip's War broke out in 1675 with severe consequences for Maine as Indians began attacking settlers. In the summer of 1676, the Indians swept through, killing colonists and burning homes. Surviving inhabitants left by boat and secured themselves on Jewell Island; some gave up and continued on to Salem. By 1716 new settlers came again to Falmouth, after Samuel Moody built a fort there. The town flourished as a trading center, exporting fish, furs, and lumber. Shipbuilding became a major industry, and masts were exported for the British Navy.

During the American Revolution in October 1775, four British vessels sailed into the harbor and demanded that the people turn in their arms and leave town. This was a punitive mission under the command of Lt. Henry Mowat, who had orders from the Admiralty to "chastize" dissident settlements; he also had unpleasant memories of an incident earlier that year in Machias, when townsmen had captured his ship and held him prisoner for a short time. Now, when the people of Falmouth refused to surrender their arms, the British fleet peppered the town with bombs, grapeshot, and cannonballs. Most buildings went up in flames, and 2,000 residents were left without homes.

One courageous lady, the Widow Grele, refused to leave her tavern, throwing buckets of water on flames all around. Thereafter the tavern was used for court sessions until a new courthouse could be built. After all of the ruin they had caused, the British chose not to occupy the town, so the remaining townspeople lived in the ruins and rebuilt. By 1786 the town was renamed Portland and commerce returned.

George Tate, who was responsible for selecting and blazing mast trees with the "King's Broad Arrow," built the **Tate House,** at 1270 Westbrook Street, in 1755. His Georgian house is unusual, with its indented clerestory gambrel roof, which is a recessed windowed section, above the second story designed to let in light. The large central chimney leads to eight fireplaces. Inside, the house is furnished with pieces that depict the life-style of a wealthy official during the eighteenth century. The hall contains a dogleg stairway and the original cove ceiling. Collections include pottery, porcelain, silver, and textiles; pewter and iron kitchen utensils are also on display. Family letters and memorabilia give insight into the Tate family. Outside, the raised-bed herb garden contains eighteenth-century-type plants. Open 10:00 A.M.–4:00 P.M. Tuesday through Saturday and 1:00 P.M.–4:00 P.M. on Sunday, July 1 to Labor Day, and 10:00 A.M.–4:00 P.M. Friday to Sunday until October 31. Call (207) 774–9781 for more information.

The first brick house built in Portland, with bricks sent from Philadelphia, was the **Wadsworth-Longfellow House,** at 485 Congress Street. It was built in 1785 by Henry Wadsworth Longfellow's grandfather, Gen. Peleg Wadsworth. Enough bricks were sent to complete one story, but the second story had to wait until another shipment arrived in 1786. The house kept growing: To the two stories with a gable roof, a third was added after a fire damaged the roof. The house contains Wadsworth and Longfellow family furnishings, including crocheted tablecloths and needlework samplers. Other period pieces are from the collection of the Maine Historical Society. The house is open 10:00 A.M.–4:00 P.M. Tuesday to Saturday, June 1–October 30; closed July 4 and Labor Day.

The Longfellows and the Wadsworths were both descended from Pilgrims who came on the *Mayflower.* Henry Wadsworth Longfellow lived in the house as a child with his seven brothers and sisters, parents, and an aunt. The Maine Historical Society Summer Gallery is next door to the house. Visitors are invited to stroll in the garden behind the house. For further information call (207) 774–1822.

Visitors can climb the 102 steps up in the tower of the **Portland Observatory** (207–774–5561) for fine views of Casco Bay, the White Mountains, and the country around Portland. The observatory, which stands at 138 Congress Street on Munjoy Hill, was built in 1807. The site had been even more important in colonial days when it was used as a lookout for incoming vessels. The observatory is open 1:00 P.M.–5:00 P.M. on Wednesday, Thursday, and Saturday and 10:00 A.M.–5 P.M. on Friday and Saturday during July and August; 1:00 P.M.–5:00 P.M. Friday through Sunday in June, September, and October. The hill gets its name from George Munjoy, who settled there around 1659. It is the site of the oldest cemetery in Portland, named Eastern Cemetery, with graves that date back to 1670.

In nearby **Freeport,** now well known throughout the East as a burgeoning and busy shopping mecca built around an enlarged L.L. Bean store, visitors can still find some semblance of colonial atmosphere in the **Harraseeket Inn** on 162 Main Street. This inn began with a building in 1798, then added a new wing in 1989 to meet the new demand. When your shopping spree is over, you'll find that the inn is a good place to recover, take tea at four o'clock, sup in one of three dining rooms, and stay the night. For reservations call (800) 342–6423 or (207) 865–9377.

A living-history museum that portrays Shaker life from the eighteenth century to the present day is located in **New Gloucester.** The **Shaker Museum,** on Route 26 in Sabbathday Lake, is one of few remaining Shaker communities. The Sabbathday Lake Shaker community was founded in 1783 and formally established in 1794. The Meetinghouse is a two-and-one-half story clapboard building with a gambrel roof. The room for worship is on the first floor. Collections include furniture, textiles, tools, farm implements, and folk art. The museum is open 10:00 A.M.–4:30 P.M. daily except Sunday from Memorial Day to Columbus Day. Call (207) 926–4597 to find out more.

The oldest wooden fort building left in New England is **Old Fort Western,** on City Center Plaza in **Augusta.** The fort dates from 1754. Wealthy Boston merchants, "Proprietors of the Kennebec Purchase," built the fort, which served as a supply depot for the military garrison at Fort Halifax, located 17 miles upriver. Capt. James Howard, the first commander of the fort, was in charge of the twenty soldiers who were garrisoned there. In 1763, after the French and Indian Wars, the fort was no longer used. James Howard bought it, and generations of his family lived in the main house. Visitors can get a glimpse into eighteenth-century life through the costumed interpreters. The fort is open 10:00 A.M.–5:00 P.M. Monday to Friday and 1:00 P.M.–5:00 P.M. Saturday and Sunday, mid-June to Labor Day; 1:00 P.M.–4:00 P.M. Saturday and Sunday from Memorial Day to mid-June and the day after Labor Day. Call (207) 626–2385 for more details.

"This Land Called Maine" tells Maine's story in five natural history settings in the **Maine State Museum** (207–289–2301). Located in the Capitol Complex on State Street, it offers a wealth of programs and displays on Maine. Visitors can see collections of gems and minerals that are found in the state. Some exhibits focus on the state's early economic industries, including fishing, lumbering, and shipbuilding. A new archaeological exhibit is entitled "12,000 years in Maine." Open 9:00 A.M.–5:00 P.M. Monday to Friday, 10:00 A.M.–4:00 P.M. on Saturday, and 1:00 P.M.–4:00 P.M. on Sunday; closed January 1, Easter, Thanksgiving, and Christmas.

Upriver through the Wilderness

A rnold's collection of volunteers began marching at General Washington's headquarters in Cambridge and passed through Medford, Salem, and Ipswich to Newburyport. They sailed from Newburyport on September 19, 1775, on eleven schooners and sloops. Pittston was the departure point for the 1,100 men who soon found themselves struggling up the Kennebec River in their 400-pound bateaux loaded with equipment.

North of Augusta they met the challenge of the Ticonic Falls, followed by Five Mile Ripples. They were able to rest at Fort Halifax in Winslow before continuing on, carrying their heavy boats up steep cliffs around waterfalls. Skowhegan Falls and Solon Falls were especially difficult. In Norridgewock, the last bit of civilization at that time, they passed the site where a priest, Father Rasle, had been murdered by the British in 1724. His monument today is a granite obelisk with a cross on top.

The army reached Caratunk Falls in Solon, maneuvered rapids, and increased their food supply by fishing. By October 10 they reached the Great Carrying Place, where they were joined by three rifle companies. They were delighted to find plentiful moose for their dinners. The next section continued through marshes, around three ponds, and through a swamp. Rain had made walking difficult through the bog, but they finally reached the Dead River, where they saw mountains on both sides, covered with snow.

Arnold ordered his men to abandon the boats and carry provisions on their backs. By then they were exhausted and hungry—so hungry that they ate candles, their leather shot pouches, and even a beloved pet dog. After six weeks of relentless hardship, they finally reached the St. Lawrence opposite Quebec on November 8 but did not attack the garrison there until December 31, 1775, with another force that had come up the easier route through Lake Champlain and the Richelieu River.

Nearby in **Hallowell** visitors can stay overnight at **Maple Hill Farm Bed & Breakfast Inn,** on Outlet Road. The land was cleared and settled in the late 1700s and was home to one of the founding fathers of Hallowell, William Oliver Vaughn. Call (207) 622–2708 for reservations.

In 1607 Sir George Popham brought a group of settlers into the harbor at the mouth of the Kennebec River. He died during the first winter, and the colony broke up and left before the year was over; the colonists, however, had built the first ship of the colonies, the *Virginia*. The present **Fort Popham State Historic Site** was built in 1861 near the site of the original Popham Colony. Displays there interpret the history of the area—the story of Popham Colony, Benedict Arnold's march through Maine, and the fort's construction. Open 9:00 A.M.–dusk daily, Memorial Day to September 30.

In 1775 Benedict Arnold left from Popham to march to Quebec. He was unlucky because the British received word that he was on the way, thereby destroying the element of surprise. The **Arnold Trail** is 194 miles long and continues from Popham to Hallowell, Skowhegan, Solon, Moscow, Stratton, Sarampus, Chain of Ponds, and Coburn Gore. Those interested in Arnold's epic march to Quebec can drive along routes 201 and 201A to see some of the sites and read panels that detail the army's struggle. Hikers can also walk on the Appalachian Trail, map in hand, from where it joins the Arnold Trail at East Carry Pond. To do this cross over the Kennebec to the west side at Bingham and continue north along the Kennebec to the southern tip of Pierce Pond.

The **Damariscotta** site was settled by John Brown in 1625 at the head of navigable water, and in 1730 three families from Boston arrived to live there. Visitors can trace the history of Damariscotta's major industry, shipbuilding, in the **Chapman-Hall House,** on Main Street, built in 1754 by Nathaniel Chapman. The wooden house has a central brick chimney and small-paned windows. The rooms are pine paneled with wide-board floors and are furnished with antiques. Open 1:00 P.M.–5:00 P.M. daily except Monday, mid-June to September.

Not far away, on the Damariscotta River, stands the **Newcastle Inn**, which is a fine place to spend the night. Fifteen rooms are furnished with antiques and crewel needlework by one of the owners. Call (800) 832–8669 or (207) 563–5685 for reservations.

If you enjoy archaeological digs, **Colonial Pemaquid Historic Site** is the place to go. It is being explored just off Route 130. Foundations that date from the early seventeenth-century settlement have been uncovered. Artifacts, including household pieces and farming implements, may be seen in the adjacent museum, which is open 9:00 A.M.–5:30 P.M. daily, Memorial Day to Labor Day, and 9:00 A.M.–5:00 P.M. on Saturday and Sunday, Labor Day to October 31. For more information call (207) 677–2423.

Here's a place to stretch your legs and do a lot of exploring. **Fort William Henry** on **Pemaquid** beach is a replica of one of the second of three English forts on the site. A stockade called Shurt's Fort was built around 1630, then burned by Indians. Fort Charles was built in 1677. Then settlers built a third fort in 1692 to defend themselves against Indians, pirates, and the French. It was destroyed in 1696 by the French. A fourth, Fort Frederick, was built in 1729 and destroyed during the Revolution. The tower of the fort contains artifacts found on the site, military equipment, and Indian deeds. A stone wall encloses the old parade ground, and about 200 cellars are visible. The Old Fort Cemetery, just outside the fort, contains old slate stones, including that of Ann Rodgers, wife of Lt. Patrick Rodgers, who died in 1758. The fort is open 9:00 A.M.–5:30 P.M. daily Memorial Day to Labor Day and then 9:00 A.M.–5:00 P.M. on Saturday and Sunday until October 31. Call (207) 677–2423 for details.

You may wonder about this bit of graffiti found during a church restoration in Pemaquid. Someone wrote, "McLain is a lying fool" and placed it on a plaster layer under the **Harrington Meeting House**. This restored eighteenth-century meetinghouse is located on Old Harrington Road. Col. David Dunbar arrived in 1696 with 200 Irish Protestants and proceeded to divide the region into three areas: Walpole, Harrington, and Pemaquid.

Pirate in Pemaquid

Dixey Bull, a pirate who was incensed after the French seized his sloop in 1632, began harassing shipping vessels, without much success. He arrived in Pemaquid harbor and destroyed the trading post and some houses, stealing as he went. With this upturn in his fortune, he continued to raid settlements and capture small vessels. Not surprisingly, he disappeared when a fleet of ships left Boston harbor to find him, and no one knows if he was ever caught.

Three meetinghouses were to be built, and in 1768 a post-and-beam framework was erected in Bristol Mills. After disagreements the framework was taken down and rebuilt on another piece of land. The Reverend Alexander McLain came to America in 1770 and traveled on horseback to service each of the three meetinghouses.

The building was jacked up in 1851 and moved over the present cemetery, leaving the stones intact. The box pews and galleries were removed, the doors and windows were relocated, and the pulpit was lowered. During renovation after 1960 the box pews were returned, the pulpit was raised, and the galleries were replaced. A historical museum now occupies the gallery area. It houses artifacts, tools, maps, period clothing, and documents contributed by local residents. Open 2:00 P.M.–4:30 P.M. Monday, Wednesday, Friday, and Saturday in July and August. The Harrington Burial Ground contains stones that date back to 1716. Call (207) 677–2193 for more information.

If you'd like to sleep in a house with both river and saltwater views, try the **Little River Inn,** on Route 130 in **Pemaquid Falls.** It was built in 1840 as a farmhouse. Call (207) 677–2845 for reservations.

Captain John Smith wrote that **Camden** stands "under the high mountains of the Penobscot, against whose feet the sea doth beat." Champlain arrived in 1605 and called the Camden Hills the "mountains of Bedabedec" on his map. Views from the ledges of the Mount Battie South Trail are worth the climb for today's visitor; there is also a toll road from Camden Hills State Park. Other trails favored by hikers include Mount Megunticook Trail, Tablelands Trail, Bald Rock Mountain Trail, Maiden Cliff Trail, and Ragged Mountain Trail.

Conway Homestead and Mary Meeker Cramer Museum, on Conway Road off Route 1, dates from 1770, with later additions in 1815 and 1825. The house has roof timbers fastened with treenails, or trunnels. Some of the beams in the cellar still are covered with bark, and there is a bake-oven, built with small bricks, in the kitchen. The entrance hall is curved and contains a "parson's cupboard." Open 10:00 A.M.–4:00 P.M. Tuesday through Friday in July and August.

Robert Thorndike had the original deed to the lot, and his son was one of the first white children born in the area. Several generations of Thorndikes lived in the house until it was sold to Frederick Conway in 1826. The barn houses a collection of carriages, sleighs, farm tools, and a saw to cut ice. The complex also includes a blacksmith shop, herb garden, maple-sugar house, and barn. The Mary Meeker Cramer Museum houses collections of antique glass, paintings, musical instruments, furniture, costumes, quilts, and ship models. To find out more call (207) 236–2257.

Camden boasts a lot of historic inns including the **Camden Harbour Inn,** at 83 Bayview Street. Built in 1874, this inn is on a hill with views of the harbor and Penobscot Bay (207–236–4200). **Edgecombe-Coles House,** at 64 High Street, is also on a hilltop with a view (207–236–2336 or fax 207–236–6227). **Hawthorne Inn,** at 9 High Street, has views and gardens (207–236–8842). **The Maine Stay Inn,** at 22 High Street, is in an 1802 house in the historic district (207–236–9636). **Norumbega,** at 61 High Street, looks like a castle and was built in 1886 (207–236–4646).

For more than 200 years, **Castine** was fought for by the French, British, Dutch, and Americans. In 1629 the Pilgrims sent Edward Ashley there to build a trading post, but it was ruined in 1631 by the French. Baron de St. Castin came from Quebec in 1673 to manage the trading post for the French. Castin had earlier arrived in New France, at the age of fifteen, to claim a royal land grant that belonged to his family. He canoed with several Abnaki Indians to the mouth of the Penobscot and decided to stay; Castin also married the daughter of a chief.

As early as 1626 people were protecting themselves by an early fort on the site of the present **Fort George,** on Wadsworth Cove Road, which was built by the British in 1779. Also in that year forty-four ships sailed from Boston in an attempt to seize the fort. Commodore Saltonstall led Paul Revere and other patriots in that flawed Massachusetts expedition. The British sent in reinforcements, and all the American ships were captured or sunk. One shipwrecked vessel, the *Defense,* is now the object of an underwater archaeological exploration.

Wilson Museum, on Perkins Street, contains anthropological and geological collections, as well as colonial pieces. It is open 2:00 P.M.–5:00 P.M. daily except Monday, Memorial Day to September 30. The **John Perkins House,** dating from 1763, is on the grounds. As the only pre-Revolutionary building in the region, it holds historical interest with its hand-hewn beams. The house contains eighteenth-century pieces, and some date from the Perkins family. Artifacts given by local inhabitants are on display, and interpreters demonstrate the work done in the blacksmith shop. Don't overlook the interesting collection of family pieces in the Hearse House. Perkins House is open Wednesday and Sunday from 2:00 to 4:45 P.M. in July and August.

In 1633 the English built a trading post at **Machias** with Richard Vines in charge, but it was quickly destroyed by the French Governor of Acadia.

Pirates used the port from 1675 when Rhodes, the pirate, arrived. Another pirate, Samuel Bellamy, went so far as to coerce a ship's crew, after he had captured it, to join his forces. He told them that shipowners were also thieves who created laws to protect their interests; therefore, crews, as well as shipowners, should be able to rob. He met his death after capturing a New Bedford whaler; he thought he had convinced the captain to join forces, but he then was surprised to find that the captain had led his ship onto the rocks, where Bellamy and his crew drowned.

The first naval battle of the Revolution took place in Machias in 1775. Colonists chose not to send their lumber to England, so the British commander of the *Margaretta,* Captain Moore, told them he would fire on the town. Jeremiah O'Brien and Benjamin Foster took a group of men and went out to fight the *Margaretta,* killing Moore and capturing his ship. The British retaliated by sending George Collier on the *Ranger* and several other ships to ravage Machias.

Burnham Tavern Museum, at Main and Free streets on Route 192, is a 1770 gambrel-roofed building. Underneath each of the four cornerstones, the builder, Job Burnham, placed a note that reads as follows: "hospitality, cheer, hope and courage." Job and Mary Burnham lived here with their eleven children and ran the tavern. The original sign is inscribed: DRINK FOR THE THIRSTY, FOOD FOR THE HUNGRY, LODGING FOR THE WEARY, AND GOOD KEEPING FOR HORSES. Open 10:00 A.M.–5:00 P.M. Monday to Friday, June 1 to early September; by appointment the rest of the year.

In 1775 the men of Machias met in this tavern to discuss action and to erect a Liberty Pole on the Village Green; here they planned their successful capture of the *Margaretta.* The tavern was also used as a hospital for the wounded. Now the tavern is furnished with period pieces. The focus of the museum is the first naval battle of the Revolution, and it displays muskets that were used then.

FOR MORE INFORMATION

Maine Publicity Bureau
P.O. Box 2300
Hallowell, ME 04347–2300
(800) 533–9595
(207) 623–0363 (within Maine)
(207) 623–0388 (fax)

Massachusetts

Historical Introduction to the
MASSACHUSETTS COLONY

Escape to Freedom

*I*n the struggle for religious uniformity that raged in England throughout much of the seventeenth century, a group of separatists from Scrooby in Yorkshire became weary of discrimination against them and sailed for Holland in 1608. Although they found greater religious tolerance in Leiden and formed close ties with the Dutch community and Leiden University, they were eventually harassed through the influence of the British Ambassador. When Leiden officials closed William Brewster's Pilgrim Press, Brewster went into hiding and the group of separatists decided to leave for America.

In July of 1620 a group of merchants and Pilgrims organized a joint stock company to finance the expedition. The Pilgrims were supposed to farm, build houses, and fish for seven years, and after that time profits would be shared jointly. Each Pilgrim had a share of 10 pounds 10 shillings in the project. After reaching Plymouth, England, they set sail on the *Mayflower* and the *Speedwell*, but when the *Speedwell* began to leak seriously, both ships put back to Plymouth; then all 101 persons crowded into the *Mayflower* for a final departure on September 16, 1620.

Landfall

Although the Pilgrims thought they were coming to the Hudson River (then described as the northern fringe of Virginia), they actually sighted land farther north, off Cape Cod. They started to sail southward for the Hudson River but wisely turned back when they "fell amongst dangerous shoals and roaring breakers" off Monomoy at the elbow of the Cape. Anchored off Provincetown on November 11, they proceeded to write the Mayflower Compact for their new life ashore, and, after a month of exploring the shores of Cape Cod Bay in their shallop, landed at Plymouth on December 21, 1620.

Foothold in the New World

On December 25, 1620, the Pilgrims started building a house to store their goods ashore, and, later, dwellings for each family, but they were entering the grimmest months of their ordeal. Bradford, the governor of the colony, calls it the "starving time": Weakened by scurvy and other diseases during the long voyage, half of the group died during the depths of the first winter. Then assistance from Indians revived the distressed colony. The first Thanksgiving was held in appreciation for their good fortune.

As an investment, the colony was not providing a good return to shareholders in England, so they agreed to sell their interests in 1626, which made distribution of land to the Plymouth shareholders possible. When the Massachusetts Bay Company arrived in 1630, Plymouth colonists gained a new market for their grain and livestock. In 1636 the colony adopted its first formal constitution, which served as the framework of government until it united with Massachusetts in 1691.

The Massachusetts Bay Company Arrives

The Massachusetts Bay Company was far larger, with more than 2,000 emigrants in 1630, and had better financing through an agreement that vested all interest in Puritans who were actually going to America. John Winthrop and his followers decided to emigrate, partly because of deteriorating conditions in England under Catholic kings and partly through religious fervor to establish a righteous "City upon a Hill" in the New World. They took over the existing Massachusetts Bay Company chartered by Charles I, and Winthrop became its governor.

The group on the *Arabella* sailed past Maine and Salem to the Charles River, which they named Boston. With more financial support than the Pilgrims, they arrived with tools, livestock, and other provisions. Their Puritan vision was both personal and theocratic. If they lived good lives, they would be saved, so they followed a strict list of rules in daily conduct. In addition, they felt obliged to make others conform to their rules or be banished from the colony—a tenet that sowed seeds for the rapid expansion of New England.

The Navigation Act Begins Dissension

The Navigation Act of 1660 unreasonably declared that goods could be brought to England from America only in English ships, with an English captain, and, in addition, three quarters of the crew had to be English. This act, followed by the Staple Act (1663) and the Plantation Duty Act (1673), caused a great deal of friction between governors and merchants within the colonies. As a result the Crown sent Edward Randolph to Massachusetts in 1676 for the specific purpose of checking up on the colonists' adherence to the various acts. He reported that Massachusetts was disobeying just about everything England had demanded.

The Politics of Charters

Existing charters were a problem to the Crown, especially the one granted to Massachusetts, which seemed to place the colony beyond royal domination. In 1682 Massachusetts was required to send representatives to London to revise this charter, but the Puritans still believed that they should hold out against the King rather than go against their religious principles. Consequently the Crown began proceedings against Massachusetts and, by October of 1684, claimed that the original charter was not valid. In 1691 a new charter provided for a Royal Governor appointed by the Crown.

Revolutionary Rumblings

During the eighteenth century Royal mandates continued to spawn rebellion in the colonies, especially when they were designed to raise money for the Exchequer. In 1765 the Stamp Act mandated that duty was to be levied on business papers, licenses, newspapers, almanacs, and other paper products.

The Sons of Liberty took it upon themselves to quash these taxes by destroying the homes of stamp collectors and other officials, and Massachusetts convened the Stamp Act Congress, which met in New York in October 1765. The Congress concluded that "no taxes ever have been, or can be constitutionally imposed on them [colonies] but by their respective Legislatures." Nine colonies met together in the congress, and feelings ran high enough for them to proclaim this rebellious position.

The real punch was felt by the home country when the Daughters of Liberty stopped buying from English merchants and made their own clothing and household items. Parliament repealed the Act but was soon busy creating even more offensive levies.

The Townshend Acts

Charles Townshend, the chancellor of the exchequer, decided to charge taxes on lead, paint, paper, glass, silk, and tea that came into the colonies from England. In protest Samuel Adams wrote the Circular Letter of February 11, 1768, for the Massachusetts legislature, and it was sent to all of the colonies. Lord Hillsborough, secretary of state for the colonies, demanded that Massachusetts rescind the Circular Letter. When he received a negative reply, he sent troops into Boston. The Daughters of Liberty again saved the day by boycotting English tea and other taxed imports. Duties on everything but tea were repealed in 1769.

Nevertheless by 1770 the air was thick with resentment over these accumulating attempts to balance the English budget through taxing the colonies. On March 5 a number of soldiers, who wanted retribution after a recent fight, broke their 8:00 P.M. curfew and went out looking for trouble. People from the town also came out, and a group of men gathered beside a sentry in front of the customhouse. More soldiers arrived, and, in the confrontation, five citizens were killed after someone thundered, "Fire!" Although Lieutenant Governor Hutchinson promised that the perpetrators of the "Boston Massacre" would be punished, sentiment was running high for the removal of British troops. Hutchinson asked the commanding officer to depart, and within a week the troops were gone.

The Explosive Tea Act

"Would you like a cup of liberty tea?" was a frequent refrain in Boston after Parliament created a British monopoly in the Tea Act of 1773. Again the Daughters of Liberty provided a grass-roots protest by making "liberty tea" from raspberry and currant leaves. After the *Dartmouth, Eleanor,* and *Beaver* had come into port laden with tea, Lieutenant Governor Hutchinson insisted that it be unloaded and marketed, against the will of the citizenry. Sam Adams and other patriots met in Old South Church to determine what to do about the tea. As the last meeting broke up on the night of December 16, 1773, some were heard to say: "Boston harbor a tea-pot tonight!" and "The Mohawks are come!" British response to the "Boston Tea Party" was immediate and punitive with the Coercive, or Intolerable, Acts, a series of new restrictions on American freedom passed in 1774. The powder keg was ready, waiting for a match.

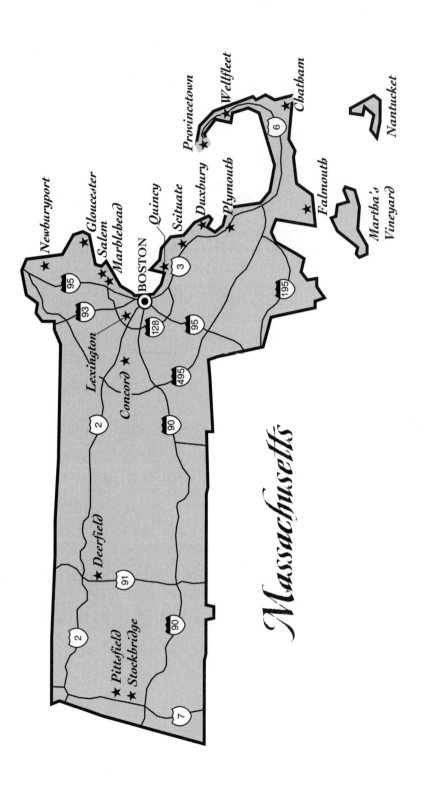

Massachusetts

Regions to Explore

We've divided the Massachusetts colony into five geographical regions: Plymouth and the South Shore, Boston, Salem and Other North Shore Ports, Central Massachusetts and the Berkshires, and Cape Cod and the Islands.

PLYMOUTH AND THE SOUTH SHORE

Plymouth

Plymouth, the spot where it all began, is still the best place to imagine what life must have been like for the Pilgrims in 1620. Their story and character has been overloaded with patriotic myths and clichés for centuries, but with the help of replicas and reenactments, they can be visualized more realistically here. After bouncing in the *Mayflower* for more than two months amid very cramped and unpleasant conditions, these steerage passengers probably walked on dry land with great expectations, but hard work followed, with severe struggles for their very existence. Many died.

Plimoth Plantation, on Route 3A/Warren Avenue, re-creates the original village established by the Pilgrims in 1620. Archaeological research, descriptions recorded by members of the group, and study of the documentation have provided an authentic reproduction of its structures in 1627. The plantation is open daily from 9:00 A.M. to 5:00 P.M., April through November. Call (508) 746–1622 for more information and a schedule of specific events.

Imagine yourself in this setting 375 years ago and walk into the Visitor Center for a glimpse of your trip backward in time. The orientation video begins with prelanding images of inhabitants in tune with nature—a pristine sunrise, complete with birds wheeling, waves splashing, and a grassy cliff. The People of the Dawn were the Wampanoags, who introduced their beautiful land to the Pilgrims. The stage is set for you to arrive as a Pilgrim.

After seeing the video, walk through the Carriage House Crafts Center, where artisans make baskets, furniture, pottery, and woven goods. A short

The first Thanksgiving is relived each year at Plimoth Plantation by convincing interpreters posing as Pilgrims and Indians.

walk along the path outside will take you to the entrance of the 1627 Pilgrim Village.

We were lucky enough to visit Plimoth Plantation on Thanksgiving Day for a number of years. Cold, blustery winds blowing down the hill, swirling the smoke from chimneys and bursting into houses through cracks brought us back into the harsh environment of daily life during the colder months. Every year interpreters in colonial dress play the parts of Myles Standish, John and Priscilla Alden, Governor William Bradford, and other persons in the plantation. If you ask them questions appropriate to the year 1627, they will answer in dialects and accents of that day. Interpreters welcome give-and-take, even if they pretend not to understand anachronistic questions, so don't be bashful in talking to them.

Inside the thatched-roof dwellings, people are baking bread, stirring up Thanksgiving dinner, spinning, and preserving food. Outside others are har-

Fashions of the Times

Women interpreters at Plimoth Plantation wear a shift (like a shirt), petticoat, gown (or waistcoat and skirt), apron and coif (linen cap that covers the hair). Men wear a shirt, breeches, stockings, and doublet (close-fitting jacket). Both women and men wear a cape, hat or cap, and low shoes tied with lappets and fastened in front.

vesting crops, shearing sheep, salting fish, making clapboards, and working in gardens. On our last visit, after a heavy rain, many men were digging small ditches to control water flow, and others were trying to drain a muddy pig-pen—all with the tools of 1627.

The "First Thanksgiving" feast probably included cod, sea bass, wild fowl, cornmeal and wheat breads, venison, and perhaps a sallet, or vegetable dish. Beverages were beer and *aqua vitae* (strong waters). You can taste bits of it in preparation as you visit various houses. Plimoth Plantation also provides original and updated recipes for many foods in *The Thanksgiving Primer.*

Sauce for a Turkie

Recipe from Gervase Markham in *Country Contentments*, 1623

Take faire water and set it over the fire, then slice good store of Onions and put into it, and also Pepper and Salt, and good store of the gravy that comes from the Turkie, and boyle them very well together: then put to it a few fine crummes of grated bread to thicken it; a very little Sugar and some Vinegar, and so serve it up with the Turkey.

Among the special events at Plimouth Plantation are the Thanksgiving Day celebration, including a Pilgrim procession from Plymouth Rock to the First Parish Church on Town Square, and the Festival of Trees in early December.

After several hours of wandering in and out of the Pilgrim houses, take a stroll down along the water to Hobbamock's Homesite, where you will meet the Wampanoag Indian interpreters. They will tell you about Hobbamock, a real Indian who lived in the area during the 1620s. You can creep inside one of their structures by lifting the leather that covers the doorway. Inside you'll find people sitting on animal skins around a fire to keep warm and listening to an interpreter in Wampanoag clothing.

Three miles north in the center of town, first-time visitors usually want to take a look at **Plymouth Rock.** Located on Water Street, it commemorates the spot where the Pilgrims landed to establish the plantation. Don't be disappointed—the rock is small. The date engraved on the stone—December 21, 1620—is accurate for this landing but not for the Pilgrims' first contact with the New World, since they had reached Provincetown on November 11. The rock is now protected from the weather by a large, columned granite building.

Across the street stands the **Pilgrim Mother,** a fountain built in honor of the women who sailed on the *Mayflower.* Gardens surrounding the statue thrive, and the language of herbs symbolizes the virtues of these women: basil for love, thyme for courage, and sage for immortality.

After you have looked at the monuments, head for a living-history conversation on board the ***Mayflower II,*** moored at State Pier. This accurate replica, built in England, sailed to America in 1955 under the command of Alan Villiers, a renowned square-rigger captain and maritime historian. It is a three-masted, square-rigged bark, 106 feet long and 25 feet wide; its headroom is 1 foot higher than the original, but don't let that keep you from ducking as you go below. The *Mayflower II* is open 9:00 A.M.–7:00 P.M., July–August, 9:00 A.M.–5:00 P.M., April–June and September–November. For more information and a schedule of special programs, call (508) 746–1622.

As you step aboard, you may be greeted by Master Christopher Jones, an interpreter dressed as Jones would have been. He might tell you about the one hundred passengers aboard with six and twenty crew and "there you be—tossing about all being seasick with pigs and goats beside you." Seaman Smith told us about the voyage in very heavy weather, how he steered a course of southwest by west and how the ship behaved. Down below we met a young lady who was sitting on a bunk, sewing. She told us that the voyage was very hard on her children—not much room to roughhouse and let off steam down there. Back on deck you may want to ask the Master about the navigating system and the seaworthiness of the vessel. Also glance over the starboard side at the ship's shallop, another accurate replica moored alongside; it was essential to the month of exploration in Cape Cod Bay that preceded the landing at Plymouth.

The captain and a crew member on the Mayflower II

If the *Mayflower II* has roused your curiosity about the ships of the era, you can see the only surviving remains of an early seventeenth-century ship, the *Sparrow Hawk,* in the **Pilgrim Hall Museum,** at Court and Chilton streets. She was wrecked off Cape Cod in 1626, silted over by sand for many years, and brought up more than 200 years later. Among other exhibits in the museum is a touching sampler that Lora Standish, a daughter of Myles Standish, stitched in 1653. The museum also contains collections of Pilgrim furniture, pewter, textiles, books, tools, weapons, and personal treasures, including Peregrine White's cradle, swords that belonged to Myles Standish and John Carver, and the Bibles of John Alden and William Bradford. The museum is open daily from 9:30 A.M. to 4:30 P.M.; closed January 1 and December 25. Call (508) 746–1620 for details.

One Thanksgiving Day we remember watching a procession winding through town and into the **First Parish Church** on Town Square. This structure was actually built in 1899, but the congregation dates back to a group who first met in Scrooby, England, then in the Netherlands, and finally in Plymouth. The figure in the window over the choir loft portrays John Robinson as he spoke to his congregation before leaving the Netherlands.

Climb up beyond the church to **Burial Hill,** the site of a 1622 fort and meetinghouse. A number of colonists—including Governor William Bradford, John Howland, and the last woman survivor, Mary Cushman—lie there. If you're fascinated by headstone inscriptions in old cemeteries, here's the place to wander and read the tales of courageous folk.

Coles Hill, closer to the water, was where the dead were placed in unmarked graves during the first winter. The colonists did not want the Indians to know how many of them had died. A granite sarcophagus now holds the remains of those who were uncovered through erosion. Its inscription reads: "In weariness and painfulness, in watchings often, in hunger and cold they laid the foundations of a state wherein every man through countless ages, should have liberty to worship God in his own way." Massasoit's bronze monument is there too, commemorating the friendship with Indians that enabled the struggling settlement to survive.

Plymouth is lucky to have a concentration of later colonial homes that didn't go up in flames. Edward Winslow, a great-grandson of Governor Edward Winslow, built his home at 4 Winslow Street in 1754, and it is now owned by the **Mayflower Society.** Nine rooms are furnished with period pieces from the seventeenth to the nineteenth centuries. *Mayflower* descendants have given family treasures including clocks, Wedgwood, quilts, and a 1670 Court cupboard that belonged to the Brewster family. The flying staircase is a highlight of the Georgian section of the house. Open daily from 10:00 A.M. to 5:00 P.M., July through August; from 10:00 A.M. to 5:00 P.M., Friday through Sunday, Memorial Day to June 30 and September 1 to mid-October. For further details call (508) 746–2590.

The oldest original house in town is the **Richard Sparrow House** (1640), at 42 Summer Street. A large fireplace dominates the original downstairs room; upstairs there was another for sleeping. Over the years Sparrow added rooms at the back, and the next owner built the entire right side of the house as it stands today. Stoneware pottery has been made in the house for years. The house is open 10:00 A.M.–5:00 P.M., Thursday to Tuesday, Memorial Day to December 24. Call (508) 747–2340 for more information.

Five generations have lived in the **Spooner House** (1747), at 27 North Street. It contains oriental rugs, period furniture, and wallpaper that once lined tea boxes, as well as Blue Canton and rose medallion china. As the family prospered, the left side of the house was added later. James Spooner could open up a window on the harbor side to watch the wharf below, and that was essential in his maritime business. The family company, Plymouth Cordage, was the largest rope company in America. Open noon–5:00 P.M., Tuesday to Sunday, June 1 to Columbus Day. Call (508) 746–0012 to find out more.

John Howland, who was saved by the "Grace of God" when he was almost washed overboard on the voyage to America, lived in the **Howland House** (1666), at 33 Sandwich Street. The house has a lot of interesting seventeenth-century pieces, including a chest thought to have belonged to the family. Ask to see the Murphy-type bed and look carefully at the stools, which have curved holes that fit the shape of a hand for easy carrying. By 1700 the family had added a kitchen, a borning room (where babies were born), and two more rooms above. The left side of the house, another addition, was built around 1750. The house is open daily 10:00 A.M.–5:00 P.M., Memorial Day to Columbus Day; 10:00 A.M.–4:00 P.M., Monday–Saturday, Thanksgiving to November 30. Call (508) 746–9590 for more information.

One more house to see before you leave Plymouth is the **Harlow Old Fort House** (1677), at 119 Sandwich Street. When the Old Fort was dismantled after 1676, some of its beams were reused to support this house—a common practice in colonial times. Inside, docents are engaged in spinning,

Burning the Candle at Both Ends

If you've wondered about the source of the potent life-style phrase "burning the candle at both ends," it may have come from the rush reeds that were dragged through tallow, placed in a holder, and then lit at one or both ends. The choice between more light for a shorter time or less for a longer quite naturally represents spendthrift and conservative human impulses. The rushlight both smoked and smelled, and it had to be watched because when the reed was consumed, the light went out. Some holders had hooks for hanging, some had legs so that they could stand on the floor, and others had a heavy bottom so that they could be placed on a table or shelf.

weaving, candle making, and other household tasks. Open noon–5:00 P.M., Tuesday–Sunday, mid-May through Columbus Day. Closed July 4. For more information call (508) 746–3017.

For a visual glimpse of the sequence of Pilgrim history visit the **Plymouth National Wax Museum** (508–746–6468), at 16 Carver Street, which mounts twenty-seven scenes from the Pilgrim story. Visitors will see them leaving England, arriving in the Netherlands, sailing on the *Mayflower*, reaching Plymouth, and celebrating the first Thanksgiving. The museum is open daily 9:00 A.M.–9:00 P.M. July through August; 9:00 A.M.–7:00 P.M. in November; 9:00 A.M.–5:00 P.M. September through October.

To top off your visit, take a look at the 81-foot granite monument called **The National Monument to the Forefathers,** on Allerton Street. The names of all 102 *Mayflower* colonists are etched on the monument. The figure that symbolizes faith is 36 feet tall; other figures depict liberty, morality, law, and education. The memorial honors the Pilgrims for their "labors, sacrifices and sufferings for the cause of civil and religious freedom."

The South Shore

Soon after Plymouth was firmly established, its first residents, and others who joined them, began to spread northward along the southwestern shore of Cape Cod Bay. Many of these communities have retained a colonial feel and look, with many fine houses surviving, because the big roads and industrial developments of later centuries went elsewhere. So if you have the time and inclination, poking northward up Route 3A from Plymouth toward Boston will be much more rewarding than flying by on Route 3.

Christopher Jones (whose persona you may have met on the *Mayflower II*) was the Master on the *Mayflower*, and he agreed to stay in Plymouth with his ship and crew until spring. He lived in **Kingston**, where the Jones River was named for him.

The **Major John Bradford House** (1674), on Landing Road at Maple, overlooks the Jones River. As the grandson of Governor William Bradford, Major Bradford was active in the town of Kingston as a selectman and moderator of the first town meeting. The west half of the house was built first, and in 1720 the Bradfords completed the other half. Governor William Bradford's original manuscript of his *Of Plymouth Plantation* was once kept in the house. Open 10:00 A.M.–noon on Sunday during July and August; by appointment at other times. For more information, call (617) 585–6300.

Shipbuilding prospered in Kingston, beginning in 1713. The *Independence* was built here in 1776 at **Holmes Shipyard** (1765), at Landing Marine on Landing Road. This sixteen-gun brig was active during the Revolution.

Just north of Kingston **South Duxbury** and **Duxbury** are loaded with sites associated with the earliest pilgrims. **Captain's Nook Hill,** on Standish Street, was the homesite chosen by Captain Myles Standish and Elder William Brewster; it looks out upon both Kingston Bay and Duxbury Bay. Nearby in the Standish Reservation on Crescent Street, the **Myles Standish Monument** overlooks the land where Standish spent the last thirty-six years of his life. His statue stands extending a hand in friendship. Visitors can walk up to the top of the monument for a fine view of Duxbury Beach, Clark's Island, and Plymouth.

William Brewster was a tower of strength for the Pilgrims during their difficult early years. The **Brewster Home** (ca. 1631), off Marshall Street at Bradford Road, is marked with a stone near the site of the home. When Brewster died in 1645, the land was inherited by his sons, Love and Jonathan.

The **Old Burying Ground** (ca. 1635), at Chestnut Street and Pilgrim By-Way, is also marked as the site of the first two meetinghouses; they were built in 1635 and in 1706. Captain Myles Standish, daughter Lora, and daughter-in-law Mary are buried there. John and Priscilla Alden rest in the Alden Corner in unmarked graves; their son Jonathan has the oldest gravestone, dated 1697.

Henry Wadsworth Longfellow's poem "The Courtship of Miles Standish" romanticizes Priscilla's reply to John Alden's brokered proposal: " . . . Speak for yourself, John." John and Priscilla Alden built their second home, the **John Alden House,** in 1653 at l05 Alden Street, Duxbury. Then ten generations of Aldens lived in the house. The front section has a large central chimney, and the back section probably incorporated the first Alden house, built in 1628, which was then moved to connect with the 1653 house. An archaeological dig confirmed this guess, and some of the excavated artifacts are displayed in the house. Alden furniture stands in the rooms. The house is open from 10:00 A.M. to 5:00 P.M. Tuesday to Sunday from late June to the day before Labor Day; by appointment at other times. Call (617) 934–6001 for more information.

When you're ready for a meal, try the **Winsor House Inn,** at 390 Washington Street in Duxbury. This 1799 farmhouse is primarily a restaurant, and it offers some colonial-style dishes. It also has rooms for guests who want to stay overnight. For reservations call (617) 934-0991.

In the next town northward, **Marshfield,** colonists chose to settle in widely separated sites where they had access to protected waterfront—Green Harbor, just beyond Duxbury, and North River, just south of Scituate. Ships wintered in the North River, and in 1645 Thomas Nichols built a ship here.

Not far from Green Harbor the **Winslow House** (1699), at Webster and Careswell streets, stands near the site of the earlier 1636 Careswell home, built by Edward Winslow. After his wife, Elizabeth, died during the first winter ashore and Susanna White's husband also died, Susanna and Edward were married in 1621. Theirs was the first wedding to take place in Plymouth. Isaac Winslow, their grandson, built the present house on the Winslow property. The common room and the kitchen each have exposed, natural beams and a large fireplace. The parlor contains eighteenth-century paneling and woodwork, complete with a delft-tile fireplace. Upstairs is the bedroom for Isaac's bride, Sarah, and also his office. The house is open 1:00 P.M.–5:00 P.M. Wednesday–Sunday, mid-June through mid-October. Call (617) 837–5753 for further details.

Much later Daniel Webster arrived to buy land from both the Winslow and Thomas families, on Webster Steet. His office did not go up in flames when the rest of his estate did, and it has been moved onto the Winslow property.

Winslow Cemetery (1641), on Winslow Cemetery Road, is the burial site for Governor Edward Winslow, Governor Josiah Winslow, and a number of other Winslows and Thomases. Near Daniel Webster's grave there is a stone on the site of the first meetinghouse in Marshfield (ca. 1641).

If you've ever approached England by ship and found your eyes drawn to the White Cliffs of Dover, you can empathize with the early settlers who arrived in **Scituate**, just north of Marshfield. It has one of the finest harbors on the South Shore, and its cliffs must have reminded them of their home in Kent. They arrived in 1628 after Timothy Hatherly and three others received the Conihasset Grant of land. A number of interesting seventeenth-century structures have survived in town.

The linsey-woolsey curtains in the **Cudworth House,** on First Parish Road and Cudworth Road, were all made on a late-1600s loom. The old kitchen's fireplace was built in 1636, and there's an oven in the back. Mordecai Lincoln, one of Abraham Lincoln's ancestors, made the gigantic pot that stands on the hearth. Look for the spit with a turning lever, a device that may have been the source of the phrase "done to a turn." The unfinished room upstairs was used as a church for a number of years. Call (614) 545–0474 or 545–1086 for more information.

Richard and Rebecca Mann came from England around 1644. Unfortunately Richard fell into a pond and drowned: "Wee find that by coming over the pond from his owne house towards the farms that he brake through the iyce and was in soe deep that he could not get out." The **Mann Farmhouse and Historical Museum,** at Stockbridge Road and Greenfield Lane, like many other colonial homes, has an eclectic history, with a late-1600s foundation under a 1700s house and an ell that was attached in 1825. The house remained in the Mann family until the last one died. Most of the furnishings you will see belonged to the Manns, including Peregrine White's high chair, marked "PW 1620 TM 1650" after it was used by Thomas Mann. Upstairs there's a sail loft that dates from 1821; see if you can find the "baggy wrinkle" up there. Horse-drawn farm equipment fills the barn. Seasonal; call (617) 545–1083 for more information.

Mystery unfolded when the last Mann heirs pulled up floorboards and found two cans that contained eighteenth-century coins. A bag with the name Holmes on it could have been buried by the Scituate pirate, Holmes, who had captured a ship, taken the treasure, and buried it. He was hanged for his pains, but perhaps one of the Manns found the treasure and secreted it in the attic.

Stockbridge Mill (ca. 1640), on Country Way, is the oldest operating waterpowered gristmill in the country. Isaac Stedman built this mill with equipment he brought from England. The mill has been restored and still grinds corn today. Samuel Woodworth, after living in Scituate, beginning in 1784, wrote "The Old Oaken Bucket," which immortalized the pond and

Baggy Wrinkle

"Baggy wrinkle," also called a "bag o' wrinkle," is used by sailors to prevent chafe between lines and sails as they rub against each other in a seaway. It was essential to keeping the rigging working on long voyages. Made from bits of old rope yarns woven with marline into longish bunches of padding, baggy wrinkle was attached to wire stays, shrouds, and other lines that might come into contact with sails and wear holes in them.

If you like mysteries, don't miss seeing the spot in the attic of the Mann house where treasure was hidden years ago.

the mill. Later while living in New York, on a particularly hot day, Woodworth yearned, "What would I not give for a drink from the old well in Scituate." The well is still there on Old Oaken Bucket Road. To find out more call (617) 545–0474.

If the idea of dining in a seventeenth-century roadside tavern appeals to you, try **Barker Tavern** (ca. 1634), at 21 Barker Road. It was built by John Williams and used as a garrison during King Philip's War (1675–76). Sections of the original house remain in the entrance and the room on the left.

The next town north, **Cohasset**, now a Boston suburb and sailing center because of its fine harbor, began with a needed industry. Mordecai Lincoln, an ancestor of Abraham Lincoln, started his ironworks there around 1704. By 1708 George Wilson and Joseph Southern began building ships. Colonists lived around the handsome common then just as residents do today; all the houses are private, and some of them date from the colonial period. Here's a place to feast your eyes on surviving beauties of colonial architecture: the homes of James Stutson (1750), at 3 North Main; Adam Beal (1756), at 7 North Main; Nehemiah Hobart (1722), at 19 North Main;

Sweeping Up Your Water

The "Old Oaken Bucket" well has a fine example of a "well sweep" poised above it. The sweep is a long pole, leaned against a Y shaped supporting fulcrum. The bucket hangs from the end of the pole over the well, ready to go down for water and be lifted, full, with minimal effort. Simple and efficient engineering didn't begin in the twentieth century!

Joseph Bates (1713), at 67 North Main; and James Hall (1750), at 31 Highland. These houses are not open to the public.

If you like reminders of the role of the sea in this area, visit the **Maritime Museum** (ca. 1760), at 4 Elm Street, which was once Bates Ship Chandlery at the Cove. It was moved to Elm Street in the 1950s. The maritime collections include paintings, photographs, scrimshaw, and ship models. Open seasonally. For more information call (617) 383–6930. The **Captain John Smith Monument,** Town Landing, marks the place where the enterprising captain and explorer landed in 1614.

Just to the west, in **Hingham,** twenty-eight colonists arrived from England with the Reverend Peter Hobart in 1635, built a meetinghouse, and named their town Hingham after their home in Hingham, England. Originally an agricultural community, Hingham diversified by adding shipyards, an ironworks, and mills.

If you'd like to visit a church that looks like a ship, don't miss the **Old Ship Meeting House** (1681), at 90 Main Street, which remains one of the oldest wooden churches still in use in the United States. Look up from the box pews to see the oak-beamed ceiling in the shape of a ship's hull, upside down. The woodwork in the church is spectacular, almost guaranteed to keep you awake through a long sermon. (Did you know that Colonials were kept awake in church by a tickle from the end of the tithingman's rod?) Open noon–4:00 P.M. Tuesday to Sunday, July and August; by appointment at other times. For more information call (617) 749–1679.

The **Old Ordinary** (1680), on Lincoln Street, began as a two-room house for Thomas Andrews. His son, with the same name, began to sell drinks in 1702; then Francis Barker bought it in 1740 and ran it as a tavern.

Today the building contains fourteen rooms of furnishings, textiles, paintings, glass, wallpaper, pewter, and clothing. The 1760 section has been kept as a taproom. Upstairs several cradles include those of two governors: Andrews and Long; a Bradford cradle is also there. Frederick Law Olmsted planned the colonial garden in the nineteenth century. The house is open 1:30 P.M.–4:30 P.M. Tuesday to Saturday, June through September. Call (617) 749–0013 for more details.

The **Ensign John Thaxter House** (ca. 1695), at 70 South Street, started life as a simple four-room house before the owner added more rooms. Inside, the original panels, painted by John Hazlitt around 1785, are still intact. The house is now the Hingham Community Center and is open during business hours.

Like Cohasset, Hingham is lucky to have an impressive collection of private homes that date from the colonial period. Most of them are on Main Street, including the Daniel Cushing House (ca. 1690), at 209 Main Street; the Hawkes Fearing House (1784), at 303 Main; the John Tower House (1664), at 518 Main; the Edward Wilder House (ca. 1650), at 597 Main; the Theophilus Cushing House, at 753 and also 757 Main; and the Daniel Shute House (1763), at 768 Main. On North Street you will find the Samuel Lincoln House (1667), at 172; the Benjamin Lincoln House (1673), at 181; and the Samuel Lincoln House (pre-1740), at 182.

In 1622 two ships, the *Charity* and the *Swan,* sailed into the adjoining town, **Weymouth.** A trading post was built there, but because the settlers did not plant crops, the settlement failed. A second wave of settlers—including farmers this time—led by Captain Robert Gorges, arrived with their families and moved into the original buildings left by the first group. In addition to farming, the new settlers soon engaged in fishing and lumbering.

North Weymouth Cemetery, at North and Norton Streets, has graves that date back to the 1600s. The parents of Abigail Adams, William Smith, and Elizabeth Quincy Smith, are buried there.

Abigail Adams Birthplace (1685), at North and Norton streets, is more than its name suggests. There Abigail, the wife of John Adams, the second president, was born in 1744, and she also became the mother of John Quincy Adams, the sixth president. The house has been renovated and restored and is furnished with period pieces. Open 1:00 P.M.–4:00 P.M. Tuesday to Sunday, July 1 to Labor Day; by appointment during June and after Labor Day. For more information call (617) 335–1067.

Just west of Weymouth lies **Quincy**, now an industrial city on the fringe of Boston but still a separate and self-sufficient port and manufacturing town in the colonial era. Called the City of Presidents, it was home to our second and our sixth Presidents. The **Adams National Historic Site** includes the farmhouses where each was born. John Hancock, President of the Continental Congress during the American Revolution, was also born in Quincy at a site that is now the **Quincy Historical Society Museum.** The museum is open daily 9:00 A.M.–5:00 P.M., mid-April through mid-November.

Anne Hutchinson and her husband, William, received a land grant in Quincy, and they lived there until she was tried and convicted of heresy, sedition, and contempt and subsequently left, in 1637, to join the settlement in Rhode Island. The Adams and Quincy families settled in the 1630s and began to produce outstanding leaders. Industry arrived in the form of tanneries that produced shoes and granite cut for monuments and churches. Shipbuilding prospered from the seventeenth century through the launching of the *Massachusetts* in 1789 and far beyond the colonial era.

Visitors can find information on the **Quincy Historic Trail,** a tour of Quincy homes and historic sites, in the City Hall, built of Quincy granite in 1844. The Adams National Historic Site was home to four generations of the Adams family. The complex includes the Adams Mansion and the birthplaces of John Adams and John Quincy Adams. Call (617) 773–1177 for further details.

The **Adams Mansion** (1731), at 135 Adams Street, bought by John and Abigail Adams in 1787 and passed down through the generations, is now run

Too Much of a Good Thing

Who would have thought that a maypole could cause a flap? Quincy's earliest beginnings date back to 1625, when Richard Wollaston arrived with settlers. Thomas Morton took over as head of the settlement and built a trading post. He was infamous for erecting a maypole and extending a drinking and dancing festival longer than necessary. By 1628 he had been sent back to England, and the maypole was destroyed.

by the National Park Service. All its furnishings were used by the family in the house; visitors can trace the development of style from colonial times to 1927. Look for the John Singleton Copley painting of John Adams, the Trumbull engraving, a 300-year-old grandfather clock, the Louis XV safe, and high-cushion chairs, specially designed for the hoopskirts of the day. A modern library next door holds the Adams collection of manuscripts and books.

There's a secret hiding place in the chimney (in case of attack by Indians) in the **John Quincy Adams Birthplace** (1663), at 141 Franklin Street. It continued to be the home of John and Abigail Adams until they returned from England, where John had been the United States minister to the Court of St. James. John Quincy Adams was born in the house in 1767. The Constitution of Massachusetts was drafted in John Adams's study in 1779; he promoted some of the structural features that characterize our federal Constitution, including the separation of powers among three branches of our government and the inclusion of a bill of rights.

Nearby, the **John Adams Birthplace** (1681), at 133 Franklin Street, was the home of Deacon John and Susanna Boylston Adams. John Adams was born here in 1735.

John Quincy Adams and his family sat in pew 54 at the **United First Parish Church** (1636), at Hancock and Washington streets. The church is an 1828 structure on the site of the original. Built of Quincy granite, the church is often called the Stone Temple. The Adams crypt contains the remains of John and Abigail Adams and John Quincy and Louisa Catherine Adams.

Look for a romantic inscription in the **Quincy Homestead** (1686), at 34 Butler Road, built by Edmund Quincy and enlarged by later Quincys in 1706. Dorothy Quincy married John Hancock, who took her diamond ring and etched on a window, "You I love and you alone." Look for the secret chamber where American patriots hid during the Revolution. Open noon–4:00 P.M. Wednesday to Sunday. Call (617) 472–5117 for more information.

There's also an etched window in the **Josiah Quincy House** (1770), at 20 Muirhead, home to six Quincys named Josiah. During the Revolution the family could watch the British coming and going. A windowpane upstairs contains a message that was etched as Josiah watched General Gage leave for London: "October 10th 1775 Governor Gage saild for England with a fair wind." The house is filled with Quincy furnishings and the fireplaces are handsome, with English Sadler tiles. The house is open Tuesday, Thursday, Saturday, and Sunday; tours at noon, 1:00 P.M., 2:00 P.M., 3:00 P.M., 4:00 P.M., June 1 through October 15. For further details call (617) 227–3956.

The **Hancock Cemetery**, on Hancock Street, was named for the Reverend John Hancock, whose son was a signer of the Declaration of Independence. The cemetery dates from 1640, and the earliest grave, that of Henry Adams, is marked 1646. Abigail Adams's grandfather, John Quincy, is buried here as well as Josiah Quincy. Sixty-nine veterans of the Revolutionary War also lie here.

Before entering Boston you might want to take a side trip southwest to **Mansfield** to visit the **Fisher-Richardson House,** on Willow Street, dating from 1704. This house is especially interesting because it portrays the lives of families who did not live in mansions but, instead, in dwellings like those inhabited by much of the population. The house was never "tampered with prior to the time of restoration after about 200 years." It is furnished with original pieces from relatives of former residents or local citizens. There is an especially poignant doll collection, reminding us of the dolls our mothers and grandmothers played with. The house is open during the summer from 2:00 P.M. to 5:00 P.M. Saturday and Sunday. Call (508) 339–8739 for more information.

BOSTON

William Blackstone arrived with Robert Gorges in 1623 to settle in Weymouth but moved across the bay in 1625 to Shawmut or "living waters." His house overlooked the present northwest corner of Boston Common. This young minister had a Cambridge University degree but chose to live a solitary existence there with his 200 books.

Meanwhile John Winthrop and his Puritan settlers in Charlestown were having trouble because they did not have pure water. An Indian brought a letter from Blackstone to Winthrop that began

Worthy Mr. Winthrop, it grieves me to know that there hath been so much sickness in your company . . . and that . . .there is dearth of good water. It is not so here, but there are good springs, and the country is pleasant to dwell in. If you will come hither with the Indian, I will show you the land. . . .

The Puritans arrived, liked what they saw, invited Blackstone to join their church, and then moved onto Blackstone's land. This was more than the reclusive Blackstone had bargained for, so he sold the rest of his land and left. The colony was called Trimountain (Tremont) until the name was changed to Boston, after the Puritans' home in Lincolnshire, England.

By 1631 a ship aptly named the *Blessing of the Bay* had been built and launched for use in the Boston area. This trading vessel set the stage for Boston's auspicious future in fishing, trading, and commerce. By the 1640s Boston ships were sailing out for the West Indies with cargoes of dried cod, flour, dried beef, and barrel staves; they returned with wine, sugar, and molasses.

Education began early and expanded vigorously in Boston, as one might expect in a mercantile colony with strong financial backing. The Boston Latin School was founded in 1635 as the first public school in the colonies, and Harvard College became the first university in America a year later. By 1647 the General Court provided for both secondary and elementary education at public expense—but only for boys until 1789, when girls were also included.

King Charles I planted the first seed of American rebellion when he reversed his decision on the self-governing charter that had been granted to the Massachusetts Bay Company in 1634. When he asked for the return of the charter, the colonists gathered a militia and placed a light on top of the highest hill in Boston, Beacon Hill, to warn of English aggression. Charles II did rescind the charter in 1684 and forced Massachusetts to become a royal colony.

As a busy and growing commercial town—loaded with well-educated merchants, lawyers, ministers, and shipowners—Boston led the resistance to incursions on its autonomy. When England imposed one tax after another on the colonists, Bostonians dug in their heels and refused to bend. The series of ill-advised Parliamentary taxes—the Sugar Act, Quartering Act, Stamp Act, Townshend Acts, and Intolerable Acts—created the climate for incidents like the Boston Massacre and the Boston Tea Party. By the time Patriots and Red Coats faced each other in Lexington, armed rebellion was inevitable.

Although Boston has grown by reclaiming land from the bays that once surrounded its narrow peninsula and recast itself many times since the colonial era, it has managed to preserve a past that you can still see, tucked in among the skyscrapers. Begin your walk on the **Freedom Trail** at the Information Kiosk on Boston Common, where you can get a map. About 2 miles long through the heart of Boston, the trail is marked with a red line on the sidewalk.

Before you start you may want to pause for a moment to appreciate where you are. No one has ever built on part of William Blackstone's land, at that time on the water's edge of Back Bay, because it was set aside as the

Boston Common in 1634. It has been a pasture for grazing cattle, a site for militia training and public executions, and a British encampment in the years just before the Revolution. Whenever the colonists had reason to celebrate, such as the repeal of one of the oppressive British taxes, they headed for the Common. And Bostonians still use this open land in their midst for a variety of gatherings and simple recreation.

The red line will lead you across the Common to the **Massachusetts State House,** on Beacon Street (617–727–3676), the "new" State House of 1795. Inside, the Archives hold precious documents such as the Charter of the Massachusetts Bay Company and the Massachusetts Constitution of 1780. The carved wooden *Sacred Cod* still hangs in the House of Representatives to remind visitors of one of Boston's first sources of prosperity.

Next on Freedom Trail you will pass the **Granary Burying Ground,** on Tremont Street. It holds the remains of many famous Americans, including John Hancock, Samuel Adams, Paul Revere, victims of the Boston Massacre, Benjamin Franklin's parents, Peter Faneuil, and Mother (Elizabeth) Goose.

King's Chapel (1754), at Tremont and School streets, built on the site of a 1689 chapel, was the first Anglican church in America; it then became the first Unitarian Church in the country. Governor John Winthrop and William Dawes lie in the burial ground next door. A death's head was carved on the stone over Joseph Tapping's grave, and the inscription on the gravestone of Elizabeth Pain was the inspiration for Nathaniel Hawthorne's novel *The Scarlet Letter.* For further information call (617) 523–1749.

As you walk down School Street, a mosaic marker indicates the site of the first **Boston Latin School.** Philemon Pormont began teaching in his home in 1635, and by 1645 a building rose on the site, but it was moved in 1754.

The Alphabet of Crime

Massachusetts Puritans clearly believed that exposure led to deterrence, so they branded anyone who violated their code of behavior. Those who were accused of a crime had to wear a signifying letter such as *A* for adultery, *B* for blasphemy, *C* for counterfeiting, *D* for drunkeness, *F* for forgery, *R* for roguery, *S* for sedition, or *T* for theft.

Also look carefully at **Benjamin Franklin's Statue,** which has a bizarre twist. It was designed by Richard Greenough to honor Franklin as a printer, scientist, and signer of the Declaration of Independence and the Peace Treaty with Great Britain. One side of the face is smiling and the other side sober.

The next building on Freedom Trail is a major landmark of the Revolution. The **Old South Meeting House** (1729), at 310 Washington Street, was originally a Puritan church, but it also accommodated town meetings—and more ominous gatherings as the Revolution approached. All day before the Boston Tea Party, thousands of citizens met here; then the secret group slipped into the night. The meetinghouse is now a multimedia museum that documents the turbulent events that led to the Revolution, and it has a model of what Boston looked like in the colonial era. Open daily from 9:30 A.M. to 5:00 P.M. April through October; 10:00 A.M.–4:00 P.M. Monday–Friday; 10:00 A.M.–5:00 P.M. Saturday and Sunday during the rest of the year. Call (617) 482–6439 for more information.

No one knows exactly which citizens were involved in the Boston Tea Party that started with the meeting here. Witnesses reported that after the meeting, one group of men gathered at Fulton's carpenter shop, another at Brewer's block-maker home, and yet another at Crane's house, on the corner of Hollis and Tremont streets, during the evening of December 16, 1773. Disguised and painted as Indians, they stormed aboard three tea ships and dumped the cargo overboard. Nathaniel Hawthorne used the incident as the basis for his powerful story "My Kinsman, Major Molineux."

The customs officials were removed from the vessels before the colonists attached a block and tackle to each chest so that it could be hoisted up to the deck. More men splintered open the tea chests with axes, poured all 90,000 pounds of tea into the harbor, and tossed the chests in as well. The water was only 2 or 3 feet deep because the tide was low, so waterlogged tea piled up next to the ships.

After about three hours their work was done, and each man was honor-bound not to take even a pinch of the valuable tea home. When one man thrust tea into the lining of his coat, others stripped him and beat him before turning him loose. John Adams noted, "The Dye is cast: The People have passed the River and cutt away the Bridge: . . . This is the grandest Event, which has ever yet happened." Each year on December 15 the Boston Tea Party is reenacted by costumed interpreters.

Lord North was so enraged that he supported the Coercive, or Intolerable Acts, which started with the Boston Port Bill. This bill closed

Boston Harbor to all shipping except for food and fuel until the East India Company had been reimbursed for the dumped tea. The next was the Justice Act, which moved the venue of trial for any official who stopped a riot from the colonies to England. Another, the Massachusetts Government Act, abrogated the charter of the colony, and the final act forced colonists to quarter British troops at the site of any incident.

Backtracking slightly, continue your walking tour from the Old South Meeting House to the **Old Corner Bookstore,** at School and Washington streets. It was the home of Thomas Crease in 1712 and later became a literary center for Boston during the nineteenth century. Before that it was the site of Anne Hutchinson's house, which burned in the fire that consumed much of Boston in 1711; Anne had been banished to Rhode Island in 1637.

If you like the sense of standing on the spot where important events occurred, look down as well as up while walking the Freedom Trail. In front of the Old State House, your eyes will be drawn to the cobblestone circles that commemorate the Boston Massacre of March 5, 1770, when five citizens were killed by British soldiers. The **Old State House** (1713), on Washington Street at State Street, on the site of the earlier 1657 Town House, stands as the oldest surviving public building in Boston. There in 1761 James Otis gave his famous speech against the "Writs of Assistance," and it was also the site for a public reading of the Declaration of Independence on July 18, 1776. Today its museum houses mementos of Boston's history as a port and center of revolutionary fervor. To find out more information, call (617) 720–1713.

A copper and gold-leaf grasshopper adorns the top of **Faneuil Hall** (1742), which was donated to the city as a market by Peter Faneuil, who had made his fortune in the slave trade. The first building burned in 1761, then was rebuilt in 1763, and enlarged in 1806. James Otis called the meeting hall on the second floor the Cradle of Liberty because it was often filled with oratory that denounced British oppression in the decades before the Revolution. Paintings of battles hang in the hall, and a military museum is housed on the third floor. Open 10:00 A.M.–4:00 P.M. Monday through Friday. Closed January 1, Thanksgiving, and Christmas. Call (617) 635–3105 for details.

Just behind Faneuil Hall on Merchants Row stands **Quincy Market,** named after Mayor Josiah Quincy and built in the early nineteenth century. Although the buildings are not colonial, they retain some of the flavor of old Boston. From the Market you can catch a shuttle bus to the **Boston Tea Party Ship and Museum** (617–338–1773), moored at the Congress Street

Bridge on Harbor Walk. The ship is a replica of the brig *Beaver,* one of the three ships raided by the colonists. An audiovisual program shows visitors how the tea was tossed into the harbor, and there are other exhibits related to shipbuilding. The museum is open daily 10:00 A.M.–6:00 P.M. March 1 to December 16. Closed Thanksgiving Day.

The Freedom Trail continues from Faneuil Hall into the North End via a pedestrian tunnel under Interstate 93. The oldest house in Boston is the **Paul Revere House** (1680), at 19 North Square. Revere, a silversmith and an engraver, owned it from 1770 until 1800 and was active as a patriot while residing here. He created an engraving of the Boston Massacre, participated in the Boston Tea Party, and finally, on April 18, 1775, rode to warn Lexington and Concord that the British were coming. Exhibits include family possessions and some of Revere's work. Next door, at 29 North Square, stands the 1711 **Pierce-Hichborn House,** built by a glass merchant, Moses Pierce. Paul Revere's cousin, Nathaniel Hichborn, bought the house in 1781. Open daily 9:30 A.M.–5:15 P.M. April 15–October 31; daily 9:30 A.M. 4:15 P.M. November 1–April 14; 9:30 A.M.–4:15 P.M. Tuesday through Sunday during the rest of the year. Closed January 1, Thanksgiving, and Christmas. Call (617) 523–2338 for more information on both houses.

The sexton, Robert Newman, placed two lanterns in the steeple of the **Old North Church** to signal Charlestown that the British were on their way across the harbor toward Lexington and Concord. Really named Christ Church (1723), at 193 Salem Street, it is the oldest church building in Boston. The bells were brought from England in 1744, and Paul Revere was one of seven boys who agreed to ring them. For details call (617) 227–6993.

Robert Newman is buried in **Copp's Hill Burying Ground,** at Hull and Snow Hill Streets, which has been a cemetery since the 1660s. William Copp owned the land before it was purchased by the town for this purpose; earlier, the Puritans had placed windmills here and called it Windmill Hill. Cotton Mather and his father, Increase Mather, are buried here. From the hill you can get a clear view of the U.S.S. *Constitution,* from a slightly later era, and the Bunker Hill Monument across the harbor in Charlestown.

The Freedom Trail continues to **Bunker Hill Monument,** on Breed's Hill, standing on the site of the first important battle of the Revolution, fought on June 17, 1775. A day earlier the Americans began digging a redoubt, or small fort, on Breed's Hill to defend their position on the hill. When the H.M.S. *Lively* crew awoke in the morning, they panicked and sent a volley of fire onto Breed's Hill, but the guns couldn't aim high enough to harm the men in the redoubt. With the Americans in control of both Breed's Hill and Bunker Hill, the British advanced and were slaughtered. A 221-foot granite obelisk towers into the sky to mark the spot. The Battle of Bunker Hill celebration is held each year on the anniversary of the battle, June 17, 1775. Call (617) 242–5641 for more information.

The St. Patrick's Day parade, held each year on March 17 in South Boston, honors the city's Irish heritage as well as Evacuation Day, the day the British troops left Boston. The Harborfest on July 4 is another festive occasion. That's when the *Constitution* leaves its berth and turns around in Boston Harbor.

Here the Freedom Trail ends, but you may want to stay on this side of the Charles River to visit **Cambridge.** Originally the village of Newtowne, later renamed Cambridge, it was founded as a fortified town in 1630 by the Massachusetts Bay Colony. The settlers built a meetinghouse, a marketplace (now Winthrop Square), and their homes around the center. Soon **Harvard College** was founded in 1636 to train Puritan clergy and political leaders. If you want to get a sense of what the College looked like during the colonial era, walk around the **Old Yard** and identify some of the buildings that remain from the eighteenth century—Massachusetts Hall (1720), Wadsworth Hall (1726), Hollis Hall (1763), and Harvard Hall (1764). For more details stop by at the Harvard Information Center, at 1353 Massachusetts Avenue, or call (617) 495–3045.

Christ Church (1761) was built by Peter Harrison, who also designed King's Chapel in Boston. In 1774 much of the Tory congregation fled to Boston. Then the church became a barracks for Connecticut troops, and its organ pipes were made into bullets. By 1775 this temporary aberration had stopped, and the church reopened for services; George and Martha Washington were present on New Year's Eve in 1775.

Cambridge Common, like its counterpart in Boston, was a center for social, political, and military events. In 1631 the land was used for grazing cattle, training soldiers, and holding public meetings. By September of 1774 patriots from New England came to Cambridge Common to raise their protests against the British. Three cannons taken from the British in 1775 are here. According to local lore George Washington reviewed troops and took command of the Continental Army here on July 3, 1775, an event commemorated by a bronze plaque, marking what is now called the Washington Elm.

The **Longfellow National Historic Site** (1759), at 105 Brattle Street, was built by John Vassall, Jr., one of many Tories who left Cambridge when it became a hotbed of revolt in 1774. George Washington and his family lived here during the Siege of Boston from July 1775 to March 1776. Later Henry Wadsworth Longfellow and his descendants lived in the house from 1837 until the National Park Service took over in 1974. Longfellow wrote "Paul Revere's Ride" and "The Courtship of Miles Standish" while he lived here. The house is open daily from 10:00 A.M. to 4:30 P.M. Closed January 1, Thanksgiving, and Christmas. Call (617) 876–4491 to find out more information.

There are several more interesting houses to visit in Cambridge. The **Hooper-Lee-Nichols House** (1688), on Brattle Street, is the oldest house in the city. The **Brattle House** (1727), also on Brattle Street, was built by William Brattle, another Tory who fled Cambridge. During the Revolution Maj. Thomas Mifflin, Commissary General of the Continental Army, lived here. The **Hicks House** (1762), on South Street, was built by John Hicks, a carpenter who may have taken part in the Boston Tea Party; it is now the library of Kirkland House, a Harvard residence. **Apthorpe House** (1760), on Plympton Street, was built for East Apthorp, the first pastor of Christ Church. General Burgoyne and his officers lived here after their defeat at Saratoga.

Boston has a variety of hotels, and we have selected several that are historic. The **Copley Plaza Hotel,** Copley Square, sometimes called the "Grande Dame of Boston," has been in business since 1912 when it was opened in the presence of John F. Fitzgerald, grandfather of the late President Kennedy. For reservations call (800) 8–COPLEY or (617) 267–5300, fax (617) 267–3547. The **Eliot,** 370 Commonwealth Avenue, resembles a European hotel and offers some suites with kitchenettes. Call (800) 44ELIOT or (617) 267–1607, fax (617) 536–9441.

If you would rather avoid the major hotels on either side of the river, the **Cambridge House B&B,** at 2218 Massachusetts Avenue, provides an alternative, and it's a good base for sightseeing in Cambridge or Boston. The rooms are individually decorated, and there is a pleasant parlor for guest use. For reservations call (800) 232–9989 or (617) 491–6300, fax (617) 868–2848.

Brookline offers two guest houses: **Beacon Street Guest House,** 1047 Beacon Street, is located just outside Kenmore Square, close to Fenway Park. **Brookline Manor Guest House,** 32 Centre Street, is composed of three separate houses built in the early 1900s. In Wellesley visitors might try **Wellesley Inn on the Square,** which is a 100-year-old Colonial type of inn. For information call (617) 235–0180.

By spring of 1775 Massachusetts was "a bonfire waiting for a match," and the conflagration quickly erupted in **Lexington** and **Concord**. Although Gen. Thomas Gage thought he would subdue the "rude rabble," the patriots were able to hear about most of his plans in advance. General Gage had secretly determined that the British must capture their cache of military supplies at Concord. As Lt. Col. Francis Smith opened his sealed orders on April 18, the patriots had already surmised where the restless British troops were going, but they didn't know which of two possible routes would be chosen.

Paul Revere sent the sexton of the Old North Church up into the tower, armed with two lanterns to be used as a signal to the patriots. Revere's signal: " . . . if the British went out by water we would shew two lanthorns in the North Church Steeple, and if by land, one, as a signal; for we were apprehensive it would be difficult to cross the Charles River, or git over Boston Neck."

A Petticoat to the Rescue

Paul Revere may have been a somewhat absentminded hero, if the stories he later told his children and grandchildren can be believed. Apparently he forgot two essential items when he left home that night—cloth to muffle the oars for crossing the Charles and spurs for the ride itself. He dared not return and risk getting caught for violating the curfew. So one of his oarsmen got a petticoat from a girlfriend, and he sent his dog back with a message for the spurs—or so the story goes, perhaps embellished a bit by the art of a good storyteller.

As the redcoats were preparing to leave Boston in secret, two lights glowed in the Old North Church, signaling their route. Revere and William Dawes galloped off to warn John Hancock and Samuel Adams in Lexington. They were sleeping in The **Hancock–Clark House** (1698), at 36 Hancock Street. When Paul Revere rode up, William Munroe warned him to quiet down. Revere shouted, "You'll have enough noise before long. The Regulars are out!" The house contains mementos from that day, including the drum that William Diamond used to march out the minutemen, so called because they had agreed to fight on a minute's notice. Call (617) 862–5598 for more information.

British troops arrived in Lexington in the early morning hours and were met by a group of minutemen. Capt. John Parker, known for his bravery as one of Roger's Rangers during the French and Indian War, had told the minutemen "not to be discovered, nor meddle, nor make with said regular troops, unless they should insult or molest us. . . ." Since the Rangers had been well known for their effectiveness in what we would now call guerrilla warfare, the advice came from experience.

Maj. John Pitcairn warned his men "on no account to fire, nor even attempt it without Orders"; nevertheless, American witnesses noted that British officers yelled, "Ye villans, ye Rebels, disperse; Damn you, disperse!" Pitcairn maintained that he heard a musket fire from behind a stone wall, and then the British fired.

No one knows who fired the first shot, but eight minutemen were killed in the skirmish. The British marched on to Concord, where the colonists had already removed arms and ammunition by ox team. The redcoats searched property, threw 500 pounds of musket balls into a pond, cracked open sixty barrels of flour, and then tossed wooden spoons and trenchers into a bonfire around the liberty pole. A reenactment of the Battle of Lexington is held in mid-April. For information phone (617) 862–1450.

The **Minute Man Statue,** sculpted by Henry Hudson Kitson, greets visitors on the eastern end of the Green, or Common. The **Lexington Visitors Center,** at 1875 Massachusetts Avenue (617–862–1450), and the Lexington Historical Society, on Meriam Street (617–861–0928), both offer dioramas of the clash on the green.

The minutemen gathered around midnight after Paul Revere rode through and adjourned to **Buckman Tavern** (1709), on Bedford Street and the Common. There muskets from the period are on display. We also noted the mugs for serving "hot flip," a popular drink in colonial times that was

The Miller and the Redcoat

When the redcoats got to Timothy Wheeler's house, Wheeler was emphatic: "This is my flour. I am a miller, Sir. Yonder stands my mill; I get my living by it. . . . This is my flour; this is my wheat, this is my rye; this is mine." The British officer replied, "We do not injure private property."

made of beer or ale with rum or other liquor, sweetened and served hot. Call (617) 861–0928 for more information.

Visitors can continue along Battle Road from Lexington to Concord, stopping at the **Battle Road Visitor Center**. Pick up a pamphlet that maps the redcoat route and events along the way. A stone marks the spot where Paul Revere was captured by a British patrol, who later released him without a horse. He and Dawes never got to Concord with the alarm, but a third rider who had joined them, Dr. Samuel Prescott, did. **Minute Man National Historical Park** is run by the National Park Service. For information call (617) 862–7753.

When the redcoats marched on to Concord, they seized the North Bridge and went on to search for munitions they thought were hidden on James Barrett's farm. In town the British set fire to some gun carriages and, by accident, a nearby building. The minutemen had forced the British to the west end of the bridge when they saw smoke from the fire and thought the town was being burned. Then the "shot heard round the world" was fired at North Bridge, where two minutemen and two redcoats fell, and nine more of the British contingent were wounded. The Revolution had begun.

As the British retreated back to Boston, the Americans sniped at them all along the way. The redcoats thought there might be a musket behind every tree; Americans had learned how to fight behind walls, trees, and buildings. They took delight in cutting across country to ambush the British at the next angle in the road. At the end of that day the British sustained seventy-three dead and twenty-six missing, the Americans forty-nine dead and five missing.

If you want to stay the night in this region, try the 1870 **Hawthorne Inn B&B,** at 462 Lexington Road in Concord. The name comes from its garden, which has larch trees planted by Nathaniel Hawthorne. Call (508) 369–5610 for reservations.

SALEM AND OTHER NORTH SHORE PORTS

Salem

Salem, like a handful of other colonial cities, prospered early but then lay dormant during later eras of urban deconstruction and rapid growth through much of the nineteenth and twentieth centuries. Thus it is a prize for those who want to recapture the sense of life in colonial and early Federal times.

Salem was founded almost by accident. Roger Conant and a group of fishermen settled first on Cape Ann, which proved to be too rocky and harborless, so they sailed southwest to a cove they called Naumkeag, later renamed Salem. In 1628 the Dorchester Company was chartered and organized there, with Captain John Endecott as leader. Then Governor Winthrop sailed in on the *Arabella* in 1630, with the charter of the Massachusetts Bay Company.

At the outset fishing was the major industry, and Salem vessels carried dry cod, whalebone, whale and fish oil, as well as furs. Shipping burgeoned in the eighteenth century, and merchants survived the Revolution through extensive privateering. The Continental Congress actually licensed privateers to harass the British and to take prizes. Salem provided 158 ships for this purpose, and its men were highly successful. Salem's peak of affluence came just after the Revolution as wealthy merchants used their fleets to develop the new and extremely lucrative trade with the Far East.

Visitors to Salem today can explore the center of the city in a number of ways. You can get oriented with a map of the **Salem Heritage Trail** (available in the Visitor's Center, Essex Street Mall) and follow the red lines on the sidewalk, or you can take a trolley along the same route. You can begin any-

The Ghost Ship

A ccording to legend men who left from Salem and died at sea always returned home in spirit. In a tale reminiscent of Coleridge's "Rime of the Ancient Mariner," a sailor on board the *Neptune* reported seeing a ship four times her size bearing down upon his vessel. He threw the wheel hard over to avoid a collision. The other vessel veered slightly and came along the starboard side without a sound. There was no rush of water, no crunch of wood splitting, no straining of lines and canvas—only a glowing silence. And there wasn't a seaman in sight. As the ship faded away in the distance, the sailor said, "It's the Ghost Ship. A proper Salem man has died somewhere, and the ship is bringing his spirit home to Salem, home for Christmas."

where, but you will best appreciate the seafaring traditions of the town by starting on the waterfront, where it all began.

Here the **Salem Maritime National Historic Site,** which also has a Visitor's Center, operates a number of buildings. They include the Central Wharf Warehouse Visitor Center (1800), where visitors can see an audiovisual orientation program, the Custom House (1819), the Scale House (1826), and three houses from the colonial period. Derby House (1762) was built for Elias Hasket Derby, and it stood within sight of his many ships. Hawkes House (1780) was Derby's warehouse during the Revolution. The Narbonne-Hale House (seventeenth century) served as home and shop for craftspersons and tradespeople. The houses are open for tours daily. Closed January 1, Thanksgiving, and December 25. Call (508) 745–1470 for more information.

A good place to begin is the massive **Derby Wharf** (1762), some 2,000 feet long and still under restoration. This wharf was once one of fifty more, all covered with warehouses, where valuable spices, coffee, tea, fabrics, ivory, and gold dust were stored.

The **Derby House** was built for Elias Derby and his wife, Elizabeth (a Crowninshield), in 1762. Classic but unostentatious in its lines, the house nevertheless represents the wealth of the town's two leading merchant families. It is filled with exotic imported woods, porcelain, and silver and brass collections, including a silver tankard and condiment set that belonged to the Derbys. Elias Derby's bed is at Winterthur, but a copy stands in his upstairs bedroom; it is short because people tended to sleep almost sitting up, leaning against pillows and bolsters.

The Drunken Elephant

As the depot for products from all over the world, Derby Wharf occasionally saw bizarre scenes. A drunken elephant? Yes, when the first elephant arrived in 1777, it apparently had been fed beer, about 30 gallons a day, throughout the long voyage. It had become addicted to this liquid diet, and money had to be raised to support the expensive habit. So, in a move that anticipated Barnum and Bailey, people were charged admission to view the elephant.

When the Revolution shut down normal trade with Europe, Derby turned to privateering, then considered a patriotic and honorable profession. Half the profits from the seizure of British vessels were kept by the owner, and many privateers became wealthy. A privateering commission was granted by the colonial governors and, by 1776, the Continental Congress. (Of course England considered privateers as dangerous pirates, suitable for hanging if caught.)

Lying Quakers

"Quakers" were sometimes not people but fake cannons! Some privateers mounted wooden cylinders on their vessels. As the ships sailed along toward a British vessel, the fake cannons looked like a porcupine of armament about to attack. And it was a cheap ruse too—in 1780 a quaker cost about 12 pounds.

Sea captains brought back exotic curiosities from around the world, and many of them are displayed in the **Peabody Museum** (1799), on East India Square. Only Salem captains who had sailed the seas near or beyond the Cape of Good Hope or Cape Horn were elegible for membership in the East India Marine Society.

The Museum is grouped into three departments: Maritime History, Ethnology, and Natural History. Visitors can see ship models, paintings, figureheads, scrimshaw, navigational instruments, and mementos given by sailors. Asian collections include pottery, jewelry, weapons, and religious artifacts. The Natural History collection focuses on New England's seashore. Recently the museum has joined forces with the Essex Institute. The museum is open 10:00 A.M.–5:00 P.M. Monday–Saturday; Sunday noon–5:00 P.M. Closed January 1, Thanksgiving, and December 25. Call (508) 745–1876 for more information.

The **Essex Institute** (508–744–3390), at 132 Essex Street, contains a research library, an art gallery, and seven period houses. The museum building houses five galleries that contain silver, glass and ceramics, lighting devices, furniture, portraits and landscape paintings, dolls, toys, and military items.

The **John Ward House** (1684), adjacent to the Essex Institute, has a seventeenth-century parlor and kitchen within its clapboard walls. A lean-to houses an apothecary shop and scent shop from a later period. Four generations of one family lived in the **Crowninshield-Bentley House** (1727), at 126 Essex Street. This gambrel-roofed house has a facade with symmetry that anticipates later Georgian styles. You can still see the room where the Reverend William Bentley, a diarist of ordinary life in Salem, lived in the years following the Revolution.

The **Peirce-Nichols House** (1782), at 80 Federal Street, was designed by Samuel McIntire for Jerathmiel Peirce, who became wealthy in the China trade. Sally Peirce married George Nichols, and they lived in the house after it had been remodeled for their wedding. The house contains family possessions of both the Peirce and Nichols families.

The **Cotting-Smith Assembly House** (1782), at 138 Federal Street, was built as a hall for assemblies. George Washington was entertained there. The **Ropes Mansion** (1727), at 318 Essex Street, was home to four generations of the Ropes family after they bought it in 1768. Although this handsome house has been architecturally altered many times, all the furniture inside belonged to the family.

While you are out exploring houses on Federal and Essex streets, it would be a shame not to return to the center by walking down **Chestnut Street,** adorned on both sides by mansions of merchants and shipowners. Most of these houses were built in the first two decades of the nineteenth century, but they represent wealth that began accumulating during the colonial era.

If you've been intrigued by Nathaniel Hawthorne's novel *The House of the Seven Gables,* there's a treat in store for you. A group of historic buildings—the **Hathaway House** (1682), **Retire Beckett House** (1658), and **Hawthorne's Birthplace** (1750) stand in a village setting on Salem Harbor next to the **House of the Seven Gables** (1668), at 54 Turner Street. The latter was built by Captain John Turner and later sold to the Ingersoll family. In the 1840s Nathaniel Hawthorne visited there and used the house for scenes in his novel: the parlor where Colonel Pyncheon sat, dying, in the oak chair; the shop in which Hepzibah sold scents and candy; and the secret staircase that led to Clifford's room.

Visitors begin the house tour in the seventeenth-century kitchen, where there's a beehive oven with a wooden door. We were told that the housewife would stick her hand in the oven for about ten seconds to test for hotness before putting her food in. Look for the "courting" candle, which the family set in advance; when the light went out, it was time for the gentle-

Visitors at the House of the Seven Gables may feel the presence of ghosts.

man to go home. Climb the twenty wooden steps up into Clifford's room. You can count the seven gables on the house model in the attic. Phoebe's room is bright and cheerful, with a view of the water and of Marblehead.

When you have finished touring the house, explore the garden; there's a great view of both garden and house from the seawall. Also don't miss the other open houses. Hawthorne's Birthplace, though far smaller and less complex than the House of the Seven Gables, has an elegant simplicity. The house is open daily 9:30 A.M.–5:30 P.M. July 1 through Labor Day; 10:00 A.M.–4:30 P.M. during the rest of the year. Closed January 1, December 25, and during the Thanksgiving period. Call (508) 744–0991 for more information.

Nathaniel Hawthorne's ancestor, Judge Hathorne, was involved in the infamous Salem witch trials of the 1690s. **Witch House** (1642), at 310½ Essex Street, was once the home of Judge Jonathan Corwin, a judge in the trials. The trials began in 1692 when local girls had fits, which, they said, were brought on by hearing stories from Tituba, a slave who belonged to Samuel Parris. These girls took to writhing and babbling, accusing Tituba, Sarah Good, Sarah Osborne, Rebecca Nurse, and others of having cast a spell on them.

By October of 1692 more than one hundred people had been accused and indicted; fifty confessed, twenty-six were convicted, and nineteen hanged. Executions took place until the governor's wife was accused; then, suddenly the witchcraft hysteria stopped. Visitors to Witch House will find the upstairs room where the hearings took place. For details call (508) 744–0180.

Pioneer Village, in Forest River Park, is a living-history museum built as a re-creation of Roger Conant's 1630 settlement. The village contains thatched homes, wigwams, log-and-mud dugouts, and gardens. A replica of Governor John Winthrop's house is here. Visitors can play with seventeenth-century toys and learn games such as Jacob's Ladder, visit the gardens, and talk with interpreters in period costumes. The museum is open 10:00 A.M.–5:00 P.M. Monday–Saturday, noon–5:00 P.M. Sunday and holidays, June through October. For more information call (508) 745–0525.

A Pinching Witch

Confessions of Sarah Carrier, age seven, 1692:

"How long hast thou been a witch?"

"Ever since I was six years old."

"Who made you a witch?"

"My mother, she made me set my hand to a book [of the devil]."

"How did you afflict folks?"

"I pinched them."

Adjacent to the Maritime National Historical Site, Salem's waterfront has begun to develop areas that are pleasant to wander through. **Pickering Wharf,** a shopping village with a range of restaurants, has the ambience of earlier times with the amenities of ours.

If you'd like to spend the night in a house that dates from 1667, try the **Stephen Daniels House** (508–744–5709), at One Daniels Street. There are ten fireplaces, and the rooms have different shapes, which reflect various stages of the house's evolution. Look for the collections of samplers, teapots, puppets, and antique furniture. Another historic B&B is the **Suzannah Flint House,** at 98 Essex Street, named after an eighteenth-century owner. It has wide-board floors and is filled with antiques. Call (508) 744–5281 for reservations.

Other North Shore Ports

Across from Salem lies another superb harbor. Fishermen from Cornwall and the Channel Islands arrived in Marble Harbor, now **Marblehead,** in 1629. The peninsula provides a sheltered deepwater harbor, with easy access to the open sea—advantages that ensured its continuity as a maritime center throughout four centuries. Marblehead's history of activity encompasses fishing, shipbuilding, privateering, blockade running, merchant voyages throughout the world, and eventually yachting. Its townspeople were extremely active during the Revolution, both as seamen and as soldiers, and

No Christmas?

I n the late seventeenth century, the Puritans caused an uproar in town by opposing the celebration of Christmas. When Dr. Pigot planned to hold an Anglican service, the Puritans held a lecture at the same time. Dr. John Barnard, parson of the Puritan church, argued that Christ was born in October and that Christmas was a pagan custom. Dr. Pigot published a paper entitled "A Vindication of the Practice of the Ancient Christian as well as the Church of England, and other Reformed Churches in the Observation of Christmas-Day; in answer to the uncharitable reflections of Thomas de Laune, Mr. Whiston and Mr. John Barnard of Marblehead." By 1681 the Puritan law against celebrating Christmas was repealed.

Gen. John Glover provided his Marblehead ship, the *Hannah,* for the use of the Continental Congress.

Visitors to Marblehead are in for a treat when they see a special painting in **Abbot Hall** (617–631–4056), on Washington Square. It's the well-known Archibald Willard painting, *The Spirit of '76.* Gen. John Devereux, whose son was the model for the drummer boy, gave the painting to the town. Abbot Hall is open 8:00 A.M.–5:00 P.M. Monday, Thursday, and Friday; 8:00 A.M.–8:00 P.M. Tuesday and Wednesday; 1:00 P.M.–9:00 P.M. Saturday; 11:00 A.M.–6:00 P.M. Sunday and holidays, June through October.

The **Jeremiah Lee Mansion** (1768), at 161 Washington Street, has a rusticated exterior, that is, a wood exterior designed to look like stone. The house still has the original hand-painted (in tempera) paper on the walls in several rooms. In the State Drawing Room, the panels feature classical ruins, with each panel designed to fit the wall. Jeremiah Lee had made a fortune in shipping. His early death was thought to have been brought on by overexposure in the opening days of the Revolution. He had been involved in a meeting at the Black Horse Tavern in Arlington when the alarm was given, and he hid in the fields as the British marched by on their route to Concord.

In 1789 and 1794 Washington and Lafayette were guests in the Mansion's Great Room, which is elegant, indeed, with its elaborately carved chimney piece and marble fireplace. Original colonial furnishings mix with pieces collected from all over the world. The museum rooms on the top floor contain paintings by a Marblehead artist, John Frost, who was once a Grand Banks fisherman. Colonial samplers are there, too, as well as a wooden codfish, a reminder of the main industry of early Marblehead. The mansion is open 10:00 A.M.–4:00 P.M. Monday through Friday; 1:00 P.M.–4:00 P.M. Saturday and Sunday, May 15 through Columbus Day. Call (617) 631–1069 for more information.

Another mansion to visit is the **King Hooper Mansion** (1727), at 8 Hooper Street, built by "King" Robert Hooper. Visitors can see colonial rooms, a ballroom, a wine cellar, and slave quarters. The Marblehead Arts Association has an art gallery on the third floor in the ballroom. The flower garden has been restored to its colonial past. Open 10:00 A.M.–4:00 P.M. Monday–Saturday; 1:00 P.M.–5:00 P.M. Sunday. For more information call (617) 631–2608.

Here's a bell that did its job too well! One of the oldest Episcopal churches in America is **St. Michael's Church** (1714), at 13 Summer Street, which was constructed with building materials sent from England. Its bell is especially meaningful because it was rung so hard and long after the news of the signing of the Declaration of Independence that it cracked and had to be recast by Paul Revere. The church is open from 9:00 A.M. to 2:00 P.M. Monday through Friday. To find out more call (617) 631–2242.

Old Burial Hill, off Orne Street, contains the graves of 600 Revolutionary War veterans. It is also the site of the first meetinghouse in Marblehead. Just a few ruins remain today of **Fort Sewall** (1742) on the northeast end of Front Street. It was first built in the seventeenth century and then updated in 1742.

The older sections of Marblehead delight the observant eye, and walking is by far the best way to enjoy its intricate streets and lanes. If you want to stop for the night, try the **Harbor Light Inn,** at 58 Washington Street, which offers fireplaces and canopied beds. Call (617) 631–2186 or fax (617) 631–2216 for reservations.

Gloucester, named for Gloucester, England, claims to be the oldest fishing port in the state, with a founding in 1623. It is the city most closely identified with the lucrative cod fishery, the staple of exports from the New World to the Old in the colonial era. Gloucester's central role in that fishery has persisted through four centuries, but it is threatened now by the rapid depletion of cod, which has led to the closure of some offshore banks. In June the town celebrates St. Peter's Festival, when the Italian-American fishermen gather for the blessing of the fleet and for fireworks.

During the Revolutionary War the town was harassed by the H.M.S. *Falcon,* a British warship that tried to capture a colonial ship. Gloucester men took thirty-five British sailors as prisoners, and a British cannonball is on display in the **Cape Ann Historical Museum** (508–283–0455). Part of the museum was the home of sea captain Elias Davis. The museum contains fishing exhibits and memorabilia and is also well known for its outstanding collection of Fitz Hugh Lane paintings of the area. Open from 10:00 A.M. to 5:00 P.M. Tuesday through Saturday.

Beyond Gloucester and northwest of the rocky outcropping of Cape Ann lies **Ipswich**, on a river surrounded by salt marshes. Twelve colonists arrived here in 1633 to found a town that would become famous for shipbuilding in the colonial era and beyond. The first American female poet, Anne Bradstreet, lived here in the 1630s with her husband, Simon Bradstreet; he was a governor of Massachusetts. The **John Whipple House** (1640), at 53 South Main Street, contains furnishings of the Whipple family. A colonial herb garden, including medicinal herbs, grows in back. Call (508) 356–2811 for more information. Seven miles inland in **Topsfield** there is another seventeenth-century house worth visiting. The **Parson Capon House** (1683), at One Howlett Street on the green, has a cantilevered second story that is typical of English houses and period furnishings. The houses are open 10:00 A.M.–4:00 P.M. Wednesday through Saturday; 1:00 P.M.–4:00 P.M. Sunday, May 1 through October 15. For further details call (508) 887–8845.

The town of Newbury was founded by settlers in 1635, and by 1646 they had established a port, **Newburyport,** on the banks of the Merrimack River. Early records note that a new ship was built as early as 1639 and that 117 more ships came from Newburyport yards between 1671 and 1714. By 1764 the shipbuilders in Newburyport had split from the town of Newbury

Prizes and Surprises

Some privateers used subtle methods to bluff the British. Capt. Jonathan Haraden of Gloucester disguised his gun ports with canvas painted the color of the hull to make it look like an unarmed vessel. An enemy ship might think this an easy mark and rush to capture its prize—until the guns poked out of the canvas and fired at close range.

because their emphasis was on the sea, not farming; approximately 60 percent of the men in town earned their living through some trade connected with the sea. In 1776 they built two frigates for the Continental Navy, the *Hancock* and the *Boston,* and outfitted a number of privateers. Unfortunately shipbuilding collapsed in the depression after the Revolution, and Newburyport launchings dropped from ninety in 1772 to three in 1788.

Newburyport has preserved the atmosphere of its maritme heritage in the **Market Square Historic District**. The **Custom House Maritime Museum,** at 25 Water Street, is in an 1835 building but dates back to an earlier era, when a group of sea captains formed the Newburyport Marine Society in 1772. They collected maritime artifacts and passed them on to the Historical Society of Old Newbury after World War I. Now these artifacts are on display along with ship models and navigational items. The museum is open 10:00 A.M.–4:00 P.M. Monday through Saturday; 1:00 P.M.–4:00 P.M. Sunday, April 1 through mid-December; there are Christmas tours available in December. To find out more call (508) 462–2681.

Architecture buffs shouldn't miss a walk along Newburyport's **High Street,** where the wealth from the harbor built handsome homes through the colonial, Federal, and later eras. Among the earliest is the **Coffin House** (1654), at 14–16 High Street, which remained the home of the Coffin family until 1929, when the Society for the Preservation of New England Antiquities took it over. The house has both a 1600 and a 1700 kitchen, and, like many that stay within a single family, it incorporates changes made by many generations. Open noon–4:00 P.M. Wednesday through Sunday, June 1 through October 15. Call (508) 227–3956 or 463–2057 for more information.

When it's time for a rest, try the **Morrill Place Inn,** at 209 High Street. It features a staircase with 6-inch risers, built to accommodate the fashionable hoopskirts of the times. For reservations call (508) 462–2808.

CENTRAL MASSACHUSETTS AND THE BERKSHIRES

In 1669, when Samuel Hinsdell arrived to farm, **Deerfield** was considered the last civilized place on the edge of New England. Hinsdell was joined by other settlers, and within six years the population grew to 125. The Pocumtuck Indians, who had used the land to raise corn, tobacco, and pumpkins, were enraged. They attacked during King Philip's War, when the Bloody Brook Massacre of 1675 took the lives of seventy-six persons; the village was almost abandoned after that outburst.

Deerfield's stormy history continued through the first part of the eighteenth century. In 1704 the French, led by Hertel de Rouville, accompanied a group of 142 Indians who invaded the town, killed fifty persons, and set fire to homes. The townspeople taken as prisoners marched for 300 miles into Canada. By 1706 some of them had come home, and in 1735 a peace treaty brought settlers back to Deerfield.

News of the Boston Tea Party pleased some but angered others. The Reverend Jonathan Ashley, who had been pastor in the Deerfield parish for forty years, felt loyalty to King George III. In defiance he held a tea party in his home and sent a pound of tea to a Tory friend in Greenfield. Whigs and Tories shouted vehemently from opposite sides of the street in Deerfield. In July 1774 patriots had a Liberty Pole ready to be erected when Tory sympathizers cut it in two during the night. The Whigs got another pole and raised it. A replica of the Liberty Pole still stands on Deerfield's main street.

By 1775 Deerfield men marched to Boston, and some of them fought in the Battle of Bunker Hill. Although Deerfield was isolated from the major population centers of eastern Massachusetts, the town was ready for independence and would fight for it. Citizens provided food for Colonials who had fought at Fort Ticonderoga; Benedict Arnold made the arrangements in Deerfield.

The attractive town you see today is largely the work of one family. The Flynt family restored many of the original homes and buildings in Historic Deerfield. Henry N. Flynt first came to town in 1936, when he brought his son to Deerfield Academy. He liked the town and bought an inn, followed by one home, then another and another, restoring each in turn. Over the next twenty-five years, Flynt and his wife oversaw the restoration and furnishing of twelve buildings, acquiring more than 8,000 antique pieces in the process.

Historic Deerfield had been born, a pioneer restoration project in New England historic preservation. Stop first at **Hall Tavern** (ca. 1760), the visitor's center, for tickets and information. Then enjoy the houses and their furnishings—among them a print shop, a tavern, a silver shop, and **Allen House** (ca. 1720), the Flynts' own home—all spread along one of the most beautiful village streets in New England. The **Frary House** (ca. 1720 and 1768) was first a home and then a tavern. The **Wells-Thorn House** (1717 and 1751) contains English ceramics, needlework, a buttery, and a garret.

The **Dwight-Barnard House** (ca. 1725) was originally a merchant's house in Springfield. The **Sheldon-Hawks House** (1743) remained in the Sheldon family for two centuries, and the **Ashley House** (ca. 1730) was the home of Deerfield's Tory minister, Jonathan Ashley. And there's much more to see in the village, so allow plenty of time for your visit. The houses are open daily 9:30 A.M.–4:30 P.M. Closed Thanksgiving and December 24–25. Call (413) 774–5581 for more information.

The **Deerfield Inn,** on The Street in Deerfield was built in 1884. It has twenty-three rooms, a dining room, coffee shop, and tavern. It is right in the center of things, so you can rest in your room between spells of touring. If you are just visiting for the day, the inn is also a nice place to have a meal. For reservations call (800) 926–3865 or (413) 774–5587.

Indians went along the **Mohawk Trail** from central Massachusetts to the Finger Lakes of New York. Then colonial troops marched the same route to New York during the French and Indian Wars, and later settlers used the trail on their way west. The trail, now Route 2, passes through the Connecticut Valley and into the Berkshires, running along the banks of the Deerfield and Cold rivers to Williamstown. Colonial soldiers may not have been looking at the views but they are spectacular, with waterfalls, gorges, cliffs, and mountains.

Just beyond the western edge of the Berkshires lies **Hancock Shaker Village**, on Route 20, 5 miles west of Pittsfield. It is one of several extant Shaker communities founded by Mother Ann Lee, who came to America in 1774. By 1780 people were becoming attracted to the Shakers, and in 1783 Mother Ann Lee preached at Hancock in a house near the village's Trustees' House. In 1790 Hancock was the third of the eighteen communities she established. Besides being pacifists, the Shakers believed in withdrawal from the world, holding property in common, confession of sin, celibacy, and separation but equality of the sexes. Today visitors can walk through twenty-one buildings, many of them designed with elegant simplicity, and appreciate the utility and beauty of Shaker furniture. Interpreters demonstrate crafts, such as weaving, woodworking, and box making, as well as cooking, farming, and gardening. There are Saturday night dinners July through October. The Shaker Village is open daily 9:30 A.M.–5:00 P.M. May through October; 10:00 A.M.–3:00 P.M. in April and on holidays. Closed Thanksgiving. To find out more call (413) 443–0188.

Farther south (just off the Massachusetts Turnpike), **Stockbridge** village was first an Indian mission in 1734. Reverend John Sergeant decided that the

Indians should live with the English settlers and perhaps become Christians. He taught them in their own language until he died prematurely in 1749. **Mission House** (1735), on Main Street, was Sergeant's home. Today it contains collections of Indian pieces and early American furnishings. He ordered an elegantly carved wooden door that was brought over the mountains by oxcart from Connecticut. John and Abigail Sergeant are buried in the cemetery nearby. The Mission House is open 11:00 A.M.–4:00 P.M. Tuesday through Sunday, open Monday holidays; closed the following Tuesday, Memorial Day through Columbus Day. Call (413) 298–3239 for more information about the house.

Also buried in the cemetery is Theodore Sedgwick, who became well known after he defended a slave named Mum Bett. She wanted him to help her claim her liberty under the Bill of Rights of the new Massachusetts Constitution. He defended her against the claims of Colonel Ashley, her owner, who was forced to pay her 30 shillings. Mum Bett was free then and chose to live with the Sedgwick family as their housekeeper.

The **Red Lion Inn,** on Main Street in Stockbridge, was built in 1773 as a tavern and stagecoach stop, and now it provides travelers with both informal and formal dining in a pleasant setting. For reservations, which are advised, call (413) 298–5545.

Seven miles south of Stockbridge, the town of **Great Barrington** was settled in 1726 as a farming community. In 1774 the citizens captured the courthouse so that the king's court could not hold a session. A stone marker describes this feat as "the first act of open resistance to British rule in America." Another attempt at individual rebellion, however, didn't pay. **Belcher Square** was named after Gill Belcher, a counterfeiter who made coins in a cave near his house in the 1770s. He was captured and hanged.

The **Knox Trail** is remembered as the route Henry Knox took from Fort Ticonderoga to Boston. He set out with sixty tons of artillery that had been seized by Ethan Allen and the Green Mountain Boys. The route through Massachusetts begins in the Alford-Egremont area in the Berkshires across Routes 71, 23, 20, 67, 9, and 20. Knox and his men traveled more than 300 miles through deep snow in the mountains, over rivers, and through forests. Oxen pulled the heavy equipment on sleds, now and then crashing through frozen rivers. The fifty-nine cannon were used to bombard the British forces from Dorchester Heights on March 4, 1776, an action that precipitated their withdrawal from Boston.

The oldest house in Berkshire County is the **Ashley House** (1735), on Cooper Hill Road in **Ashley Falls**. John Ashley and other townsmen drafted the Sheffield Declaration in his home in 1773. His slave, Mum Bett, won her freedom after hearing talk in the house of personal rights. The house contains period furnishings and has a collection of early farm tools. The Ashley House is open 1:00 P.M.–5:00 P.M. Wednesday through Saturday, end of May to Columbus Day. Call (413) 229–8600 for information.

CAPE COD AND THE ISLANDS
Cape Cod

Bartholomew Gosnold first landed on Cape Cod in 1602. Although he didn't stay long, he was impressed with the number of cod in the surrounding waters. On November 11, 1620, the *Mayflower* sailed to the end of the Cape and anchored near the present Provincetown, then spent about five weeks there before continuing on to Plymouth. In 1627 a trading post opened at Aptuxcet, at the base of the Cape. The Council for New England annexed Cape Cod to Plymouth in 1630, and four towns were established: Sandwich, Yarmouth, Barnstable, and Eastham. During the 1630s and 1640s, Plymouth colonists moved onto Cape Cod. By 1644 Governor William Bradford of Plymouth announced that he felt lonely, as if children had left their mother.

A historic tour can circle the Cape on a counterclockwise route that heads outward along the outer perimeter (Nantucket Sound and the Atlantic) and returns along Cape Cod Bay. You can also choose to enjoy the smaller roads by crisscrossing the mid-cape highway from ocean to bay.

The cradle of American commerce was the Aptucxet Trading Post, which Pilgrims from Plimoth Plantation built in 1627 because they needed a place to trade with the Indians from Cape Cod and with the Dutch from New York. A replica of the original building, the **Aptucxet Trading Post Museum,** now stands on Shore Road in **Bourne.** The museum contains seventeenth-century furnishings, Indian artifacts, and pieces used during colonial times. The grounds include a windmill and an herb garden. The museum is open 10:00 A.M.–5:00 P.M. Monday through Saturday, 2:00 P.M.–5:00 P.M. Sunday, July through August; closed Mondays May through June and September 1 to mid-October. Call (508) 759–9487 for more information.

Quakers arrived in **Falmouth** in 1660, led by Isaac Robinson, who had been a Congregational minister. He and his followers brought with them religious tolerance for those who had been persecuted in other parts of Massachusetts. A Quaker cemetery dating from 1720 is located near the Friends Meetinghouse.

The **Falmouth Historical Society Museum,** on Palmer Avenue, was built in 1790 by Dr. Francis Wicks. Two restored houses contain pieces from Falmouth's early history, period furnishings, paintings, and china. The property also has a colonial herb garden. The museum is open 2:00 P.M.–5:00 P.M. Monday through Friday, June 15 to September 15. Closed holidays. For more information call (508) 548–4857.

When it's time to stop for the night, there is a wide choice of historic inns to try: **Captain Tom Lawrence House,** at 75 Locust Street, was built as a whaling captain's home (508–540–1445); **Coonamessett Inn,** at Jones Road and Gifford Street, dates from 1796 (508–548–2300; **Mostly Hall Bed & Breakfast Inn,** at 27 Main Street, has a widow's walk room at the top (508–548–3786); the **Palmer House Inn,** at 81 Palmer Avenue, furnishes its rooms with a four-poster or sleigh bed (508–548–1230); and the **Village Green Inn,** at 40 West Main Street, has a collection of brass rubbings from England and large porches for rocking (508–548–5621).

Mashpee Indians, belonging to the Wampanoag Federation, had lived in **Mashpee** long before the settlers arrived. Richard Bourne appealed to the Massachusetts legislature on their behalf, and in 1682 they received a land grant. The **Old Indian Meeting House,** on Route 130, was built in 1684; it is the oldest meetinghouse on the Cape. Wampanoag Indians are buried in the cemetery here. Call (508) 477–1536 for details.

Yarmouth was the third village to be founded on the Cape, in 1639. The **Winslow-Crocker House** (1780), on Route 6A, was put up in West Barnstable, then taken down and moved to Yarmouth in 1935. The house features furnishings made by New England craftspersons. Open noon–5:00 P.M. Tuesday, Thursday, Saturday, and Sunday, June 1 to October 15. For more information call (617) 227–3956.

For a good B&B in this region of the Cape, try the **Isaiah B. Hall House,** at 152 Whig Street in Dennis, a 1857 Greek Revival farmhouse built by a cooper. The rooms are decorated with antiques. Call (800) 736–0160 or (508) 385–9928 or fax (508) 385–5879 for reservations.

Pollock Rip Passage, off Monomoy Point in **Chatham,** tricky with riptides and shoals, is the only way to get into Nantucket Sound from the east. These treacherous shoals played an interesting part in determining the history of the United States: They forced the *Mayflower* to change course. A sign at Chatham Lighthouse reads: "About nine miles SE of this place are the shoals of Pollock Rip which turned the *Mayflower* back to Provincetown Harbor and caused the Pilgrim Fathers to settle in Plymouth instead of on the Jersey Coast, their original destination."

The shifting sands of the region make these feared shoals difficult to chart, and they have taken a deadly toll in wrecks and lives through four centuries. As an illustration, in October 1770 a number of ships foundered during a violent storm; a sloop, returning from a whaling trip, was wrecked near Eastham, another at Race Point; and a whaling schooner foundered in Chatham.

Moreover in 1778 the *Somerset,* a sixty-four-gun British man-of-war, was caught in the area between the Highlands in Chatham and Pollock Rip Shoals, and she crashed onto a reef. (Longfellow wrote about the *Somerset* and her captain, George Curry, in the third verse of "Paul Revere's Ride.") The captain surrendered himself and his crew to men from Provincetown who had come to salvage the wreck. Revolutionary history recalls the winter-long march of the 500 prisoners across the Cape to Boston. More than a hundred years later, the *Somerset's* timbers appeared in the sands of Peaked Hill Bars in Provincetown, and in June 1973 her bones appeared again.

The **Old Atwood House** (1752), at 347 Stage Harbor Road, is the home of the Chatham Historical Society. The house contains a collection of items from the Chatham Light, as well as antique household pieces. Call (508) 945–2493 for more information.

Looking for a spot for the night? The **Cranberry Inn,** at 359 Main Street, dates from the 1830s. The bedrooms offer four-poster, canopy, and antique brass beds, and there are lots of fireplaces. For reservations call (508) 945–9232. The **Queen Anne Inn,** at 70 Queen Anne Road, has a view of Oyster Pond Bay. Visitors can have a complimentary cruise around the harbor and the use of bicycles. Call (800) 545–4667 or (508) 945–0394 or fax (508) 945–4884 for reservations.

The *Mayflower* Pilgrims met their first Indians in **Eastham**. A marker on Samoset Road describes the attack on Myles Standish's scouting group. These Indians were not friendly because, earlier, some of their people had been captured and taken to Spain. Squanto was one of them, but he managed to get to England and then back home, where he became very helpful to the Pilgrims.

The **Old Windmill** (1793), on Route 6, is the oldest working windmill on the Cape. It was actually built in Plymouth, then moved to Truro and finally to Eastham. Some Pilgrims from the *Mayflower* were buried in **Old Cove Cemetery,** on Route 6. The Old Windmill is open from 10:00 A.M. to 5:00 P.M. Monday through Saturday, 1:00 P.M.–5:00 P.M. Sunday, June 1 through Labor Day.

An interesting place to stay the night nearby is the **Ship's Knees Inn,** on Beach Road in East Orleans, formerly the home of a sea captain. A "ship's knee" is a piece of wood that braces deck beams to the frames of a ship, preferably cut from sections of trees with curved grains. For reservations call (508) 255–1312 or fax (508) 240–1351.

The **Pilgrim Monument,** on High Pole Hill in **Provincetown,** is a 250-foot-tall granite column that serves as a memorial to the Pilgrims. Climb up to the observation deck for a panoramic view of the sea and Cape Cod. The Pilgrim Room in the adjacent Provincetown Museum contains *Mayflower* mementos, ship models, and collections of colonial china, silver, and pewter. Open daily 9:00 A.M.–7:00 P.M. July and August, 9:00 A.M.–5:00 P.M. April 1 through June 30 and September 1 through October 30. Call (508) 487–1310 for details.

Sandwich is the oldest settlement on the Cape: The first group arrived in 1627 from Plymouth, followed by another in 1637 from Saugus. The historic district contains houses from the late 1600s. **Dexter Mill** (1654), on Main Street, grinds corn daily 10:00 A.M.–5:00 P.M. Monday to Saturday and 1:00 P.M.–5:00 P.M., mid-June to early October. **Hoxie House** (1635), on Water Street, a restored saltbox, may be the oldest house on Cape Cod. Call (508) 888–1173 for more information on both the mill and the house.

Riding into Eternity

A 1677 grave on Wilson Road, that of Edmund Freeman, is unusual because his stone is a saddle and that of his wife a pillion, or chair that can be attached to a saddle so that two persons can ride at once.

The **Wing Fort House** (1641), at 69 Spring Hill Road, originally built by a Quaker and partially fortified, was owned and occupied by members of the Wing family through three centuries until 1942. The rooms now contain period furnishings. For more information call (508) 833–1540.

The **First Parish Meeting House,** on Main Street, is known for its bell and town clock, given by Titus Winchester. He was a slave who received his freedom when his master, Abraham Williams, died in 1749. Winchester specified that the bell was to ring on the hour in memory of Williams.

The **Benjamin Nye House** (1685), on Old Country Road (508–888–4213) is one of the few remaining colonial structures on the Cape and has early construction exposed. The house is furnished with period pieces.

When you're looking for a place to spend the night, try the **Daniel Webster Inn** (508–888–3622), at 149 Main Street, which has a conservatory with a view of the garden and a display of Sandwich glass, or the **Captain Ezra Nye House,** at 152 Main Street, located in an 1829 vintage captain's house (800–388–CAPT or 508–888–6142; fax 508–888–2940).

The Islands

Martha's Vineyard

According to tradition Leif Eriksson stopped on this island in the eleventh century, calling it Straumey, which means island of currents. Verrazano arrived in 1524 and called it Luisa. But the name that stuck came from Bartholomew Gosnold, who stepped ashore in 1602 and named the island after his daughter Martha and the wild grapes that grew there.

Gay Head, on the southwest tip of Martha's Vineyard, is marked by varicolored cliffs, a national monument. Each colored layer records a part of history that took place before the Ice Age. The layer of black at the bottom indicates buried forests; red and yellow layers are clay; a layer of green sand, which turns red when exposed to the air, contains fossils of crabs and clams; the gravellike layers contain sharks' teeth, whale bones, and animal skeletons.

In 1642 Thomas Mayhew, a Puritan leader, bought Martha's Vineyard, Nantucket, and the Elizabeth Islands. He brought Christianity to the Wampanoag Indians. Christiantown Cemetery in Vineyard Haven has a large plaque, which states that the "Ancient township of the praying Indians" was set apart in 1660 by Josias, the sachem of Takemmy, and was later called Christiantown. Mayhew Chapel in West Tisbury was built as an Indian chapel in 1910.

Moshop, a mythical hero to the Indians, was said to have built the Devil's Bridge, a reef of glacial boulders that reach out from the Gay Head cliffs toward Cuttyhunk. On January 18, 1884, the steamship *City of Columbus* crashed into the reef; 121 passengers and crew lost their lives that night. The English thought of Moshop as the devil. You can drive along Moshop's Trail, with its wind-battered vegetation, but you can't stop to swim or walk over the dunes because of possible damage to the environment.

Vineyard Haven, also called Tisbury, was harassed by a British fleet of eighty-three ships during the Revolution. They pulled into port and almost destroyed the town. Hearing that the British wanted to use the flagpole standing in town for a mast, three young ladies got rid of it.

Edgartown was founded in 1642 by the Mayhew family, who named it Great Harbor. The **Thomas Cooke House** (1765), at Cooke and School Streets, was the home of the customs keeper. The house is furnished with period Vineyard furnishings. Call (508) 627–4441 for more information.

The **Vincent House** (1672), on Pease's Point Way, is the oldest house on the island. Some of the walls are left exposed to show the original construction. It is owned by the Martha's Vineyard Historical Preservation Society. The house is open from 10:00 A.M. to 2:00 P.M. Monday through Friday, July through late August. For information call (508) 627–8017.

There are many places to stay on the Vineyard that have historic interest. The **Ashley Inn** (800–477–9655), at 129 Main Street, dates from 1860. **Captain Dexter's House** (508–627–7289), at 35 Pease's Point Way, was built in the 1840s. The **Daggett House** (508–627–4500), at 59 North Water Street, consists of twenty-six rooms in three buildings, the oldest dating to 1660. It also has a secret stairway. The **Kelley House,** on Kelley Street, dates back to 1742; for reservations call (800) 225–6005 or (508) 627–4394 or fax (508) 627–7845.

Nantucket

Nantucket was settled by early colonists who learned from the Indians how to capture whales. The Indians watched for whales coming close to shore and harpooned them from land or from small boats. In 1712 Capt. Christopher Hussey's ship had been blown farther out to sea in a gale. He nabbed a sperm whale and found that it gave more oil than the right whales that swam near shore. Nantucketers began to use larger ships that could accommodate offshore work. By 1740 the island was considered the whaling capital of the world. Merchants sold oil in Europe and became wealthy enough to build grand homes on the island.

Visitors new to Nantucket will enjoy taking **Gail's Tours,** offered by a seventh-generation native. The narrated tours cover all the important sights. This is a good way to survey the island and then choose where you want to spend more time. Call (508) 257–6557 for schedules and more information.

Moshop's Cloud

There are several legends that describe the birth of Nantucket, but our favorite is the story of Moshop, the first inhabitant of Martha's Vineyard. One day an Indian maiden came to him. She was from a poor family, and the parents of the boy who wanted to marry her would not allow it. Moshop promised to meet the young lovers on Sampson's Hill, on Chappaquiddick. As they were trying to think of some way to marry, he took out his pipe and began to smoke. Because he was a giant, his pipe was filled with many bales of tobacco. When he knocked the ashes out into the sea, clouds of smoke and vapor filled the air. The fog lifted to reveal an island gilded by the rising sun. With this island as a dowry, the young people were allowed to marry.

The **Nantucket Historical Association** maintains eleven buildings on the island, including houses, museums, a gaol, and a mill. Some of the houses are closed for renovation, so call for current details (508–228–1894). The **Oldest House** (1686), on Sunset Hill, was built by Jethro Coffin. The horseshoe pattern on the brick chimney was thought to protect the family from witches. This wooden saltbox has a secret hiding place in the closet.

The **Nantucket Whaling Museum,** on Broad Street, is housed in a former candle factory. It documents every aspect of the major economic enterprise on Nantucket in the colonial period and beyond. Here visitors will find an outstanding collection of whaling gear, a whaleboat, models, paintings, and some fine examples of scrimshaw.

Special events on Nantucket include the Garden Club house tour in August (for information call 508–228–6879); the Nantucket Harborfest with tours in June; Nantucket Noel in November; and Christmas Stroll in December (for information on these three call the Nantucket Chamber of Commerce at 508–288–1700).

No one should have trouble finding accommodations of historic interest on Nantucket. The **Anchor Inn** (508–228–0072), at 66 Centre Street, was owned by a whaleship captain. The **Carlisle House Inn,** at 26 North Water Street, dates from 1765 (508–228–0720; fax 617–631–2216). The **Jared Coffin House** (800–248–2405 or 508–228–2400), at 29 Broad Street, is a complex of historic buildings. **Martin House Inn** (508–228–0678), at 61

Centre Street, dates from 1803. **Nantucket Roosts,** at Nine Cliff Road, has two guest houses including one built for a sea captain; call (508) 228–9480 or fax 508–228–6038). The **Roberts House Inn,** at 11 Indian Street, is a Greek Revival inn (508) 228–9009. The **Manor House, Periwinkle,** and **Linden** are owned by the same company; call (800) 992–2899, (508) 228–9009 or (508) 228–0600 or fax (508) 325–4046.

FOR MORE INFORMATION

Massachusetts Office of Travel and Tourism
100 Cambridge Street, 13th floor
Boston, MA 02202
(617) 727–3201
(800) 447–6277
(617) 727–6525 (fax)

New Hampshire

Historical Introduction to the
NEW HAMPSHIRE COLONY

Early Enticements and Land Grants

C apt. Martin Pring reported "goodly groves and woods and sundry sorts of beasts, but no people" when he explored up the Piscataqua River in 1603. During his cruise along the New England shore in 1614, Capt. John Smith noticed the Piscataqua River as "a safe harbor with a rocky shore." In 1623 the first settlement in New Hampshire was established on Odiorne Point at the mouth of the Piscataqua.

In 1620 the Plymouth Company, reincorporated as the Council of New England, provided grants to John Mason and Ferdinando Gorges for Maine, David Thomson for Odiorne's Point, and Edward Hilton for Hilton's Point, Dover. Then in 1629 John Mason received an additional grant for coastal land south of the Piscataqua River all the way to the Merrimack and named it after his home county of Hampshire. Like many venture capitalists who obtained similar land grants in England, Mason was more interested in profit than settlement and never came to inspect the land. Others did, however, and although the early enticements were sometimes illusory, the settlement of New Hampshire had begun.

New Hampshire under Massachusetts Rule

By 1641 New Hampshire's four towns—Portsmouth, Dover, Exeter, and Hampton—chose to place themselves under the jurisdiction of Massachusetts. The decision began a political seesaw that lasted until New Hampshire finally became an independent colony in 1692.

People who chose to settle in New Hampshire had to be persistent in their struggle to tame the rocky soil, clear forests, and cope with long winters. Although farming was difficult, there were other economic opportunities. New Hampshire had produced ten cargoes of masts by 1671, highly valued by the expanding British fleet, in addition to other lumbering products. Shipbuilding and fishing were also profitable.

Endless Indian Wars

King Philip, named Metacomet, succeeded Massasoit as chief of the Wamponoags in 1662. During King Philip's War (1675–76; see sidebar on page 144), Major Waldron, formerly a friend of the Indians, set the stage for poor relations with the Indians by seizing their weapons; they retaliated later by killing him and many of the inhabitants of Dover in the Cocheco Massacre of 1689.

Just a decade after Indian King Philip's War, English King William's War (1689–97) stirred up more trouble between colonists and Indians, who attacked settlements in Salmon Falls, Exeter, Durham, and Portsmouth. The Fourth Indian War (1721–25) is also known as Lovewell's War. It started when Captain Lovewell and his soldiers met a group of Indians near Conway in 1725, and Lovewell was killed in the encounter.

Governing New Hampshire

John Cutt became president of the New Hampshire Province in 1679 and reported to the king. New Hampshire was the only colony to have this type of royal government. By 1741 there was an independent governor, Benning

Wentworth, who had an unusual method of granting townships. Each time he granted a tract he kept a lot of five hundred acres for himself. He also took a fee for each transaction; seventy-five townships were either granted or incorporated in the colony during his tenure. He also took to granting land west of the Connecticut River (later Vermont); New York, which also claimed the territory, followed suit. The result was a jurisdictional dispute that lasted until Vermont became a state in 1783.

The Wentworth family was also involved in the founding of Dartmouth College when Eleazar Wheelock moved his school for Indians from Connecticut to Hanover in 1769. Governor John Wentworth II, a nephew of Benning Wentworth, granted the college a royal charter and endowed it with 40,000 acres. During his tenure as governor, the legislature also agreed to a lottery for the benefit of the college in 1773 (so the twentieth-century New Hampshire lottery has historical precedents!).

Revolutionary Warriors

"Live free or die," written by Gen. John Stark, New Hampshire's Revolutionary War hero, is now the state motto. During the Revolution New Hampshire men served in most battle areas, but the colony did not suffer any fighting on its soil. New Hampshire men were busy as privateers along the Atlantic coast and as far away as the English Channel and the North Sea. Portsmouth was an active center for shipbuilders; the *Raleigh,* the *America,* and the *Ranger* were all built there.

As the British continued to attack harbors and rivers, George Washington first ordered his men to build a boom of masts and chains to throw across the Narrows in the Pascataqua. When the current destroyed the boom, an old ship was scuttled and sent to the bottom to block the entrance, and, finally, fire rafts were sent downstream to consume enemy ships in flames.

Regions to Explore

T he New Hampshire Colony has been divided into three regions: the New Hampshire Shore, the area of initial settlement around Portsmouth, Dover, and Exeter; the Merrimack River Valley, including the towns of Concord, Warner, and Franklin; and Western New Hampshire, where Keene, Charlestown, Enfield, and Hanover were early towns.

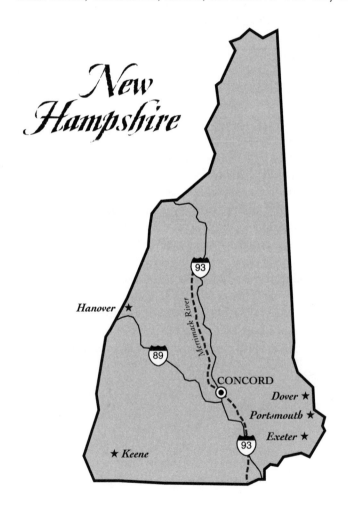

THE NEW HAMPSHIRE SHORE

The centerpiece of this region is **Portsmouth,** which was much less exposed than the colony at Odiorne Point. One can imagine the delight of the first settlers when they disembarked from the *Pied Cow* and found wild strawberries growing in great profusion along the banks of the Piscataqua River. With admirable directness they called their settlement Strawbery Banke, a name that remained until 1653, when it was abandoned for the more pedestrian Portsmouth. The town prospered as a deepwater seaport, fishing center, shipbuilding site for clippers, and lumber depot.

Today visitors can stroll through a living-history museum, **Strawbery Banke,** located on ten acres in the Puddle Dock section of town. Residents wisely chose to restore the area rather than let the wrecking hammer destroy an unusually rich cluster of forty-two historic buildings. It is truly a "museum in progress," working at archaeological digs, building restoration, designing exhibits, and engaging in historical research. When you enter Strawbery Banke, you will receive a Visitors' Map that indicates which houses are furnished and can be explored; others are available for external view only because they have yet to be restored. There are also a number of shops where

Colonial boat building at Strawbery Banke

craftspersons work at colonial trades, including boat building, cabinetmaking, cooperage, weaving, and making pottery. Colonial recipes from the eighteenth century, handwritten by Mehitable Wendell, are part of the Strawbery Banke Collection. Take a look at the orientation film and exhibits before you begin to get a sense of the whole museum.

You can wander into a wide range of colonial structures, including the 1695 **Sherburne House,** which has an exhibit on seventeenth-century construction; the 1790 **Joshua Jackson House**; the 1720 **Marden House**; the 1795 **Winn House**; the **Dinsmore Shop**, where the museum's cooper makes barrels; the 1790 **Jones House**; and the 1762 **Chase House.**

The 1780 **Wheelwright House** was built during the Revolution by Captain John Wheelwright, master of the brig *Abigail* on eight voyages to the West Indies. His death inventory included "1 sea bed, 1 quadrant, 3 sea coats and 1 old sea chest." Furnishings inside the house reflect the life of an eighteenth-century middle-class family.

The 1766 **William Pitt Tavern** was built by John Stavers; it was a popular gathering place for local residents who exchanged news, read newspapers, and conducted business. The first stagecoach service from Portsmouth to Boston, The Portsmouth Flying Stage Coach, left from this tavern. John Stavers, however, was more loyal to the Crown than to his adopted country. By 1775 an angry mob had destroyed the sign in front and broken the windows. Stavers fled to Greenland, was arrested, and jailed. In 1776 he signed the Association Test, which was an oath of allegiance to the colonies, and reopened his tavern. St. John's Masonic Lodge met there on the third floor, where members of the secret society used a stairway accessible only from the rear of the building.

If you're keen on archaeological digs, you can see artifacts recovered from the Marshall Pottery site, the Sherburne House, and other local sites in the Jones House. The museum is open daily 10:00 A.M.–5:00 P.M. May through October. Call (603) 433–1100 for current information on this developing site and a schedule of Strawbery Banke events such as Revolutionary War reenactments in September, when people dress in period costumes and partake in drills, musket firing, and camp life.

Before you leave Strawbery Banke for the center of Portsmouth, walk across the street into the attractive gardens of Prescott Park and visit the **Sheafe Warehouse** (ca. 1705), a remnant of the busy colonial waterfront. Here John Paul Jones supervised the outfitting of the *Ranger*; now it houses a museum of folk art.

Historic recipes from Strawbery Banke

Marmalade Quince

Take the pairing and cores, cover them well with water and boil four hours, then rub it through a wire sieve. Take ⅓ the quantity of stewed apples strained in the same way and mix them well together. Weight it and put a pound of brown sugar to a pound of the mixture. Add the sugar and let it stand 24 hours, then boil it till clean, taking care not to let it burn, or boil it too much. The hand will have to be used in rubbing it through the sieve.

Fish Balls

Take equal quantities of potatoes and boiled halibut or cod, mix them well together with the hand. To about 4 pounds of the mixture add a tablespoonful of powdered sugar and half pound of butter, and salt and pepper to taste. Then beat up three or four eggs light and mix with it. Being careful not to make it too soft, make it into cakes about as large as a tea cake and fry in lard.

Strawbery Banke is only one indication of the city's passion for historic preservation: There is more to see in the center, where economic forces often make old houses an endangered species. This is not so here, and a number of the best survived. The **Portsmouth Trail** (603–436–1118) leads you to six historic houses, which you can see in any order you like on a single ticket available at any one of them. Most are mansions that represent the affluence of the city's mercantile and shipping interests in the eighteenth century. For information on historic walking tours in Portsmouth, call (603) 431–5388.

The **Moffatt-Ladd House** (1763), at 154 Market Street, was built as a wedding gift for Samuel Moffatt from his father, an English sea captain named John Moffatt. The cost of the house, before the Revolution, was $12,000. There may have been a tunnel from the house to the waterfront at one time. Later John's son-in-law, William Whipple, a signer of the Declaration of Independence, lived in the house. There are three floors of eighteenth-century furnishings and beautifully terraced gardens. Don't for-

Time for a Drink

Mrs. Stavers lies dead in the house of John her Husband, who, by her being there is impeded from vending his Punch, he therefore determined to put her under ground this afternoon or tomorrow . . . & then I suppose we may again assume our Lodge, that, Since last Wednesday, has been cover'd with the Show of Sorrow.

—John Wentworth, 1757

get to pause in the stairwell to admire both the murals and the carving on the staircase. The house is open 10:00 A.M.–4:00 P.M. Monday through Saturday, 2:00 P.M.–5:00 P.M. Sunday, June 15 to October 15. Call (603) 436–8221 for more information.

The **John Paul Jones House,** on the corner of Middle and State Streets, is large but fitted out more modestly. As you might expect, John Paul Jones stayed here while he was supervising the outfitting of the *Ranger* in 1777 and the *America* in 1781. The house was built by Captain Purcell, who lived here with his wife, Sarah, niece of Governor Benning Wentworth. After Purcell's death in 1776, Sarah took in boarders, and John Paul Jones was the one most remembered today. The house contains eighteenth-century furniture, cookware, silver, glass, ceramics, portraits, guns, and a wooden leg—not an uncommon aftermath of naval warfare. Open 10:00 A.M.–4:00 P.M. Monday through Saturday, noon–4:00 P.M. Sunday, Memorial Day to October 15. To find out more call (603) 436–8420.

The **Governor John Langdon House,** on Pleasant Street, was built in 1784. John Langdon was a prominent statesman and patriot, both governor of New Hampshire and later the first president of the United States Senate. His fortune came from shipbuilding and privateering during the Revolution. The house is a Georgian mansion with an imposing facade, and it contains beautiful carving. George Washington visited the house in 1789 and wrote about both the house and his host with compliments. Open noon–5:00 P.M. Wednesday through Sunday, June 1 to October 15. Call (603) 436–3205 for further information about the house.

Another Georgian mansion, the **Wentworth Gardner House** on Mechanic Street, was built in 1760 for Thomas Wentworth, brother of John

Wentworth II, the last of the Royal Governors. Look for the windmill spit in the great fireplace in the kitchen, Bristol tiles in blue or mulberry around most of the fireplaces, hand-painted Chinese wallpaper in the North parlor, and French wallpaper in the dining room. It has eleven fireplaces and fine carving throughout. Open 1:00 P.M.–4:00 P.M. Tuesday through Sunday, mid-June through mid-October. For details call (603) 436–4406.

The **Warner House** (603–436–5909), on the corner of Daniel and Chapel streets, was built 1n 1716 for Capt. Archibald MacPhaedris from brick carried as ballast in the hold of his ship. Original painted murals are still in place on the staircase, and portraits by Blackburn hang on the walls. Look for the two murals on the stair landing that portray American Indians who were taken to London to meet Queen Anne in 1710. The lightning rod on the west wall may have been installed under the watchful eye of Benjamin Franklin in 1762. The Warner House is unusual because it is one of four brick buildings built before the Revolution, when New Englanders thought such construction to be damp and unwholesome. The house is open 10:00 A.M.–4:00 P.M. Tuesday through Saturday, 1:00 P.M.–4:00 P.M. Sunday, June through October. Call (603) 436–5909 for more information.

Captain MacPhaedris was related to the Wentworth family by marriage. Benning Wentworth had been appointed Royal Governor by King George II in 1741, and he rented the Warner House for ten years while building a mansion on Little Harbor. During that interval one of the parlors was used as a council chamber for the province. For further information call (603) 436–5909.

If you're ready to rest for the night, try **The Inn at Strawbery Banke,** at 314 Court Street. This nineteenth-century sea-captain's home is in the historic district. Call (603) 436–7242 for reservations. Another good choice is the **Sise Inn** (603–433–1200), at 40 Court Street. This 1880s inn is decorated in Queen Anne style.

Historic restaurants in Portsmouth include the **Dolphin Striker,** at 15 Box Street (603–431–5222), located in what was an eighteenth-century warehouse and specializes in seafood; the **Oar House Restaurant,** at 55 Ceres Street (603–436–4025); and the **Strawbery Court,** at 20 Atkinson Street (603–421–7722), which serves French cuisine.

Ten miles farther upstream on the Piscataqua, the emphasis shifts from shipbuilding and seafaring to fishing, farming, and lumbering in **Dover.** By 1622 this was the spot David Thompson chose to set up his fishery because salmon came to spawn near Dover Point. The next year the *Providence* sailed into Dover Point with Edward and William Hilton and Thomas Roberts, who had grants from the Plymouth Council; a decade later Captain Thomas Wiggin brought settlers to Dover Neck. Farmers and fishermen were joined by loggers, including Richard Waldron, who made use of the falls of the Cocheco for lumbering. Gradually the friendly relations with the Cocheco tribe, which at first had been friendly, deteriorated and finally exploded in the Cocheco Massacre of 1689.

The **Woodman Institute,** at 182–192 Central Avenue, has three buildings: two brick structures and the old Damm Garrison. The 1675 **Damm Garrison House** is fitted with portholes for guns to defend it against Indian attacks. The museum is furnished with cooking pots, farm equipment, clothing, and colonial furniture. The institute is open 2:00 P.M.–5:00 P.M. Tuesday through Saturday, April to January. Closed January 1, July 4, Labor Day, Thanksgiving, and December 25. Call (603) 742–1038 for more information.

The **New Hampshire Farm Museum** in **Milton** offers a farm complex with antique implements and a living-history farm. The 1780s Jones Farm house was home to Levi Jones, who came from Maine to work in a tavern owned by Joseph Plummer. He married Plummer's daughter, Betsey, and finally became the owner of the tavern. The buildings display a variety of architectural styles, beginning with colonial, and old farm implements date back to that period as well. Visitors may tour the house, barn, blacksmith shop, cobbler shop, and country store. Old Time Farm Day with sixty artisans demonstrating their craft and several workshops is held in August. For more details call (603) 652–7840.

Farther south and not far from the sea, a third early colonial settlement developed at **Exeter.** The moving force was the Reverend John Wheelwright, brother-in-law of Anne Hutchinson, who had been banished from Boston for his religious nonconformity. He chose to settle in Exeter and became head of the first church in town. The deed for his huge tract of land in Exeter is stored at Exeter Academy.

Exeter was one of the first towns to speak openly of independence, object to demands of the Crown, and even burn effigies of British Lords Bute and North. Perhaps the most interesting act of rebellion foreshadowed the Boston Tea Party, half a century later. The Mast Tree Riot took place here in 1734 when David Dunbar, surveyor for the Crown, ordered ten of his men to carve the King's Arrow on all trees in the Exeter mill to reserve them for the Royal Navy. In response Exeter men disguised themselves as Indians, broke into Samuel Gilman's tavern, grabbed the surveyor's men and tossed them out of town. Such events established the reputation of the town, and the capital of the province was moved from Portsmouth, which had a lot of Royalists, to Exeter in 1775.

The **American Independence Museum,** at 225 Water Street, is in the 1721 home of the Colonial Governor of New Hampshire, John Taylor Gilman. Among the three purple hearts given during the Revolution, one rests in this house, as well as an original copy of the Declaration of Independence. If you plan to visit in July, ask about Exeter's Revolutionary War Days, which feature a militia encampment wih colonial troops, demonstrations, farm animals, boat builders, and blacksmiths. Open 10:00 A.M.–4:00 P.M. Tuesday through Saturday, noon–4:00 P.M. Sunday, May through October; noon–3:00 P.M. Tuesday and Saturday during the rest of the year. Call (603) 772–2622 for more information and schedules of events.

The **Gilman Garrison House** (603–436–3205), at 12 Water Street, also called "the old logg house," dates from 1690, when it was constructed as a fortified garrison by John Gilman. The walls were built of enormous logs, and pulleys released a portcullis, or strong door, behind the main door. Peter Gilman added another wing in 1772 to make the Royal Governor comfortable when he chose to visit Exeter. The house is open noon–5:00 P.M. Tuesday, Thursday, Saturday, and Sunday, June 1 to October 15.

A Recipe for Yankee Individualism

Jeremy Belknap assessed the character of colonists and the nature of their daily life in his *History of New Hampshire*, published in 1784:

The inhabitants of New-Hampshire . . . [have] firmness of nerve, patience in fatigue, intrepidity in danger and alertness in action. . . . Men who are concerned in travelling, hunting, cutting timber, making roads and other employments in the forest, are inured to hardships . . . their children are early used to coarse food and hard lodging. . . . By such hard fare, and the labour which accompanies it, many young men have raised up families, and in a few years have acquired property sufficient to render themselves independent freeholders; and they feel all the pride and importance which arises from a consciousness of having well earned their estates.

When you're looking for accommodations in this attractive town, try the **Inn by the Bandstand,** at 4 Front Street. This 1809 inn has working fireplaces in every room. Call (603) 772–6352 for reservations. If you want to be closer to the sea, another choice is the **New Grayhurst,** at 11 F Street in Hampton Beach. This 1890 gambrel-roofed beach house has a cottage, an apartment, studios, rooms, and suites. For reservations call (603) 926–2584.

THE MERRIMACK RIVER VALLEY

Lack of access to the sea and Indian troubles slowed settlement in inland New Hampshire, but it began to develop along major rivers like the Merrimack. There was a trading post at **Concord** by 1660, and some colonists arrived during the succeeding years. Settlement began in earnest in 1727, with an influx of strict Protestant, Anglo-Saxon people. They got on well with the Indians until 1746, when five men were killed in the Bradley Massacre. The men were on their way from Rumford to a garrison when a large group of Indians suddenly appeared and shot them. The **Bradley Monument,** on Route 202, is inscribed with the names of those men.

Nearby, in Canterbury Center, is the **Canterbury Shaker Village,** where twenty-four Shaker buildings are open as a living-history museum. The village was founded in the 1780s as the sixth of nineteen Shaker communities. Shaker furniture includes simple but aesthetically remarkable beds, chairs, chests, work tables, benches, baskets, and more. The Shakers devoted their "hands to work and their hearts to God." Visitors can watch craftspersons weaving, spinning, printing, making brooms, and engaging in woodworking, tinsmithing, and basket making. You can also sign up in advance for workshops and learn how to make brooms, herbal wreaths, baskets, or engage in woodworking or weaving. When you're hungry, try the **Creamery Restaurant** on the grounds, which serves Shaker-inspired meals. The village is open 10:00 A.M.–5:00 P.M. Monday through Saturday, noon–5:00 P.M. Sunday, May to October; 10:00 A.M.–5:00 P.M. Friday and Saturday, noon–5:00 P.M. Sunday, April 1 and November. Call (603) 783–9511 for information or reservations.

If you're heading north from Concord and want to stop at some interesting accommodations for the night, there are a number of choices. One (in

Recipe from Canterbury Shaker Village

Shaker Rhubarb Tea

8 cups diced, peeled rhubarb, with red skin   8 cups water

Grated rind of 2 lemons or oranges   1 1/2 to 2 cups sugar

Simmer rhubarb in water until very tender, about 20 to 25 minutes. Strain, add grated lemon or orange rind and sugar. Stir until sugar has dissolved. Cool well and serve.

spite of the trendy name) is **The Inn at Golden Pond** (603–968–7269), in Holderness. Dating from 1879, the inn property includes fifty-five acres and fronts on the beautiful lake where *On Golden Pond* was filmed. Another, **The Manor on Golden Pond,** also in Holderness, looks like an English estate with carved and paneled walls and fireplaces; call (800) 545–2141 or (603) 968–3348. A short distance southeast, in Meredith on Lake Winnipesaukee, is **The Inn at Mill Falls,** which was a gristmill in the early 1800s; from the windows you can watch water cascade down through a series of channels; for reservations call (800) 622–MILL (622–6455) or (603) 279–7006 or fax (603) 279–6797. Farther north **The Mill House Inn** in Lincoln is part of the historic old mill complex at Loon Mountain—the former mill drying shed has been converted into comfortable accommodations (800–654–6183 or 603–745–6261). Still farther north **Adair,** off Route 302 in Bethlehem, is a mansion on a hilltop complete with an all-weather tennis court and landscaping designed by Olmsted on 200 acres (603–444–2600; fax 603–444–4823).

WESTERN NEW HAMPSHIRE

Western New Hampshire was frontier territory, far removed from colonial support, through the seventeenth and much of the eighteenth centuries and thus considered too dangerous during the almost incessant Indian wars. Early settlers lived in **Keene** in the 1730s, after Nathan Blake built the first log cabin in 1736. Forty families arrived in 1737 but found it hazardous to go into the fields near their homes because of Indians. In 1747 two people were killed when the fort was attacked, Nathan Blake was captured, and homes were burnt. The entire population then left town, and the Indians burned the village to the ground; nevertheless, by the 1750s settlers were back.

The 1762 **Wyman Tavern,** at 399 Main Street, was built by Isaac Wyman. He was a staunch patriot who led his friends to Lexington, Concord, and Boston; these Keene minutemen met in the tavern before beginning their march. Inside the tavern visitors will see the restored taproom, two parlors, a ballroom, a kitchen, an office, and bedrooms. For more information call (603) 352–1895.

Swing Your Partner

"Contra-dances" were very popular in New Hampshire; the word doesn't mean "country dances" but stands for dances in which two lines of dancers face each other. Imagine early settlers bringing joy into their lives—after working hard all day—by an evening of contra-dancing at Wyman Tavern. Contra-dancing is still popular today in many parts of New England.

To the north a log fort was built at Charlestown on the Connecticut River in 1744, but as the northernmost white settlement, it was continually invaded by Indians. Later the fort, called No. 4, was a rendezvous spot for colonial troops on their way to Crown Point and Bennington.

Today visitors to **Old Fort No. 4** will find a living-history museum of the 1740s and 1750s. Buildings include a blacksmith shop, cow barn, great stockade building, watchtower, Hasting house, Parker/Sartwell lean-to, Willard house, Spafford lean-to, Sartwell house (the cooking area), Parker house, Killam/Hastings lean-to, Farnsworth house, Parker/Putnam lean-to, Stevens house, and the Great Hall with its second floor used for church services and town meetings and as a barracks during wartime. With a map in hand, visitors may wander in and out of the buildings. Costumed guides will tell you about the daily life in the fort during this era. The fort is open 10:00 A.M.–4:00 P.M. Wednesday through Monday, Memorial Day to Labor

Day and September 21 to Columbus Day; 10:00 A.M.–4:00 P.M. Saturday and Sunday after Labor Day to mid-September. Call (603) 826–5700 for more information.

Farther north on the Connecticut River, Eleazar Wheelock came to **Hanover** to establish an Indian school in 1769 and built a log cabin here in 1770. His school eventually became Dartmouth College. The school continued to grow, with a number of colonial buildings, including those on Dartmouth Row. Dartmouth is the ninth oldest college in the country and the northernmost of eight Ivy League institutions. **Webster Cottage** dates from 1780 and is famous for the fact that Daniel Webster lived there when he was an undergraduate. To find out more call (603) 643–3512.

Try **The Hanover Inn,** an elegant nineteenth-century inn, for a meal or overnight stay. The Daniel Webster Room serves memorable dinners. Call (603) 643–4300 for reservations.

FOR MORE INFORMATION

Office of Vacation Travel
172 Pembroke Road
P.O. Box 856
Concord, NH 03301
(603) 271–2343

Rhode Island

Historical Introduction to the
RHODE ISLAND COLONY

The Quest for Religious Tolerance

*T*he rebels who fled the rigid structure of the Massachusetts Bay Colony for Rhode Island established and maintained a level of tolerance for nonconformist beliefs that was almost unimaginable in the early seventeenth century. What kept the various religious groups from struggling for predominance, and why did they not proclaim the need for religious orthodoxy, which was the hallmark of the century? For reasons not clearly understood, tiny Rhode Island became the refuge of the unwanted and expelled, the model for cooperation among religious denominations, and a puzzle for historians, who are still trying to explain why an unusual degree of tolerance emerged at this time in this place.

Apart from the extraordinary freedom of religious belief that the colony afforded, its topography was unusually attractive. In an era when access to protected harbors meant access to world sea trade, Narragansett Bay was truly a godsend. Here was not only a marvelous sea harbor, at Newport, but also a string of protected harbors that reached far inland on both sides of the bay. In an era when transport by sea was far more efficient than rudimentary land conveyance, this was indeed a magnificent find, a region that invited settlement.

Roger Williams

Roger Williams was forced to leave the Massachusetts Bay Colony in 1636 because he would not submit to the strict Puritans, who ruled every aspect of life there. Never cautious in his words, he wrote, "Yourselves pretend liberty of conscience, but alas! it is but self, the great god self, only to yourselves." Williams felt that church and state should be separate: Magistrates should deal with civil offenses but leave religious matters to the church. He advocated respecting all religions, instead of persecuting them, and not forcing other sects to attend Puritan services. Forced worship, he said, "stinks in God's nostrils."

Payment to the Indians

Williams also held an extraordinary and dangerous conviction that would not be taken seriously for most of three centuries: He believed that the king could not grant land to his subjects unless the Indians were paid for it. He wrote, "James has no more right to give away or sell Massasoit's lands . . . than Massasoit has to sell King James' kingdom." As the authorities were about to send him back to England, Williams escaped to the Narragansett Bay area, where he lived with friendly Indians during the winter of 1636. He founded the first settlement in Providence in the same year.

Williams opened a trading post and proceeded to make friends with the Indians. He was fascinated with the Narragansetts and kept records of their language; crops, such as corn, squash, beans, and tobacco; cooking, including strawberry bread, which became a favorite in colonial kitchens; and work, like the method for building stone walls. He also noted their ball games, somewhat similar to modern football, and other warlike sports like tomahawk throwing, bow-and-arrow competition, and races on horseback. Williams was upset to learn that the Narragansetts gambled among themselves and frequently lost everything they had saved.

Anne Hutchinson

Anne Hutchinson, an intelligent, energetic, and charismatic woman who lived in the Massachusetts Bay Colony, was clearly a danger to the establishment. She used her front parlor for discussions of the local ministers' sermons, which she thought reached far beyond the intent of Christianity. Devout Christians could commune directly with God, she felt, instead of believing that God had spoken only once through the Scriptures. Such heresies added to the general discomfort with strict theocratic rule. Merchants in the Massachusetts Bay Colony were upset with government restrictions and eager to side with her rational approach to civil government.

Inevitably she was arrested and brought to trial, where she stood her ground against the strict interpretation of the Bible advocated by the Puritan magistrates. John Winthrop wrote that she had a "nimble wit and active spirit and a very voluble tongue." Anne was convicted of heresy, sedition, and contempt in the Massachusetts Bay Colony and subsequently left with her husband, William, and others to join the settlement at Portsmouth, which William Coddington and John Clarke had founded.

Aquidneck

Roger Williams of Providence was instrumental in negotiating a contract for the island of Aquidneck as a home for the exiles from the Massachusetts Bay Colony. It was named Portsmouth, and later some of the group split off to settle Newport. There was also a newcomer, Samuel Gorton, to whom the Earl of Warwick had granted land called Shawomet, on the west side of Narragansett Bay. Although the four settlements had their differences, Roger Williams acted as a mediator; and, finally, in 1647 they united, leading to a charter as the Colony of Rhode Island and Providence Plantations from Charles II in 1663.

Regions to Explore

F
or your convenience in exploring this small but always energetic colony, built on the islands and shores of a beautiful bay and ocean coastline, we divide it into four geographical regions: Providence Area, East Bay, Newport County, and South County. All are within easy reach of one another, so you can use any one of them as a base for day trips throughout the original colony.

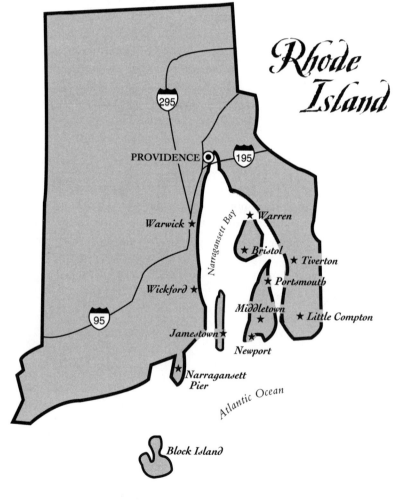

PROVIDENCE AREA

William Blackstone, a bull-riding minister, who also left the Massachusetts Colony because of its overpowering Puritanism, arrived in Rhode Island in 1635. He developed a 200-acre estate on the Blackstone River north of Providence, where he planted the first apple orchard in the colony and introduced the first dairy cattle. He also kept hogs. His wandering hogs were often swept up by Indians, and one Indian named Nahanton had to give him two beaver skins "for damage done him in his swine, by setting of traps."

The world of Blackstone's estate and Roger Williams's trading post is hard to imagine in the midst of Providence today, but one magnificent remnant of the colony is quite visible. The "mile of history" advertised in brochures about Providence is more than the usual claim of tourist authorities. **Benefit Street** backs it up, offering a treasure in its almost unbroken string of colonial, Georgian, and Early Federal buildings.

Not only Benefit Street but the whole hill above it in the eastern section of Providence is loaded with mansions and houses, most of them marked with dates and names of the original owners. If you are an architecture buff, this is manna indeed, and anyone will enjoy the time warp made visible. You can walk up all the streets that intersect Benefit Street to imbibe the atmosphere of the last quarter of the eighteenth and the first half of the nineteenth century.

Originally the street developed in the 1760s to house the overflow from Town Street, now called Main Street. Benefit Street, first given the homely but accurate name Back Street, provided a pathway "for the benefit of all," as people walked to family burial sites, orchards, and gardens along the back of their properties. Soon shipowners, sea captains, merchants, and persons skilled in marine trades built their homes all along the street.

During the era of Providence's preeminence as a seaport, the street glowed with the evidence of prosperity. Like Chestnut Street in Salem, it saw the construction of elegant mansions such as the John Brown House and the Nightingale-Brown House. Later, as the source of this prosperity—world trade—moved to other deep-water ports and was not replaced by comparable economic bonanzas, the port section of Providence gradually slid into decline.

Before the wrecking ball could swing, the Providence Preservation Society had already begun its work in the 1930s, rescuing some almost-doomed historic buildings along the neglected street that had fallen into disrepute. The transformation we see now was the first large-scale historic restoration project in America, a model for other major efforts in the heart of cities like Philadelphia, Charleston, and Savannah. The best part is that people actually live and work here every day—it's not just a museum to visit on Sundays.

As you walk along Benefit Street—and walking is the only way to appreciate it properly—you will want to allow time for poking up and down interesting side streets, like Thomas Street. You might begin at the **Brick School House** (1769), at 24 Meeting Street, the home of the Providence Preservation Society. Here a guide to Benefit Street is available, as well as other tourist information. Call (401) 272–2760 for details.

Both Washington and Lafayette were entertained in the **Old State House** (1762), at 150 Benefit Street. On May 4, 1776, the colony renounced its allegiance to King George III, an event that took place two months before the Declaration of Independence was signed. For information call (401) 277–2678.

From the middle of Benefit Street walk down to the **First Baptist Church** (1775), at 75 North Main Street, where the first congregation was formed by Roger Williams. James Manning was the minister and also the president of Brown University. He stated that the building was created for two purposes: "for the publick worship of Almighty God; and also for holding Commencement in."

For more Roger Williams sites, walk along North Main Street to the **Roger Williams National Memorial** at Smith Street. The original settlement in Providence took place here in 1636. The Roger Williams Spring is now a well, and the Visitors Center here has exhibits, including a three-minute slide show about Williams's life and the history of the area plus several videos, one of them narrated by Charles Kuralt. The memorial is open daily 8:00 A.M.–4:30 P.M. Closed January 1, Thanksgiving, and December 25.

For a skyline view of downtown Providence, head for **Prospect Terrace,** at Congdon and Cushing streets, which contains a Roger Williams memorial statue; his remains are also buried here. From this park you can also see the State Capitol, with a statue of the *Independent Man* on top—another signal that the state continues the colony's penchant for going its own way.

For a dollar a week during colonial days, twenty-five students were served "three good meals per day" in **University Hall** (1771), just up the hill where College Street meets Prospect Street. It was built for Brown College, first chartered in 1764 as Rhode Island College. During the Revolution

University Hall was used as a barracks and hospital by the Continental army until 1780, then by the French until 1782, when it was returned to the college. The building, which was modeled after Nassau Hall at Princeton, is now used for administrative offices. Open 8:30 A.M.–5:00 P.M. Monday through Friday during the academic year; 8:00 A.M.–4:00 P.M. during the rest of the year. For information about the hall, call (401) 863–2453.

When you're on Brown's central quadrangle, you may want to visit the **John Carter Brown Library,** an elegant, monumental building that houses the collection of its founder, who was born at the end of the eighteenth century and began gathering Americana in the nineteenth. With a focus on the discovery and later development of the Americas during the colonial period, the library has an extensive collection of books that draws scholars from all over the world. Originally kept in the Nightingale-Brown House (see below), which it outgrew, the collection was moved from Benefit Street to the Brown campus in 1904. Exhibits, as well as public lectures and other events, are open to visitors. The library is open 8:30 A.M.–5:00 P.M. Monday through Friday, 9:00 A.M.–noon Saturday during the academic year. Hours vary during the summer and holidays. Call (401) 863–2725 for details.

This area of Providence was at the heart of Revolutionary events. Here Stephen Hopkins signed a copy of the Declaration of Independence with a shaky, palsied hand. On that occasion he said, "My hand trembles, but my heart does not." Visitors can see the copy in the **Governor Stephen Hopkins House** (1707) at 15 Hopkins Street at the corner of Benefit. Hopkins was a member of the Continental Congress, ten-time governor of Rhode Island, chief justice of the superior court, and first chancellor of Brown University. This house was eventually moved up the hill, and Hopkins added the two-story gable-roof section after 1743.

The house is open, and docents give guided tours. In the large fireplace you will see an assortment of cooking necessities, including pot hooks and a trammel (a long rod with teeth for setting the height of a pot), common to many colonial homes. The Keeping Room also contains many utensils: a revolving toaster, a foot stove (taken to church with hot coals in it to help worshipers endure long sermons), a waffle iron, and a pastry roller. A decanter set was given to Hopkins by George Washington, who visited in 1776, 1781, and 1791. The study contains a fireplace with maroon-colored Dutch tiles that depict biblical stories and are covered with a manganese glaze.

Climb upstairs to see the Washington Room, where George stayed overnight. An inscription in a book on the bedside table reads: "Sarah Wells her book given to her by her Mama January of 1700." Tabatha Hopkins's sampler, now hanging on the wall, was stitched when she was five years old. Stephen Hopkins's baby cap, baby shoes, porringer, and a buckle are on display in a case.

Outside, the eighteenth-century colonial garden is open to the public for a welcome respite after climbing up and down the hills of Providence. A sundial rises from the middle of symmetrical gardens. Stephen Hopkins proclaimed the site "A garden that might comfort yield," which indeed it does. For more information call (401) 884–8337 or 751–1758.

In the area surrounding the southern half of Benefit Street, restoration fever has spread all the way up the hill to Brown and beyond. If you have time to walk streets like Charlesfield, Power, Williams, John, Arnold, and Transit, and the lanes connecting them, you will find yourself wandering back into the ambience of the late eighteenth and early nineteenth century.

The first house built on the hill above Benefit Street was the **John Brown House** (1786), 52 Power Street at the intersection of Benefit Street. Originally John Brown had a magnificent view of the sea and his own ships in the harbor. His three-story mansion has a balustrade around the roof and a Palladian window on the second floor. John Quincy Adams wrote that the house was "the most beautiful and elegant private mansion that I have ever seen on this continent."

John Brown and his family created a commercial dynasty in the China trade, and they were astute enough to shift their activities as old industries declined and new ones emerged. Thus as shipping became less lucrative in the middle of the nineteenth century, they also spurred on the growth of textile manufacturing in Rhode Island. The family became an institution in the city, and much of its wealth went toward supporting Brown University and various charitable institutions.

In the house you will find an impressive collection of colonial furniture, much of it made by Rhode Island craftspersons. One of the finest pieces is a Rhode Island nine-shell, blockfront desk. Squirrels as a motif in the study symbolize the family industriousness. The hall contains lithographs from England dating from 1740, marble busts, photographs of John Brown, and vases and urns from the China trade that built their fortune.

Upstairs you will see some symbolic Revolutionary war items, including John Brown's walking stick, made from wood taken from the *Gaspee*. (For an account of the *Gaspee* affair, see Warwick, page 141.) Brown, a staunch American patriot, was involved in the burning of the ship, and a goblet taken from the the *Gaspee* is displayed as spoils of war among the collection of family silver.

If you are a vehicle buff, don't miss the carriage house, which contains the first (1782) American-made vehicle to be ordered. It is handsomely painted in turquoise and gold and has gigantic wheels. The John Brown House is open 11:00 A.M.–4:00 P.M. Tuesday through Saturday, 1:00 P.M.–4:00 P.M. Sunday, March to December; 11:00 A.M.–4:00 P.M. Saturday, 1:00 P.M.–4:00 P.M. Sunday during the rest of the year. For more information on the house, call (401) 331–8575.

The elegant yellow mansion filling the next block down Benefit Street, the largest wooden house still standing from eighteenth-century America, also belonged to the Brown family domain. The **Nightingale–Brown House** (1792), at 357 Benefit Street, was among five mansions built on College Hill just after the Revolutionary War. Nicholas Brown bought the house in 1814 from the heirs of Col. Joseph Nightingale, a merchant who had made his fortune in the China trade. It was home to the Brown family for 171 years until deeded to the John Nicholas Brown Center for the Study of American Civilization in 1985. The house was designated a National Historical Landmark in 1989.

The house almost didn't survive. At the time of the transfer, engineers discovered extensive damage from termites, rot, and successive alterations to such a large post-and-beam structure. Seven years of restoration began, largely financed by the sale of a single, original Rhode Island shell desk for $11 million (now replaced by a first-rate replica). The house is unusually interesting not because it is authentic to the colonial period—or any other era in decoration or furnishing—but because it evolved through nearly two centuries of use by a single family.

In this sense the house is Winterthur in miniature, a record of the changing tastes of generations. The last redecoration, in the 1920s, adopted the colonial Revival style and installed eighteenth-century paneling in the dining room. The second floor of the renovated house provides study space for visiting scholars at the John Nicholas Brown Center, but the first floor has been left as the family used it and is open to the public one day a week, usually Fridays, or by appointment. Call ahead for specific times: (401) 272–0357.

Transit Street was named for the transit of the planet Venus in 1769, which was observed by Joseph Brown, Stephen Hopkins, and Jabez Bowen through a telescope. They were standing on the corner of Transit and Benefit

Streets, near the location of the "lightning splitter house," with a steep gabled roof (1781), at 53 Transit.

Just a block downhill toward the river, **South Main Street** runs parallel to Benefit Street, and here some buildings of historic interest still stand. **Joseph Tillinghast's House** (1770), at 403 South Main, was built by a sea captain, then used as a tavern for sailors during the China trade era. The **Axel de Fersen House,** at 312 South Main Street, is named after a flamboyant aide-de-camp of Rochambeau who stayed there when the French were in residence during the later stages of the Revolutionary War. A Swedish nobleman, he was also a lover of Marie Antoinette and drove the carriage in which she unsuccessfully tried to escape from France in 1791. These houses are not open to the public.

The **Joseph Brown House** (1774), at 50 South Main Street, was also used by Rochambeau's officers. It was the scene for male high spirits when one young officer reputedly "rode his spirited charger up the flight of steps" that led to the front door; when the horse refused to turn and head down the steps, he rode through the house and exited by the rear door.

If you'd like to stay overnight in this area, there are several possibilities nearby that will keep you in historical settings. Try the **Old Court,** at 144 Benefit Street, which was designed in 1863 as a rectory for St. John's Episcopal Church. For reservations call (401) 751–2002 or (401) 351–0747. Another good choice is the **State House Inn,** at 43 Jewett Street, a colonial Revival ten-room bed-and-breakfast inn that once stood where the Capitol is now. Call (401) 785–1235.

Warwick, lying just south of Providence on the western shore of Narragansett Bay, is now a sprawling bedroom community. Its old center, however, had an important role in the colonial era, and it is still well known for its June Gaspee Days, which celebrate the capture and destruction of the *Gaspee,* a British revenue schooner that had been harassing the patriots. Beginning with the 1993 celebration, the Rhode Island Mace, which contains a piece of wood from the *Gaspee,* was carried in the parade. There's also a colonial muster of fife and drums that follows the parade. A Revolutionary War battle reenactment and the burning of the *Gaspee* takes place the next day at Salter Grove State Park.

The town of Warwick had an earlier history of rebellion. Samuel Gorton, who founded it in 1642, was regarded as extremely outspoken, a troublemaker who had been exiled from both Plymouth and Portsmouth. The site

Baiting the British

The *Gaspee* affair occurred off Namquid Point (now called Gaspee Point), Warwick, in 1772. It has been compared to the Boston Tea Party by some historians because it represents the response of a maritime community to British interference with trade. The affair started when Captain Thomas Lindsay of the packet sloop *Hannah,* one of the vessels harassed by the *Gaspee,* had purposely led the deeper revenue schooner aground on a sandspit during the afternoon of June 9. Lindsay got the news to John Brown, who gathered a group of leading Providence merchants in the Sabin Tavern that evening to organize the burning of the stranded *Gaspee* before the next high tide could get her off.

Capt. Abraham Whipple led sixty-four men in a successful attack that captured and burned the ship. So much secrecy surrounded the plot that none of the patriot suspects were ever found, in spite of the obligatory proclamations of Governor Wanton and the arrest of Brown. How could a band of prominent citizens steal through the night unobserved? The investigating commission reported that not a soul in Rhode Island knew anything about the mysterious conflagration.

of the **Samuel Gorton House** is located at 190 Warwick Neck Avenue, Warwick Neck, where there is a bronze plaque and a newer home built by the Gorton family.

The **John Waterman Arnold House** (1760), at 25 Roger Williams Circle, stands on land originally owned by Israel Arnold, who supplied Continental troops with cattle, wood, and tobacco during the Revolution. It is an authentic example of a central-chimney colonial farmhouse that grew as the family prospered; at one time the Arnolds owned nearly 10,000 acres of land and paid the highest taxes in the colony. Quite appropriately the house now serves as home for the **Warwick Historical Society,** which rescued it from threatened destruction for an initial $1.00, then began restoring it for a good bit more.

The structure has paneled doors, six-over-six windowpanes, and thumb latches on the doors. Look for the niche in the stairway that allowed the inhabitants to move large pieces upstairs, such as coffins. It has colonial furnishings, textile and clothing exhibits, and a beehive oven that dates from 1770. Open Wednesdays 9:00 A.M.–1:00 P.M. For more information call (401) 467–7647 or 737–8160.

EAST BAY

Roger Williams canoed on Narragansett Bay from Providence to various sites along the way south to Portsmouth and Newport. The East Bay towns of Warren, Bristol, and Barrington are among the finest residential areas in greater Providence. Proud of their past and assiduous in preserving it, these attractive towns provide a feast for those interested in colonial architecture.

Water Street in **Warren,** a National Register Waterfront District, is located on the eastern bank of the Warren River. Once the site of an Indian village, **Burr's Hill Park** contains Indian burial mounds. Massasoit ruled the whole region, including southeastern Massachusetts and the lands bordering Narragansett Bay, when the Mayflower arrived in 1620. Some Indian artifacts are in the **Charles Whipple Greene Museum** in the George Hail Library. The museum is open Wednesdays 2:00 P.M.–4:00 P.M. or by appointment. For more information call (401) 245–7686. Massasoit's Spring is located on Baker Street near the water. Warren is now restoring the historic buildings where its residents were once involved in whaling and sea trade. It was the fifth largest whaling port in the country during the early eighteenth century.

Maxwell House (1755), at 59 Church Street, was built by Samuel Maxwell as a brick colonial-gable house and is now owned by the **Massasoit Historical Association.** Inside there are two beehive bake ovens, which still produce colonial-style fare periodically. Open 5:00 P.M.–8:00 P.M. Friday, July through August 1 and by appointment. The Massasoit Historical Association also conducts a tour of historical buildings in Warren's historic district, usually in October. For exact dates of tours and information on activities in the house, call (401) 245–7652.

Other houses still standing in town are remembered for specific events during the Revolution. One is the **Rogers-Hicks House,** on School Street, built by Peleg Rogers in 1765. Josias Lyndon, the governor of Rhode Island from 1768 to 1769, escaped British troops during the Revolution and fled to this house. He survived until 1778, when he died of smallpox. He is buried in Kickemuit Cemetery in Warren. The house has been the rectory

Baking in Beehives

A beehive bake oven is made of brick in an arched shape on one side of a colonial kitchen fireplace; it does look just like a beehive. Cooks experienced in using them say this particular shape contributes to holding proper temperatures for baking over long periods.

of St. Mark's Church since 1921. Open by appointment Sunday, 7:00 A.M.–noon. Call (401) 245–3161. The **Jesse Baker House** (1753), at 421 Main Street, is remembered for the courage of its owner, Mrs. Jesse Baker, who used blankets to curtail the flames as the British were burning the nearby Baptist Meeting House.

When you're ready for a taste treat in an elegant colonial home, try the **Nathaniel Porter House,** at 125 Water Street, named by the current owners for an ancestor who fought at the Battle of Lexington. Built by a sea captain, the house was meticulously restored by owners Robert and Vi Lynch over a period of years; here they used their experience garnered in earlier preservation projects. Now the house serves as an authentic colonial inn and has bedrooms furnished with antiques—some with canopied beds, and all with the fireplaces that were once essential. The Nathaniel Porter House is especially noted for its fine cuisine, and it also serves plain colonial fare amid original murals and period antiques in separate dining rooms, including two formal parlors, a tavern room, and a courtyard. The Sunday Champagne Brunch draws people from miles around. For reservations call (401) 245–6622.

Visitors know they're in **Bristol** when they spot the red, white, and blue stripe down the center of the principal through-street (Highway 114). Bristol was the first town to hold a Fourth of July parade, in 1785, and today the red, white, and blue centerline is a proud reminder of that tradition. The whole town looks like a Norman Rockwell painting, brimful of restored homes that are really lived in.

Bristol was a focal point of both peace and war as settlers and Indians lived side by side during much of the seventeenth century. The chief of the Wampanoag Indians, Massasoit, had his headquarters in the Mount Hope Lands that included Bristol. Although he had sold much of his land to the colonists, the Wampanoags retained the eastern shore of Narragansett Bay, the southern Massachusetts coast, Cape Cod, Martha's Vineyard, and Nantucket. Massasoit's son, Metacom, or King Philip, led the war named after him in 1675–76; near its end a search party under Capt. Benjamin Church ambushed him, and a Sakonnet ally killed King Philip in a swamp below Mount Hope.

King Philip's War

King Philip's War was by far the bloodiest confrontation between Indians and New England colonists. The Wampanoags attacked fifty-two of ninety settlements, destroyed thirteen entirely, burned houses, and killed more than 600 colonists, including women and children. The peaceful relations between coexisting settlers and tribes that had persisted through Massasoit's life deteriorated after his death in 1662 as the Wampanoags harbored grievances about unfair treatment of individual Indians and trickery in land deals. The attacks began in June of 1675 and spread to include the Narragansetts, who controlled most of mainland Rhode Island, after the Great Swamp Fight. In this raid on December 19, 1675, New England colonists overwhelmed the Narragansett winter camp near West Kingston and destroyed their food supplies. The war did not begin to wind down until July 1676, after a battle at Warwick.

Each of three colonies—Rhode Island, Massachusetts Bay, and Plymouth —wanted Bristol because of its fine harbor and ideal location on Narragansett Bay. Plymouth was granted the lands in 1680 by King Charles II, and people began to buy parcels as householders. By 1690 fifteen ships called Bristol home port, and a local shipyard built both the *Grampus* and the *Dolphin* in 1696.

By 1747 Rhode Island had won back Bristol as well as Cumberland, Tiverton, Little Compton, Warren, and part of Barrington. During the Revolution Bristol supported the independence movement and paid for it. After fifteen British ships came into the harbor in 1775, demanded provisions, and fired upon the town, citizens built fortifications along the harbor for some protection in their exposed position. In May of 1778, however, 500

British soldiers landed on Bristol Neck, burning and destroying buildings in both Warren and Bristol.

Those readers who are especially interested in colonial architecture will find a tour of Bristol illuminating. A good place to start is the **Bristol Historical and Preservation Society Museum and Library,** at 48 Court Street, built from stone ballast sent over on Bristol sailing ships. Group walking tours are offered by appointment, and the society sells a book with detailed descriptions of the town's restored homes, many of which are opened up during special tour days. A House and Garden Tour is held in September. Call (401) 253–7223 for dates and schedules.

Bristol is a perfect place to take a long walk, either with or without a camera in hand, and you can enjoy the exteriors of these fine houses at any time. Use a town map to locate the colonial buildings you are particularly interested in. **Hope Street**, stretching from end to end of the town, is lined with a panoply of fine restored houses; if your time is limited, walk this street to get an overview of colonial Bristol. Altogether about fifty eighteenth-century homes are still standing in Bristol, making the town a kind of living museum of late colonial life.

One of the oldest and best preserved of Bristol's historic houses is the **Joseph Reynolds House** (1693), at 956 Hope Street, which fortunately was saved from destruction and is now a bed and breakfast. Although it began as a two-room, center-hall house, additions created a three-story home. The Marquis de Lafayette lived with the Reynolds family here for three weeks in 1778, and Rochambeau, Jefferson, and Washington visited

Gables and Gambrels

Most of the houses in Bristol were built in typical Rhode Island style (five bays, five rooms) as wood-framed structures with gable or gambrel roofs. The chimney was usually in the center of the house, and the five rooms surrounded it. This pattern had evolved from simpler two-room houses in the seventeenth century that were only one room deep, with a single room on each side of the chimney. By the eighteenth century larger, more elaborate houses added a second chimney, more bays, and other refinements.

him here. Guest rooms are located on the second and third floors; the keeping room is available as a lounge, and breakfast is served in the second parlor. Ask about the ghosts! For reservations call (401) 254–0230.

If you get enthralled with this town, and it is easy to do so, another good place to stop for the night is the **Williams Grant Inn,** at 154 High Street. Built in 1808, it was given to the grandson of Deputy Governor William Bradford. Call (401) 253–4222 for reservations.

Two other rural properties not far from the town center are also worth a visit. Across the harbor in Colt State Park stands **Coggeshall Farm** (1750), on land first bought by Samuel Viall in 1723 and worked by the Coggeshall family in the 1830s. Today the Coggeshall Farm Museum portrays rural life in the late eighteenth century complete with period farm animals, including working oxen. This salt-marsh farm includes a saltbox house, barns, a weaving shed, a blacksmith shop, and exhibits of agricultural implements and tools. For information call (401) 253–9062.

Just east of Bristol's town center lie the heights of **Mount Hope,** with deep roots in early colonial and Revolutionary history. This was the site of King Philip's village and his death in the marsh below; here also Elizabeth and Isaac Royall lost their home a century later because they remained staunch royalists. **Mount Hope Farm** was built in 1745 as a two-and-a-half story, five-bay, gambrel-roofed house with later additions. In 1776 the farm was confiscated by the state after Royall had fled to Nova Scotia. William Bradford bought it in 1783, and George Washington visited him here in 1789.

Energy-Efficient Homes

Coggeshall Farm's saltbox construction has two stories in front and only one in back, resulting in a shorter roof on the facade and a longer one behind. Familiar to colonists from East Anglia and Kent in England, this design was a way of rebuilding small houses to add sleeping space above and a lean-to kitchen shed (usually unheated) behind. It was economical and efficient, with two rooms for living on the ground floor and small bedrooms above, all drawing heat from a single central chimney stack, and it soon became a common design in New England colonies—the "split-level" of its era.

The property was given to Brown University in the 1950s and is now the site of the **Haffenreffer Museum of Anthropology.** Visitors can see artifacts and displays of Native Americans from the area as well as other locations in the world, including South America, Middle America, Africa, Asia, the Middle East, and Oceania. The museum is open from 10:00 A.M. to 5:00 P.M. Tuesday through Sunday, June to August; 10:00 A.M.–5:00 P.M. Saturday and Sunday, March through May and September through December. For more information call (401) 253–8388.

NEWPORT COUNTY

If you approach Newport County from Fall River on Route 24—a normal way to get there from Interstate 95 since Rhode Island and Massachusetts cannot be divorced in this region—you may want to pause for a pleasant side trip down the east shore of the Sakonnet River to Tiverton and Little Compton. This is great territory for wandering in unspoiled land. It is curious that this pocket of almost timeless rural New England, both in Rhode Island and across the border in southern Massachusetts, remains untouched by suburbia and shopping malls since it is less than an hour's drive from Providence, Fall River, and New Bedford.

The lovely, quiet roads of the east shore area resemble English lanes—many of them unsigned. When driving through this undisturbed pleasant landscape, we followed our instincts and our noses to get from one place to another; a good map and a compass would make it easier. It is also superb for cycling, with many almost deserted country roads to explore.

In **Tiverton** you may want to stop at **Fort Barton,** on Highland Road, the colonial army's staging point for the invasion of Aquidneck Island and Newport in the 1778 Battle of Rhode Island, when the patriots unsuccessfully tried to expel the British. An observation tower and 3 miles of walking trails await visitors. Nearby the **Chase Cory House,** at 3908 Main Road, stands at Tiverton Four Corners. This gambrel-roofed building offers special exhibits of paintings, clothing, and model ships during the summer season. Call (401) 624–4013 or 624–8881 for the exhibitions schedule.

Farther south in **Little Compton,** a monument to Elizabeth Pabodie stands in the **Commons Burial Ground.** Elizabeth was the first white girl born in New England, a daughter of pilgrims John and Priscilla Alden. The

Wilbur House, Barn, and Quaker Meeting House, on West Road, was begun in the seventeenth century and completed in the nineteenth century. The house contains period furnishings, and the barn displays New England farm tools and vehicles. Open 2:00 P.M.–5:00 P.M. Tuesday through Sunday from late June to Labor Day. For more information call (401) 635–4559.

In **Adamsville,** northeast of Little Compton on the Massachusetts border, **Gray's Store** (401–635–4566), at 4 Main Street, was built in 1788 by Samuel Church. It is one of the oldest operating stores in the country. Here country-story buffs will find the original soda fountain, aged cheddar cheese, penny candy, antiques, vintage clothing, and collectibles.

Aquidneck

Visitors driving onto Aquidneck, the island of Rhode Island that gave the colony and state its name, usually head toward Newport and fly right by some other sites of colonial significance in Portsmouth and Middletown. Entering **Portsmouth** on Route 114 from the north or Route 24 from the east, you get little sense of the older town that has been cut into pieces by the new roads, portions of which are cluttered with shopping malls and other supporting services for the Portsmouth Naval Base. Nevertheless you can still find remnants of the earliest settlement and the major Revolutionary War battle fought there.

Anne Hutchinson and her followers settled in 1638 at **Founder's Brook,** off Boyd's Lane. A bronze and stone marker bears the inscription of the Portsmouth Compact, which outlined the first democratic form of government in the colony, and the names of its twenty-three signers. **Butts Hill Fort,** off Sprague Street, has redoubts left over from the Revolutionary War battle on August 29, 1778. Generals Lafayette, Hancock, Greene, and Sullivan were all there. A memorial to soldiers of the first black regiment to fight for the American flag on that day stands at the junction of routes 114 and 24.

The "Hessian Hole" is now a depression in the earth in Leheigh State Park, where thirty German mercenaries were buried in a common grave after the 1778 Battle of Rhode Island. According to local tradition a group of tall Hessian ghosts continues its march on foggy nights.

The **Old School House,** at the corner of East Main Road and Union Street, dates from 1716 and contains antique desks, school bells, and textbooks. The **Portsmouth Historical Society,** at the corner of East Main Road and Union Street, displays early household objects and farm tools.

Open 1:00 P.M.–4:00 P.M. Saturday and Sunday, Memorial Day through Labor Day. Call (401) 683–9178 for information.

Middletown, between Portsmouth and Newport, served as a base for the British at **Green End Fort** during the two-year occupation of Newport in the Revolutionary War. The fort has disappeared, but a plaque remains. **Prescott Farm,** at 2009 West Main Road, has colonial farm buildings, British General Prescott's Guard House, a working 1812 windmill, a medicinal herb garden, free-ranging geese and ducks, and a country store. The farm is open daily 10:00 A.M.–4:00 P.M. April through November. For more information call (401) 847–6230, 849–7300, or 849–7301.

The town also contains a site associated with the mainstream of European intellectual life in the eighteenth century. Dean George Berkeley—philosopher, educator, and, later, Anglican Bishop—lived in town from 1729 to 1731 and built a home that became **Whitehall Museum House,** at 311 Berkeley Avenue. His arrival was fortuitous, one of the vicissitudes of eighteenth-century seafaring, since he had set out for Bermuda to found a seminary there.

While in Middletown Berkeley pursued the same purposes in America, unsuccessfully, and began a philosophical treatise; after returning to England he became one of the greatest metaphysicians of the century. Whitehall, named after its London counterpart, contains period furnishings and portraits. When Berkeley returned to England, his library and the house were given to Yale College. Later, while British troops occupied Newport during the Revolution, the house became a pub and barracks. Whitehall is open daily 10:00 A.M.–5:00 .m. July 1 through Labor Day and by appointment during the rest of the year. To find out more information, call (401) 846–3790, 847–7951, or 846–3116.

Newport

Although Newport was one of the earliest and most important settlements in Rhode Island, its colonial history is often overshadowed in a visitor's imagination by more recent eras—especially the grand showpiece "cottages" of industrial magnates newly minted in the boom after the Civil War. Newport is the acknowledged yachting capital of the eastern seaboard, home of the America's Cup for decades, the Bermuda Race, two major boat shows, as well as extravaganzas like the Newport Jazz Festival. And there's more—a string of regattas, concerts, parties, and special tours in the cottages, conferences throughout the year—enough to justify construction of new convention hotels and a large visitor's center. Almost everyone can find a good excuse to come to Newport.

The city, still a popular place to "summer," was first enjoyed by South Carolina plantation families, who came in 1720 to escape the heat. Even more important than Newport's long history as an elegant summer resort is its colonial heritage. A great many houses built in the seventeenth and eighteenth centuries are still standing and lived in today. Clustered around the green and adjoining streets, the historical district encompasses one of the finest collections of colonial houses in America.

From the beginning Newport and the bay beyond attracted visitors. While on a journey sponsored by the King of France, Giovanni da Verrazano recorded in his journal an impression of beautiful Narragansett Bay and declared, "I've decided to linger for a fortnight." Verrazano's visit may have been the first two-week vacation with pay. He was struck by how much Aquidneck looked like Rhodes; in 1644 the fledgling settlements of Portsmouth and Newport, now united, renamed Aquidneck the Isle of Rhodes.

Before that could happen, the groups at both ends of the island had to quell their own wrangling about the form of government that would prevail. The first Portsmouth group, led by John Clarke and William Coddington, bought Aquidneck from the Narragansett Indians and settled there in 1638. They favored the theocracy they were accustomed to in Massachusetts, whereas those who came later with Anne Hutchinson favored a separation between church and state. In 1639 some of the first group pulled out of Portsmouth and founded Newport.

As any visitor today can see, their choice of site was fortunate. With a marvelous harbor near the sea, Newport prospered, especially in the lucrative "triangular trade" to Africa with rum, to the West Indies with slaves, and back to Newport with molasses. Easy access to and from the sea had its dangers, too, and the city was vulnerable during the Revolution. It was occupied by the British from 1776 to 1779, an unhappy time as British soldiers were quartered in colonists' houses and proceeded to vandalize the town. In 1780 Comte de Rochambeau and 4,000 French soldiers arrived with a fleet that helped the colonial forces win the war.

The best way to appreciate the colonial heart of Newport is by walking, either on your own or with a guide. **Newport on Foot** tours, conducted by Anita Rafael (401–846–5391), begin at Gateway Center and lead visitors through a "window peeping" historical exploration, since the colonial district is still very much lived in. As the seaport developed, Newport captains also prospered and built these handsome houses. Some were privateers with smuggling tunnels from their homes to the water, others ran the slave trade from Africa, and still others ferried summer vacationers to Newport from the Carolinas and the West Indies. The captains' feet trod the walks you will wander along, and their families peered out of the windows you will see. If you'd like to attend the annual Secret Garden Tour, in June, call (401) 847–0514.

Eighteenth-Century Ark

Like mysteries? In 1750 local fishermen noticed a ship that headed for shore and then beached itself without a crew in sight. The fishermen went on board and found a dog on deck, a cat in the cabin, and coffee boiling on the stove. Not a soul was on board the Newport-bound vessel *Sea Bird*.

The oldest house in Newport is the **Wanton-Lyman-Hazard House** (1675), at 17 Broadway. This dark red house has a steeply pitched roof, typical of the time when roofers built them that way so that water would run off easily when they were thatched. Colonial governors lived there, and it was the site of the Stamp Act Riot in 1765 when its tenant, a Scottish physician, was run out of town with other Royalists who had supported the Stamp Act. The house is open 10:00 A.M.–4:00 P.M. Thursday through Saturday, 1:00 P.M.–4:00 P.M. Sunday; 10:00 A.M.–4:00 P.M. Friday and Saturday, June and September. Hours by appointment during the rest of the year. Call (401) 846–0813 for more information.

The **Old Colony House** (1739), on Washington Square, was the meeting place for the General Assembly from 1739 to 1776 and then became the State House from 1779 to 1900. During the Revolutionary War the British used the building as a barracks, hospital, and stable. When the French arrived in 1780, they continued to use it as a hospital, and chaplains held the first Roman Catholic Masses in Rhode Island in the building. The house is open by appointment only. For further information call (401) 846–2980.

The **Second Congregational Church,** on Clarke Street, dates from 1735. It was known as "Dr. Stiles' Meeting House" for Ezra Stiles, who served as minister during the troubled pre-Revolutionary years from 1755 to 1771. Stiles was a philosopher and diarist who later became the president of

Yale from 1778 to 1795. During the British occupation Redcoats burned the pews for firewood and used the church as a riding rink.

The Artillery Company of Newport, headquartered in the **Military Museum** at 23 Clarke Street, was chartered in 1741 to protect Newport from invasion. John Malbone was elected Captain of the Company and conducted drills with his men in full uniform, including gun, pouch, ball, and cartridge. These men were trained to take command of other units should the need arise in the colony. The museum, in an 1836 building, contains uniforms and memorabilia from 1741 to the present. There's a three-pounder shot that was found at George Washington's post-Revolutionary encampment area and a 1700 red model of a French Vallière cannon with carriage. Guns on carriages are stored and kept ready for colonial reenactments. For dates of special events and other information call (401) 846–8488.

If you like Christopher Wren's churches, there's one here that was designed as an adaptation of his work. **Trinity Church,** on Queen Anne Square at Spring and Church streets, is the home of a congregation assembled in 1698. The first church was built in 1702 and the present one in 1726, with an addition completed in 1762. During the Revolutionary War the British did not destroy the church because of the gold bishop's miter (a symbol of the British monarchy) on top. It contains the only three-tiered, wineglass pulpit in the country. George Washington worshiped in Pew 81 in 1756, 1781, and 1790. It is said that Handel approved the organ before it left England, and the casework and some of the pipes were donated by Bishop George Berkeley in 1733, several years after he had left Middletown. For more information call (401) 846–0600.

The **First Congregational Church** (1729), on Mill Street, is now owned by the Knights of Columbus. Its minister, the Reverend Samuel Hopkins, was instrumental in banning slavery in 1774. His genuine antislavery interest is reflected in a report that when two slaves bought a lottery ticket and won enough money to buy freedom for only one of them, Reverend Hopkins paid for the other.

Touro Park is the site of the **Old Stone Mill.** No one knows for sure the origin and date of the mill—perhaps it was built by Norsemen before Columbus arrived or by a colonial farmer or by Benedict Arnold, who once owned the land. It was used as a watchtower and a munitions storage depot by the British during their occupation of Newport.

Redwood Library, at 50 Bellevue Avenue, is the oldest continuously used library building in the country. Abraham Redwood gave £ 500 for books, and the library was built in 1750 in Greek Revival style. The statue in front somewhat anachronistically represents George Washington. Inside you'll find a grandfather clock made by William Claggett of Newport in 1723 and some of Gilbert Stuart's portraits on the walls. The library is open 9:30 A.M.–5:30 P.M. Monday through Saturday. Closed holidays. For information call (401) 847–0292.

The oldest synagogue in the North American continent is **Touro Synagogue,** at 85 Touro Street. It was founded in 1758 by Rabbi Isaac Touro to serve Jews arriving from the Caribbean. They had fled from the Dutch colony in Brazil after the Portuguese took it over and forced conversion to Catholicism. They first settled in British Barbados but were not allowed to own property there and so eventually left for Newport. The building was dedicated in 1763. Inside, the Ark of the Covenant, the cabinet that contains the tablets of the Ten Commandments, faces east, toward Jerusalem. A secret passage, which leads out to Barney Street, was used by anyone who needed to leave in a hurry. The General Assembly and the Supreme Court met in this building until the Old Colony House was repaired after the Revolution. The synagogue is open 10:00 A.M.–5:00 P.M. Sunday through Thursday, 10:00 A.M.–3:00 P.M. Friday, mid-June through Labor Day; 1:00 P.M.–3:00 P.M. Sunday, October to May. Call (401) 847–4794 for more information.

While in Newport, be sure to have a meal at the most authentic colonial tavern in America, located right in the heart of the historic district. The romance of dining in a colonial setting is topped only by delectable tastes at the **White Horse Tavern,** at the corner of Marlborough and Farewell Streets. It is the oldest operating tavern in the country and has an extensive menu. Built before 1673, it was first called the William Mayes House after its first proprietor, reputedly a pirate on the side, and later the Nichols House. In 1708 the Newport Town Council began to meet here, as well as the General Assembly and the Criminal Court. By 1730 Jonathan Nichols had purchased the tavern and placed a "white horse" sign in front. Reservations are recommended, especially for dinner (401–849–3600).

Most visitors to Newport spend a good bit of time on the waterfront, and that was of course the center of economic activity for the growing settlement, just as it is today for sailors and shoppers. Buildings in such districts are notoriously subject to change and demolition as one enterprise succeeds another, but some harbor installations remain in different forms, like the wharves. **Bannister's Wharf** and **Long Wharf** have long histories, the latter stretching back to 1685, when it was called Queenhithe. During the

Revolution Washington and Rochambeau reviewed the arriving French troops here, and it was also the site of Admiral de Ternay's funeral procession. While you are in this part of town, try another good colonial era restaurant, the **Clarke Cooke House** on Bannister's Wharf. Call (401) 849–2900 for reservations.

Also in this area is a gem that survived rebuilding along the waterfront area, **Hunter House,** at 54 Washington Street near Goat Island Causeway. Saving and restoring it was the first project of the Preservation Society of Newport County, which later went on to salvage some of the magnificent cottages from the late nineteenth century. Hunter House has both historic and architectural significance: It was the Revolutionary War headquarters of the French Admiral de Ternay and faithfully represents the most elaborate interior decorations of its era.

The house, which dates from 1746, was built by Jonathan Nichols, Jr., a prosperous shipowner, privateer, merchant, landowner, and deputy governor of Newport when he died. Then in 1756 Col. Joseph Wanton, Jr., purchased the house and built an addition. When Wanton, a Loyalist, escaped to New York during the Revolution, the colonists took over the house. It is named for William R. Hunter, a U.S. Senator who bought the house in 1805.

Inside there are collections of Townsend-Goddard furniture, silver, and portraits. The keeping room contains seventeenth-century furniture, including a William and Mary table, a Jacobean chest, and a Carver chair. The staircase is made of mahogany with a Jacobean balustrade. Upstairs the master bedroom has a Goddard chest with one shell and ball-and-claw feet.

A Navy Twice Born

Officially, Newport was the birthplace of the United States Navy in 1775. An Act of Congress provided for the Continental navy, and Esek Hopkins was named the first admiral and commander-in-chief. Of course this is not an uncontested claim in such a momentous historic matter: Whitehall, New York, also advertises itself as the birthplace of the American navy, based on Benedict Arnold's Whitehall schooner *Liberty,* which captured a British sloop in a naval engagement on Lake Champlain on May 17, 1775, as well as the building of the naval fleet in Whitehall during the spring and summer of 1776.

Hunter House was the Revolutionary War headquarters of French Admiral de Ternay.

Eighteenth-century maps of Newport and Narragansett Bay line the hall walls. Open 10:00 A.M.–5:00 P.M. daily in May through September, and Saturday, Sunday, and holidays in April and October. Call (401) 847–1000 for more information.

Newport's July 4 celebration includes a twenty-one-gun salute on Washington Square. Freebody's Turtle Frolic, a dinner dance featuring eighteenth-century cuisine, is a highlight of the Christmas season.

Newport has a wonderful array of colonial inns and B&Bs—no one with a yen for historic atmosphere needs to settle for a chain motel here. The **Admiral Benbow Inn,** at 93 Pelham Street, was built by Captain Littlefield in 1855 and contains a collection of English barometers (800–343–2863 or 401–846–4256) . The **Admiral Farragut Inn,** at 31 Clarke Street, has a great snowy egret painted on the wall just inside the door (800–343–2863 or 401–846–4256). The **Admiral Fitzroy Inn,** at 398 Thames Street, was built in 1854 by an architect, Dudley Newton (800–343–2863 or 401–846–4256). The **Benjamin Mason House,** at 25 Brewer Street, was built by Benjamin Mason in 1740 (401–847–8427). The **Melville House,** at 39 Clarke Street, is right around the corner from the Brick Marketplace (401–847–0640). The **Cliffside Inn,** at 2 Seaview Avenue overlooking the Atlantic, was built in 1880 by Governor Swann of Maryland as a summer residence (800–845–1811 or 401–847–1811). The **Jailhouse Inn,** at 13 Marlborough Street, is a renovated 1722 Newport Jail (401–847–4638). It is light and airy, and the jail signs make it a fun place to stay. The **Pilgrim House,** at 123 Spring Street, in the Historic Hill district has a deck over-looking the harbor (800–525–8373 or 401–846–0040).

Just across the Newport toll bridge, with a sweep upward to magnificent views of Narragansett Bay and Rhode Island Sound, lies **Jamestown,** also known as Conanicut Island. It was settled in the 1650s by Quakers who made a living raising sheep and farming. During the Revolution the British camped on the island until they were removed by French and American troops.

Captain Kidd reputedly buried some of his treasure here in Pirate Cave. He often visited Jamestown to see his friend Thomas Paine, whose house still stands on the north end of the island. Pirate Cave is located in **Fort Wetherill State Park,** across the main channel from Fort Adams State Park in Newport. **Fort Getty State Park,** on the other side of the island facing the Narragansett mainland, has earthworks left over from the Revolutionary War that are still visible on Prospect Hill.

The striking rock formations at the southernmost tip of Jamestown have always been a landfall for seamen and the site of a lighthouse since the eighteenth century. At **Beavertail,** the present Beavertail Lighthouse was built in 1856, but the foundations of a 1749 lighthouse are still there. The 1938 hurricane exposed them to view.

In the middle of the island, on North Road off Route 138, is the **Jamestown Windmill,** which dates from 1787. The windmill was in use until the end of the nineteenth century. Open 1:00 P.M.–4:00 P.M. Saturday and Sunday, mid-June to mid-September. Call (401) 423–1798 for information. Also on North Road, the **Sydney L. Wright Museum** (401–423–7380) contains collections of Native American and colonial artifacts. The museum is open 10:00 A.M.–5:00 P.M. and 7:00 P.M.–9:00 P.M. Monday and Wednesday; noon–5:00 P.M. and 7:00 P.M.–9:00 Tuesday and Thursday; 10:00 A.M.–5:00 P.M. Friday and Saturday; 10:00 A.M.–1:00 P.M. Saturday, June 15 to September 15.

SOUTH COUNTY

The communities in almost the lower half of Rhode Island west of Narragansett Bay make up Washington County, locally referred to as South County. Inland it includes the Great Swamp and the beautiful campus of the University of Rhode Island, but its most notable features are old lower-bay settlements and an almost unbroken coast of superb ocean beaches backed by salt ponds. There are many traces of colonial America in the region, including historic homes, museums, and old trails to explore.

In North Kingstown, **Wickford,** on the lower bay opposite Jamestown, dates from 1674, and its historic colonial homes still stand. It was named for the birthplace of Elizabeth Winthrop, the wife of the governor of Connecticut, in Wickford, England. One of the first houses was built in 1711, and a number of others followed. They were called "one-room houses" and were one story high, with a steeply pitched gable roof. A large stone chimney was built into one end of the house and served to heat the whole house as well as provide a fire for cooking. By 1725 "central chimney" houses of one or two stories were being built.

Smith's Castle, also called Cocumscussoc, at 55 Richard Smith Drive, Wickford, is the oldest building in South County. Richard Smith used to invite William Blackstone to conduct monthly Church of England services at his home, known as "Smith's Castle." The minister would ride his beige-colored bull from his home along the Pequot Path to Cocumscussoc.

As a friend of Richard Smith, Roger Williams spent time with him in Cocumscussoc and also preached in Smith's home. Both Roger Williams and Richard Smith established trading posts in 1637. The plantation house was built on an estate that covered 27 square miles of coastal land. The first house was burned by the Indians in 1676 at the end of King Philip's War. Richard Smith, Jr., rebuilt it in 1678.

The castle became the military headquarters for Massachusetts, Plymouth, and Connecticut troops in 1675. The Great Swamp Fight, at the Indian winter encampment on Great Swamp west of Kingston, saw the colonists victorious and the Narragansetts almost eliminated. The common grave for forty of the dead colonists from that battle is on the grounds of Smith's Castle. The "grave of the forty" was, at one time, under the Grave Apple Tree, which blew down during a gale in 1815. Now it is marked by a large stone with a bronze tablet, inscribed, "Here were buried in one grave forty men who died in the Swamp Fight or on the return march to Richard Smith's Block House, December, 1675." Not far from the grave site there is a green box, about 6 by 8 feet, with a lid you can lift to reveal an ongoing archaeological dig. In 1993 part of a wall had been excavated.

Smith's Castle is furnished with seventeenth- and eighteenth-century antiques, china, and utensils. The keeping room has a large fireplace, complete with a recipe for Rhode Island johnnycakes on the hearth. Upstairs there is a ballroom, which was used for line dancing. Roger Williams owned a chair that is now in the house.

Lodowick Updike, a nephew of Richard Smith, inherited the castle when Smith died in 1692. The property continued down the Updike line from Lodowick I to Daniel, Lodowick II, and Wilkins. Over the years the family entertained the Marquis de Lafayette, Benjamin Franklin, and General Nathaniel Greene, among others, in the castle. Open noon–4:00 P.M. Thursday through Monday, June through August; noon–4:00 P.M. Friday through Sunday, May and September. For more information call (401) 294–3521.

Old Narragansett Church, on Church Lane off Main Street in Wickford, is one of the oldest Episcopal churches in the country. It was built in 1707 and was moved to its present location in 1800. The church organ dates from 1660; the wineglass pulpit looks out onto square box pews. Her Majesty Queen Anne sent a silver baptismal basin and communion service inscribed with the royal insignia and ANNA REGINA. Unfortunately the baptismal bowl was melted down and made into a number of plates after the Revolution, by order of the vestry. James MacSparren baptized Gilbert Stuart here on April 11, 1756. The church is open 11:00 A.M.–4:00 P.M. Friday through Sunday, mid-June to mid-September. Call (401) 294–4357 for further details.

If you're curious about snuff, visit the **Gilbert Stuart Birthplace,** at 815 Gilbert Stuart Road, in **Saunderstown** near Wickford, the site of his father's snuff mill and Gilbert's birth in 1755. The snuff mill stands on the bank of Mattatuxet Brook in a picturesque setting and is equipped with a waterwheel and a fish ladder. During spring herring swim up to the pond above the mill dam.

A Pinch, Anyone?

The snuff mill on the lower floor of the Gilbert Stuart Birthplace is alive with large wooden gears and meshing teeth to supply the power for grinding tobacco into the fine powder called snuff. A heavy pewter-covered iron ball roller does the job. Throughout the seventeenth and eighteenth centuries in both Britain and America, it was fashionable for gentlemen to inhale this powder in their nostrils, and they often carried small quantities of it on their persons in snuffboxes. In colonial days women took snuff as well as men, but behind closed doors.

Also on display downstairs in the mill are household pieces, including a 1680 spinning wheel, a cooper's bench and draw knife, a butter skimmer, a cottage-cheese press, a weasel to measure yarn, and a butter churn. Upstairs there are several Gilbert Stuart paintings of George Washington, including one of a first sitting and another unfinished portrait. Stuart painted six presidents and their wives. The rooms contain period furnishings such as a rope bed, a 1740 cradle, a tripod candle holder, a bed warmer, and a trundle bed. The mill is open 11:00 A.M.–4:30 P.M. Saturday through Thursday, April to mid-November. Call (401) 294–3001 for more information.

In 1679 or 1680 Theophilus Whalley arrived from Virginia and moved into a cottage about half a mile south of Snuff Mill Pond. An air of mystery about him led some to say that he was the Colonel Whalley who was one of the regicide judges of King Charles I. He lived quietly, making his living by fishing and by writing for other settlers. Men from Boston used to visit him once a year; after they left, he had money, but he never told a soul about his past.

Wickford is a pleasant place to spend the night. Try the **John Updike House,** at 19 Pleasant Street, which was built as the grandest home in town in 1745. The bedrooms have fireplaces and period decor. For reservations call (401) 294–4905.

Casey Farm, south of Wickford on Route 1A in Saunderstown, is an eighteenth-century farm on Narragansett Bay. The area was included in the Boston Neck Purchase of 1636 but not settled until 1702 because of King Philip's War and disputes with Connecticut. The current house was built in the 1740s by Daniel and Mary Coggeshall of Newport as the country seat of a well-to-do merchant. It contains the original 300 acres and is large enough to be considered one of the South County plantations.

In 1789 the Coggeshall's daughter, Abigail, moved into the house with her husband, Silas Casey, and the house was kept in the family until 1955, when it was bequeathed to the Society for the Preservation of New England Antiquities. Now renovation is in progress, and the house will be open in the near future; until then visitors are welcome to walk around the grounds. Call (401) 227–3956 for more information on the renovation and opening date.

In **South Kingston** just a few miles south of Saunderstown, **Hannah Robinson's Rock** is located at the intersection of Route 1 and Route 138. There's an observation tower there which provides a view of Narragansett Bay, the campus of the University of Rhode Island, and the surrounding countryside. Hannah Robinson fell in love with a French dance teacher, Peter Simon, who serenaded her from the lilac bushes below her window. Her father was not pleased with the match, so she eloped after telling him that she was going to a dance given by her uncle, Lodowick Updike, at Smith's Castle. Later she fell upon hard times, returned home ill, and paused on her litter at this spot for a final view of the countryside she loved. Hannah died the same night she arrived at her childhood home.

At the foot of **Tower Hill** near the Pettaquamscutt River, Thomas Carter, a notorious convicted murderer, was hung in chains in 1751. His body, then his bones, swung there for many years, a grisly reminder of colonial justice. After the gallows rotted, the irons that contained his bones were taken to the blacksmith shop of Joseph Hull, who had made the irons; he removed the bones and salvaged the irons.

When it's time for a meal or an overnight rest, try the **General Stanton Inn,** on Route 1 in **Charlestown,** which dates from 1667. Rooms are available in the older section, with hand-hewn beams and low ceilings, as well as in a newer addition. Call (401) 364–0100 or fax (401) 364–5021 for reservations.

In the same area call ahead to see when **Carpenter's Grist Mill** is grinding. Samuel E. Perry built the mill in 1703 on Moonstone Beach Road, and it is still a working mill where Whitecap Flint Corn is stone-ground by waterpower. Johnnycake meal can be used in any recipe that calls for cornmeal, and you can buy it at the shop. For the working schedule call (401) 783–5483.

Accommodations in **Narragansett** include **The Four Gables,** at 12 South Pier Road (410–789–6948), an 1890s summer home with four fireplaces; **Murphy's Bed & Breakfast,** at 43 South Pier Road (410–789–1824),

Very good, Mr. Watson . . .

A pparently Thomas Carter, who had lost all when his cargo vessel was shipwrecked, was trying to return to Newport when he met William Jackson, a wealthy Virginia merchant, on the road. Carter pretended to be ill and played on Jackson's sympathy enough to ride his horse while Jackson walked. They stopped for the night at Mrs. Nash's house, and she noticed a round spot on Jackson's hair; during another stop, Mrs. Combs noticed a mismatched button on his vest. Near Tower Hill Carter hit Jackson on the head with a stone; then Jackson ran, but Carter caught him and beat him to death. He dragged the body down the hill and pushed it under the ice. After a fisherman found the body, Mrs. Nash identified Jackson by the spot on his head, and Mrs. Combs recognized the mismatched button. Carter was convicted of killing Jackson and robbing him of £1,080.

is in a one-hundred-year-old building and decorated with marine art, antiques, and orientals; and **The Richards,** at 144 Gibson Avenue (410–789–7746), has antique and wicker furniture and some fireplaces.

Block Island

Although Block Island is miles offshore and reachable only by sea or air, it is technically a part of South County. Long a mecca for sailors, fishermen, and vacationers who want to roam over its uncrowded beaches, the island has a history that stretches back into the early colonial era. Dutch navigator Adrian Block discovered the island in 1614, and the first settlers landed in Cow Cove in 1661. They were from the Massachusetts Bay Colony and had each paid £25 for a share in the island. Settlers' Rock is inscribed with a memorial to the brave people who chose to stake their futures on an exposed and isolated island.

In 1662 Block Island became part of Rhode Island at the settlers' wish, but that did not protect them from continued depredations by privateers. One of the most notorious was the raid by the Frenchman William Trimming, who tricked the islanders, imprisoned them, and plundered their houses in 1689. Sarah Sands, the first woman physician in the colonies, tended to the ills of isolated settlers. Privateer raids lasted throughout most of the eighteenth century, and even the Revolution brought little relief since deserters from both armies flocked to the island.

Shipwrecks were frequent on an island that then had no sheltered deep-water harbor, and one of them became infamous. In 1732 the *Palatine* left Rotterdam, laden with Dutch families who were on their way to Philadelphia. It was to be a voyage of incredible hardship through winter storms, polluted drinking water, starvation, extortion, maltreatment, then abandonment by the crew after the captain died (or was killed), and, finally, stranding on the reefs of Block Island during a blizzard. **Palatine Graves,** 1½ miles southwest of Cooneymus Road near Dickens Point, is the spot where those who died were buried. The rough-hewn stones are now over-grown by brush.

The Wreck of the Palatine

By one account Block Island wreckers lured the *Palatine* onto the rocks, and the passengers dived into the water and drowned; by another the wreckers just boarded to claim salvage, rescued the few passengers remaining alive, and then set the ship afire when a gale stopped their salvage efforts. There is agreement that one woman refused to leave the ship, and her screams were heard as the burning ship drifted out to sea. In island legend her screams can still be heard and the burning ship seen during storms. John Greenleaf Whittier's ballad "The Palatine" depicts the events of this fearsome wreck.

FOR MORE INFORMATION

Rhode Island Tourism Division
7 Jackson Walkway
Providence, RI 02903
(800) 556–2484
(401) 277–2601
(401) 277–2102 (fax)

Vermont

Historical Introduction to
VERMONT

*V*ermont's relatively short history is full of unsolved questions and undocumented claims, but most historians agree that Samuel de Champlain was the first white man to explore the western side of the territory. In 1609 he emerged from Canada, discovered the lake that was later named after him, and, aided by the Algonquians, fought the Iroquois. He killed two Iroquois chiefs and a number of warriors. The Iroquois never forgave him for humiliating them with "white man's lightning" and for the next century and a half continued to fight against the French in the long struggle for domination of the territories north and west of the New England colonies.

Champlain sketched that first fight and portrayed the Indians in the nude, because that is how Europeans imagined savages. He also added some palm trees—certainly a curiosity for the Lake Champlain shore—an addition that raises some questions about his professional role as a geographer. Champlain had been appointed Royal Geographer by King Henri IV, and he christened the north country around the St. Lawrence "New France" in his report to the king.

Mystery or Hoax?

Further confusion about Champlain's role as the first white man to see the lake emerged from a find in the middle of the nineteenth century. Near Swanton, Vermont, at the mouth of the Missisquoi River and Lake Champlain, two workmen discovered a lead tube in 1853. A note inside read:

Nov. 29 AD 1564

This is the some daye
I must now die this is
the 90th day sine we
lef the Ship all have
Perished and on the
Banks of this river
I die to (or, so) farewelle
may future Posteritye
knowe our end

JOHNE GRAYE

Although this note indicates an earlier English presence on the lake, the claim can't be substantiated by any known voyage to this part of the New World. At this time British expeditions, like those of John Hawkins, were too busy with the West Indies, and Martin Frobisher's three voyages did not begin until 1576.

First Settlement

The first French settlement was that of Captain La Motte, who built a fort and shrine to Saint Anne on Isle La Motte in 1666. Next Capt. Jacobus Ten Warm, a Dutchman, developed a British post at Chimney Point in 1690. Neither of these settlements lasted very long. Throughout the seventeenth century and much of the eighteenth, Vermont was mostly uninhabited land, trod by the French and Indians on their way to attack English settlers in the south and east.

Massachusetts residents built Fort Dummer, near Brattleboro, in 1724, now considered the first permanent settlement. The French built both a fort at Crown Point and a village on the Vermont side in 1731 but did not concentrate on settling this area. Throughout the first half of the eighteenth century, England and France battled for domination of the Champlain valley. The emphasis was still on forts, and in 1755 the French built a major one, named Carillon, at Ticonderoga to guard the strategic portage between Lake Champlain and Lake George.

The Land Grab

Vermont land was in constant turmoil over ownership, as both kings and governors gave it away before either actually owned it. King George II handed over to Benning Wentworth, Governor of New Hampshire, land "extending due West Cross the said River [Merrimack] till it meets with our other governments" in 1741; however, the "government" on the other side, that of New York, had not received word of its eastern boundary from the king. New Hampshire and New York were supposed to meet—but where? Governor Wentworth made the assumption that he had control of land as far to the west as Massachusetts and Connecticut did to the south, but Governor Clinton opposed this expansion as an intrusion on New York territory.

Both governors agreed to abide by the decision of the king, which was a long time coming. And Wentworth continued to make grants over a large portion of Vermont, which he called the New Hampshire Grants. Finally in 1770 the king declared "the Western Banks of the River Connecticut to be the Boundary Line between the said two Provinces of New Hampshire and New York." New York then insisted that Wentworth's grants were invalid and issued their own New York grants for the same land.

The king's edict and the New York response created the "unruly mob" that we remember as the Green Mountain Boys in another context. Ethan Allen had been elected by a group called the Bennington Nine to organize the legal defense of their New Hampshire titles before the supreme court in Albany. When Chief Justice Robert Livingston (with some New York titles in his own pocket) refused to hear the evidence, Allen went back to Bennington and gathered some 200 vigilantes to protect New Hampshire grants. Thus the origin of the Green Mountain Boys had more to do with a lasting grievance against neighboring "Yorkers" than with revolutionary fervor against the king.

The Struggle for Autonomy

In April 1775, one month after a nasty fracas over land foreclosures in which two men were killed, the Cumberland County Convention at Westminster voted to petition the king for a new province. At this time, however, the Revolution started, and New Hampshire and New York had more important business to attend to. Ethan Allen and Benedict Arnold slipped across Lake Champlain and seized Fort Ticonderoga. The land dispute had merged into the issue of separate statehood, and that had to wait until the Declaration of Independence was read on July 4, 1776.

Even then the dispute was not quickly settled, remaining a very live controversy for fifteen more years. The New Hampshire grantees were considered the "inhabitants of Vermont" by Dr. Thomas Young of Philadelphia, who encouraged them to form a new state. In April 1777 the Constitution of New York State was published, but people in Vermont did not care for its claims, so in July 1777 seventy delegates adopted a Constitution for the State of Vermont. By 1781 Ethan Allen and some other Vermonters were threatening secession and even negotiating with the British. The final tremors of the land disputes did not subside until boundaries were drawn and Vermont was admitted to the Union as the fourteenth state on March 4, 1791.

"The Birthplace of Vermont": Old Constitution House in Windsor, tavern where the republic of Vermont was declared in 1777

Regions to Explore

W e've divided the Vermont Territory into the two regions that were most important during the late colonial era. The first region borders Lake Champlain, encompassing the areas of early settlement on the northern islands and the towns that grew along or near the shore. The sec-

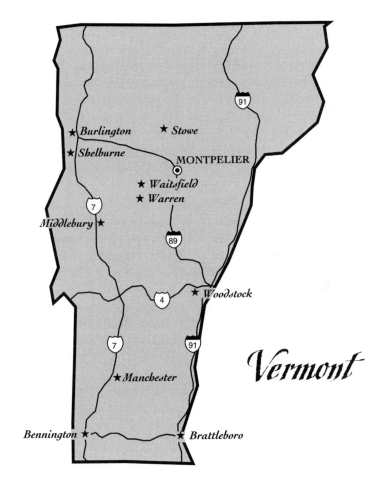

ond region is southern Vermont, accessible by land from Massachusetts and the Connecticut River valley. On the edges of these regions or beyond them lie many towns of great historic interest, deriving from later eras— Middlebury, Stowe, Woodstock, and Manchester, for example. Throughout Vermont you are likely to focus less on specific historic houses than on whole towns and villages, many of which seem virtually unchanged from earlier centuries.

LAKE CHAMPLAIN

The **Isle La Motte,** controlling the northern reach of Lake Champlain as it narrows toward the Richelieu River, was one of two sites on the lake with continuing historic importance in the colonial era; the other was Ticonderoga, controlling the portage into Lake George. Both were check-points on the major water highway between the St. Lawrence and the Hudson during two centuries of intensive use by the French, the British, and various Indian tribes, who had already used this route long before any Europeans arrived.

In 1666 Captain de La Motte and his French troops of the Carignan Regiment built **Fort Sainte-Anne** on Isle La Motte as a defense against the Mohawks. A garrison of 300 men, including a number of Jesuits, celebrated Mass in the chapel of Fort Sainte-Anne, and in 1668 Bishop Laval of Quebec traveled by canoe to say Mass there. The fort was abandoned after eight years. Visitors to the **Shrine of Saint Anne** will see the open-air chapel and perhaps be on hand for Mass; crowds come, especially on feast days and on Sundays. An A-frame structure covers a marble statue of Saint Anne. Call (802) 928–3362 or 3385 for more information.

A statue of Samuel de Champlain, sculpted for Expo '67 in Montreal, is located where Champlain probably landed on Isle La Motte in 1609. The statue stands in a grove of trees that overlook the lake. Nearby **Burying Ground Point** memorializes Revolutionary War soldiers who are buried there, and a memorial plaque describes some of the history of the island. There is also an open-air chapel and a statue of St. Anne.

Benedict Arnold anchored his fleet off the western shore of Isle La Motte just before proceeding to engage the advancing British forces in the Battle of Valcour Island on October 11, 1776. This was the first major naval battle of

A Seventeenth-Century Fish Story

Samuel de Champlain wrote about a creature he spotted that was 20 feet long and as thick as a barrel, with a head like a horse and a body like a serpent. Thus the legendary "Champ" was born, perhaps a relative of Scotland's "Nessie." Times haven't changed much.

the Revolutionary War, and a crucial one. The British strategy sought to split the colonies in two, with General Burgoyne's army moving down the Champlain waterway until it joined General Howe's army moving up the Hudson. Arnold's fleet was outnumbered by the British fleet under the command of Capt. Thomas Pringle. Quite predictably Arnold could not hold against the larger fleet. He escaped in a dense fog but lost most of his ships as the British chased them down afterward; he and his men escaped to Fort Ticonderoga. Arnold's resistance at Valcour Island deflected a British strategy that might have won the war for the Crown.

Farther south in the Lake Champlain island chain, the **Hyde Log Cabin** stands on the main road (Route 2) in **Grand Isle.** Dating from 1783, it is thought to be the oldest extant log cabin in the country. Jedediah Hyde, Jr., who fought in the Revolution, built the cedar cabin with a large fireplace. It has been restored to its original appearance. Inside visitors will see furnishings of early colonial life collected by the Grand Isle Historical Society. Open 10:00 A.M. to 5:00 P.M. Wednesday through Sunday, June 1 through Labor Day. Call (802) 828–3226 for more information.

The omnipresent Allen family had been active in the **Burlington** area at least since 1772, when Ira built ships there while Ethan was struggling against New York land claims from Bennington. With others, they left town to fight during the Revolution but returned shortly afterward. Ebenezer Allen, a cousin of Ethan's, arrived in 1783 and settled on Allen's Point. He ran a ferry service for many years and in 1787 turned his home into a tavern. Prince Edward of England stopped there on his way from Montreal to Boston. The last time Ethan Allen was seen alive was the night of February 10, 1789, when he came to Ebenezer's tavern for a load of hay. It has been surmised that they spent the night with bottles of rum, which may have contributed to Ethan's demise.

For a glimpse into Allen's life, visit the **Ethan Allen Homestead** in Burlington (just off Route 127 northbound at the exit sign labeled NORTH AVENUE, BEACHES). The house has been reconstructed and is furnished with period pieces. Visitors can see a multimedia program and also stroll along hiking trails. Open 10:00 A.M.–5:00 P.M. Monday through Saturday, 1:00

Vermont's Paul Bunyan

L egends about Ethan Allen mix fact and fabrication. Those who believe that tall tales belong only to the American West may change their minds after hearing some of these Vermont whoppers:

Once when he was walking through the woods, a huge bobcat sprang and landed on his back; Allen reached behind and wrenched the cat onto the ground, then strangled it. When he arrived where he was going, he explained his delay by blaming the "Yorkers" for training and setting varmints against him.

Another time he was said to have killed a bear by jamming his powderhorn down the animal's throat. Even a rattlesnake didn't get the better of Ethan Allen. One night after too much elbow bending, Allen and a friend stopped for a nap. A rattler coiled on Allen's chest, struck him several times, then rolled off, staggered, burped, and fell asleep. The next morning Allen complained about the pesky "mosquito" that kept biting him during the night.

Allen's drinking caused him some trouble at home, too. His wife, Fanny, finally worked out her own method for checking his sobriety. She pounded a nail high on the wall of their bedroom. In the morning, if she found his watch hanging on the nail, she knew he'd come home sober; if not, he was in for it. It didn't take Allen long to put one and one together. After a while, no matter how much he was weaving about, he'd get that watch hooked on the nail before he went to sleep.

When news leaked out of an impending real estate auction, Ethan, his brother Ira, and the sheriff announced the sale would be delayed until one o'clock the next day, and it was—until one in the morning. Just after midnight the three men met. At the stroke of one, Ethan bid $1.00 for the house, barn, and hundred acres; Ira bid $2.00, and the gavel fell.

P.M.–5:00 P.M. Sunday, late June through Labor Day; 1:00 P.M.–5:00 P.M. daily through late June, and the day after Labor Day to late October. Call (802) 865–4556 for more information.

If you're interested in Americana collections and American folk art, head south to the **Shelburne Museum,** on Route 7 in **Shelburne.** The thirty-seven buildings, spread out on forty-five acres of land, house collections of quilts, textiles, tools, glass, ceramics, scrimshaw, decoys, weather vanes, furniture, dolls, carriages, circus memorabilia, and wagons. There are seven restored period homes; the oldest is the **Prentis House,** dating from 1733. Built in saltbox style, the house has a colonial kitchen with a large fireplace. This house contains seventeenth- and eighteenth-century furniture, decorative arts, and textiles. The **Dutton House,** which came from Cavendish, Vermont, dates from 1782. The 1786 **Sawmill** has an operating waterwheel and an up-and-down saw. The **Stagecoach Inn** was built in 1782 in Charlotte, Vermont. Visitors will enjoy the cigar-store figures, weather vanes, whirligigs, and trade signs here. The museum is open daily 10:00 A.M.–5:00 P.M., mid-May to mid-October. To find out more call (802) 985–3344.

The **Lake Champlain Maritime Museum,** located farther south in **Basin Harbor,** off Route 22A west of Vergennes, is home to a replica of the Revolutionary War gunboat *Philadelphia.* The orginal vessel was part of Benedict Arnold's fleet that was sunk after the Battle of Valcour Island in 1776. Visitors can climb all over her, even help hoist a sail. Call ahead to be sure the vessel is in her home port. The museum also has a replica of an eighteenth-century bateau that was modeled on a wreck recovered from the lake. In the boat shop you can watch boat builders working on replicas, and you can see a blacksmith use a forge to make typical eighteenth-century boat fittings. Open daily 10:00 A.M.–5:00 P.M., mid-May to mid-October. Call (802) 475–2317 for more information.

To the east of the lake over the mountains, **Waitsfield** and **Warren** are a goldmine of historic inns and B&Bs for visitors who avoid hotels on principle, as well as those who just want to transport themselves backward in time. The most interesting (but not the fastest) way to get there from the lake takes you over the **Appalachian Gap** on Route 17, which passes between two "colonial" peaks, Stark Mountain and Molly Stark Mountain. The views at the summit of the pass are worth the dozens of switchbacks it takes to get there, and the whole trip will remind you of how difficult it was to travel east or west in the colonial era. Early settlers quite sensibly stayed along the lake or poked up river valleys.

Workboats of the Wars

ateaux ("boats" in French) were general-purpose vessels used to transport goods and people on the rivers and lakes of French Canada and the Adirondacks. They were built with flat bottoms for capacity and double ends for maneuverability, and they were usually rowed, though some were rigged with sails. During the French and Indian War and the American Revolution, they ranged from 25 to 35 feet in length and were used primarily as troop transports. As many as 260 of them lie buried in the mud at the bottom of Lake George, where the British sank them in the fall of 1758, hoping to recover them in the spring for the campaigns of 1759. Seven bateaux have been listed on the National Register of Historic Places.

When you arrive, the choice of accommodations is wide indeed. The **Beaver Pond Farm Inn,** on Golf Course Road in Warren, is a country inn with down comforters and lovely views (802–583–2861). **The Inn at the Round Barn Farm,** on Route 1 in Waitsfield, offers luxurious suites including fireplaces, Jacuzzis, and an indoor pool (802–496–2276). **Lareau Farm Country Inn,** on Route 100 in Waitsfield, is located beside the Mad River and is filled with lots of antiques (800–833–0766 or 802–496–4949). **Mad River Inn B&B,** on Tremblay Road in Waitsfield, offers afternoon tea in an 1860s inn (802–496–7900). **Newton's 1824 House Inn,** on Route 100 in Waitsfield, has cross-country skiing on site (802–496–7555). **The Sugartree,** on the Sugarbush Access Road in Warren, is a country inn with atmosphere and a roaring fire on cold days (800–666–8907 or 802–583–3211). **Tucker Hill Lodge,** on Route 17 in Waitsfield, is a country inn with herb and flower gardens (call 800–543–7841 or 802–495–3983 or fax 802–496–3032). The **Waitsfield Inn,** on Route 100 in Waitsfield, is in an 1825 parsonage (800–758–3801 or 802–496–3979). If you want to stay in any of these inns during during peak times—ski season and leaf season—be sure to call for advance reservations.

If you want to stay closer to the lake west of the mountains, visit **Middlebury,** where there is no dearth of interesting accommodations. The **Middlebury Inn,** at 14 Courthouse Square in Middlebury, is an 1827 village inn; afternoon tea is served (800–842–4666 or 802–388–4961). In East Middlebury **Waybury Inn** was originally built as a stagecoach stop; meals include Sunday brunch (802–388–4015). Although Middlebury was founded in 1761, it was not permanently settled until near the end of the Revolution, so its interesting historic district represents the early Federal and later eras. While you are here, take the time to walk down Main Street and through the lovely campus of **Middlebury College,** founded in 1800.

Farther south along the Champlain lakeshore, **Chimney Point** got its name after settlers, who had been threatened too long by the British, set their homes afire and left, leaving just blackened chimneys. Earlier, Dutchman Jacobus Ten Warm had brought a contingent of British troops from Albany and built a fort in 1690. By 1730 a group of French colonists arrived and rebuilt the fort, adding more homes as well. The eighteenth-century **Chimney Point Tavern** has displays of archaeological artifacts found on the site. The focus is on Native American and French settlers in the area. The site is open 9:30 A.M.–5:30 P.M. Wednesday through Sunday, Memorial Day to Columbus Day. Call (802) 828–3226 for more information.

SOUTHERN VERMONT

Mount Independence, located west of Route 22A in **Orwell,** was once the scene of an important Revolutionary War military compound. It was planned for a garrison of 12,000 men in 1776, one of the largest in North America. A floating bridge provided access across Lake Champlain to Fort Ticonderoga. During winter it became very difficult to send supplies there, so the force was reduced to 3,000 soldiers. Then in July of 1777 the fort was taken by the British when the Americans retreated. A rearguard action was fought at nearby Hubbardton. Today, remains include the blockhouse, gun batteries, a stockade, and a hospital. Visitors should bring their walking shoes and enjoy the trails in the park. Open 9:30 A.M.–5:30 P.M. Wednesday through Sunday, June to mid-October. Call (802) 828–3226 for more details.

After General Burgoyne took Mount Independence and Ticonderoga, the Continentals fled to **Hubbardton,** where Seth Warner's Green Mountain Boys covered the rear as the main army continued to escape. Warner's men were cooking breakfast on July 7, 1777, when the British burst upon them. They defended their position Indian style, by hiding

Toasting the Tories

C apt. William Watson of the American Revolutionary Army raised his glass at the Eagle Tavern in East Poultney, Vermont, in 1790 with the following toast: "To the Enemies of our Country! May they have cobweb breeches, a porcupine saddle, a hard-trotting horse, and an eternal journey."

behind trees and in brush, and seemed to be forcing the British back until Baron von Riedesel's German soldiers arrived on the scene. Seth Warner, however, knew that he had caused heavy losses on the British side. The Battle of Hubbardton was the only Revolutionary War battle fought in Vermont. It was also the beginning of the end for General Burgoyne's campaign to split the colonies, leading to his defeat at the Battle of Saratoga in the fall, a major turning point in the war. The museum at the **Hubbardton Battlefield,** seven miles off Route 4 in East Hubbardton, has exhibits that show how this battle fit into the Revolutionary War. Visitors can walk around the battlefield to see markers for each event. The Hubbardton Battlefield Monument is placed on the grave of Colonial Ebenezer Francis, a patriot from Massachusetts. The musuem is open Wednesday through Sunday, late May to mid-October.

Following is a nice selection of inns to be found throughout this section of Vermont. Towns and lodgings are scattered in rural Vermont, so check your map for locations of the inns. The **Inn at Long Last,** in Chester, is an attractive Vermont country inn located on the green (802–875–2444). **The Woodstock Inn,** in Woodstock, is built on the site of the original 1793 inn (800–448–7900 or 802–457–1100). The **Darling Family Inn,** on Route 100 in Weston, is a restored 1830 farmhouse with both European and American antiques (802–824–3223). **The Inn at Weston** on Route 100 is an 1848 farmhouse that offers cross-country skiing from the door (802–824–5804).

Since one of the best ways to appreciate the history of Vermont is simply wandering around and finding interesting places to stay, we offer more possibilities. The **Quechee Inn at Marshland Farm,** located on Clubhouse Road in Queechee, is a 1793 country inn with plenty of colonial atmosphere (800–235–3133 or 802–644–8851). **Echo Lake Inn,** north of Ludlow on Route 100, offers rooms, suites, and new condominiums built in an old cheese factory (800–356–6844 or 802–228–8602). **Wilson Castle Inn,** on routes 103 and 33 in Proctorsville, is located in a former governor's mansion (802–226–7222).

Farther south, the **Barrows House** on Route 30 in Dorset is almost 200 years old. The inn is furnished with antiques, including rockers in front of the fireplace (802–867–4455). Also in Dorset the **Dorset Inn** is right on the green; early guests had a view of parades as well as the departure of the Green Mountain Boys in 1775 (802–867–5500). **The Inn at West View Farm** on Route 30 offers guest rooms with country antiques (802–867–5715).

The **Equinox Hotel** on Route 74 in **Manchester** has been revitalized again. The first hotel on the site was built in 1769, and since that time historic events have swirled around it. On the green stands a statue of one of Ethan Allen's Green Mountain Boys; a group of them met here just before the Battle of Bennington in 1777. Call (800) 362–4747 from outside Vermont or (802) 362–4700 from within Vermont for reservations. The **1811 House** in Manchester Village once belonged to Abraham Lincoln's granddaughter. English and American antiques, fireplaces, oriental rugs, and canopied beds make the house inviting. For reservations call (802) 362–1811.

The Old Tavern at Grafton (802–843–2231), on Main Street in Grafton, dates from 1801; over the years it has been popular with writers. The pretty town of Grafton is a village frozen in time. It was settled in 1780, prospered, and then faded, but has been restored by the Windham Foundation. To go to Grafton is to step back in time.

The **Highland House,** on Route 100 in Londonderry, was built in 1842; the house is surrounded by 200-year-old maples (802–824–3019). **Three Mountain Inn,** on Main Street in Jamaica, dates from the 1780s. It has walls and floors of wide, planked pine, a fireplace, and a library for reading (802–874–4140). The **Arlington Inn,** on Route 7A in Arlington, is filled with antiques and oriental rugs. Guest rooms and suites are attractively furnished with antique pieces (802–375–6532).

In **Bennington** itself, the center of Revolutionary activity, stands the **Bennington Battle Monument,** a 300-foot-high obelisk, built in 1891. It commemorates Gen. John Stark's victory over the British forces, led by Gen. John Burgoyne. Both British and Germans were following the Continentals as they left Mount Independence. Burgoyne wanted to replenish his supply of ammunition and food and demanded that the Hessians seize both in

The Bennington Battle Monument watches over the Vermont countryside.

Bennington. General Stark and the Green Mountain Boys attacked the Hessians and defeated them. Burgoyne then beat a retreat to Saratoga. The American flag was first carried in battle at Bennington. This flag is now on display in the Bennington museum, which is worth a visit for its small but impressive collection of glass, military memorabilia, Grandma Moses paintings, and early Vermont furniture. If you visit Bennington in August, you can witness the celebrations of Bennington Battle Day Weekend, which includes a reenactment of the battle. Take an elevator to the top of the monument for a view of the countryside. The monument is open daily 9:00 A.M.–5:00 P.M., mid-April to October 31. Call (802) 447–0550 for further details.

The **Molly Stark Trail,** heading east on Route 9 from Bennington, was named for the wife of Gen. John Stark, who was called out of retirement during the Revolution to lead a thousand men across Vermont to protect munitions stored in Bennington. Stark wrote to his wife:

Dear Molly: In less than a week, the British forces will be ours. Send every man from the farm that will come and let the haying go.

She did as he asked and more; she sent 200 townspeople along, too. As he went into battle, General Stark said, "There are the Redcoats, and they are ours, or this night Molly Stark sleeps a widow"—but she didn't. He won the battle and brought home a brass cannon, one of six taken from the British.

The Molly Stark Trail is now known as Route 9, and it curves around the hills of southern Vermont from Bennington to Brattleboro. It crosses the Appalachian trail at Woodford and skirts the northern edge of Harriman Reservoir as it descends into the Deerfield River Valley. About 3 miles east of the town of Wilmington is the Molly Stark State Park, with walking trails and a campground. A few miles farther along, near Hogback Mountain, is the three-state, one-hundred-mile view. Driving along this road you can imagine what it was like for the New Hampshire volunteers as they set out to meet John Stark.

Four Chimneys Inn, at 21 West Road (Route 9) in Bennington, is a restored 1910 estate. Call (802) 447–3500 for reservations.

FOR MORE INFORMATION

Department of Travel and Tourism
134 State Street
Montpelier, VT 05602
(802) 828–3236

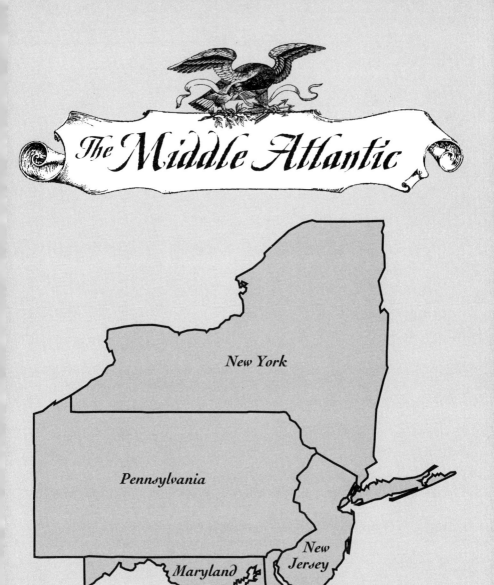

The Middle Atlantic

New York

Pennsylvania

New
Jersey

Maryland

Delaware

Delaware

Historical Introduction to
DELAWARE

Although Henry Hudson sailed the *Half Moon* into Delaware Bay in August of 1609, he circled around and did not proceed farther because of shoals. In 1631 a group of Dutch settlers, who had previously arrived at Cape Henlopen, settled in Lewes. The Lenni Lenape Indians in the area at first welcomed the Dutch, but after a dispute over a theft in which an Indian lost his life, the unlucky colonists were murdered by the Indians.

Swedish, Dutch, and English Tag

The next settlers in Delaware were Swedish, and they chose to live in Wilmington in 1638. Dutch settlers built Fort Casimir at New Castle, and the fort went back and forth between the Dutch and Swedish several times before the English took over. In 1664 King Charles II gave the land between the Connecticut and Delaware rivers to his brother, the Duke of York. Then William Penn received his land in Pennsylvania from King Charles in 1681 and, in addition, was granted Delaware by the Duke of York. The Calverts of Maryland, however, also thought they owned parts of Delaware, so disputes continued throughout the seventeenth century and recurred sporadically in the eighteenth century.

Delaware's Firsts

In 1704 Delaware became a separate state when Pennsylvania determined that each of its counties could have its own legislature. Maintaining the tradition, Delaware became the "First State"—its favorite name—by quickly ratifying the Constitution of the United States in 1787.

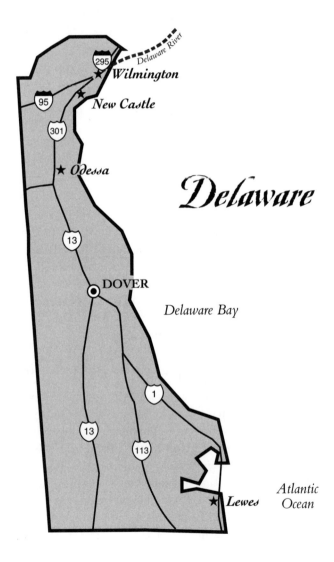

Regions to Explore

We've divided Delaware into two regions. We begin in the southern part of Delaware, with the early Delaware Bay settlement at Lewes, the first in the state; then we continue up Delaware Bay and slightly inland to Dover and Odessa. Finally we move into the Delaware River Valley to the competing settlements of New Castle and Wilmington.

DELAWARE BAY AREA

Although the first colony of Dutch whalers in **Lewes** (1631), then called Zwaanendael, was obliterated by an Indian massacre in the year of its founding, more settlers arrived in 1659. Visitors can take the Pilottown Road to see the **deVries Monument and Fort Site;** the monument is placed on the site of the north bastion of the fort. Its inscription reads: THAT DELAWARE EXISTS AS A SEPARATE COMMONWEALTH IS DUE TO THIS COLONY.

Lewes led a maritime existence through its involvement with shipwrecks, pirates, and privateers during the Revolution, but it had been fair game for pirates long before that. In 1698 French pirates laid siege to the town, then broke into every house and made off with family treasures. In 1708 pirates burned and sank three vessels off Cape Henlopen within four days, causing William Penn's secretary to write, "The coast begins to be intolerably infested."

Take a look at **Zwaanendael Museum,** with its spectacular stair-step roof, and wonder if you're in the Netherlands. In fact, the building is a replica of the town hall in Hoorn, Holland. It was constructed in 1931 to commemorate the 300th anniversary of the first settlement in Delaware.

Inside, the exhibit of the vessel H.M.S. *DeBraak* is exciting for those persons fascinated with nautical archaeology. The *DeBraak* existed prior to 1781, when she sailed in Dutch naval operations from the North Sea to the Mediterranean. The British captured her in 1795, and the Admiralty converted her rig from a single-masted cutter to a two-masted brig-sloop. When sailing off Cape Henlopen in 1798, the vessel sank, perhaps because she was "overmasted" and therefore top-heavy. After her discovery in 1984, the State of Delaware provided specialists to study her hull and artifacts. Among the

The Zwaanendael Museum, with its stepped roof, looks just like the houses on the canals of Amsterdam.

pieces recovered from the sea were barrel staves, barrel end pieces and hooping, and earthenware and stoneware jars and pots.

Other museum exhibits include a 1625 logbook, written by Robert Jewett, describing the bay as seen from the deck of Henry Hudson's *Half Moon*. You'll learn about the lighthouse, built in the 1760s, from displays. Made of granite, it stood almost 70 feet tall; on April 23, 1926, the lighthouse toppled into the sea.

Look for the "merman" in a glass case; it has the head and arms of a monkey and the tail of a fish. Such stuffed animals were known as devil fish and were displayed as oddities. Upstairs you'll see collections of coverlets, samplers, china, silver, models, dolls, doll cradles, accordions, puzzles, and a

Cutters and Smashers

The H.M.S. *DeBraak* was originally a single-masted vessel called a cutter. These ships were able to move into shallow waters and also assisted larger ships at sea. Her hull was covered with overlapping copper plates to keep marine organisms from demolishing the wooden bottom. A kentledge (iron ballast bars) provided weight below for stability. She carried two long guns, which fired six-pound projectiles, and fourteen guns called smashers, which fired twenty-four-pound projectiles. Her smashers were very destructive at short range.

Dutch costume from Marken, Holland. The museum is open 10:00 A.M.–4:30 P.M. Tuesday through Saturday, 1:30 P.M.–4:00 P.M. Sunday. Closed holidays. Call (302) 645–9418 for more information.

Next door the **Fisher-Martin House** dates from 1730. It was moved from Coolspring as part of the 350th anniversary festivities of the first settlement and now serves as a visitor center. The center is open 10:00 A.M.–3:00 P.M. Monday through Friday, 10:00 A.M.–2:00 P.M. Saturday. The Martin family lived here from 1736 until 1959. The **Lewes Presbyterian Church,** across the street, was founded in 1692; it is the third building on the site. If you love strolling around old cemeteries looking at interesting headstones, try this one.

Several private houses not open to the public date from the colonial era. These include the 1760 **Marvil House,** at 124 Gills Neck Road. Captain Richard Howard, a Delaware Bay and River Pilot, built the house, knowing he could watch for ships from the upper floors. Head along Front Street to 202 West Third Street to see the late eighteenth-century **Metcalf House,** once a blacksmith shop. The **Daniel Nunez House,** at 208 West Third Street, was once an inn. The **Lewes Historical Society Complex,** at Shipcarpenter and Third, has more information (302–645–7670), or call the **Lewes Chamber of Commerce and Visitor Bureau** (302–645–8073) for dates of the open-homes tour in December when a selection of these homes and some others are on view.

When you're ready to stop for the night, try the **Inn at Canal House Square,** at 122 Market Street (800–222–7902), which contains eighteenth-century reproduction furniture.

Dover was originally proclaimed the seat of Kent County in 1683 by William Penn. It became the state capital after the British captured New Castle in 1777. The **Green,** laid out by William Penn, was the site of public events. A portrait of King George III was burned here after the ratification of the Declaration of Independence. Also on the Green stood Red Hannah, the last whipping post to be used in the United States.

The **Old State House,** on the eastern side of the Green, dates from 1792, but its bell was cast earlier, in 1763. There's a large portrait of George Washington in the Senate Chamber. Call (302) 739–4266 for more information. While you're on the Green, stop in at the **Hall of Records** (302–739–5314) to see the original Royal Grant from King Charles II. The Old State House and the Hall of Records are both open Monday through Friday 8:30 A.M.–4:30 P.M. except holidays.

The **John Dickinson Plantation,** located 6 miles south of Dover on Kitts Hummock Road, contains a 1740 Georgian mansion, a reconstructed farm complex, a "log'd dwelling," and a visitor center. John Dickinson, sometimes called the "Penman of the Revolution," was a prolific writer for the colonists. It has been reported that he drafted the Articles of Confederation in 1778. This colonial home, restored to the era of Dickinson's boyhood, contains furnishings of the period and has a formal English garden.

John Dickinson inherited both the slaves and the land when his father died in 1760. By 1777 he had freed his slaves with a manumission document. This document required them to serve him for twenty-one years in exchange for food, clothing, shelter, and remuneration, but by 1785 he had freed all his slaves. The John Dickinson Plantation has interpreters to

The Simple Life

The "log'd dwelling" on the John Dickinson Plantation shows the life-style of slaves, free blacks, and poor whites in Kent County in the late 1700s. Most of these one-room dwellings were 20 by 16 and 18 by 16 feet. Their sides were made of oak or pine clapboards, sheathed with oak roof shingles, and the floors were either planked or dirt. A brick chimney topped the structure.

demonstrate various aspects of colonial life. The plantation is open Tuesday through Saturday 10:00 A.M.–3:30 P.M., Sunday 1:30 P.M.–4:30 P.M. Closed holidays. For more information call (302) 736–3277.

For overnight accommodations try the **Inn at Meeting House Square,** at 305 South Governors Avenue in Dover. It's on the National Register of Historic Places, and the charm of this 1849 residence is here for you to enjoy. Call (302) 678–1242 for reservations. Friends recommend meals in the **Blue Coat Inn,** at 800 North State Street (302–674–1776), which takes its name from the coats worn by the Delaware regiment as they marched from Dover Green in 1776.

Odessa, named for the Ukrainian seaport on the Black Sea, has a historic district of restored and preserved eighteenth- and nineteenth-century homes. Many of them are in private hands but are open for tours at various times of the year, usually in May, July, October, and December. For information and schedules for these special events, call **Historic Houses of Odessa** at (302) 378–4069.

Tours of some properties in the historic district are available throughout the year. Winterthur Museum owns and operates several houses from the colonial era as well as the Brick Hotel gallery, a nineteenth-century tavern. The 1774 **Corbit-Sharp House** was built by William Corbit, a Quaker tanner who had his business on Appoquinmink Creek. Some of the furnishings still in the house belonged to the Corbit family; others were made by local Delaware craftspersons. David Wilson, a local merchant and the brother-in-law of William Corbit, owned the **Wilson-Warner House,** which is furnished as it was when a bankruptcy inventory was prepared in the early nineteenth century. The homes in the historic district are open 10:00 A.M.–4 P.M. Tuesday through Saturday, 1:00 P.M.–4:00 P.M. Sunday, March to December. Closed Easter, July 4, Thanksgiving, and Christmas. Call (302) 378–4069 for more information.

THE DELAWARE RIVER VALLEY

Fort Casimir was the first name for the attractive town of **New Castle,** then New Amstel, and finally New Castle. The **Green,** laid out by Peter Stuyvesant in 1655 during the years when it was called Fort Casimir, is still here; weekly markets and "great fairs" took place on it. Restored buildings that line the sides of the Green include the **Old Court House,** between Market and Third Streets, which dates from 1732; the Colonial Assembly met here until 1777. Visitors can get information on walking tours and special events such as A Day in New Castle in May and Christmas in New Castle in December by calling (302) 323–4453.

Immanuel Episcopal Church, on Harmony Street, was built in 1703; inside, the high vaulted ceiling draws the eye upward. The graveyard has a lot of early headstones to find and enjoy. On Second Street the **Old Presbyterian Church** dates from 1707. Records indicate that it was the successor of the original Dutch Reformed Church of 1657. The church is open daily from 8:00 A.M. to 4:00 P.M.

Dutch House, at 32 East Third Street, may be the oldest brick house in Delaware, dating from the late seventeenth century. Now a museum, the house offers historical displays and artifacts. Look for the hutch table, a sixteenth-century Dutch Bible, and the courting bench. If you're there around the Christmas season, you'll see it decorated as it would have been for a Dutch celebration of Twelfth Night. Open 11:00 A.M.–4:00 P.M. Tuesday through Saturday, 1:00 P.M.–4:00 P.M. Sunday, March to December; 11:00 A.M.–4:00 P.M. Saturday, 1:00 P.M.–4:00 P.M. Sunday during the rest of the year. Closed holidays. Call (302) 322–2794 for more information.

Amstel House, on Fourth and Delaware streets, dates from the 1680s and the 1730s. Don't miss one of the earliest fanlight windows in the colony, which highlights the colonial furnishings. The house is open Tuesday through Saturday 11:00 A.M.–4:00 P.M., Sunday 1:00 P.M.–4:00 P.M. March to December; Saturday 11:00 A.M.–4:00 P.M. and Sunday 1:00 P.M.–4:00 P.M. during the rest of the year. Closed holidays. For more information call (302) 322–2794.

Take time to walk around town and look for **Packet Alley,** between The Strand and the river, where you'll see a sign that tells you what happened here:

Packet boats from Philadelphia met stagecoaches here for Maryland, the chief line of communication from the north to Baltimore and the south. Andrew Jackson, Daniel Webster, Henry Clay, David Crockett, Lord Ashburton, Louis Napoleon, Stonewall Jackson, Sam Houston, and Indians led by Osceola and Blackhawk en route to visit the Great Father in Washington all passed this way.

As you stroll around these streets, you will see window boxes filled with impatiens, heavy door knockers, painted shutters and doors, and a variety of iron fences. New Castle's charm is undeniable but partly accidental, since much of the town's growth was stunted by a great fire in 1822 and the diversion of main railroad lines to Wilmington later in the nineteenth century. Thus the inevitable demolition of old buildings to make way for the new ones stopped, and there are many colonial and Federal houses to enjoy.

Turfs, Twigs, and Taking Possession

Another sign along the river marks the landing place of William Penn and describes the ceremony of taking possession:

Near here Oct. 27, 1682 William Penn first stepped on American soil. He proceeded to the fort, performed livery of seisen (the act of taking legal possession of property), he took the key thereof. We did deliver unto him one turf with a twig on it, a porringer with river water and soil in part of all.

Among several places to stop for the night, you might try the **David Finney Inn,** at 216 Delaware Street in New Castle (302–322–6367). This 1683 inn was increased in size by several owners and maintains its colonial heritage. Meals are also served in the colonial dining room or courtyard. The **Jefferson House B&B,** at 5 The Strand, dates from colonial times and stands on the wharf; call (302) 322–8944 or 322–0999 for reservations. For lunch or dinner try the **New Castle Inn,** on Cobblestone Market Street (302–328–1798), which stands on the Green. It was built prior to 1809 and contains colonial-style furnishings.

The New Sweden Company founded **Wilmington** as Fort Christina in 1638; the name was changed by Quakers, who developed the town a hundred years later. The **Fort Christina Monument,** by sculptor Carl Milles from Stockholm, stands where Peter Minuit landed after his voyage from Sweden.

Holy Trinity (Old Swedes) Church, at 606 Church Street, dates from 1698; it is the oldest active Protestant church in North America. The iron numerals (1698) are now on the belfry although originally they were on the west wall over the main door. Inside, the pulpit, dating from 1698, is the oldest known pulpit in the country; Joseph Harrison carved it from black walnut wood, which was donated by the congregation.

During the 1700s men sat on the right and women on the left. A number of graves lie inside the church, including that of Peter Tranberg, a Swedish pastor. His portrait hangs with others of early pastors on the balcony railing. Don't miss the model of the *Kalmar Nyckel,* the ship that brought the first Swedish settlers to Wilmington in 1638. Outside, the graveyard has a number of interesting stones; the oldest marks the grave of William Vandever, who died in 1718. Call (302) 652–5629 for further information.

Next door to Holy Trinity Church, you'll find the **Hendrickson House,** originally built by Andrew Hendrickson on Crum Creek, near Chester, Pennsylvania, in 1690. He built it for his bride, Brigitta, and they filled it with eight children. In 1958 the house was taken down and reassembled next to Holy Trinity Church. The curved staircase was reconstructed by following old marks on the wall. Now a museum, the house contains colonial furniture, a spinning wheel, and pewter dishes and cooking utensils commonly used in Sweden. For more information call the number for Holy Trinity Church. The church and Hendrickson House are open Monday, Wednesday, Friday, and Saturday from 1:00 P.M. to 4:00 P.M.

Winterthur Museum and Gardens, northwest of Wilmington on Route 52, is one of the most remarkable museum complexes we have ever visited. It emphasizes decorative arts made or used in North America between 1650 and 1850. No pains (or costs) were spared to make this one of the most complete and representative collections of Americana ever assembled. For example, one room was carefully removed from a 1680s house in Essex, Massachusetts, and meticulously put back together as a room in the museum.

Winterthur took its name from the Swiss city of Winterthur, home of James Antoine Bidermann. His son, James Irénée Bidermann, inherited the estate but lived in France; his uncle, Henry Du Pont, bought the property in 1867. The Bidermann's great-nephew, Henry Francis Du Pont, was the moving force behind the further development of the mansion to house his growing collection of American art objects.

He started with the purchase of a Pennsylvania-made chest dated 1737, studied American crafts at a time when little research had been done, and continued collecting. Du Pont also became interested in the decorative art objects found in early American homes. His collection expanded to include textiles, needlework, ceramics, glassware, metalwork, paintings, prints, books, and newspapers. Going further he collected interior woodwork, paneling, fireplace walls, and doors from houses built between 1640 and 1840. Interiors from houses all along the Eastern seaboard were purchased, dismantled, and reassembled in his mansion. A newspaper reporter once asked Du Pont who his collection agent was and received the reply, "You're looking at him." The museum and gardens are open Tuesday through Saturday from 9:00 A.M. to 5:00 P.M., Sunday from noon to 5:00 P.M. Closed January 1, July 4, Thanksgiving, and December 24 and 25. Call (800) 448–3883 or (302) 888–4600 for more information.

Although the focus of other magnificent museums and gardens northwest of Wilmington is not primarily colonial, it would be a pity for any visitor interested in American history to miss them. Most of them are associated with the Du Pont family. **Hagley Museum,** on Route 141, on the original site of Du Pont mills along Brandywine Creek, is one of the best industrial museums in the country, and it also includes workers' homes and a Du Pont home built in 1803 (302–658–2400). The museum is open daily 9:30 A.M.–4:30 P.M., March 15–December 31; 9:30 A.M.–4:30 P.M. Saturday and Sunday during the rest of the year. Closed Thanksgiving and December 25 and 31. Beyond Winterthur, on Route 52 just over the Pennsylvania border, lies **Longwood Gardens,** a vast and magnificent horticultural collection, both indoors and outdoors, with elaborate fountains (215–388–6741). The gardens are open daily 9:00 A.M.–6:00 P.M., April to October; 9:00 A.M.–5:00 P.M. during the rest of the year. Other notable manor and garden estates in the area include the **Nemours Mansion and Gardens** (302–651–6912), on Rockland Road, and **Rockwood Museum** (302–761–4340), at 610 Shipley Road. Nemours Mansion is open Tuesday through Saturday with tours at 9:00 A.M., 11:00 A.M., 1:00 P.M., and 3:00 P.M.; Sunday tours at 11:00 A.M., 1:00 P.M. and 3:00 P.M., May to November. The Rockwood Museum is open Tuesday through Saturday from 11:00 A.M. to 3:00 P.M. Closed holidays.

For lunch or dinner try **Columbus Inn,** at 2216 Pennsylvania Avenue; call (302) 571–1492 for reservations. Dating from 1798, this building has colonial charm within its stone walls.

FOR MORE INFORMATION

Delaware Tourism Office
99 Kings Highway, P.O. Box 1401
Dover, DE 19903
(302) 739–4271 or (800) 441–8846

Maryland

Historical Introduction to
MARYLAND

Proprietary Charter

When we think of America as a "new" world, we often forget how much was simply transposed from the old. Maryland began with a medieval land arrangement. In 1632 a charter for the colony was granted to the first Lord Baltimore, George Calvert. He convinced Charles I to issue a proprietary charter, which was feudal in nature, giving Baltimore title as "absolute Lord and Proprietor." And he did not need to pay duty to the Crown, other than a symbolic two arrows each year. He worked out his own subsidiary land grants that offered manorial rights, which meant that purchasers could collect rent and also a portion of yearly income. This system of manorial rights was an inducement for the aristocracy and gentry to buy land, thereby avoiding the need to finance the enterprise through selling shares.

After his father's death, the second Lord Baltimore, Cecil Calvert, organized the expedition to America and put his younger brother, Leonard Calvert, in charge of managing the colony. In March of 1634 two vessels, the *Ark* and the *Dove,* sailed up into the St. Mary's River with 140 settlers aboard. Some were gentlemen who had bought land, but most were servants or indentured laborers who had to work to pay for their passage to the New World. The Yoacomaco and Piscataway Indians cooperated with the settlers as they built St. Mary's City, hoping to receive protection against the Susquehannocks.

Plantations, Indentured Servants, and Slaves

Within two years Leonard Calvert had begun organizing farming, the principal activity of the colony, on a manorial basis. From the outset tobacco was the important crop for export, and plantations to grow it developed along the tidewater rivers of Chesapeake Bay, where the crop could easily be shipped to England. By the turn of the century, many large plantations, like Sotterley, were thriving and growing; however, many of the indentured servants, who had signed on for opportunity died, and the survivors were still living in poor conditions. Even after they had worked off their debts and become free, many did not have enough money to begin their own farms. As more indentured servants succeeded in buying and working small parcels of land, especially when tobacco prices rose after mid-century, they were replaced with African slaves.

Religious Troubles

The Calverts, as well as most of the early settlers in Maryland, were Catholics who were tired of persecution in England. They had endured political and financial hardships throughout most of the Elizabethan era, fanned by the papal excommunication of the queen, the threat of the Spanish Armada, and Guy Fawkes's gunpowder plot. Yet, unlike the similarly persecuted Puritans of the Massachusetts Bay Colony, they established religious tolaration in Maryland from the beginning. Perhaps it was, in part, a practical strategy to attract needed settlers from a largely Protestant England, or as insurance against future intolerance aimed at Catholics.

Even wise colonial policies can fail, as this one did, twice, under the weight of turbulent events in the home country. When Charles I was executed and rule passed to a Protestant Parliament, there was a split between Catholic authority in the southern counties of St. Marys and St. Georges and Puritan control of the northern ones, Anne Arundel and Kent. Religious toleration returned in a compromise reached in 1657 and was reinforced by the restoration of Catholic kings in England, but by the time Protestants William and Mary regained the throne of England after the "Bloodless Revolution" of 1688, Protestants outnumbered Catholics in Maryland. They managed to get rid of Lord Baltimore's governor of St. Mary's City and substituted Francis Nicholson as governor. They also managed to stop Catholics from voting—an ironic disenfranchisement that lasted until after the Revolution.

Moves Toward Independence

Beyond the question of religion, the split between the life-styles of southern and northern counties (plantation life and mercantile endeavors) widened during the eighteenth century. Annapolis, settled by Puritans from Virginia in 1649, had gained enough political clout from events in England to have the capital shifted from St. Mary's City by 1694 and thereafter prospered as the principal port and business and social center of the colony. Thus it is no surprise that the colony's reactions against the financial exactions of the mother country were parallel to those in other ports like Boston, Providence, New York, or Philadelphia. The independence question began to come to the fore by 1765, when Marylanders objected to English taxes and, in fact, made the tax collector leave Annapolis. In 1774 they sent the *Peggy Stewart* up in flames because the tax had been paid on the tea she carried. The first constitution in the state was ratified in 1776.

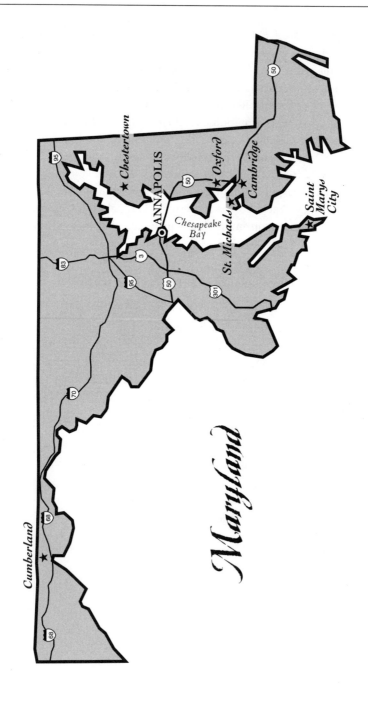

Regions to Explore

Maryland's most rewarding colonial regions include St. Marys County on the lower Potomac, where the first settlers landed and established their homes; then Annapolis, capital for three centuries; and finally the Eastern Shore, on the other side of Chesapeake Bay.

ST. MARYS COUNTY

In November 1633 two ships, the *Ark* and the *Dove*, left Cowes, England; the *Ark* was said to be "a shippe as strong as could be made of oake and iron, king built, making faire weather in great storms."

Yet the two vessels did survive a long and arduous voyage, landing on the shores of the St. Mary's River, a tributary of the lower Potomac. There, in March 1634, they founded Lord Baltimore's colony at **St. Mary's City,** first capital of Maryland and now a major archaeological site for colonial history. The Visitor Center offers a helpful slide show and displays for orientation before your visit. Archaeological exploration has uncovered a number of ruins from the original city; more are waiting for future generations to excavate in open fields that were once filled with houses and other structures.

The museum that adjoins the Visitor Center displays a wealth of military artifacts, ranging from 1645 iron shot, cannon fragments, and English flint to a 1650 sword and parts of armor. House bits include a 1675 door hinge, iron keys, handmade nails, wall plaster made of oyster shells, pale green leaded glass, and a 1650 Dutch brick. The food display features a large 1661 pitcher by Morgan Jones, knives, pewter spoons, slipware cups from Staffordshire, England, and other ceramics. Medical instruments include a lancet for bleeding, forceps, and a bleeding porringer.

Most visitors enjoy a walking tour of the site, which begins with the newest discovery—three lead coffins. In 1992 Project Lead Coffin undertook the process of determining whether the coffins still contained original air from the 1600s, taking a preliminary look inside by means of a fiberscope, lifting the coffins from the ground of Chapel Field, opening them, and analyzing the remains. NASA scientists were involved, and the procedure was carried out within a medical tent.

The small coffin contained the remains of a small female child, along with traces of finely woven linen. The second coffin contained an older woman, who is considered perhaps the best-preserved skeleton of a seventeenth-century colonist in North America. She was lying in a shroud, with silk ribbons at her wrists, knees, and ankles. The third coffin revealed the skeleton of a man who wore a leather piece of clothing. Smithsonian Institution scientists have recently established the identity of these three individuals; Governor Philip Calvert; his wife, Anne Wolsley; and an infant daughter, probably from the governor's second marriage. The museum and nearby houses are open 10:00 A.M.–5:00 P.M. Wednesday through Sunday. April 1 to the last Friday in November; closed Thanksgiving.

A walking trail will take you to the Governor's Field area, where you can visit the **Brome-Howard House, Farthing's Ordinary** (an inn), the 1676 **State House,** and **Trinity Church.** Visitors to St. Mary's City are encouraged to "keep seventeenth-century time" to blend in with the interpreters, who want to speak with them in language of that era and follow its customs. You may meet Dan Clocker as he comes to town to drink, smoke, and tell stories; or you may run into Mrs. Nuthead, who loves to gossip as she runs the printing press. Chancellor Phillip Calvert tries Capt. Fendall for treason in the State House; Capt. Miles Cook sells indentured servants from the transom of the *Dove;* and the Spray family continues cultivating its tobacco. All the buildings on St. Mary's follow the same schedule as the museum (above). For more information call 800–762–1634, 301–862–0990, or 301–862–0960.

Don't miss walking down to the river to go on board the *Maryland Dove* and talk with her crew, unless she is out on a training cruise. As the faithful sailing replica of a small square-rigged ship from the 1630s, she gives visitors a chance to visualize a typical merchant vessel of the era. These vessels carried lumber, tobacco, corn, furs, household items, and people. Now the *Dove's* primary mission is educating people of all ages as she follows a busy schedule of port visits and cruises throughout maritime Maryland and adjoining states. In the process she has served as a vehicle for experimental nautical archaeology, teaching maritime historians much about the capabilities of such vessels.

Also don't miss the **Godiah Spray Plantation,** located down the road on the other side of the Visitor Center. When we were there, a group of schoolchildren were quizzing interpreters and getting good seventeenth-century answers. In between gardens, orchards, and barns stand the planter's house, a freedman's cottage, and tobacco houses; a path leads to slave quarters a hundred yards away.

St. Mary's has a number of annual special events, including Maryland Day Weekend in March, Charter Days in June, Grand Militia Muster in October, and Harvest Home, also in October. Call (301) 862–0990 for the schedule and more information, or write to the Chamber of Commerce, St. Mary's City, MD 21686.

Across the St. Mary's peninsula on the Patuxent River lies **Sotterley,** one of Maryland's many tidewater plantations during the colonial era. Lord Baltimore issued a manorial grant in 1650 to Thomas Cornwallis, who arrived on the *Ark* or the *Dove,* and James Bowles built the first house there in 1717. After the latter's death, his widow married George Plater II, who named Sotterley after his ancestral home in Suffolk, England. George Plater III was a delegate to the Continental Congress and one of the first governors in Maryland. Because Sotterly was a port of entry for the colony, the resident in the house was also the customs officer.

George Plater V was only five years old when he inherited the house, but he lost it later in a roll of the dice. He wanted to die in the house but didn't

Sotterley Plantation offers a glimpse into the colonial past.

make it—his body was found in a nearby ditch. Some say that they can still hear the hoofbeats, see footprints, and even hear the fatal roll of the dice—George is apparently a friendly spirit when he comes to visit his plantation.

Richard Bolton created the Chinese Chippendale staircase and the ornate shell woodwork in the Drawing Room. The staircase has a break in the rail; its purpose may be to signal a curve coming or to prevent a child from sliding down! The Drawing Room, furnished with Adam and Hepplewhite pieces from London, is considered one of the hundred most beautiful rooms in America. In the front hall Chinese lattice-back mahogany chairs match the Chinese trellis stair. Like other great houses of the colonial era, it has an almost necessary feature of the colonial era—a secret staircase, which leads from the bright red small parlor to an upstairs bedroom.

Sotterley is a working plantation, and you can visit the outbuildings, including tenant houses, a smokehouse, and a tobacco shed. Open 11:00 A.M.–4:00 P.M. daily except Monday, June to September; by appointment in April, May, October, and November. Special programs and candlelight dinners are held at Sotterly at various times during the year. For the schedule and more information, call (301) 373–2280.

ANNAPOLIS

Annapolis always has been and is now a thriving waterfront city with salt water washing right up into the town dock (the original British meaning of the word *dock* is waterway) at the center of its business district. This narrow slip of water juts in to meet the bottom of Main and Cornhill streets. Almost everyone gravitates at one time or another to the dock area—always a busy place with fishing, charter, excursion, and pleasure boats going in and out. Forty years ago it was filled with bugeyes and skipjacks, among the last work boats to operate under sail; now it and the surrounding creeks are filled with sailboats, which make Annapolis the premier sailing center in the Middle Atlantic states. Of course Annapolis has been home to another premier nautical institution, the United States Naval Academy, since 1845.

Such continued vitality and the change that it inevitably brings somehow have not obscured the colonial past of the city, either in ambience—it's still primarily a walking town—or in surviving buildings. Somehow the allure of an active port and capital city manage to coexist with a rich historical heritage that stretches back to the city's founding in the seventeenth century, and that enables visitors to enjoy both worlds simultaneously.

Annapolis was first established under the name of Providence, chosen by its Puritan settlers. Then a ship's captain was honored by the choice of his name, Proctor, for the town. Later it was called City by the Severn, the river on which it is located. Some records refer to it as Anne Arundel Town, Arrundell Towne, or Arundelton, all variant names of the surrounding county.

In 1694 it became the capital of Maryland, when Governor Francis Nicholson moved the seat of government from St. Mary's City to this site, nearer the center of the colony. Nicholson directed his commissioners "to survey and lay out in the most comodius and convenient parte and place of the said Towne six Acres of Land intire for the erecting a Court House and other buildings as shall be thought necessary and convenient." In 1694 Annapolis was chosen as the city's name to honor Queen Anne of England.

The city became an important and strategically located seaport, in addition to serving as the administrative center of Maryland during the Revolution. Ships sailed in and out of the harbor, right past the blockade of English vessels. The Continental Congress met in the State House in 1783 and again in 1784 to ratify the Treaty of Paris, which ended the Revolution.

You can begin to discover the sometimes hidden treats of Annapolis through a walking tour with Three Centuries Tours of Annapolis, at 48 Maryland Avenue (410–263–5401). This is by far the best way to see a city full of narrow lanes and one-way streets. Your family may enjoy being directed by a guide in colonial costume who will pull relevant objects out of her basket as she reaches each new location. Our guide had a great deal of precise information, interspersed with anecdotes and stories, to make the history of Annapolis come alive. Historic Annapolis (410–267–8149), located in the **Old Treasury Building** right next to the State House, also offers walking tours. The Treasury itself, built in 1735, has the distinction of being the oldest building in Maryland.

Annapolis will captivate architecture buffs, and it serves as a useful school for the evolution of architecture in America. As you walk around Annapolis, you'll notice buildings marked with historic district plaques that are color-coded according to date and style. Colors signify time periods as follows: provincial green (seventeenth century), terra-cotta (eighteenth-century colonial), blue (Federal), verdigris (Greek Revival), aubergine (Victorian), and ocher (twentieth century).

The earliest structures are plain, unadorned seventeenth-century houses like the one at 130 Prince George Street. This house was patterned after the utilitarian wooden-frame houses common in English villages. The gambrel roof is topped by a very large central chimney, typical of early colonial homes. Take a stroll down the smaller lanes like Pinkney, Fleet, Cornhill, and Francis Streets to spot more of them; then walk on the broader avenues—King George, Prince George, East, and Duke of Gloucester streets—and around State Circle to spot some of the plaques on later and larger structures.

The **Maryland State House,** built in 1772, has a distinguished history. It is the oldest state house in use in the United States and also served as the U.S. Capitol from November 1783 to August 1784. George Washington resigned his commission as commander in chief of the Continental armies in the Old Senate Chamber. Look for the bronze plaque on the floor that marks the spot where Washington stood on that day. Patriotic fervor for this admired leader was expressed during a celebration the day before the resignation, given by Governor William Paca. Supplies for the evening were furnished by Mann's Hotel, as follows: "ninety-eight bottles of wine, two and one-half gallons of spirits, nine pounds of sugar, a lot of limes, music and waiters, and a dozen packs of cards."

The official end of the Revolutionary War came with the signing of the Treaty of Paris in the State House in 1784. Charles Willson Peale painted a number of portraits for the State House, including one of George Washington with Tench Tilghman, his aide-de-camp, which hangs over the fireplace in the Old Senate Chamber. Open daily 9:00 A.M.–5:00 P.M.; closed December 25. Call (410) 974–3400 for more information on the State House, its exhibits, and opportunities for visiting its elegant chambers while the legislature is sitting.

From the State House be sure to walk up the short block of School Street that links State Circle to Church Circle and visit **St. Anne's Church.** King William III contributed the communion silver, with his coat of arms on it, in 1695. Nearly two centuries later, in 1893, the Sands Memorial Window won first prize for ecclesiastical art at the Chicago World's Fair. The oldest grave in the cemetery is that of Amos Garrett, the first mayor of Annapolis, who died in 1727.

From Church Circle continue east along College Avenue to **St. John's College,** founded in 1696, and famous in the twentieth century for its demanding liberal arts curriculum based on the classic texts of Western civ-

The Maryland State House is the oldest state house in use in the United States.

ilization. There is a legend that the treaty of peace with the Susquehannock Indians was signed under the large 400-year-old tulip-poplar tree called the **Liberty Tree,** located and marked on the front campus.

From St. Johns turn right onto King George Street to reach the **Chase-Lloyd House,** which was partially built by Samuel Chase, a signer of the Declaration of Independence. Francis Scott Key married Mary Taylor Lloyd there in 1802. The house is open 2:00 P.M.–4:00 P.M. Tuesday to Saturday.

There's a mystery in the **Hammond-Harwood House** across the street, which was designed by William Buckland for Mathias Hammond in 1774. Hammond reportedly was having the house built for an unknown bride-to-be, who then eloped with someone else, so he resolved not to live in the house and left Annapolis. He died at the young age of thirty-eight, and the mystery of his forlorn love has never been solved. Ask about the tunnel under the house, which may have led down to the water. Two ancient keys were also found under the floor, one labeled "to the Secret Chamber" and the other "to the Secret Burying Place." Doesn't that stir your imagination? Open 10:00 A.M.–4:00 P.M. Monday to Saturday; closed Janulary 1, Thanksgiving, and December 25.

Around the block on Prince George Street is the **William Paca House,** which was originally designed as a home and office for Paca in 1763. The restored house is now open and furnished in period decor. The original Paca gardens have also been replanted. Look for the unusual Chinese trellis bridge that matches the staircase in the house. Open 10:00 A.M.–4:00 P.M. Monday through Saturday, noon–5:00 P.M. Sunday and holidays, March to December; 10:00 A.M.–4:00 P.M. Friday and Saturday and noon–4:00 P.M. Sunday and holidays the rest of the year. Closed Thanksgiving and December 24 and 25. For more information on the house and gardens, call (410) 269–1714.

On the other side of Main Street, the **Charles Carroll House,** at 107 Duke of Gloucester Street, was opened for visitors in May of 1993. Charles Carroll the Settler owned the property of St. Mary's Parish, where the house and the church now stand. He built his home in the 1720s, perhaps using an older structure within the building. This two-and-a-half story house was then among the largest in Annapolis. Carroll's son, Charles Carroll of Carrollton, was born in the house in 1737; it is the only surviving birthplace of a signer of the Declaration of Independence in Maryland.

The house is open 10:00 A.M.–4:00 P.M. Friday; 10:00 A.M.–2:00 P.M. Saturday, and noon–4:00 P.M. Sunday and holidays. Closed Thanksgiving, Christmas, and Easter. Workshops, concerts, and candlelight tours are scheduled at various times during the year. Call (410) 269–1737 to find out details and to confirm hours.

The calendar of special events is loaded in Annapolis. If you visit in June, you may be there for the Children's Colonial Festival, with hands-on events

History from Trash

The story of the Carroll House is not over yet. During archaeological exploration the foundation of the "Frame House," possibly a seventeenth-century building, was uncovered. Objects from the 1660s were unearthed in the adjacent "builder's trench," and broken dishes from the same era were also found on the property near the Eastport bridge. Inside the house the East Wing archaeological dig uncovered pieces from the late 1700s that may indicate that slaves lived and worked in that room.

Outdoors the discovery an eighteenth-century cistern on the west side of the house began a series of archaeological finds. Excavations continue in the gardens and along a 400-foot eighteenth-century stone seawall. Core samples were taken to ascertain the makeup of the terraced gardens, which may eventually be restored to their original appearance.

and lectures for chilren, offered by the Historic Annapolis Foundation (410–267–7619). For schedules and information on other events, call the Annapolis & Anne Arundel County Conference and Visitors Bureau at (4l0) 280–0445.

Annapolis is a delight for those who seek accommodation in historic buildings. **Prince George Inn,** 232 Prince George Street (410–263–6418), is centrally located and offers four Victorian town-house rooms, all decorated differently. **Historic Inns of Annapolis,** 16 Church Circle (800–847–8882), also operates five historic inns, all conveniently located in the center of town. **Magnolia House Bed & Breakfast,** at 220 King George Street (410–268–3477), is a Georgian house built of brick using "header bond" style, in which only the head of the brick shows. **Reynolds Tavern,** at 7 Church Circle (410–626–0380), is an eighteenth-century tavern with four antique-filled rooms and suites. For dining in historic surroundings, try **Middleton Tavern**, City Dock (410–263–3323), **King of France Tavern** in the Maryland Inn (410–263–2641), or **Reynold's Tavern.**

THE EASTERN SHORE

The Eastern Shore region, remote from urban expansion in the Baltimore-Washington corridor on the other side of the Bay, escaped most intrusions of the modern world on a more relaxed rural life-style throughout the nineteenth century and the first half of the twentieth. Then in 1952 the completion of the Bay Bridge began changing all that, but not quickly or irreparably. The pace is still slower on the other side of the bridge, and the people who have lived there for generations value their traditions. Thus the Eastern Shore is peppered with colonial homes, still lived in, wonderful harbors and creeks to explore by boat, and a number of old inns and museums to preserve its agricultural and maritime heritage. Like the South Shore in Massachusetts or Bucks County in Pennsylvania, it's an area that invites you to wander around and savor the colonial atmosphere of old towns, as well as the virtually unchanged land- and seascape of winding tidewater rivers.

Wye Oak State Park is famous for its 400-year-old Wye Oak, which overlooked the colonists when they first arrived. It is now 95 feet high, has a trunk 21 feet in circumference, and stretches to a horizontal spread of 165 feet. This white oak is Maryland's state tree.

Wye Mill was built in 1671, reconstructed in 1720, and then again in 1840. It is the earliest industrial-commercial building in continuous use in Maryland. Robert Morris, major financier of the American Revolution, bought flour for the American troops in Valley Forge from it and paid £ 10,000, which was about $50,000 then. Today visitors will see old equipment and new in Wye Mill. You can try weaving, broom making, and hand milling here if you wish. Call (301) 827–6909 or 685–2886 for more information.

Easton was settled in the late seventeenth century. The oldest frame house still standing in America is the **Third Haven Meeting House,** on South Washington Street. It was built at the headwaters of the Tred Avon, and people arrived by boat for the meetings; monthly meetings lasted all day long. William Penn preached here, and Lord Baltimore attended services. The **Historical Society Complex**, at 29 South Washington, includes a Quaker cabinetmaker's cottage from the 1700s, a period garden, and a museum. To find out more call (410) 822–0773.

St. Michael's, on the Miles River, is remembered for its legendary naval trick during the War of 1812, when its residents foiled a British attack by snuffing out all lights at ground level and hanging lanterns in the tops of trees. This caused the British ships to aim their guns high and shoot over the town. The town was very much alive as a colonial shipbuilding center during the late seventeeth and early eighteenth centuries; thus it is an appropriate site for the **Chesapeake Bay Maritime Museum,** on Mill Street, an eighteenth-century complex that focuses on the maritime history of the area and the bay. Open 9:00 A.M.–6:00 P.M. daily, June to September; 10:00 A.M.–4:00 P.M. daily, April, May, October, November, and December; and 10:00 A.M.–4:00 P.M. Saturday and Sunday, January to March (410–745–2916).

As you enter the museum, you'll see an overview of the Miles River—a "drowned river," in geological terms—and its many uses and vessels. The Indians made their canoes by burning and then scraping out the inside of a log with oyster shells; the sample on display is partly finished to show the process. Colonists arrived and planted tobacco, with sassafras as a secondary crop during poor tobacco years, and they used the river to bring in supplies and ship out the crop. To harvest the wealth of the bay, fishermen, oyster-men, and crabbers developed distinctive craft that are exhibited throughout the museum—sailing log canoes, bugeyes, and skipjacks—maintaining one of the few continuous traditions of sailing workboats in America. The museum traces the culture of Chesapeake watermen who have worked the bay long and hard for generations; some have family roots that go back to the seventeenth century.

Accommodations in keeping with the historic atmosphere of St. Michaels include **The Inn at Perry Cabin** (410–745–5178), a large and luxurious early nineteenth-century house on the river; **The Parsonage** (410–745–5519) at 210 North Talbot Street, which dates from 1883; and

Superstition at Sea

Among maritime superstitions are beliefs that bad luck will come to a boat that contains anything blue; a hatch cover upside-down; a red brick used as ballast; and a leaf, nut, or twig from a walnut tree. Worse luck comes from having a woman on board, changing the name of a boat, or watching three crows fly across the bow.

Wades Point Inn (410–745–2500), on Wades Point Road in nearby McDaniel, built by a shipwright in the nineteenth century. **Chesapeake House** (410–886–2123), located on the Bay at Tilghman, some 15 miles from St. Michaels, is an 1856 inn on the water.

Oxford, on the Tred Avon River, was once a stamping ground for pirates, including Stede Bonner and Blackbeard Teach, when they needed repairs on their ships. Because of its location and sheltered anchorage, it was popular as a port of entry for the colony. London and Liverpool stores started branches in town, where traders exchanged goods for tobacco.

One of the town fathers, Robert Morris, for whom the main street is named, was killed unexpectedly by the wadding from a ceremonial cannonball; his son was a signer of the Declaration of Independence. The **Robert Morris Inn,** located right on the river, has a fine reputation for dining and overnight stays. Apart from the wonderful food, you will enjoy looking at its architectural features. It was built in 1710 by ships' carpenters and has wooden-pegged paneling and hand-hewn beams. Call (410) 226–5111 for reservations.

Tench Tilghman, another Oxford resident, rode from Yorktown to Philadelphia on October 17, 1781, to tell the Continental Congress that Cornwallis had surrendered. As Washington's aide-de-camp he was well known for his bravery. He was buried in the Oxford Cemetery, and a monument stands by his grave as a memorial. Look across the cove to see **Plimhimmon,** which was the home of his widow, Anna Maria Tilghman.

The **Oxford-Bellevue Ferry,** on North Morris Street and The Strand, has been operating since 1683—continuously—the only one in the country with such a record. Even if you have no pressing reason to get to the other side (most visitors don't), it's worth the ride just for the fine views down stretches of the Tred Avon.

Cambridge was founded on the Choptank River in 1684, mostly for the purpose of collecting customs fees. High Street is brick paved and lined with houses from the eighteenth and nineteenth centuries. Stop in the **Dorchester County Historical Society** for a map of the walking tour. Call (410) 228–7953 for more information or the **Dorchester County Tourism** office at (301) 228–1000.

If you'd like a view of **Cambridge Creek,** where skipjacks moor, climb to the rear of the Dorchester County Office Building, at 120 High Street. Skipjacks are, unfortunately, vanishing as the last sailing fishing fleet in the country.

Chestertown was founded in 1706 on the banks of the Chester River, although it had been designated as a town as early as 1668. Many waterfront homes were built during the 1700s, and a number of them are identified on a walking tour. (Other homes elsewhere in town are also on the tour.) Stop in the **Kent County Chamber of Commerce** for a brochure or call (410) 778–0416 for details and a schedule of special events.

The **Hynson-Ringgold House** on the corner of Cannon and Water streets dates from 1743 and is now the home of the Washington College president. At the end of the block and across the street is the **Customs House,** which has Flemish bond brick construction. Nearby, furious citizens met before boarding the *William Geddes,* Chestertown's own version of the Boston Tea Party: On May 23, 1774, angry citizens boarded the brig, moored in front of the Customs House, and threw the cargo of tea into the river. The Chamber of Commerce sponsors a reenactment of the 1774 Tea Party in May.

The house across the street is called **Wide Hall;** this Georgian house was the scene of much action during the Revolution because the owner, Thomas Smythe, was the head of Maryland's provincial government from 1774 until the state's first constitution emerged in 1776. An unusual free-standing staircase was built in the house.

The house at 107 Water Street, called **River House,** was built by Richard Smythe between 1784 and 1787. Woodwork from one of the second-floor rooms now resides in the Chestertown Room of Delaware's Winterthur Museum. (It is open at times specified by the Maryland Historic Trust.) The **Historical Society of Kent** offers historical candelight tours through town in September. For the schedule and more information call (410) 778–3499.

Washington College was founded in Chestertown in 1782 and is now the tenth-oldest institution of higher learning in America. George Washington was instrumental in the founding of the college and in 1789 he received a doctor of laws degree there.

FOR MORE INFORMATION

Maryland Office of Tourism
217 East Redwood Street
Baltimore, MD 21202
(410) 333–6611
(410) 333–6643 (fax)

New Jersey

Historical Introduction to
NEW JERSEY

*H*enry Hudson sailed his ship, the *Half Moon,* into New York Bay in 1609 and anchored off Sandy Hook. Since the initial reception of the Indians had been friendly, his crew began to explore the New Jersey side of the bay along the Staten Island shore. After discovering Newark Bay, which they thought to be an open sea, the men turned back toward the ship. Indians in two canoes chased them; John Colman was shot in the throat with an arrow, and two other crewmen were wounded. After dark, Hudson's men were not able to find their ship, and they rowed back and forth until daybreak. Thus began the continually changing story of one of the greatest harbor complexes in the world.

Early Settlers under Various Flags

The Dutch West Indian Company followed the New Netherland Company as merchant-navigators continued to seek wealth through the flourishing fur trade. In 1624 Captain Cornelis Jacobsz May sailed for America in the *Nieu Nederlandt,* with thirty families on board to settle in the new land. Two families and eight single men were the first to live in New Jersey, on Burlington Island in the Delaware River, but by 1630 these people had moved to New

Amsterdam. A few men lived in Fort Nassau, now the city of Gloucester across from Philadelphia. In fact the company had trouble enticing any potential Dutch emigrants to move from their comfortable homes in the Netherlands.

Dutch families established a settlement on the Delaware in 1638 under a Swedish charter, and the energetic Johan Printz ruled as governor of New Sweden from 1643 to 1653. He built Fort Elfsborg, also called Mosquito Castle, on the eastern shore of the Delaware; the fort was obliterated as the river changed its course. Several Indian wars decimated the settler population, but more settlers arrived around 1655 to live under the rule of Peter Stuyvesant.

Troubles under English Rule

Without warning in August of 1664, four British warships arrived in New Netherland, and Dutch authorities quickly surrendered their settlements, which included the Dutch across the Hudson and the Swedes on the Delaware. King Charles II gave New Jersey to his brother James, Duke of York, and granted the land in between the Hudson and Delaware rivers to John Berkeley, Baron of Stratton, and Sir George Carteret. The name "Jersey" came from Carteret, the former governor of the Isle of Jersey in the English Channel. In 1673 the Dutch captured New Netherland again, but the Treaty of Westminster gave it back to the English in 1674. The remainder of the century was filled with disputes between proprietors and settlers over land titles, rents, voting rights, and self-government, as well as struggles with New York over control of East Jersey; in 1680 Governor Philip Carteret, a distant cousin of George Carteret, was abducted and tried in New York, and in 1681 he dissolved a legislature that threatened his constitutional authority.

Political conditions got worse rather than better after the turn of the century. Queen Anne appointed her cousin Edward Hyde, Lord Cornbury, governor of New Jersey on a whim in 1703. The first recorded bribe in New Jersey was delivered to Cornbury's home that year, with more to follow. In the politics of the colony, he sided with the proprietors and found ingenious ways to defeat the antiproprietors—such as making them stand outdoors all day in winter weather before allowing them to vote. Cornbury later ignored both parties and put his own henchmen, the "Cornbury Ring," into power; some of them held positions in both New York and New Jersey.

The Cornbury "Magot"

The Cornbury Ring, reputedly a bunch of unsavory characters, brought political corruption to the colony in a big way. Some of them had official posts, and pay, in two colonies. Others were embezzlers and crafty land speculators. By 1707 most people had caught on to their tactics and wanted to get rid of the Cornbury Ring. The assembly compiled a list of grievances against Lord Cornbury—some called him a "detestable magot"—until he was recalled to England.

Inching toward Independence

With this independent spirit and long history of grievances against the Crown, it is somewhat surprising that New Jersey resentment against the imposition of new controls and taxes remained dormant in the years before the Revolution, but there are good reasons for New Jersey's moderation. William Franklin, son of Benjamin Franklin, was governor from the end of the French and Indian War in 1763 to the time of the Declaration of Independence in 1776, and his sympathies remained with the Crown, even including emigration back to England in 1782. Also, parliamentary measures that affected land claims or commerce excited Virginia and Massachusetts more than New Jersey. The Stamp Act of 1765, however, changed all that because it placed heavy burdens on citizens in all colonies. New Brunswick was the site of the first provincial congress held in 1774 to appoint delegates to the Continental Congress in Philadelphia. By 1776 the provincial congress had adopted its own declaration of independence and a state constitution.

Once in the fray, the new state was occupied by British troops and battered incessantly as both sides struggled for control of the territory between New York and Philadelphia. During the Revolution the Continental army advanced through the state four times. General Washington and his men spent two winters in Morristown and one at Middlebrook; crucial battles were fought in Trenton, Princeton, and Monmouth. After the British capitulation the Continental Congress met in Princeton in 1783 and in Trenton in 1784. Trenton became the state capital in 1790.

New Jersey

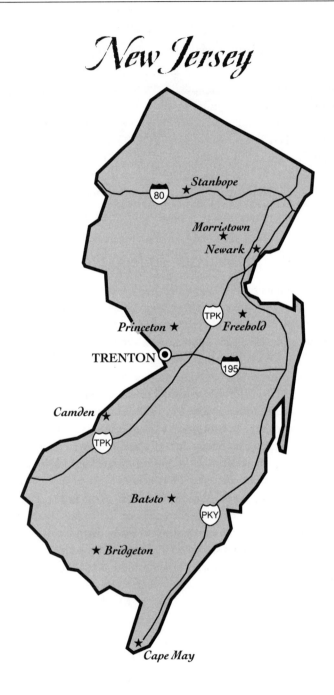

Stanhope

80

Morristown

Newark

Princeton

TPK

Freehold

TRENTON

195

Camden

TPK

Batsto

PKY

Bridgeton

Cape May

Regions to Explore

We've divided the colony into three regions. We begin with the first settlements in the southwest along the Delaware, then move to the Pine Barrens in the southeast, and finally to important Revolutionary War sites in the central counties of Mercer, Monmouth, and Morris.

DELAWARE RIVER AND BAY SETTLEMENTS

The expansive reaches of the Delaware River and Delaware Bay first tempted explorers as the beginning of the northwest passage to Asia, but later the river and bay, with its network of tributaries, provided the needed water transport for colonial development. **Bridgeton** was settled by Quakers in the late seventeenth century and still retains an extensive historic district that represents all succeeding eras. For information on self-guided walking tours, stop in at the Bridgeton/Cumberland Tourist Center, at 50 East Broad Street, or call (609) 451–4802. The **New Sweden Farmstead Museum,** in Bridgeton City Park, at the intersection of West Commerce Street and Mayor Aitken Drive, is noted for its replicas of seventeenth-century structures that reflect the Swedish culture of the people who lived here. The museum is open weekends during the summer. For more information call (609) 455–3230.

By 1763 Bridgeton residents had bought a liberty bell, and they rang it with vigor on July 7, 1776, when townspeople gathered to hear the Declaration of Independence read. Farther downstream on the Cohansey River, New Jersey's only tea party took place in **Greenwich** in December 1774. Patriots in Indian disguise gathered on the square to burn tea, snatched from the East India Company. Visitors will see the **Tea Burners Monument,** which stands on the square.

Nicholas Gibbon built his home on Ye Greate Street in Greenwich, in 1730. It looks like a London town house from the outside and is now the home of the **Cumberland County Historical Society.** Inside, the house contains eighteenth- and nineteenth-century furnishings, including rush-seated Ware chairs that were made in the area. Don't miss the 1650 **Swedish**

Granary, a Swedish log cabin built by early settlers. The house and cabin are open Tuesday through Saturday noon–4:00 P.M., Sunday 2:00 P.M.–5:00 P.M., April to November. Call (609) 455–4055 for details.

The oldest village along the Delaware River, **Salem,** was built on land bought by Quaker John Fenwick in 1675. To conclude the purchase, Lenape Indians met him under the **Salem Oak,** estimated to be more than 500 years old, in the **Friends Burying Ground.** The **Salem County Historical Society** owns the 1721 **Alexander Grant House,** at 78 Market Street. If you're interested in genealogical research, visit the library in the house. Twenty-one rooms contain pieces from the colonial and Federal periods, and you will also see a colonial garden, a stone barn, and a law office that dates from 1736. The house is open Tuesday through Friday from noon to 4:00 P.M. and every second Saturday of the month from noon to 4:00 P.M. Call (609) 935–5004 for more information.

The 1734 **Hancock House,** located a few miles south of Salem, was the site of a massacre during the Revolution. In 1778 Major John Simcoe ordered a retaliatory raid on the town because its Quaker residents had supplied food to Washington's troops at Valley Forge. In a surprise attack a British force of 300 killed thirty local militiamen who were sleeping there. Although you can't go inside the house, it's an interesting site to visit.

Just across the Delaware from Philadelphia, the British occupied **Woodbury** in 1777, and General Charles Cornwallis lived in the home of John Cooper, a member of the Continental Congress. **Red Bank Battlefield Park** is the site of **Fort Mercer,** on a strategically important bluff that overlooks the river. Here 400 American defenders held their fire and drove off more than 1,200 attacking Hessians on October 22, only to evacuate the fort a month later when Cornwallis approached with an overwhelming force. In the park you can visit the restored home of **Ann Whitall,** who reportedly sat, calmly spinning wool, during the battle. The park is open dawn until dusk and the Whitall home is open Wednesday through Friday from 9:00 A.M. to noon and Saturday and Sunday from 1:00 P.M. to 4:00 P.M., April to September. To find out more call (609) 853–5120.

Just to the north **Camden** was founded in 1681, when William Cooper started a ferryboat service across the Delaware River to Philadelphia. **Pomona Hall** (1726), on Park Boulevard at Euclid Avenue, was home to his descendants. The **Camden County Historical Society** owns the home, which contains period furnishings, and an adjacent library. Open 12:30

P.M.–4:30 P.M. Monday to Thursday, 2:00 P.M.–4:00 P.M. Sunday, September through July. Closed holidays. Call (609) 964–3333 for more information.

When you're ready for lunch, dinner, or Sunday brunch, head for **Chateau Silvana,** on Route 541 in Medford. The restaurant is in a 1774 building built by the Wilkins family; the cuisine is northern Italian and southern French.

THE PINE BARRENS

In a state of constantly evolving transportation systems, as well as expanding commercial and suburban development, the Pine Barrens may be New Jersey's only "natural" museum of the past. Now protected and treasured for its canoeing, hiking, fishing, and hunting, its rivers and woods were once scenes of considerable industrial activity. Charles Read built the **Batsto Furnace** in 1766; it was a major supplier of munitions during the Revolutionary War.

Visitors to the Wharton State Forest, east of Hammonton on Route 542, can tour the restored thirty-six-room **Ironmaster's House** (1766); Joseph Wharton, a financier from Philadelphia, restored the house as a summer home. Inside, the house is fully furnished with period pieces. Seventeen workers' homes are also open, and you may wonder why they are black; they were built of Jersey cedar clapboards that blacken with age and the weather. A sawmill, a gristmill, and a general store are open to visit, too. When you get to the horse barn, look at the vertical slots in the walls, which were

Jersey Witches and Devils

"Pineys," the people who live deep in the forest, have tales to tell about Peggy Clevenger, known as the Witch of the Pine. They say that she could turn herself into a rabbit and that she had a treasure of gold. Residents also tell about various strange creatures that inhabit the forest, including the Jersey Devil, who supposedly carried off farm and domestic animals and left cloven tracks behind.

Workers' homes made of Jersey cedar clapboards, which blackened over the years.

designed to prevent hay inside from molding. Open daily 10:00 A.M.–4:00 P.M., Memorial Day to Labor Day. For details call (609) 561–3262.

Legends abound about the "Pine Robbers" who fled into the forest to safety. Some stories are based on historical fact, whereas others are embellished fiction—believe what you will. According to one tale, Joe Mulliner, who was hanged in 1781, was known as the Robin Hood of the Pine Barrens. Apparently he was finally captured because he could not resist coming out of hiding to dance in a local tavern.

For a local overnight stay, try the **Henry Ludlam Inn,** at 1336 Route 47 in Woodbine, south of the Pine Barrens in Cape May County (609–861–5847). This eighteenth-century B&B has stenciled pineapples, a sign of welcome, above the wainscoting. Shipwrights originally built this home on a site in colonial Dennisville, just south of Woodbine.

REVOLUTIONARY WAR SITES IN CENTRAL NEW JERSEY

The swath through central New Jersey that lies between Philadelphia and New York—now a highly developed segment of the northeastern megalopolis—has always been extraordinarily important, and never more so than during the Revolution. To disrupt British control of this strategic pipeline for troop reinforcements and supplies, Washington made his famous crossing to attack **Trenton.** (For details of the crossing, see Washington Crossing in the Pennsylvania chapter.)

A master of surprise attacks after his experience in the French and Indian War, Washington led his men across the Delaware on Christmas night, while Hessian Col. Johann Rall and his men were imbibing spirits and playing cards well into the night. When Washington and his militia arrived in **Trenton**, the guards on duty were hardly awake or sober. By the time Rall tried to organize his troops, the Americans had the distinct advantage over the Germans, who turned and dispersed, leaving 918 prisoners.

The **Battle Monument** is a 155-foot granite obelisk, located on the site of Washington's clash with the Hessians. The **Old Barracks Museum,** on Barrack Street, is the only British colonial barracks in the United States to survive. Built in 1758, the museum is a natural site for docents in costume to explain life in Revolutionary War days. The enlisted-men's room has bunk beds in three levels. Upstairs, dioramas recall the battles from the Christmas Eve crossing of the Delaware to the Battle of Princeton. The museum is open Tuesday through Saturday 11:00 A.M.–5:00 P.M., Sunday 1:00 P.M.–5:00 P.M. Closed January 1, Easter, Thanksgiving, and Dec. 24 and 25. Call (609) 396–1776 for more information.

"Bagging the fox" was the goal of British General Cornwallis, who considered himself the hunter, but Washington, the "fox," had taken his men to **Princeton** immediately after the Trenton victory. As Washington and his men headed through country lanes toward Princeton, the muddy tracks that had slowed down Cornwallis on his way to Trenton froze with a drop in temperature, so Washington's men were able to make more speed, even though they were exhausted.

They arrived on January 3, 1777, and the Battle of Princeton began. Ahead of the main body of troops, Gen. Hugh Mercer's forces planned to demolish the wooden bridge across Stony Brook on the King's Highway, leading into Princeton. There they encountered two British regiments and were forced to retreat to a position near the Thomas Clark House. General Washington, however, saved the day with his soldiers, who arrived just beyond the ridge on the other side of the Thomas Clark House. "It's a fine fox chase, my boys!" was Washington's call to his men as they rode through British regiments and assured an American victory. He went on to capture the British headquarters at Nassau Hall in Princeton, before moving north to winter quarters in Morristown. At the junction of Nassau, Mercer, and Stockton streets, the marble **Princeton Battlefield Monument** stands tall, with a figure of Liberty encouraging Washington.

The **Thomas Clark House,** in Battlefield Park, is remembered as the place where General Mercer died after being stabbed seven times by British soldiers during the battle. Thomas Clark, a Quaker farmer, had built his home in 1770. Today visitors may tour the house and see its Revolutionary War role in a special exhibit area. Don't miss the Carroll collection of Revolutionary War firearms and weapons. Open 10:00 A.M.–noon and 1:00 P.M.–4:00 P.M. Wednesday through Saturday, 1:00 P.M.–4:00 P.M. Sunday. Closed January 1, Thanksgiving, and Christmas. For more information call (609) 921–0074.

The town of **Princeton** was first called Stony Brook, then Prince's Town by 1724, and finally Princeton. **Nassau Hall** dates from 1756, when it served **Princeton University** (chartered in 1746) as classrooms, dormitories, dining rooms, and professors' quarters. During the Revolution Nassau Hall was occupied by both British and American troops at various times, serving as a hospital and a barracks.

Bainbridge House, at 158 Nassau Street, houses the Historical Society of Princeton, where visitors can get information on walking tours, the university campus, and the Revolutionary War route. Built in 1766, it was the birthplace of William Bainbridge, captain of the USS *Constitution* during the War of 1812. The facade is handsome, with Flemish bond brick. The house is open Tuesday through Sunday noon–4:00 P.M. For further details call (609) 921–6748.

Morven, at 55 Stockton Street, was built in 1751 by one of the signers of the Declaration of Independence, Richard Stockton. When the Continental Congress convened in 1783, Washington, Madison, Hamilton, and others met in this house. At this writing the rooms have not been furnished, but there are plans for period rooms to chronicle three generations of Stockton family life. In 1987 a team of archaeologists began digging for artifacts to shed more light on the past history of Morven. The ongoing dig, which has uncovered foundations and artifacts, is worth a visit. Call (609) 292–6300 to find out more.

Rockingham, also known as the Berrien Mansion, is 5 miles north of town on Route 518. Martha and George Washington lived here in 1783 while the Continental Congress was convening in Nassau Hall. Washington's

"Farewell Address to the Armies" was written in Rockingham, which has been restored with period furnishings. We were told that the site will be moved within a few years, so please call (609) 921–8835 for more information. Rockingham is open from 10:00 A.M. to noon and 1:00 P.M. to 4:00 P.M. Wednesday through Saturday, from 1:00 P.M. to 4:00 P.M. Sundays and closed January 1, Thanksgiving, and December 25.

If you're ready for lunch or dinner, head for the **Nassau Inn,** in Palmer Square (609–921–7500). There are three restaurants in the inn to choose from: The Greenhouse, Palmer's, and the Yankee Doodle Tap Room. Palmer's is the most expensive. The "Nass" is also a great place to stay the night. For eating, **J. B. Winberie** (609–921–0700) is also on Palmer Square. Nearby on Witherspoon Street, **Lahiere's** (609–921–2798) is another traditional restaurant in Princeton noted for its fine French cuisine. The **Peacock Inn,** at 20 Bayard Lane (609–924–1707), dates from 1775 and offers both rooms and gourmet meals.

Washington brought his men north to **Morristown** for the winter and spring of 1777 and again for the winter of 1779–80 because its position in the hills, just west of the New York–Philadelphia track, allowed him to move easily to counter any British movement. The area was agricultural so he knew his men would be fed; and besides that, there were furnaces and forges to make his cannon and ammunition. If you visit in mid-March, you can see a reenactment of Washington's Winter Encampment; in August don't miss the Colonial Country Fair. Call (20l) 539–2085 for more information and exact schedules of events.

The large **Morristown National Historical Park,** the first to be established in the United States, has three units. The **Ford Mansion,** on Washington Place, dates from 1772. General and Mrs. Washington lived here during the winter of 1779–80, along with the owner, recently widowed Mrs. Theodosia Ford and her four children. This large house is furnished with Chippendale furniture. Guided tours are available on the hour from 10:00 A.M. to 4:00 P.M. Across the lawn the **Washington Headquarters Museum and Library** documents the history of the period with an orientation film, exhibits, and an extensive collection of books and manuscripts that relate to the colonial era and the Revolution. The museum is open daily from 9:00 A.M. to 5:00 P.M. The library is only open by appointment. **Fort Nonsense,** on Washington Street, was built by Washington's soldiers during the first encampment in 1777 as a defense for supplies in town. According to the scuttlebutt of the time, probably apocryphal, he had his men build it just to keep them busy—therefore the name.

Jockey Hollow, the third venue of the park, on Western Avenue 5 miles southwest of town, is the principal site of the later encampment. Here the Continental Army spent the miserable winter of 1779–80, enduring a succession of blizzards. Now five reconstructed huts represent the twelve hundred that at one time filled the hollow. Here you can also see the **Wick House,** a restored farmhouse formerly occupied by Maj. Gen. Arthur St. Clair, commander of the Pennsylvania Line. For more information about the park and exact schedules of its events, call (201) 539–2085.

If you're heading west from Morristown and looking for colonial-era accommodations, try the **Inn and Millrace Pond,** just south of Interstate 80 on Route 519 near Hope. This restored 1769 gristmill on Beaver Brook has additional rooms in adjoining buildings and a restaurant. Going north from Morristown you may want to stop overnight at the **Apple Valley Inn,** at the junction of Route 517 and Route 565 in Glenwood, near the New York border. This historic mansion was built in 1831 alongside the Pochuck Brook (201–764–3735).

The long and crucial **Battle of Monmouth** took place in 100-degree heat on June 28, 1778, when Washington's soldiers, arriving from Valley Forge, intercepted Sir Henry Clinton's men as they were retreating from Philadelphia to Sandy Hook. **Monmouth Battlefield,** in **Freehold,** has a visitor center with an audiovisual presentation and an electronic relief map so that you can follow the route of the troops during the battle. The center is open daily 8:00 A.M.–6:00 P.M., Memorial Day to Labor Day; 8:00

Molly under Fire

The heroism of Mary Ludwig Hays, who took over firing her husband's cannon after he was overcome by the heat during the Battle of Monmouth is legendary. She also carried water into the battlefield for the soldiers, a deed that earned her the nickname "Molly Pitcher." As a reward she was presented to General Washington. Look for the marker at Molly Pitcher's Well.

A.M.–4:00 P.M. during the rest of the year. **Craig House,** dating from 1710, is on the grounds; it was built by Archibald Craig for his family of eleven children and used as a field hospital by the British during the battle. Call (908) 462–9616 for more information.

Tennent Church, dating from 1751, stands on a hill that overlooks the battlefield, and you can get your bearings here. The churchyard contains bodies of Americans who died in the Battle of Monmouth. New headstones have replaced the old crumbly ones, including that of Capt. Henry Fauntleroy of Virginia, felled by a cannonball on his twenty-second birthday. British General Sir Henry Clinton stayed at **Covenhoven,** at 150 West Main Street in Freehold. The house has been restored and is open to visitors. For further information call (201) 462–1466.

FOR MORE INFORMATION

New Jersey Department of Commerce and Economic Development
Division of Travel and Tourism
CN826
Trenton, NJ 08625
(800) JERSEY–7 (537–7397)

New York

Historical Introduction to the
NEW YORK COLONY

Henry Hudson

enry Hudson had heard from his friend Capt. John Smith
of Virginia that there was "a sea leading into the western
ocean, by the north of the southern English colony." When
the Dutch East India Company hired Hudson to find a
speedy route to China, the usual European visions of instant wealth through
trade in spices, pearls, and silk were persuasive. Not daunted by three failures
to reach China through a northeast passage, he shifted his attention to finding a northwest passage.

By September 2, 1609, Henry Hudson had reached Lower New York
Bay off Sandy Hook, then sailed up "the great river of the mountain." The
Half Moon anchored when it came to a section that was only seven feet deep.
Hudson surmised that he was on a river and was not going to find the western ocean, but he sent men in a small boat upstream as far as they could go
in half a day; the mate returned and confirmed his suspicions. As Hudson's
dreams of spices and pearls faded, they were replaced by the skins and furs
that the local Indians were willing to trade for trinkets.

Mutiny on Hudson Bay

Henry Hudson set sail on his final polar expedition in 1610, again seeking the tantalizing northwest passage through the bay named after him. After a long winter locked in ice, Henry Greene led discontented crew members in a mutiny and forced Hudson, his son, and some others into a small boat before sailing for England in June of 1611. Hudson Bay must have claimed their lives; they left no trace and were never recovered.

A Promising Start for New Netherland

Adrien Block, a Dutch trader and explorer, sailed into Narragansett Bay and Long Island Sound on the *Tiger* in 1613 and continued up the Hudson to Castle Island, just south of Albany, where he built Fort Nassau. Block returned home with a shipload of furs—a new form of wealth—and a more detailed map. His company, the United New Netherland Company, received the right to make four more trading trips over a three-year period. The West India Company obtained a charter in 1621, and by 1624 its first group of settlers arrived in New Netherland. Most of them were French-speaking Huguenots, called Walloons, who had been persecuted in Belgium and France for being Protestants.

Clearly the Dutch were serious about establishing New Netherland. Three months later forty-five Walloons arrived with cattle, sheep, horses, hogs, and farm equipment. The Manhattan Island colony now numbered about 200 persons. New Amsterdam was planned by West India Company engineers down to the last street, school, and the Dutch Reformed Church. Those persons who were persecuted in other colonies found the New Netherland colony a safe place to settle in the 1630s and 1640s.

From New Netherland to New York

New Netherland was under the control of the Dutch for forty years until Governor Peter Stuyvesant had to turn it over to the British in 1664, beginning a seewaw of trade-offs during the Anglo-Dutch Wars. The change was not unwelcome to the colonists, whom Stuyvesant had annoyed by his autocratic manner and "foul language better fitting the fishmarket than the council board." The Dutch recaptured the colony in 1673, then ceded it to England again the following year in the Treaty of Westminster. King Charles II gave New Netherland to his brother James, Duke of York, hence the name New York.

Profit Lodes: Fur, Lumber, and the Spoils of the Sea

New Yorkers were not slow to exploit the resources around them—an omen of things to come for the Big Apple. Governor William Burnet, who was in control in 1724, decided to garner furs from the western part of the colony by building a trading post at Oswego, an attempt to encroach upon Indian trade with Montreal. Such trade wars sowed seeds of the larger struggle between England and France for control of the vast resources of North America.

Europeans' desire for furs was matched by their navies' insatiable demand for masts. The British Royal Navy turned to the colonies to supply its expanding fleet with spars during the seventeenth and eighteenth centuries. Lumbering had already begun to deplete this new resource in the forests of the upper Hudson valley as early as 1699, and eventually lumbering moved northward into the larger forests of the Adirondacks.

Another "resource"—privateering—was both legal and very profitable for

The Respectable Pirate

Most people would never guess that the most notorious donor to the building fund of Trinity Church, on Wall Street, was none other than William Kidd, better known as Captain Kidd. He was clearly part of the New York establishment until he turned to piracy. The borderline between privateering and piracy was thin indeed, and Kidd had won renown for his success as a privateer. At one point his crew mutinied and he then became a pirate—or so he said. In the midst of his second career, conducted under cover of the first, he was arrested in Boston in 1699, sent to London for trial, and executed in 1701.

New Yorkers during the colonial era. The king of England granted privateer's commissions, and the captain and crew eagerly divided up the spoils of capture. Some privateers became pirates when they seized a ship that belonged to a neutral country: The trick was to off-load the cargo from the seized ship into an unarmed New York ship; faked papers completed the job.

Revolutionary Rumblings and Action

New York's reputation as a haven for Tory sympathizers during the Revolution was not undeserved, but it's only half the truth. For some time before the Revolution, colonists in the ports that were major centers of trade had chafed under English regulations, and New Yorkers often led the dissidents. To make matters worse, the British Army had been headquartered in New York through the long French and Indian War. By its end in 1763, England was trying to get the colonies to help pay for the war that had drained the Royal Treasury. Prime Minister Lord George Grenville started with an import tax, then the infamous stamp tax, and soon followed with a host of other measures designed to wring money from the colonists.

By 1765 New York's merchants had had enough and decided to boycott British goods. The Stamp Act Congress met in the city in October of 1765, with delegates from nine colonies, and proclaimed the right to self-determination in matters of taxation. A group that called itself the Sons of Liberty emerged, and its members had no compunction about using force to obstruct British measures. In 1774, 2,000 Yorkers jumped on board a ship, burst open the tea cases, and threw the cargo in the river.

About a third of Revolutionary War battles were fought in New York, including many important disasters and victories. A major disaster came first with the occupation of New York City, lost to British forces under Lord Howe in a series of battles during the late summer and fall of 1776. Upstate along the water route—the Hudson River, Lake George, Lake Champlain, and the Richelieu River—the record was mixed but better for the patriots. The water route played a major role in crucial campaigns, just as it had in the French and Indian War, because the British wanted to use it to cut the colonies in half.

In a symbolic victory, but almost by accident, Ethan Allen seized Fort Ticonderoga in 1775. The next year Gen. John Burgoyne was more successful, capturing Fort Ticonderoga and moving southward along the water route until he was stopped and finally surrendered at Saratoga, a battle that many regard as the turning point of the war.

Regions to Explore

The New York Colony has been divided into five geographical sections: New York City, Long Island, the Hudson River Valley, Forts in the Adirondacks, and the Mohawk River Valley.

NEW YORK CITY

Recreating the colonial life of New York City is a bit like starting to assemble a jigsaw puzzle that has been in the attic too long, with many key pieces lost by generations of careless children. All the sites of major events are still there—from the first Walloon settlement at the Battery in 1625 to the route of Washington's parade down Bowery Lane when the British finally evacuated the city in 1783—but most have been transformed beyond recognition. New York, more than most large cities of the world, has always used the wrecking ball freely to make room for the new on an island much too small for its ambitions. Finding where the pieces that remain unchanged fit into the cityscape is not an easy task. The best place to start is in museums, where you can see the pattern that no longer exists as a whole.

In **The Museum of the City of New York,** on Fifth Avenue at 103rd Street, you can trace the history of the city from its days as a Dutch trading post. Exhibits include a model of Henry Hudson's *Half Moon,* dioramas that show the age of Dutch exploration in the sixteenth century, Dutch life in New Amsterdam, a model of a Dutch fort, and a scale model of Nieuw Amsterdam in 1660. The English and Revolutionary War Gallery explores the history of New York after the British arrived in 1664. Two Gilbert Stuart portraits of George Washington hang here. The Toy Gallery on the third floor features dolls' houses and furniture that date from 1769. Call (212) 534–1672 for more information.

For further immersion in the colonial history of the city, visit the **New-York Historical Society,** on Central Park West at West Seventh-seventh Street. The American silver collection has pieces from the seventeenth and eighteenth centuries, and period rooms from those centuries are open as well. Don't miss the collection of eighteenth-century toys. The third floor houses American crafts, including weather vanes, pottery, and household utensils. At this writing the museum is closed; potential visitors should call for information on an opening date (212–873–3400).

In the years before the Revolution, wealthy loyalist families often built country estates outside of the "city," as it was defined in the eighteenth century. The remnants that survive have been swallowed by the gargantuan metropolis of the twentieth century, among them the **Morris-Jumel Mansion,** on Edgecombe Avenue at West 160th Street. Roger Morris and his wife, Mary Philipse, built it as a summer house in 1765. Morris had fought under Edward Braddock during the French and Indian War and was also a friend of George Washington. As the Revolution approached, however, the Morris family remained staunch loyalists and fled to England. George Washington used the house as his headquarters during the fall of 1776 as he unsuccessfully struggled to preserve Manhattan from British occupation.

Afterward the house became a tavern; then Stephen and Betsy Jumel purchased it; the lady, a famous beauty remembered for her affairs and later marriage to Aaron Burr, created a new history for the house in the first half of the nineteenth century. Her ghost has appeared quite often on the balcony. Inside, the house still contains its original fireplace in the old basement kitchen. Some of the furniture dates from the Morris period, before the Revolution, and some from the Jumel period. Call (212) 923–8008 to find out more. For visitors unfamiliar with the city a visit via commercial bus tour is suggested.

Another colonial remnant on Manhattan is the **Dyckman House,** at 4881 Broadway at 204th Street, a Dutch colonial farmhouse situated at one time in the midst of 300 acres but now surrounded by apartment houses and shops. The present house was rebuilt in 1783 after the British had burned it during the Revolution. Jan Dyckman emigrated from Germany in 1661 and began acquiring land for the farm in 1677, and it continued in cultivation until 1868. Dyckman's descendants reacquired the house in 1915, filled it with colonial furnishings, family heirlooms, clothes, and toys and then presented it to the city to represent Manhattan's past. The authentic colonial garden was one of two places chosen by Queen Elizabeth to visit on her trip some years ago. The seeds used are traded among historic places. The plants include Thomas Jefferson's hollyhocks. For more information call (212) 304–9422.

The original Dutch settlement of New Amsterdam and its British successor, now Lower Manhattan, flourished for many years, but inevitably most of the buildings have disappeared. Among them the City Hall, begun by the British in 1699 and razed by Americans in 1812, was the center of eighteenth-century political activity in New York—the Stamp Act Congress of 1765, the Congress under the Articles of Confederation from 1785 to 1790, and the inauguration of George Washington as the first President of the United States. Now on the site at 26 Wall Street sits an 1842 Custom House, the **Federal Hall National Memorial,** housing a museum of memorabilia from Washington's inauguration, a copy of the Bill of Rights, and items related to the historic events in the original hall. Call (212) 264–8711 for more information.

Sometimes only a name suggests what was there—Wall Street refers to the wall Peter Stuyvesant built in 1653 as the northern boundary for New Amsterdam—but a few colonial buildings do survive in nearly their original form. The **Fraunces Tavern Museum,** on Broad and Pearl streets, is a reconstructed 1719 structure. Stephen De Lancey built it as his home, then sold it to Samuel Fraunces, who opened it as the Queen's Head Tavern in 1763. Fraunces became chief steward for George Washington, and his tavern was used to commemorate the General's retirement in 1783. Forty-four officers attended the dinner in the Long Room, which is still set for a dinner as it would have been laid out that night. After the dinner Washington walked to Whitehall, took a boat to New Jersey, then went to Annapolis, Maryland, and resigned his commission at a ceremony in the State House.

The museum houses a permanent collection that includes Chinese export porcelain, silver, documents, prints, paintings, maps, clocks, weapons, and sculpture. Special exhibitions are held, as well as a full roster of educational programs on topics such as science and witchcraft in colonial times, Native American fare, eighteenth-century etiquette, New York City folklore, and medicinal plants in colonial America. For more information call 212–425–1778. You can also have lunch or dinner downstairs in the colonial style **Fraunces Tavern Restaurant** (212–269–0144), a favorite spot for those working on Wall Street.

In the shadow of banks at Wall Street and Broadway, you can't miss another important site in colonial New York, **Trinity Church,** now in its third incarnation. The first was built in 1697, when taxes collected from all citizens paid for it. In addition, William Kidd (better known as "Captain Kidd") subscribed heavily to the building fund. In 1705 a large land grant from Queen Anne made the parish one of the wealthiest in the city. The Great Fire of 1776 demolished the church, and it has risen twice since, the last time in 1846. The graveyard contains many beautiful old stones; the oldest is that of Richard Churcher, who died as a child in 1681. The church is open 9:00 A.M.–11:45 A.M. and 1:00 P.M.–3:45 P.M. Monday through Friday, 10:00 A.M.–3:45 P.M. Saturday, and 1:00 P.M.–3:45 P.M. Sunday. Call (212) 602–0872 for more information.

St. Paul's Chapel, on Broadway at Fulton Street, which dates from 1766, resembles St. Martin's-in-the-Fields, the beautiful Georgian church in Trafalgar Square, London. It is the oldest public building in continuous use in Manhattan. After Trinity Church burned in the fire of 1776, St. Paul's became the favorite Anglican church in New York. Perhaps because of its resemblance to St. Martins, British officers worshiped there during the occupation instead of turning it to other uses, as they did with other sanctuaries. It was the site of the service after George Washington's inauguration, and his pew is still preserved. The elaborate tomb of Brig. Gen. Richard Montgomery, who was killed in the Battle of Quebec in December 1775, is on the east porch. Inside, the pulpit, communion rail, organ exterior, and the Waterford crystal chandeliers all predate the Revolution.

Although the Statue of Liberty was not dedicated until 1884, the **Statue of Liberty Museum,** on Liberty Island, offers immigration displays dating back to 1600. The island itself belonged to Isaack Bedloo, a merchant and "select burgher" of New Amsterdam. Bedlow's Island (an anglicization of Bedloo) remained in the family until 1732, when it was sold for five shillings. Bedlow's Island was first a quarantine station, then a summer home in 1746, and became a smallpox quarantine station in 1756, when the disease was raging through Philadelphia. During the British occupation it became a haven for Tory sympathizers, who found safety from the wrath of fellow citizens here. The museum contains personal items brought by immigrants as well as computer data on families that immigrated to the United States. Visitors can look up family names. To find out more information, call (212) 363–3200.

From the outset the growth of the New York port was a paradigm for the commercial expansion of the city. Much of the maritime activity centered on the East River, which provided shelter in the lee of Manhattan and was therefore less exposed to strong westerly winds, flooding, and ice floes than the Hudson River. The **South Street Seaport Museum,** at Fulton and Front streets, has been restored as a port, reflecting life here from early days into the nineteenth century. Although most of the historical buildings that remain date from the nineteenth century, the focus of colonial times on wharves, warehouses, and sailing ships is still here. Visitors may board three vessels, the *Wavertree, Peking,* and *Lettie G. Howard,* as well as explore the former warehouses in the Schermerhorn Row buildings that date back to 1810. There are many shops and boutiques as well as very interesting ships of later dates. Call (212) SEA PORT (212–732–7678) or (212) 669–9400 for more information.

If you have a strong interest in ferreting out other colonial buildings that remain hidden in the jigsaw puzzle of New York City's expansion, head for the other boroughs. In the Bronx you will find the **Van Cortlandt Mansion,** at Broadway and 242nd Street. This house, built around 1748 by Frederick Van Cortlandt, has rich holdings that represent much of the colonial history of New York and many of its key families. Frederick's grandfather came to New Amsterdam in 1638 with the Dutch West Indies Company and built a fortune; the Van Cortlandts established connections through marriage with the Philipse, Jay, Schuyler, Van Rensselaer, Livingston, and Astor families. The house was headquarters for Washington at one point during the Revolution, and he dined there with Rochambeau before leaving for Yorktown. With this history it is not surprising that the house is filled with antiques, portraits, and mementos from the Dutch, British, and American eras of New York life. For more details call (718) 543–3344.

On Staten Island **Historic Richmond Town** at 441 Clarke Avenue in Richmondtown, contains structures from the late seventeenth through the nineteenth centuries spread over ninety-six acres. The Staten Island Historical Society began restoring the decaying village, originally called Cocclestown, in 1939 and moved other houses of historic interest to the site. Of particular interest from the colonial era are the Voorlezer's House (ca. 1696), the Christopher House (ca. 1696), the Treasure House (ca. 1700), the Guyon-Lake-Tysen House (ca. 1740), and the Boehm-Frost House (ca. 1770). The houses are open Wednesday through Friday from 10:00 A.M. to 5:00 P.M., Saturday through Monday from 1:00 P.M. to 5:00 P.M. Call (718) 351–1611 for more information.

If you haven't had enough poking about the boroughs, you can head to Brooklyn to see the 1652 **Pieter Clasesen Wyckoff House,** at Clarendon Road and Ralph Avenue (718–629–5400), or the **Lefferts Homestead,** in Prospect Park, burned by the Americans during the Revolution and rebuilt in 1783 (718–965–6505). The Wyckoff House is open Thursday and Friday from noon to 5:00 P.M., noon to 4:00 P.M. during the winter. The Lefferts Homestead is open noon–4:00 P.M. Wednesday through Saturday, noon–5:00 P.M. Sunday and holidays, April to December; Saturday and Sunday noon–4:00 P.M. during the rest of the year. Closed January 1, Thanksgiving, and December 25.

LONG ISLAND

Long Island has a split image in the twentieth century. At the western end Brooklyn and Queens are part of the city proper, and just beyond lies Levittown, archetype of the suburbia that enveloped everything within commuting distance of the city after World War II and spawned a network of clogged arterial roads. At the eastern end lie the "forks" of Montauk and Orient, lovely sand beaches, the posh Hamptons, and miles of potato fields and vineyards—the unlikely combination of a bucolic retreat for frazzled city folk and a productive agricultural region within easy reach of its markets.

A split between west and east has always characterized the culture of the island. The first settlement came in the east as Puritans from Massachusetts, Connecticut, and England came to towns like Southampton and Cutchogue from 1640 on; the west was in the hands of the Dutch. The split between the two parts was formally recognized in a treaty of 1650 that drew a boundary that stretched southward from Oyster Bay to the Atlantic. That line had no political relevance after the British took over in 1674, but the two cultures, one associated with New York and the other with New England, remained distinct. As the Revolution approached, the west remained Tory in its sympathies, whereas the east was aligned with the patriots.

Thus it may be no accident that a spy ring operated in the old border town, Oyster Bay, during the Revolution. In 1738 Samuel Townsend had bought **Raynham Hall,** on West Main Street in **Oyster Bay,** for his wife, Sarah, and their eight children. Samuel was the town clerk and the justice of the peace; he also controlled a fleet of trading ships, a store, and a small farm. In 1778, when the Queens Rangers, a regiment of Loyalists, took over the town and fortified it against an expected attack by the patriots, Lt. Col. John Simcoe made Raynham Hall his headquarters. The head of George Washington's Culper Spy Ring was Robert Townsend, with the code name of "Samuel Culper Jr." Entertainment of British officers in the house led to the capture of Major Andre and thwarted Benedict Arnold's plan to sell West Point to the British. Visitors can see five colonial and five Victorian period rooms. Call (516) 922–6808 for more information on the house.

George Washington as James Bond

In hatching the Culper Spy Ring, George Washington gave instructions "not to divulge the names of those involved to anyone. . . . Two years ago I sent a captain into New York without adequate preparation and he was caught and hanged."

Long before Long Island's political sympathies were divided by the approaching Revolution, those people living in the east had more affinity with the Puritan culture of Connecticut than with the Anglo-Dutch society of New York. Traces of their New England roots can still be seen in the architecture. The oldest English house still standing in New York State is **Old House,** built in 1649 on the Village Green in **Cutchogue,** on the North Fork. Exposed sections inside the house let visitors see the English Tudor construction. The furniture was all handmade by the early settlers who lived in the area. **Wickham Farmhouse,** also on the Village Green, dates from 1720. Both houses contain colonial furnishings. For details call (516) 734–6532.

Farther east on the North Fork you can take a ferry from Greenport to **Shelter Island,** formerly a peaceful haven for Quakers who were fleeing persecution in New England. The **Havens House Museum,** on South Ferry Road, was the home of James Havens, a member of the provincial congress who lived there beginning in 1743. The pleasant white house, located on a curve in the road, stayed in the family until 1925. It is not open often, and visitors should call (516) 749–0399 to find out more. The site of the first meetinghouse, dating from 1743, is on North Ferry Road next to the present Presbyterian church.

A bit farther along North Ferry Road you'll come to a side road that leads to the **Quaker Cemetery.** A memorial sign at this point states that Nathaniel Sylvester and other Quakers came to Shelter Island to escape persecution. You can drive into the woods to the cemetery, which has a large stone table in the center and a number of grave markers, surrounded by a fence.

Across from Shelter Island on the South Fork, **Sag Harbor's** first inhabitants, the Indians, settled on a site that is now the center of town. They called it Wegwagonock, which means "foot of the hill." Later as the place became a port, there was opportunity to take advantage of commodities going in or out, and by 1707 the British Crown was concerned enough about rum-running to appoint an officer to monitor this illegal activity. Sag Harbor became a major whaling center in the late eighteenth and early nineteenth centuries. The call "Ship in the bay!" almost rings in your ears as you reminisce about the old days of whaling in town.

Visit the **Sag Harbor Whaling Museum** to learn more about whaling and the people who spent their lives in that wild profession, which seems ill-matched with the quietism of Quakers. Inside you'll see rooms chock-full of items brought back from long voyages, made by whalers, or enjoyed by their families back home. Both Sag Harbor and Nantucket inhabitants tried beach whaling, which they learned from Native Americans, long before they ventured onto ships with their equipment. In the museum you'll see a collection of harpoons, ships' logs, and lots of scrimshaw. There are lectures on whaling and a July 4 parade to celebrate whalers. Open 10:00 A.M.–5:00 P.M. Monday through Saturday, 1:00 P.M.–5:00 P.M. Sunday, May to September. Call (516) 725–0770 for more information.

The **Custom House,** on Garden Street, was the home of Henry Packer Dering, who held the post of U.S. Custom Master, in addition to raising nine children in his home. The office contains a history of Sag Harbor as one of two ports of entry—the other was New York. The kitchen must have been warm, with a huge fireplace and an oven for baking bread. For more information call (516) 725–0250. For a memorable meal in Sag Harbor, try the **American Hotel,** on Main Street, a Victorian hotel in the center of town which dates from 1846. Call (516) 725–3535 for reservations.

Near the end of the South Fork, **Second House Museum** (516–668–2428) was built in **Montauk** by 1746 and rebuilt in 1797. The First House, dating from 1744, burned in 1909. The eighteenth-century kitchen is a highlight of the house.

In 1648 settlers purchased **East Hampton** for "20 coats, 24 hatchets, 24 hoes, 24 looking glasses and 100 muxes [an early tool used for making wampum]" from the Shinnecock Indians. The **Osborn-Jackson House,** at 101 Main Street, dating from 1735, contains eighteenth- and nineteenth-century furnishings. Some rooms are used for galleries for temporary exhibits, and quilting and weaving are featured during summer. Call (516) 325–6850 for more details. **Clinton Academy** on Main Street was the first chartered academy in New York State; it opened in 1784 as a preparatory school for boys from New York City. The house now contains East Hampton historic exhibits. It is open 10:00 A.M.–5:00 P.M. Monday through Saturday, July and August; open weekends during June and September.

Across the Green stands **Mulford Farm,** dating from 1680. Here's a house with enough examples from colonial households to illustrate a glossary of domestic practice. A costumed interpreter will take you around the house, telling stories about how people used the items displayed here, as well as bits of gossip about their life-style. Look for the patch of eel grass that protrudes from a hole in the wall up near the ceiling; although it was handy for insulation, inhabitants found that little creatures from the woods would hunker down in it during the winter and then find it difficult to get out. Displays include one on the maritime triangle trade, a chart of cattle ear marks that enabled villagers to find their own animals, and collections of wine bottles, silver, a delft platter in blue and white, and a pewter platter.

This is a great place to recover the feel of everyday life in the colonial era. You can see the "ghosts" of missing parts of hinges where the outline still reveals their original shape. Here's a chance to collect a lot of vanished old words that were once in daily use. Did you know that "spiles" were curly wood shavings used to light the fire? Look for the "fleam," which was used to bleed people who became sick: They had to hold onto a pole so tightly that the veins stood out for bleeding; then blood ran down the fabric wrapped around the pole, and the end result looked like a "barber pole." For more information call (516) 325–6850.

The Bassett House in East Hampton is a nice place to spend the night while you're exploring the Hamptons. Dating from 1830, this B&B has charm and a variety of decoration, including a red-leather barber's chair and a wooden sea chest. Call (516) 324–6127 for reservations.

Sleeping Tight

The rope bed has straw on top and then a feather mattress. There's a twister to crank up the ropes on the bed—hence the phrase "sleep tight."

Southampton began the British heritage of eastern Long Island; English settlers arrived there in 1640 from Lynn, Massachusetts. The Earl of Southampton chose the name, which perpetuates his own, to commemorate the colonization of America.

A murder took place in the **Old Halsey**, on South Main Street; Thomas Halsey, one of the town founders, built this English frame house in 1648. Phebe, the wife of Thomas, was murdered there by Connecticut Indians. It is now the oldest house of its type in the state, with furniture from the seventeenth and eighteenth centuries. Local garden clubs maintain the colonial herb and border gardens. The house is open from 11:00 A.M. to 5:00 P.M. Tuesday through Sunday, mid-June to mid-May. To find out more call (516) 283–3527.

While you are in Southampton, you may also want to visit some of the buildings maintained by the **Southampton Historical Museum and Colonial Society,** at 17 Meeting House Lane (516–283–2494). East of town the **Water Mill Museum** operates a working gristmill from 1644 (516–725–4625).

This interpreter at Old Halsey takes visitors inside and tells them stories about the items found there.

THE HUDSON RIVER VALLEY

The Hudson River Valley has always lured and seldom disappointed visitors. In 1609 Henry Hudson sailed up the Hudson River as far as Albany; although frustrated in his original search for a northwest passage through the continent, he nevertheless returned to Holland with enthusiastic reports of the fertile valley. Soon Dutch settlers and traders led the way for other immigrants to follow. Both traders and settlers, however, had problems with the French, who came from the north, and the Indians, who objected to the snatching of their land. England would not tolerate French claims to land lying between their possessions, especially the vital water routes that linked the Hudson with Lake George and Lake Champlain and westward along the Mohawk. Thus the French and Indian War began in 1754 and continued until 1760, when the French surrendered in Montreal.

Before the Revolution the Iroquois Confederacy also blocked full use of the river: Surrounded by steep cliffs, travelers and settlers along the river valley did not have a chance against attacking Indians. During the Revolution about one third of the battles took place somewhere along the Hudson-Champlain water route, since it was the main channel of communication between Canada and the colonies. Twice the British tried to use it as an invasion route to split the colonies in two, a strategy that foundered only with their defeat at Saratoga in 1777.

In spite of British control after 1674, strong Dutch influence survived in place names, architecture, legends, and customs along the Hudson. For a glimpse of a writer who both mocked and perpetuated that influence, visit **Tarrytown.** Here the Van Tassel family built a stone house of sixteen rooms in 1656; Washington Irving bought it in 1835 and called it **Sunnyside.** Irving made his literary reputation by poking fun at the Dutch who lived along the Hudson River. He published *A History of New York* under the pseudonym Diedrich Knickerbocker when he was only twenty-six; thereafter New Yorkers were tagged as "knickerbockers." *The Sketch Book* portrayed some of the characters that Irving is best remembered for—Ichabod Crane, the Headless Horseman, and Rip Van Winkle.

At Sunnyside Irving planted the wisteria vine beside the front door, and the iron benches on the porch were housewarming gifts. He worked on *The Life of George Washington* in this house and completed it just before his death. Irving's desk and books are still in the study as he left them. The house is completely furnished, with his favorite chair poised by a window for the view and the dining room table set for dinner. Interpreters in costume, including one representing Irving himself, are there to tell visitors stories about Irving. Open daily 10:00 A.M.–5:00 P.M. except Thursday, April to December; weekends in March from 10:00 A.M. to 5:00 P.M. Closed Thanksgiving and Christmas. Call (914) 631–8200 for more information.

Irving is buried nearby in the Sleepy Hollow Cemetery. The **Old Dutch Church of Sleepy Hollow,** on Route 9 in North Tarrytown, dates from the late seventeenth century; the congregation was organized in 1697. Reverend Guiliam Bertholf became its minister and dedicated the church in 1697. The stone building, with about fourteen pews and an old-style high pulpit, sits on a hill. The church is open 2:00 P.M.–5:00 P.M. Saturday and Sunday, June through August. For more information call (914) 631–1128.

Philipsburg Manor, also on Route 9 in North Tarrytown, re-creates the period from 1720 to 1750. Built as a fort in 1682 for Frederick Philipse, it was not a major residence for the family members, who lived in Yonkers, but the house was used as headquarters for his business. After you leave the visitors' center, you will cross a bridge over the river into that earlier era.

Ducks and geese float and dive in the pond, and a mill wheel turns with a splashing sound. The interior is quite spartan, with bare floors and no curtains. In the parlor stands a Dutch cupboard with painted scenes on it. You can visit the gristmill for a demonstration. **Historic Hudson,** which operates Sunnyside, Philipsburg Manor, and Van Cortlandt Manor, offers a variety of programs throughout the year. For more detailed information call (914) 631–8200.

The tavern you might have flocked to for news during colonial times still stands in **Croton-on-Hudson,** farther north on Route 9. In 1697 Stephanus Van Cortlandt's land was chartered by Royal Patent of King William III as the Lordship and Manor of Cortlandt. It included 86,000 acres at the junction of the Croton and Hudson rivers. In 1749 Pierre Van Cortlandt, a grandson of Stephanus, lived in the **Van Cortlandt Manor House** (not to be confused with the Van Cortlandt Mansion in the Bronx). He enlarged the estate by adding a gristmill, store, church, school, and the **Ferry House,** an inn at the ferry crossing. Travelers came here on the Albany Post Road and crossed the river on a family-owned ferry, so local inhabitants frequented the taproom in the inn to get the latest news from peddlers and other more respectable folks from the city. In December Van Cortlandt Manor holds an early English eighteenth-century Christmas complete with carolers, musicians, and a bonfire. Call (914) 631–8200 for more information and a schedule of special events.

For a good meal or an overnight stay, try the **Bird and Bottle** in **Garrison-on-Hudson,** across the river from West Point. The building dates from 1761, when it was known as Warren's Tavern. The inn maintains colonial charm, with wide-plank floors and antique furnishings. For reservations call (914) 424–3000.

West Point, high land that overlooks a narrow section of the river, was occupied by the Continental army from 1778 on because George Washington understood its strategic importance in controlling navigation on the Hudson. The "Great Chain" was draped across the river to stop British ships in 1778, and Washington established headquarters here in 1779. Benedict Arnold commanded the post in 1780 and almost lost West Point to the British by betraying his country to Major John Andre, an aide to Gen. Sir Henry Clinton. Arnold made plans to sell the plans of West Point's fortifications to the British general for £20,000, but the plan backfired when Americans captured Andre near Tarrytown. The incriminating papers, which he had hidden in his boot, were sent to General Washington. Arnold then fled to the British ship *Vulture* and later served in the British army. Andre was tried and hanged as a spy.

At the **United States Military Academy,** stop in the Visitors' Information Center, located just outside the south gate (Thayer Gate) in Building 2607, for information on touring the grounds. Of particular interest is the **Military Academy Museum,** which includes some Revolutionary War exhibits, and the cemetery. A collection of military weapons and relics was begun in 1777, starting with British weapons used during the Battle of Saratoga. The museum is open daily from 9:00 A.M. to 4:45 P.M. Closed Thanksgiving, December 25, and January 1. Call (914) 938–2638 for more information.

Did Washington want to be king? From April 1782 to August 1783, Washington's headquarters were in the **Jonathan Hasbrouck House,** located at Washington and Liberty Streets in **Newburgh.** The army remained encamped at New Windsor while negotiations prior to the Treaty of Paris were in progress. Washington turned down a proposal by some of his men to turn America into a monarchy with him as king. For more information on the house and adjoining museum, call (914) 562–1195.

The First Purple Heart

George Washington originated the Order of the Purple Heart in 1782 in his headquarters in Newburgh. On May 3, 1783, he awarded the first Badge of Military Merit for acts of bravery.

New Windsor Cantonment is located south of Newburgh, on Route 300, in **Vails Gate.** Seven hundred log cabins at one time filled the land that was the site of the last encampment of soldiers during the Revolution. One of the original cabins remains, and some buildings have been reconstructed. Military reenactments take place on the grounds. Call (914) 561–1765 for more information. In the same region, on Route 94, is **General Henry Knox's Headquarters,** representing life in the field for officers. This 1734 house was built as a hunting lodge for John Ellison and is furnished with period pieces. For details call (914) 561–5498.

New Paltz is lucky to have a collection of original buildings and exhibits that tell the story of the Huguenot colony from its birth in France to the burial of the orginal patentees in the local cemetery across the road from the Hasbrouck house. In 1677 the heads of twelve families signed a treaty with the Esopus Indians for land. Four months later Governor Androw issued a patent for the land, named a township, and in 1678 the twelve families arrived to settle on their patent. These settlers had originally come from Lille and Calais, where, as members of a Protestant sect founded by Besançon Hugues, they were persecuted in Catholic France. They had first taken refuge near Speyer and Mannheim, Germany, in the province of *Die Pfalz,* and so named their town New Paltz.

Abraham Hasbrouck, their leader, had been able to obtain a large tract of land for his people, some 39,683 acres. The Esopus Indians advised the twelve families to build on high ground because the river sometimes flooded the valley, so they settled on what is now Huguenot Street. Here they lived in log cabins until 1692, when they had enough stone to build stone houses like their homes in France. The group set up a unique form of government called the *Duzine,* which means "rule of the elders." One representative from each of the twelve families was elected to the Duzine.

The **Jean Hasbrouck House,** one of the six that survive, has his initials carved in stone to the left of the door. In the living room the table is covered with a rug or tapestry, a dulcimer stands in the corner, and a snodnose lamp (very early brass oil lamp) perches on the desk. The kitchen contains furnishings that were in the family before 1700. A large Dutch *kaas* (cupboard) has several delft spice jars on top. The Huguenot Historical Society (914–255–1889 or 255–1660) manages and conducts tours of the houses on Huguenot Street, as well as two others in Gardiner.

Elbows Off the Bar!

There's a bar in the Hasbrouck House that has a little picket fence on top. Could it be so that patrons could not lean their elbows too long as they imbibed? No, it was used to dry clean glasses.

The cemetery contains the graves of all the patentees and their wives. Look for the stone with primitive angels done by a local stonecutter. Another stone embellishes the first letter of each word in the epitaph.

If you're ready for a meal or an overnight stay try the **Beekman Arms,** across the river in **Rhinebeck.** The oldest continuously operating hotel in the country, it dates from 1700 and exudes colonial charm (914–876–4001). Another good choice of more recent vintage is the **Mohonk Mountain House,** on Lake Mohonk in New Paltz, established in 1869. The hotel is set in the midst of mountains beside a crystal-clear lake with views of cliffs (914–255–1000 or 255–4500). Farther north in the Catskills, **Winter Clove**

Inn, at Round Top, has been in the same family for five generations (518–622–3267).

Does a thirteen-sided barn arouse your superstitious curiosity? The **Bronck Museum** in **Coxsackie** has one, as well as a house built by Pieter Bronck in 1663 and other buildings from 1663, 1685, and 1738. Inside, period furnishings fill the houses, as well as an art collection. The unusual thirteen-sided barn has a center-pole construction; there's also a more conventional Dutch barn. Call (518) 731–8862 for more information.

The **Van Alen House,** on Route 9H in **Kinderhook,** may have been inhabited by the model for one of Washington Irving's characters, Katrina Van Tassel. The 1737 farmhouse, built of red brick, reflects typical Dutch architecture, with gables, separate outside doors for each room, and a steep roof. Inside a collection of delft and Hudson Valley paintings, period furniture, and eighteenth-century decorative arts is on display. For more information call (518) 758–9265.

The Shaker Museum and Library in **Old Chatham** preserves the history of one of the communities Mother Ann Lee began founding in 1774. Their members lived by Millennial Laws that prescribed celibacy, separate schools for boys and girls, and communal ownership of property. The Shakers were noted for the elegant simplicity of their architecture, the design and workmanship of their furniture, and the high quality of all their products. This museum has exhibits of Shaker furniture, a blacksmith shop, a schoolroom, a collection of tools, nine rooms that contain furnishings of that time, and a craft gallery. Call (518) 794–9100 for more information and a calendar of special events that includes an herb fair on Memorial Day weekend and an antiques festival in August.

Rensselaer was founded in 1631 by Dutch settlers, and **Fort Crailo** dates from 1705. The Continental army had its cantonment in the field here in June 1775, and it served as headquarters for General Schuyler during the Revolution. Today the fort contains the Museum of Dutch Culture in the Hudson Valley, a fine place for an overview of Dutch settlements and culture in the area. To find out more call (518) 463–8738.

Philip Van Rensselaer built **Cherry Hill** in **Albany** in 1787. Fortunately, because the house had never been sold outside the family, all of the Van Rensselaers' personal belongings and clothing were saved. Visitors enter the house through an orientation room, where a family tree outlines the generations of those who lived in the house. Philip and Maria Van Rensselaer were the first to do so, beginning in 1787. They were merchant farmers who also owned a town house on North Pearl Street, and they assured the continuity of the family with thirteen children. The house is open Tuesday through Saturday from 10:00 A.M. to 3:00 P.M., and Sunday from 1:00 P.M. to 3:00 P.M., February to December. Closed all major holidays. Call (518) 434–4791 for more information.

Want to see a tomahawk's grisly gash? The **Schuyler Mansion** has one that may be genuine. The house, built in 1761 by Philip Schuyler, a Revolutionary War general and later a U.S. senator, sits high on a hill and at one time had a fine view of the river; it is also called The Pastures, and two acres of lawns and gardens affirm the name. As you tour the house, look for the gash on the stair rail, which may have been made by an Indian tomahawk. Tories tried to kidnap General Schuyler during the Revolution, but he heard of their plot in advance and was able to hire guards to thwart the attack. The legend of the gash involves one of Schuyler's daughters, who had run downstairs to grab her baby sister from the cradle and was on her way back up with the baby when, reportedly, an Indian tomahawk thrown at her missed and hit the stair rail. The house is furnished with period furniture, including some from the Schuyler family, Chinese export porcelain, delftware, and English glassware. Open 10:00 A.M.–5:00 P.M. Wednesday through Saturday, 1:00 P.M.–5:00 P.M. Sunday, mid-April to October 31. Closed Columbus Day. For more details call (518) 434–0834.

Accommodations in old buildings is scarce in the Albany area, but colonial ambience has been re-created in a few, including the **Desmond Americana,** at 660 Albany-Shaker Road. The hotel looks like an eighteenth-century village with a variety of building styles (518–869–8100). The Desmond offers fine dining with colonial flair in the dining room and lighter meals in another restaurant. As an alternative, try the **Inn at the Century,** at 997 New Loudon Road, which features fine dining in a colonial atmosphere (518–785–0931). For the treat of dining in an eighteenth-century Shaker farmhouse try **Olde Shaker Inn,** 1171 Troy-Schenectady Road, Latham (518–783–6460). Another fine restaurant is **Olde Dater Tavern,** Route 9, Clifton Park (518–877–7225). This building was on the property by 1760, built by William Schouton; George Dater bought it in 1848.

FORTS IN THE ADIRONDACKS

A key site to visit for Revolutionary War lore is the **Saratoga National Historical Park** in **Schuylerville,** located 12 miles southeast of Saratoga Springs and 8 miles south of Schuylerville on the Hudson. The visitors' center has an audiovisual presentation, a museum, and a special lecture series available on topics such as Archaeology at the Saratoga Battlefield. In addition you can watch eighteenth-century crafts demonstrated by guides in period costume. The visitors' center is open daily from 9:00 A.M. to 5:00 P.M. Closed January 1, Thanksgiving, and Christmas.

The battles that are regarded as the turning point of the Revolution took place here during the fall of 1777, when Gen. Horatio Gates led the Continental army to victory over Gen. John Burgoyne's invasion force. The latter had come down the Champlain-Hudson waterway in his attempt to split the colonies in two, overrunning Fort Ticonderoga, Fort George, and Fort Edward. In early September Burgoyne crossed the Hudson and moved down the west bank toward Saratoga. Benedict Arnold attacked the British at Freeman's Farm on September 19, 1777, and was relieved of his command by Gates for refusing to wait. Arnold stayed near his troops, however, and reappeared in his general's uniform on October 7, riding his white horse at the head of his men. His courage enabled the Americans to take a redoubt located in an important position.

Burgoyne's men were demoralized and hungry because the commissaries had not given them provisions, and they were now badly outnumbered by Continental forces. Having lost 1,200 men and surrendered 5,700 more, Burgoyne retreated to Schuylerville in a downpour, with his men slogging through the mud. On October 17 he signed the thirteen articles of surrender. When news of his defeat arrived in France, French military advisers decided to side with the Americans.

Apart from its historic interest, the well-maintained battlefield park is now a marvelous site for outdoor recreation. You can take a self-guided tour on foot, by car, by bicycle, or on cross-country skis in winter. Along the route you will see markers for **Freeman Farm, American River Fortifications, Chatfield Farm, Barbers Wheatfield, Balcarres Redoubt, Breymann's Redoubt,** and **Burgoyne's Headquarters.** Call (518) 664–9821 for more information.

Schuyler House, on Route 4, is on the southern edge of **Schuylerville.**

Gen. Philip Schuyler lived in this pleasant estate setting during summers; the original house was burned by the British during the Saratoga battles but was rebuilt in 1777 after the victory. The front door lock, with its enormous key, is one to admire, and the front parlor contains original Schuyler wallpaper. The house is open 9:00 A.M.–5:00 P.M. Wednesday through Sunday, Memorial Day to Labor Day; 9:00 A.M.–5:00 P.M. Saturday and Sunday from Labor Day to September 30. To find out more call (518) 695–3664.

The 1877 **Adelphi Hotel,** at 365 Broadway in **Saratoga Springs** (518–587–4688) is a favorite gathering place for locals. Guest rooms are decorated with antiques in a Victorian setting. The **Gideon Putnam Hotel** (518–584–3000) is located in Spa State Park. The building dates from 1930 and has elegant public rooms. **Union Gables,** 55 Union Avenue (800–398–1558 or 518–584–1558), is a restored 1901 Queen Anne home, now a B&B.

You might also want to stop for the night at the **Wayside Inn,** at 104 Wilton Road in nearby **Greenfield;** call (518) 893–7249 or fax (518) 893–2884 for reservations. Built in 1786 by Capt. John St. John, the inn was once a station on the underground railroad. The inn is furnished with pieces from the Middle East, Europe, and the Far East. The Center for Arts in the Country is on the grounds; visitors can see demonstrations by a resident potter, candle maker, and more.

Restaurants in Saratoga Springs include **Olde Bryan Inn,** 123 Maple Avenue (518–587–2990), which is in one of the oldest buildings in town. The **Inn at Saratoga,** 231 Broadway (518–583–1890) is another favorite. The **Old Firehouse,** 543 Broadway (518–587–0047), is, as you might expect, in an old firehouse and offers a casual atmosphere. The **Springwater Inn,** corner of Union and Nelson avenues (518–584–6440), reminds one of turn-of-the-century Saratoga.

The Battle of Saratoga stopped Burgoyne in an invasion that would have been impossible without his control of two portages farther north. One was the Great Carrying Place at **Fort Edward.** Boats came up the Hudson River to this head of navigation, situated below a series of falls, and then had to be pulled out and portaged overland to Lake George, and then again over a shorter portage to Lake Champlain. Since these two portages were both essential and vulnerable links in the great waterway from New York to Montreal, it is no accident that Fort Edward and Fort Ticonderoga were built to guard them in the French and Indian War and later rebuilt and occupied during the Revolution.

If you've ever had a yen to become involved in an archaeological dig, you can do it on Rogers Island at Fort Edward. The barracks area on Rogers Island has been left in overgrowth to protect artifacts and historical data that are still preserved underground. British soldiers lived here in large barracks, some as long as 300 feet. Some officers, provincial soldiers, and Rogers Rangers often lived in small huts. Here the dig site promises to yield traces of their lives and provide some answers to fascinating historical puzzles. One of the discovered huts was framed by wooden planks with hand-wrought nails and two fireplaces. Soldiers lost or dropped items in and around the hut: Lead pieces from their bullets, coins, a silver shoe buckle, nails, and stoneware have been found. Outside the hut a valuable "midden," or trash dump, yielded all sorts of items such as musket balls, buttons, a Spanish coin, pottery, animal bones, and two pig skulls. In addition excavators found a Native American layer, with arrowheads and spear points, that could date back to 2000 B.C. For more information on Rogers Island Archaeological Site call the Fort Edward Chamber of Commerce at (518) 747–3000. To find out more about the Rogers Island Archaeology Field School call (518) 793–4491, extension 236.

Maps show a hospital near the end of Rogers Island where 892 men were placed in quarantine to die of smallpox. Duncan Campbell, of the Black Watch at the Battle of Ticonderoga, was in the hospital after he was wounded in his arm in the great battle on July 8, 1758. He died on July 17 and is now buried in **Union Cemetery** in Fort Edward. He lies next to Jane McCrea, a young local girl who was shot and scalped near Fort Edward on July 26, 1777, while on her way to meet her fiancé, a British officer.

The Fort Edward Historical Association, located in **Old Fort House Museum,** has a collection of books that contain information on Jane McCrea, a piece of her shawl, a number of objects made from the wood of the tree near where she died, an 1834 print of her scalping, and a large painting of the scene of her death. Dr. Asa Fitch collected information on Jane McCrea from a number of settlers in the area.

The Old Fort House, which dates from 1772, is one of the oldest frame buildings in this area. During the Revolutionary War both sides used the house as a headquarters. Benedict Arnold, Henry Knox, and John Burgoyne all lived in the house at different times, and George Washington had dinner here in July of 1783. The Fort Edward Historical Association displays artifacts from the colonial period up to the present day. One of the rooms in the house has a rocking horse and old school desks.

Jane McCrea

There are many accounts of the death of Jane McCrea, who lived with her brother, John McCrea, on the west bank of the river several miles below Fort Edward. She was engaged to a British officer, David Jones, and went to the home of Mrs. McNeil in hopes of getting from there to the British camp. Some say that the two ladies were sewing outside near the house when a group of American soldiers went by; then musket shots were heard, and the Americans ran by, with Indians from Burgoyne's army right behind them.

The women went into the house and down a trapdoor into the cellar, along with a young man. Indians raised the trapdoor and hauled everyone out by the hair. Miss McCrea was placed on a horse (sent for her from David Jones) by Indians who thought they would get a reward for bringing her to the camp. Another group of Indians came along, and in a tussle over the bridle of her horse, one of the Indians shot her.

Baldwin Barn is part of the museum and displays artifacts from the colonial period that were unearthed in the early 1900s by people who were digging to build their homes. Among the artifacts are spades, hinges, axes, wedges, hooks, iron rings, a claw hammer, eighteen-, eight-, and four-pound cannonballs, a bullet mold, buckshot, a French musket, lock flints, a powder horn, a compass case, ice creepers for walking on ice, and more. We were fascinated by the collection of commemorative spoons, including one given by Dr. Little with a pill on the bowl of the spoon. For more information call the Old Fort House Museum (518–747–9600).

The next crucial link in the Hudson-Champlain waterway is **Lake George,** with a spectacular mountain and island topography that stretches 32 miles from Lake George Village in the south to Ticonderoga in the north. This scenic area lends itself to long walks, and if you go for a couple of miles along the waterfront and into **Lake George Battlefield Park** in the early morning, it's not hard to imagine a French bateau, a British sloop, or an Indian canoe appearing through the mist, for this lake, now a magnificent and peaceful playground, was torn by campaigns throughout the French and Indian War and the Revolution, with major and subsidiary forts at either end as the prize.

The bottom of the lake is littered with the remains of amphibious expeditions—bateaux used as troop transports, gunboats, and sloops—that were sunk between campaigns to keep them out of the hands of the enemy. The most spectacular find of recent years is an almost perfectly intact *radeau* called the *Land Tortoise,* a large gunship accidentally sunk in deep water by the British in the fall of 1758. Surveys by nautical archaeologists have been completed and the radeau is now protected in an underwater preserve, accessible only to controlled diving. You can find out more about its story on the surface by visiting the **Lake George Historical Association,** in the Old Courthouse on Canada Street (518–668–5044). Certified divers who want to view the *Land Tortoise* must register at Encon headquarters on Long Island. Call the New York Department of Environmental Conservation (518–897–1200) for further details.

On shore, controlling the portage at the head of the lake was so important that Gen. Jeffrey Amherst began work on Fort George in 1759 to replace Fort William Henry, which had been destroyed by the Marquis de Montcalm two years earlier. As he prepared to move north against the Lake Champlain forts, he urgently needed a base here and completed two or three acres of foundation within three weeks. A provincial officer reported that a month later "the Walls [are] about 14 Feet thick Built of Stone & Lime." In 1767 someone reported that Fort George was a "redoubt amounting to 12 guns, about 200 yards from shore, and some barracks." Although more work was done during the Revolutionary War, only one bastion was ever completed.

This bastion is now buried in the woods that have overgrown the cleared land in Battlefield Park. Fort George is located east of the old fort (now the restored Fort William Henry) on higher ground, farther from the lakeshore. The rock foundation remains today, and visitors can clamber up the high side and look out over the park (but please don't move or remove any of the ruins, which are currently being surveyed in an archaeological field school similar to the one in Fort Edward). Call (518) 793–4491, extension 236 for more information about the field school.

During the 1760s Fort George was used as an artillery depot, but no more construction occurred in the short interval between two wars. At one point early in the Revolution, Ethan Allen and other colonists weighed the strategic importance of three strongholds that guarded important waterways: Fort George located at the head of the lake, Crown Point at the narrows of Lake Champlain, and Fort Ticonderoga at the portage to Lake George. He was determined to win all three for the patriots.

In July of 1775 Philip Schuyler came to Fort George and was shocked to find the garrison in disorder. He cleaned it up and set firm regulations before leaving for Ticonderoga. Schuyler also built vessels on Lake George for use in his attack on Canada, as well as for defending the lake against British invasion.

By 1780 the British had learned the cost of neglecting the Hudson-Champlain waterway and were again on the move, in collaboration with Indians, raiding and burning as they went. A force under Maj. Christopher Carleton took Fort Ann, raided Saratoga, and then came north again to the Fort Edward–Fort George Military Road. Capt. John Chipman and sixty Vermonters held Fort George until they heard reports of Indian snipers near **Bloody Pond,** on the Old Military Road (now Route 9) south of Lake George, the site of a ferocious engagement during the French and Indian War. When Capt. Thomas Sill and forty-eight men left the fort to go out after the snipers, they ran right into Carleton's men, and only thirteen escaped. With a meager twenty-five left to stand against more than ten times that number in Carleton's force, Chipman was forced to surrender the fort, which was then burned. This was to be the last significant battle during the twenty-five years when military action swirled around Lake George.

The first had occurred at the outset of the French and Indian War. Sir William Johnson defeated the French Baron Dieskau in the Battle of Lake George on September 8, 1755, and began the construction of **Fort William Henry** before the month was out. The site, on a 50-foot bluff that looks up the lake to the Narrows, had obvious military advantages and still has one of the most spectacular views in the East. Although the fort was ready and manned by the campaign season of 1756, no major battle occurred until the following summer.

In June of 1757 the Marquis de Montcalm's troops moved south from Ticonderoga, by land and on the lake, for a sustained attack. As Montcalm bombarded the fort, Col. George Munro realized that explosions within the fort had ruined his northwest bastion and that he had lost many guns; also, he did not receive the reinforcements he expected from Fort Edward, and so he finally chose to surrender to Montcalm. Under the terms of the surrender, Munro's men had permission to leave with "honors of war" and their personal possessions to head for Fort Edward.

What happened next, the infamous massacre of Lake George, has been told and retold ever since by James Fenimore Cooper in *The Last of the Mohicans* and by historians who provide varying accounts. At the sound of a war whoop, the Indians in Montcalm's forces ambushed the surrendered men, women, and children and slaughtered them. Ens. John Mayhem called it a "hell whoop" in a poem he wrote seven months later. From the perspective we are most familiar with, the Indians violated the rules of war and abandoned minimal human decency, but there is another side of the story. The terms of surrender denied the Indians the war rights of their own culture, leaving them without the booty that was their only pay.

Montcalm burned Fort William Henry when he abandoned it after the battle, but it has been reconstructed on some of the original foundations. Now demonstrations bring alive eighteenth-century means of defending its walls. A grenade throw is one, complete with commands and marching into position before lobbing it at the enemy. The musket-fire demonstration, using a Kings Arm or Land pattern musket, includes the complicated steps that precede firing. A careless man could lose it all—"lock, stock, and barrel"; if he did not follow the procedure, he could "go off half-cocked" or be injured by "a flash in the pan." The most dramatic demonstration is a single shot fired from an eighteen-pound cannon located on a bastion facing Lake George. One interpreter had just explained the firing procedure to our group as another placed powder down in the barrel. He tamped it down, lit the fuse, and the blast followed in a few seconds. Heads swiveled all along Beach Road, which runs in front of the fort. Standing near the cannon, we had our ears covered, but gunners in the 1750s could lose their hearing after repeated doses of firing. Cannons could recoil as much as 5 feet, requiring a crew of eight to push them back into the port, and they often blew up, killing and wounding the crew with fragments of flying iron.

After the demonstrations you can wander in the courtyard, where there is a well that is said to contain a payroll of gold and silver or the bodies of soldiers—who knows? A crypt nearby formerly held the bones of soldiers, most of whom died of diseases such as smallpox, which ravaged men living in cramped and often unsanitary quarters. A number of skeletons that had been displayed for years were reinterred during a respectful ceremony in 1993.

Walk down into the dungeon where soldiers were imprisoned. You'll find a model of a prisoner in a tiny cell, a pillory, and a guard room. A fireplace from 1755 is still here. A long ramp leads from the courtyard down into the underground powder magazine, where kegs of black powder were stored. Curtains made of leather were hung here and kept wet with water to defuse sparks.

Museum exhibits are found in each of the buildings that line the courtyard. The James Fenimore Cooper exhibits are in the West Barracks. Walk

Visitors always cover their ears as the cannons are fired at Fort William Henry.

up the steps to see living areas of soldiers as they were in 1755. The North Barracks and East Barracks house more of the collection. Don't miss a display of Jack Binder's work. He created illustrations for comic books such as Marvel, and his original paintings include a collection of figures of soldiers during the 1750s. Open daily 10:00 A.M.–5:00 P.M., May to October, 9:00 A.M.–10:00 P.M., July to August. For more information call Fort William Henry at (518) 668–5471 or 668–3081.

You can also take tours of the surrounding area, choosing from those that explore history, culture, science, or nature. Call **Overlook Tours** at (518) 793–7914 for more information. Lake George's historic hotels, which began appearing as early as 1800, have all burned down, but visitors can stay in resorts along the west shore between Lake George Village and Bolton Landing. One of our favorites is **Canoe Island Lodge** (518–668–5592), a rustic resort with many activities and a private island for excursions on the lake. Another is **Dunham's Bay Lodge** (518–656–9242) on the quieter, mostly residential east side of the lake. Interesting accommodations can also be found in Warrensburg at the **Merrill Magee House** (518–623–2449). This nineteenth-century Greek Revival house serves gourmet meals. Peek into the ladies' room for a surprise in the bathtub.

For a special treat book in at the **Omni Sagamore Resort,** an elegant replica of one of many hotels that lined the lakeshore during the last half of the nineteenth century. The original Sagamore Hotel opened in 1883 and burned ten years later; the second building opened in 1894 and lasted until 1914, when it also burned. The third, built in 1922 and restored and expanded in the early 1970s, is undisputed queen of the lake in appearance, amenities, and resort facilities of all kinds. The complex now includes a conference center and restaurants at every level, from a casual poolside setting to the formal and sophisticated Trillium, as well as dinner cruises on board a replica of earlier lake streamers. Call (518) 644–9400 or (800) 358–3585 for more information.

Horns of Plenty

At the north end of the lake, Robert Rogers and his Rangers—after whom special forces were named in World War II—watched the French while they were building **Fort Ticonderoga** (then named Fort Carillon) from a little distance away in 1757. Rogers sneaked up close and managed to kill a number of French cattle, then left a note on the horns of one of them: "I am obliged to you, sir, for the repose you have allowed me to take. I thank you for the fresh meat you have sent me. I will take care of my prisoners. I request you to present my compliments to the Marquis de Montcalm."

The crucial battle for **Fort Ticonderoga** the following summer went entirely to the French defenders and took a terrible toll on the massive British expedition sent to retake the lakes after the defeat at Fort William Henry the year before. British and provincial forces, under Gen. James Abercromby, numbered more than 15,000, the largest force ever assembled in North America up to that time, and they proceeded 32 miles up Lake George from the ruins of Fort William Henry in an armada of more than a thousand bateaux and whaleboats. This invasion force outnumbered the French defenders four to one, but it was to fail utterly through a series of military blunders.

British delay for a day and a half after landing gave the French time to build a clever and impregnable outer breastwork from felled trees with sharpened branches. When the fighting began on July 8, 1758 Abercromby ordered repeated infantry assaults against this deadly abatis of trees without bringing up cannon to bombard it, leading to the fruitless slaughter of large numbers as each assault was cut down by French fire. When the Black Watch of the 42nd Highlanders finally pushed their way past part of the abatis to the enemy, there was no support left, and 647 were felled by bayonets and bullets. It is said that one courageous piper continued to play after he had lost his leg. The King's Royal Rifle Corps also fought valiantly before Abercromby called for retreat—too late. That retreat back to Lake George was disorderly and frenzied, with many dead and wounded left behind. The next day the Marquis de Montcalm and his men buried the dead, both French and British, before celebrating a victory that had repelled the British invasion of Canada.

Fort Ticonderoga is also remembered for another famous raid—hardly a battle—at the beginning of the Revolution. After the news of fighting in Massachusets reached Vermont colonists who were enmeshed in land disputes with the colonial government in New York, their discontent finally erupted in a plot hatched by Ethan Allen. As leader of the Green Mountain Boys, Allen combined with Col. Benedict Arnold to capture Fort Ticonderoga in a surprise raid on the morning of May 10, 1775. Because there were few boats available, only eighty-three men and some officers had been ferried across to a site north of the fort before daybreak.

Allen and Arnold—an uneasy combination of egoists—nevertheless cooperated momentarily in the raid. With dawn coming on they could not wait for more reinforcements and so began the charge on one of the gates. According to Allen, "My party who followed me into the fort, I formed on the parade in such a manner as to face the two barracks which faced each

Ethan Allen's Toast

The irrepressible Ethan Allen burst into an oratorical toast that celebrated the raid on the day of its success: "The Sun seemed to rise that morning with a special luster; & Ticonderoga and its dependencies smiled on its conquerors, who tossed about the flowing bowl, and wished **SUCCESS** to Congress & the liberty and freedom of America."

other. The garrison being asleep, [except the sentries] we gave three huzzas which greatly surprised them." Allen and Arnold then ran up the steps and pounded on the door of the commanding officer, Captain Delaplace, ordering him to surrender the fort. Some say that Arnold yelled, "Come out, you damned old rat!"

This extraordinarily important fort has been restored through the efforts and imagination of members of the Pell family, who have owned the fort and surrounding grounds since 1820. Excavation took place carefully as artifacts such as firearms, buttons, pottery, china, cutlery, cannonballs, grapeshot, tomahawks, axes, sword blades, keys, and more were found. Visitors may walk through the museum to see priceless relics such as the breastplate of a French suit of armor from the eighteenth century, as well as a blunderbuss used by Ethan Allen.

Don't miss the silver bullet with a real, if dreadful, spy history. Sir Henry Clinton had given this hollow bullet, with instructions inside, to a messenger on his way to Burgoyne just before the Battle of Saratoga. When he was captured, the messenger swallowed the bullet and refused to take an emetic until his captors threatened to "rip his bellie" to get it. Then he disgorged it, swallowed it again, and was forced to disgorge it for the second time. After all of that he was hanged as a spy.

A colorful diorama in the museum features the Black Watch regiment at Ticonderoga, wearing their red jackets and kilts. The Black Watch collection includes a sporren, clay pipes, a broadsword, a highland pistol, buttons, bagpipe ferrules (which go around the pipes), and a camp axe.

Visitors can also see George Washington's spurs; swords belonging to Israel Putnam, Arthur St. Clair, and Alexander Hamilton; Benjamin Warner's knapsack; miniature toy soldiers that belonged to Montcalm as a child; and a punch bowl that belonged to Sir William Johnson. An original American flag, possibly made by Betsy Ross, is also here. The library contains letters, diaries, papers, and books from the period. Upstairs there's more to see, including a boatswain's pipe from the World War II aircraft carrier U.S.S. *Ticonderoga*. Look for the photograph of Stephanie Pell Dechame as a young girl, cracking a bottle over the bow to christen this memorable ship.

From the Place d'Armes, or central parade ground, visitors can walk into the cellar of the East Barracks to see two gigantic ovens that formerly were used to bake bread for the entire fort. The West Barracks contains an armory in its cellar. Guns are displayed within the time periods of their use. Swords are also in the collection.

Activities at the fort include cannon firings, fife-and-drum performances, reenactments, and a tattoo in summer. The cannons on display along the south curtain wall include some late seventeenth-century and early eighteenth-century Spanish models. The British government sent fourteen 24-pounders to Ticonderoga. Twelve French bronze guns and mortars are here along with some from other countries. The fort is open daily 9:00 A.M.–6:00 P.M. in July and August; 9:00 A.M.–5:00 P.M., May 7 to the day before Labor Day and September to October 16. Call (518) 585–2821 for more information about the fort and a current schedule of activities.

For accommodations and fine dining in the southern Adirondacks, try the **Balsam House** (518–494–2828 or 494–4431), on Friend's Lake near Chestertown. This nineteenth-century inn has rooms furnished with antiques and "grandmother" spreads. Just before this book went to press, a fire destroyed part of the Balsam House; it will reopen in late 1995 or in 1996. Also noted for cuisine on Friend's Lake is the **Friend's Lake Inn,** which dates from the 1860s. Some of the rooms have a lake view; during winter there is an extensive system of cross-country trails for skiing (518–494–4251). Farther north in the High Peaks region, the **Bark Eater,** on Alstead Mill Road in Keene, was a stagecoach stop. Rooms are furnished with country antiques, and there is a sleigh bed (518–576–2221). **Mirror Lake Inn,** at 5 Mirror Lake Drive in Lake Placid, dates from before the turn of the century. An 1895 grandfather clock was saved from a 1988 fire (518–523–2544).

THE MOHAWK RIVER VALLEY

Branching off the Hudson just north of Albany, the Mohawk River was a gateway to territories in western New York. Algonquian Indians first lived on the land that is now **Schenectady;** then the Iroquois battled their way to the site. In 1661 Arendt Van Curler bought 128 square miles from the Indians and banded together with fifteen other families to form a patroonship, where they built homes within a stockade for protection against the French. The 1662 stockade is bounded by State, Front, and Ferry streets and Washington Avenue. By 1690 there were sixty houses and 400 persons living in the stockade.

On February 8, 1690, the people in the stockade were unaware of danger that was imminent. During January 114 Frenchmen and 96 Indians began an arduous trek by snowshoe from Montreal to Albany. The Indians, however, preferred to attack Schenectady instead of Albany. At a fork in the road (now Schuylerville), the choice was made, and the French and Indians turned toward Schenectady. When they were within 6 miles of the stockade, they stopped and talked with four squaws, living in a bark hut, who told them all they needed to know. Advance scouts found that there were only two sentries and both of them were snowmen! They reached the stockade, found the gate open, and sneaked around the houses in silence until a "single hideous and horrendous warwhoop" broke the silence and began the slaughter of inhabitants. Sixty persons were killed, twenty-seven were taken captive, and many others fled into the woods and died from the cold after their homes were burned. Prudently the few survivors built the **King's Fort** after the massacre, where they lived along with their Mohawk allies. After that miserable night, the stockade prospered through the colonial era and is still a visible remnant of the past today.

A new audiocassette, which accompanies a map of a walking tour, affords the easiest way to see the stockade. Called "Colonial Schenectady: An American Crucible," the cassette opens with colonial-style music and dialogue read by actors who play the parts of local people. The cassette and tape player are available from the Schenectady museum, Nott Terrace Heights (518–382–7890). There are twelve stations, sounded by a bell at the end of each. The first one reminds visitors of the massacre, with stories told of that terrible night by three residents. The second station is the site of the **Glen House,** on Washington Avenue, a typical Dutch homestead owned by the "foremost trading family" in town. After the bell sounds, continue on around the walking tour to the rest of the stations. It's nice to see lovely eighteenth-century homes and buildings still standing and lived in today.

Take some time to visit the **Schenectady County Historical Society,** at 32 Washington Street, which maintains a museum of exhibits from the area, a library, a genealogical collection, and files of many historical documents. The walls are hung with fascinating paintings of the stockade. Don't miss the "senility cradle," a bed for older family members, used for John Sanders II, who was born in 1757. Visitors will be interested in the needlework collection, complete with pincushions, lace, and Dutch bobbin lace from the seventeenth century. Toys and dolls are on display from several centuries. There's a "Liberty flag" and arms of the Revolutionary War upstairs. Indian artifacts include arrowheads, a 1720 axe head, Iroquois dolls, and a beaded bag. Call (518) 374–0263 to find out more.

The society also conducts a "walkabout" of the stockade every September. One house has a tablet inscribed as follows: "Oldest house in City built before 1700 by Hendrick Brouwer, a fur trader, who died here 1707. Sold 1799, to James Rosa, Superintendent of Mohawk and Hudson Railroad, 1831." Hendrick's wife was Maritie Borsboom, and they were married two years after the massacre. The house passed on to several sons and grandsons, also named Hendrick. A grandson of the first Hendrick served in the Revolutionary War as a member of the Albany County Militia. James Rosa, who bought the house in 1825, was descended from Heymense Rosa, who came to the new world on the *Spotted Cow* in 1661. The house is not open except during special house tours, but it is lovely to look at from the outside.

For lunch or dinner stop at the **Glen Sanders Mansion** in **Scotia,** just across the river. Some sections of the mansion date from the 1680s, including the Deborah Glen Room, which has original woodwork, mantel, and door paneling. The Great Room, now the main dining room, was built in 1713. An interior Dutch door is original, as are the small paned windows. The colonial style menu is nicely presented; call (518) 374–7262 for reservations.

West of Schenectady, the Mohawk River provided navigation all the way to Rome and, after portages, farther to Lake Ontario. Sometimes regarded as the heartland of New York State, the Mohawk River Valley has been called the "Leatherstocking" region because woodsmen in the region wore leather leggings to protect themselves from branches and thorns while blazing trails through the forest. The Mohawk River has a source just north of Rome and cuts a path through the Alleghany Plateau. Long before the Erie Canal was dug, it provided the closest connection between the Hudson River and the Great Lakes through Oneida Lake and the Oswego River.

Mohawk Indians lived here as "Keepers of the Eastern Door." These aggressive members of the Iroquois Confederacy protected the central part of New York State. Many of them prospered by farming their fertile land. As fur trade grew, the valley absorbed increasing numbers of men who transported pelts by canoes, bateaux, and barges. German settlers arrived in the 1720s, building sturdy stone houses as a deterrent against fire during Indian raids. In 1755 the British built a series of forts to interrupt French trade along this crucial route.

Rome was originally called "the carrying place" by the Indians; there is a portage right in the center of town. **Fort Stanwix,** also in the center of town, was built in 1758 during the French and Indian War, then abandoned until 1776, when American soldiers rebuilt it. As you look at this star-shaped structure, you can imagine the defenders inside, using a pattern of cross fire to mow down attackers.

In the visitors center you can watch a film that sets the stage for the twenty-one tense days during the siege of August 1777. By withstanding the siege the defenders, under Col. Peter Gansevoort, delayed the British Gen. Barry St. Leger and thus prevented him from reinforcing Gen. John Burgoyne at the Battle of Saratoga. You can walk all around inside the fort to see the officers' quarters; the men's quarters, where as many as ten men would sleep in one platform bed; the Surgeon's Day Room, where soldiers would go for possible amputation, bleeding, or quarantine; and the museum, which houses a number of artifacts found during the archaeological dig. Open daily from 9:00 A.M. to 5:00 P.M., April to December. Closed Thanksgiving and Christmas. Call (315) 336–2090 for more information.

Can you imagine anyone continuing to direct a battle while sitting under a tree with a shattered leg? Gen. Nicholas Herkimer did just that on **Oriskany Battlefield,** on Route 69, the scene on August 6, 1777, of one of the bloodiest battles of the Revolution. The British had planned a three-part invasion to take control of New York State from the north, west, and south. Gen. Barry St. Leger, who was to travel from Oswego down the Mohawk Valley to Albany, found a strong opposing force when he got to Fort Stanwix. When the resulting siege continued without resolution, Herkimer gathered 800 Tryon County militia and set off to Fort Stanwix. St. Leger sent troops, including some Mohawk Indians, to ambush Herkimer. General Herkimer's horse was shot and his leg was shattered, but he continued to direct the battle while sitting under a beech tree, resting on his saddle and smoking his pipe. Eventually the British withdrew, and the patriots returned home. General Herkimer traveled by raft down the Mohawk River; his leg was amputated when he reached home in Little Falls, and he died eleven days later. The Oriskany Monument marks the site where patriots fought and held the British force. To find out more call (315) 768–7224.

Farther west on Lake Onondaga, just north of Syracuse in **Liverpool, Sainte Marie among the Iroquois** is a living-history museum on the site of a 1657 French mission. In 1639 Jesuits came from Quebec to the area, but their first mission burned. By 1656 fifty Frenchmen had left Quebec for Onondaga, where they built another mission. They had been invited by the Iroquois nation to found a permanent settlement, which would enable them to travel to nearby villages and teach Christianity. They worked for about two years, building a stockade, chapel, workhouse, garden, and barn. Within twenty months it was abandoned after the Onondagas, members of the Iroquois nation, warned them to leave. They traveled in four canoes of Algonquian pattern and four of Iroquois, plus two other boats for shooting the rapids.

Today visitors will see a reconstructed mission that depicts mission life in the year 1656. Costumed interpreters speak to visitors as though they were living in the seventeenth century. One of them told us that they all expected to serve in the mission for life, that they worked very hard, and that they were tired enough to sleep when the sun went down. One said that after his ordination two years ago, he came to the New World. The blacksmith was at work with his bellows; he described his difficult journey along the St. Lawrence River—down small rivers and across the portages—before he arrived at the mission. The carpenter was making a wooden shoe called a *sabot,* as well as wooden nails and trunnels. As he worked, we talked with him and found that he viewed the Dutch as heretics who spread lies among the Iroquois. One mission resident, who was cooking over the fire in the huge fireplace, said that he especially liked eating the flesh of a beaver, which swam like a fish. The mercenary soldier told us that he enjoyed hunting and fishing, as well as woodworking, and did not believe in being idle. He hunted deer, elk, wild cows (moose), squirrels, rabbits, and beaver. Some of the inhabitants talked about leaving because they felt uneasy. The mission presents special programs throughout the year. Regular hours are 10:00 A.M.–5:00 P.M. Tuesday through Sunday, May to December; 10:00 A.M.–5:00 P.M. Wednesday through Sunday during the rest of the year. Closed January 1, Thanksgiving, and December 25. For further details call (315) 453–6767.

When it's time to stop for the night, try **Lincklaen House,** at 79 Albany Street in **Cazenovia.** Dating from 1835, this house features Williamsburg chandeliers, delft tiles, and fireplaces (315–655–3461). In **Skaneateles** try **The Sherwood Inn,** at 26 West Genesee Street. It was built in 1807 as a tavern; the guest rooms contain period furnishings (315–685–3405).

FOR MORE INFORMATION

Department of Economic Development
Division of Tourism
One Commerce Plaza
Albany, NY 12245
(800) 225–5697 (fifty states and possessions)
(518) 474–4116 (overseas and Canada)

Pennsylvania

Historical Introduction to
PENNSYLVANIA

First Swedish Settlers

One can imagine the astonishment in the minds of the first settlers of New Sweden when their governor, Johan Printz, arrived on shore in 1643. Pieter de Vries wrote that he was "a man of brave size, who weighed over four hundred pounds." The Indians called Johan Printz affectionately "big guts" or "big tub"; in addition, he was rumored to eat, drink, and swear more than most others in Gustavus Adolphus's army. His professional capacities, however, were just as great as his physical ones; John Winthrop reported that Printz was an experienced leader with "furious and passionate" ideas who pursued his projects vigorously.

Printz was aggressive in making changes, such as planting tobacco as a cash crop instead of corn, which could be purchased from the Indians. Printz set about eliminating English settlers as he allied himself with the Dutch. He built forts on Delaware Bay and on the Schuylkill in order to have control of traders and Indians who passed by.

Wars in Europe led to Sweden's neglect of the New Sweden colony, and no supply ships were sent for years. Consequently the colony ran out of trinkets and goods, which were used for bartering with the Indians, and, more important, the flow of immigrants to America stopped. Finally in 1653 Printz decided to return to Sweden with his family.

Enter William Penn and the Quakers

William Penn left the Church of England and became a Quaker, to the consternation of his father, who had been a principal admiral under Cromwell and later Charles II. Lady Penn reported that the Admiral "had intended to make William a great man, but the boy would not hearken." While at Christ Church, Oxford, Penn reacted against the "debauchery" of the students and refused to wear the obligatory gown or attend chapel, thus earning expulsion for nonconformity in 1662. Four years later, at the age of 22, he became a Quaker and wrote a book that led to his imprisonment in 1668. While in the Tower of London he wrote his most famous book on Quakerism, *No Cross, No Crown.*

After serving his time until 1681, Penn was granted land from Charles II, who wanted to pay his debt to Penn's father, Admiral Sir William Penn. Penn knew that the king could refuse his request for a grant because he was a Quaker, but because of his debt to the admiral, the king could also reasonably grant his request. Later Penn wrote that "the government at home was glad to be rid of us at so cheap a rate as a little parchment to be practiced in a desert three thousand miles off."

Penn and Charles II had been friends since they were young, and Penn kept up the friendship even though he and the king disagreed fundamentally on the amount of royal power and religious tolerance that should prevail in the colony. The territory, originally destined to be called Sylvania ("woods") was named Penn's Woods, or Pennsylvania, to honor Penn's father, the admiral, at the king's request. Penn was required to pay two beaver skins to Windsor Castle every year.

The main body of Quaker immigrants arrived between 1680 and 1710, with religious convictions that led them to establish a peaceful life of coexistence with the Indians in Pennsylvania. Not only would they buy land from the Indians, as Roger Williams did in Rhode Island, but they would treat the Indians as equals, without distinctions of rank or race. Such convictions were anathema in Britain and in most of the American colonies. As Quakers in England, they had refused to sign the Toleration Act of 1689, which includ-

A Quaker Come-on

Penn appealed to potential settlers by reporting that "the Air is sweet and clear, the Heavens serene, like the South-parts of France, rarely Overcast. . . . Of Fowl of the Land there is Turkey (Forty and Fifty Pound weight) which is very great; Phesants, Heath-Birds, Pidgeons and Partridges in abundance." Passengers would pay "six pounds per head for masters and their wives, five pounds for each servant, and fifty shillings for each child under ten, suckling children traveling free. Each passenger could ship one chest free and additional freight at forty shillings per ton. Land was to be granted outright, except for a small quitrent reserved for the security of the title."

ed an oath of allegiance to the Crown, and in Wales persecution drove their meetings underground. Welsh immigrants continued to arrive as late as 1720, and Dutch Quakers came in 1682 and settled in Germantown.

A Haven for Nonconformists

Penn's founding principles of tolerance encouraged immigration. Nonconformist religious groups had been persecuted by Protestants as well as Catholics in Europe, but they were welcomed in Pennsylvania. Other displaced Germans arrived in 1708 and continued streaming in until 1750. A century of European wars had devastated their lands, with army after army looting and destroying villages and crops. In 1714 Mennonites, called the Amish, arrived in Berks County. Later Moravians arrived from Poland, Hungary, and Czechoslovakia, and some moved north to found the town of Bethlehem.

The Scotch-Irish immigration began in 1717 and continued until 1776. In the earlier years some of these people had come to escape religious persecution. Later, those who had been tenant farmers arrived because "rack-renting" had driven them off the land they worked. In this growing practice landlords raised the rent when long leases expired, and tenants who could not afford more expensive short-term leases lost their homes.

Kudos for the Work Ethic

Thomas Penn, one of William Penn's sons, wrote:

This province has for some years been the asylum of the distressed Protestants of the Palatine, and other parts of Germany, and I believe it may with truth be said that the present flourishing condition of it is in a great measure owing to the industry of these people; and should any discouragement divert them from coming hither, it may well be apprehended that the value of your lands will fall, and your advances to wealth be much slower; for it is not altogether the goodness of the soil, but the number and industry of the people that make a flourishing country.

Quaker Pacifism and Preparations for War

Pennsylvania settlers were not very concerned with the French and Indian War, although the French had forts on their land in the west, and Quakers were against involvement in any war. Benjamin Franklin told them that they would have to give up their religious principles to the extent of passing a militia bill, and some Quakers compromised by withholding their votes. The militia bill of 1755 did not change much, and, in fact, the Privy Council vetoed it much later, but it broke Quaker dominance of politics in the colony.

Residents quickly formed militia groups and built stockades for defense against attack by the French and Indian forces. In between the stockades, they built blockhouses at 5-mile intervals as refuges for families scattered throughout the countryside. Such elaborate defenses were never needed during this war, fought mostly north and west of the the heavily settled territories, but they did prepare Pennsylvanians for the wider war that would begin to engulf them two decades later.

Battles for Independence

To combat the Declaration of Independence and suppress rebellion in the colonies, the British planned a tripartite strategy. First they wanted to seize major commercial centers like New York and Philadelphia and continue moving along the coast to the south. Second they planned to move down Lake Champlain and Lake George into the Hudson Valley, which would seal off New England from the rest of the colonies. Third, they planned to capture the less populous and more isolated colonies in the south.

Capturing Pennsylvania was part of the first plan. The British occupied New York in September 1776, then spent the winter in New Jersey on the way to Philadelphia. Gen. William Howe arrived in Maryland in August 1777, and by September met George Washington's forces west of Paoli. Patriots had already removed important government records and the Liberty Bell by the time Howe marched into Philadelphia.

Washington and his troops settled in for a dismal winter at Valley Forge, but by March they were in training under Baron von Steuben, who was able to transform diverse and undisciplined groups of citizens into well-trained soldiers. When the British left Philadelphia, Washington's army followed and won the Battle of Monmouth in New Jersey. Involvement did not stop in Pennsylvania, however; during this war, unlike the previous one, there were battles all over the state.

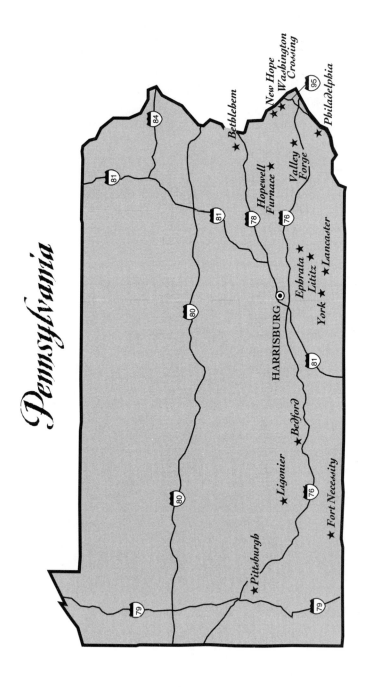

Regions to Explore

The Pennsylvania Colony has been divided into four regions. Philadelphia and the area around it played an important role in the colonial period and the Revolution. Southeastern Pennsylvania—including the Brandywine Valley, Bucks County, Bethlehem, and Valley Forge— became the center of many ethnic settlements as more immigrants came from Europe to escape religious persecution or war. The Susquehanna River Valley, in south-central Pennsylvania, became the destination of later groups of immigrants, who moved farther from the coast. Western Pennsylvania was the center of military action during the French and Indian War because the French, British, and Colonials all wanted control of the forts in this area.

PHILADELPHIA

Although the birth of the United States took place in Philadelphia on July 4, 1776, when the Declaration of Independence was adopted in Independence Hall, William Penn had started the process almost one hundred years before that.

Penn's 1682 "Frame of Government" provided freedom for its people: "Any Government is free to the People under it where the Laws rule, and the People are a Party to those Laws." A council was elected by the freeholders; they drew up laws with the governor and sent them for approval to the popular assembly. The Privy Council in London approved laws made in Pennsylvania.

Penn signed the Charter of Privileges in 1701, just as he was leaving for England. This new constitution provided for an assembly of four men from each county; they were elected yearly by the freemen. The governor and his advisory council made up the executive branch. The assembly comprised the legislative branch, and the judicial branch consisted of judges and officers elected within each county. This tripartite division of powers was a powerful model for the U.S. Constitution that emerged from the convention in Philadelphia in 1787.

Today visitors can take a walking tour of the "most historic square in America," in **Independence National Historic Park.** The National Park Visitor Center, at Third and Chestnut streets, offers a film for orientation as well as consultation with park rangers on your choice of tour. Call (215) 597–8974 for more information.

The **Liberty Bell Pavilion,** on Market Street between Fifth and Sixth Streets, is an appropriate place to begin. The bell is housed in a glass-enclosed structure so that visitors can see it twenty-four hours a day. Records from January 1750 detail the need for a steeple superstructure as a "suitable place thereon for hanging a bell." It arrived on board the vessel *Myrtilla*, but as luck would have it, the bell cracked the first time it was rung. The bell was recast in 1752, and because the tone was not ideal, it was recast again. During the Revolution the bell resided in Allentown, where it stayed until June 1778. Then it was placed in the tower until 1846 and later moved several more times until our bicentennial year, 1976, when it reached its present pavilion. This peripatetic bell deserves a rest!

Independence Hall, on Chestnut Street, dates from 1732 and has been renowned since as the site of many crucial events in United States history. Here the Second Continental Congress met; George Washington was appointed commander-in-chief of the Continental army; the Declaration of Independence and the Articles of Confederation were adopted; and the end of the Revolutionary War was announced in the hall. The Rising Sun chair in the Assembly Room was used by George Washington at the Constitutional Convention in 1787. Look for the silver inkstand on his desk, used by signers of both the Declaration of Independence and the Constitution.

As you tour Independence Hall and the other colonial sites in Philadelphia, think of the oppressions by the Crown that led to its appropriate name—Independence Hall. The Stamp Act angered those who lived in the eastern part of Pennsylvania because it required the payment of a tax on all legal documents, newspapers, and almanacs. Consequently lawyers took matters into their own hands, believing the law to be unconstitutional, and decided not to use stamps, and merchants agreed to refuse British goods. As a result the Stamp Act was repealed in 1766, but the string of offensive and costly regulations and taxes on the colonies did not stop. In 1767 the Townshend Acts became law: Taxes were to be collected on imported glass, lead, paint, paper and tea. This money was supposed to pay for British officials living in America, but in fact it financed more officials who were needed to enforce the new rules.

Construction of Independence Hall was begun in 1732. The bell arrived in 1752 and was finally installed in 1753.

By 1770 the Townshend taxes had been dropped on all items except tea, after much protest. Parliament rescinded the export tea tax in 1773, and, at the same time, the East India Company decided to sell tea at bargain rates. Suspicious colonials in Philadelphia printed sheets from "The Philadelphia Committee on Tarring and Feathering." When the expected ship, the *Polly*, arrived in Chester, her captain was escorted to a town meeting, where it became obvious that he was to sail his unloaded ship out of the bay.

In 1774 the First Continental Congress met in Philadelphia, where the colonists agreed to a trade boycott enforced by the Continental Association. The Second Continental Congress met in 1775 and asked Pennsylvania for six companies of riflemen to travel to Boston. A Pennsylvania navy was formed, and defenses were built along the Delaware River.

These preparations for passive and armed resistance put Pennsylvania in the forefront of colonial rebellion. This sentiment was further fanned in January 1776, when Thomas Paine published the first edition of *Common Sense* in Philadelphia, which openly encouraged independence. The new Constitution of 1776, written by radicals, created an independent Commonwealth of Pennsylvania, and it also gave more power to freemen rather than restricting it to men of property.

Benjamin Franklin was eminent among those associated with Philadelphia during the Revolution. He came to town in 1723 and, within five years, had bought a printing business, then a newspaper, *The Pennsylvania Gazette,* and, at the age of twenty-seven, began to publish *Poor Richard's Almanack.* **Franklin Court** is the site of his home, which was razed in 1812; the National Park Service has conducted archaeological digs to uncover the foundations. Visitors can see the restored office of his grandson's newspaper, as well as demonstrations of eighteenth-century printing and bookbinding. There's also a colonial post office, where you can buy commemorative stamps.

After you've visited some of the many sites in the Park, you may want to have lunch in **City Tavern,** at Second and Walnut Streets, a reconstructed eighteenth-century tavern that serves colonial-style food. For reservations call (215) 923–6059.

Society Hill is a historic district near the river that has been meticulously restored by its residents. Walk on the cobblestone streets past Georgian and Federal houses, lighted by Franklin lamps. **Head House Square** was originally a marketplace, dating back to 1745; now renovated, it is a red-brick collection of shops and restaurants. For a good meal try **Dickens Inn,** on Second Street between Pine and Lombard. The original name, **Harper House,** dates from 1788. Call (215) 928–9307 for reservations.

There are many interesting historic accommodations in town, including the **Thomas Bond House,** at 129 South Second Street, near Walnut. This 1769 house was the residence of a Philadelphia physician and is within Independence National Historic Park (800–845–2663 or 215–923–8523; fax 215–923–8504). The **Independence Park Inn,** 236 Chestnut Street, was built by a dry goods merchant named John Elliot and is listed on the National Register of Historic Places (215–922–4443; fax 215–922–4487). The **Society Hill Hotel,** 301 Chestnut Street, was built as an oyster house in 1832 (215–925–1394).

SOUTHEASTERN PENNSYLVANIA

Southwest of Philadelphia, in Delaware County, a landscape of rolling hills and fertile valleys surrounds tributary rivers that flow into the Delaware. Among them the lovely, meandering **Brandywine River** attracted settlers in colonial times and artists in the twentieth century, including the remarkable Wyeth family. Today visitors enjoy the valley and its galleries and flock to the many historic B&Bs and inns for a peaceful country weekend. One such inn is **Fifer's Folly** (215–353–3366), at 3561 North Providence Road in **Newton Square,** a 1715 Quaker farmhouse next to Ridley Creek Park. Not far from Longwood Gardens is another inn, **The Flower Farm,** at 453 Bayard Road in **Kennett Square.** Built on land once owned by Penn and sold to Price in 1700, this 1828 stone farmhouse is surrounded by eight acres of terraced gardens (215–444–5659).

At the center of the valley is **Chadds Ford**, now home to the Brandywine River Museum, which is loaded with Wyeth paintings. Its history stretches much further back, however, and visitors who come in September will enjoy a colonial experience in **Chadds Ford Days.** Call the Chadds Ford Historical Society at (215) 388–7376 for more information and a schedule of events. In the village the **Brandywine River Hotel,** on Route 1 and Route 100, offers comfort within a colonial setting (215–388–1200). **Chadds Ford Inn,** also located at the juncture of routes 1 and 100, is a pleasant place for a meal and has an interesting colonial history. It was built for Francis Chadsey in the early 1700s as a home and later used by his son, John, as a tavern. John's nephew, Joseph Davis, entertained American officers here just before the Battle of Chadds Ford on September 11, 1777. Call (215) 388–7361 for reservations.

The valley has not always been tranquil. **Brandywine Battlefield** is the site of an encounter between Washington's soldiers and a British force in September 1777. The visitors' center offers a slide narration and exhibits. You can visit the farmhouse that the Marquis de Lafayette used, and his carriage is also here. Next door is the house Washington stayed in for two nights before the battle. Unfortunately Washington was unable to stop Gen. William Howe's advance after many attempts, but neither was Howe successful in crushing the less experienced American militia. Washington reported to Congress as follows: "Notwithstanding the misfortune of the day, I am happy to find the troops in good spirits; and I hope another time we shall compensate for the losses now sustained." Open daily 9:00

A.M.–8:00 P.M. during the summer; 9:00 A.M.–5:00 P.M. Tuesday through Saturday, noon–5:00 P.M. Sunday during the rest of the year. For more information about the battlefield, call (215) 459–3342.

North of Philadelphia, **Bucks County** has been significant in American history for more than 300 years. You can stand on the spot where William Penn built his original summer mansion and visit a rebuilt **Pennsbury Manor,** at 400 Pennsbury Memorial Lane, near **Morrisville.** James Harrison began to build the house in 1683 while carrying on correspondence with Penn, who had returned to England. Penn moved into the house in 1700. The original house was destroyed, but the present buildings were reconstructed according to old records. Rooms are furnished with period pieces; one armchair belonged to William Penn. The house is open Tuesday through Saturday from 9:00 A.M. to 5:00 P.M. and Sunday noon–5:00 P.M. Call (216) 946-0400 for further information.

For ovenight accommodations try the **Brick Hotel** (215–860–8313), on the corner of Washington Avenue and State Street in Morrisville. This 1746 hotel was once owned by Joseph Archambault, an aide to Napoleon Bonaparte; and, of course, George Washington slept here. Another good choice is **Ye Olde Temperance House,** at 5–11 South State Street, the site of temperance gatherings in 1772; call (215) 860–0474 for reservations.

If you have the time, take a stroll around nearby **Falsington,** where some of the houses date back 300 years and are still lived in by descendants of the first settlers. The **Burgess-Lippincott House** (1780) has a remarkably handsome doorway. The 1685 **Moon-Williamson House** is one of the oldest houses in Pennsylvania that still stands on its original site. Two fieldstones on the **Schoolmaster's House** bear the date 1758. Call (215) 295–6567 for more information about the historic houses in Falsington.

Washington Crossing Historic Park, which is seven miles south of **New Hope,** memorializes one gleam of hope in the early, desperate days of the Revolution. At that stage George Washington worried about the morale of his men, who were near starvation after the winter of 1776; he knew that a victory was needed more than ever before. Fortunately Washington was experienced in handling riverboats; only the weather could defeat his daring plan to surprise the British at Trenton. If the river froze, all would be lost, for the ice would not be thick enough to support troops, horses, and heavy equipment. On Christmas Day 1776 the password among the troops was "Victory or Death" as they prepared to advance into a dark, gray, ice-strewn river. As they walked toward the boats 200 yards north of McConkey's Ferry, men without adequate shoes left blood on the snow. They embarked at 6:00 P.M. to ensure the six hours of darkness needed to get all the troops and equipment across. The weather turned from snow to sleet, slowing their progress through the ice floes, but they made it—and surprised the Hessians who were still groggy from Christmas celebrations.

A reenactment of this crossing is held at 1:00 P.M. on December 25 every year. Visitors shiver as they imagine the pain of that night. Within the park you can see the famous painting *Washington Crossing the Delaware,* by Emanuel Leutze, in the **Washington Crossing Memorial Building.** The **Thompson-Neely House,** dating from 1702, was the site of important strategic meetings to prepare for the Delaware crossing. Open daily 9:00 A.M.–5:00 P.M. Park buidings are open 9:00 A.M.–5:00 P.M. Monday through Saturday, noon–5:00 P.M. Sunday. **McConkey Ferry Inn** has been restored; Washington is thought to have dined here before the crossing. Call (215) 493–4076 for more information. You can have a picnic in one of several pavilions in the park or try **The Blue Ram,** near McConkey's Ferry. For reservations call (215) 493–1262.

Farther upstream the charming town of **New Hope** is a favorite haunt of antique hunters—you may not find anything from the colonial era, but then again, you might. The **Van Sant House** (1743), on Mechanic Street, was peppered by British shelling in 1776, and grapeshot can still be seen in the attic walls. The **Parry Mansion,** on Main and Ferry streets, built in 1784 by Benjamin Parry, a wealthy lumber mill owner, is open to visitors. The New Hope Historical Society has restored this stone house and furnished the rooms in different styles, including that of the 1775–1800 period. Call (215) 862–5148 or 862–5652 to find out more.

There's a concentration of inns and B&Bs in this retreat for artists, writers, and city folk on getaway weekends. The **Centre Bridge Inn,** on Route 263 right on the river, has nine guest rooms decorated in colonial style (215–862–2048 or 862–9139). **Hotel du Village,** on the corner of North River Road and Phillips Mill Road, is located on part of a tract of land granted to the Ely family by William Penn in the seventeenth century (215–862–9911 or 862–5164). The **Inn at Phillips Mill,** on North River Road, was originally a stone barn, dating from 1750 (215–862–2984). **Logan Inn** (215–862–5134), at 10 West Ferry Street, dates from 1727, and—no surprise—George Washington did visit here. **Pineapple Hill,** at

1324 River Road, dates from 1780; the ruins of a stone barn have been preserved to frame the swimming pool (215–862–9608). The **Wedgwood Inn,** at 111 West Bridge Street, was built in 1870 over the ruins of an earlier structure where Gen. Alexander Lord Stirling encamped in December 1776; call (215) 862–2570 for reservations.

Farther north on the Lehigh River, a tributary of the Delaware, **Bethlehem** was founded on December 24, 1741, when Count Nicholas Ludwig von Zinzendorf celebrated a communion service with a group of newly arrived Moravian settlers in their first house. This Protestant sect began with the teachings of Jan Hus during the fifteenth century in Czechoslovakia, and some of its members came to America to spread the gospel among the Indians. The Moravians brought their traditions with them, and lighted Advent stars, with twenty-six points, still beam from almost every front porch during Advent. Their distinctive Christmas music combines voices, organs, woodwinds, strings, and brass.

Moravian community "putzes" (miniature nativity scenes) are displayed in a sound-and-light show during the Christmas season. The putzes are assembled by volunteers, who do everything from arranging the tiny wooden and ceramic figures and gathering pine boughs for decorations to crawling under the stage to install the lighting. Visitors enter a darkened and quiet room, waiting for the spotlight to illuminate a scene, while unseen narrators tell the various parts of the nativity story; each scene fades into the next to create a continuous, living experience. For more information call 610–868–1513.

Traditionally on December 1 the city is suddenly illuminated with thousands of white lights on the north side and with colored lights on the south side. An 81-foot-high star gleams from the top of South Mountain. Guides in Moravian dress lead tours through the historic district.

The **Gemein Haus,** the oldest building in town (1742) and the first place of worship in Bethlehem, was a communal house that held all fifty-six settlers. The original concept of the church was its communal plan—all worked for the church and lived in separate "choirs" according to sex and age. By 1700 this plan was no longer needed, as families chose to build their own homes. The Gemein Haus is now the Moravian Museum. Saal Hall, the original place of worship, is within the house; services were conducted two or three times every day. A 1530 Nuremberg Bible is on display there. Count von Zinzendorf's room is intact, complete with a brown leather chair and ornate black wrought-iron hinges on the door. Quilts, like the one attributed to "Christine," were made from scratch; members of the community sheared the sheep, dyed the wool, carded the yarn, and wove the cloth. The music room—an important place in Moravian culture—contains an old flute, trombones with their cases, and a serpentine-shaped wooden horn covered with leather. Open Tuesday through Saturday from 1:00 P.M. to 4:00 P.M. Call (215) 867–0173 for more information about this extraordinary communal house.

The **Old Chapel,** the second place of worship in Bethlehem, dates from 1751. Movable wooden benches provided flexibility for arranging the congregation. An open Bible stands on a table where Indians were baptized during the early years of the settlement. Our guide explained the color code for ribbons on women's caps: red was for little girls, burgundy for teens, pink for those confirmed, blue for married women, and white for widowed women. All wore a gray jacket, gray skirt, gray woolen cloak, and white apron.

Private residences include the Sisters' House (1744), where single women lived and worked, and the Widows' House. The Brethren's House for single men, dating from 1748, is now part of Moravian College's music department.

Overnight accommodations in town may be found in the **Hotel Bethlehem,** at 437 Main Street, a renovated historic hotel (215–867–3711). Also **Wydnor Hall Inn,** on Old Philadelphia Pike, which dates from 1810, is now fully restored and open as a European-style inn (215–867–6851). Stop for a meal at the **Sun Inn,** at 564 Main Street, where you can dine in a colonial setting in a 1760 building (215–974–9451).

Not far away to the east, in **Kintnersville,** stands the **Bucksville House B&B,** at 4501 Durham Road and Buck Drive; the house dates from 1795, when it was built for Capt. Nicholas Buck (215–847–8948). To the west just beyond Allentown, an old stone-and-timber bank barn, in a bosky field (see sidebar, p. 278), has been converted into an elegant inn, the **Glasbern,** on Pack House Road in **Fogelsville.** The open barn is now the Great Hall, used for fine dining, with the orginal hand-hewn beams, shale walls, and farmers' ladders, which formerly led to the haymows, left intact. Guest rooms are located in the Carriage House, Farmhouse, Gatehouse, and Barn; they are also built with old beams and wide-board floors, and most have Jacuzzis. Ask for a map of surrounding walks. For reservations call (215) 285–4723 or fax (215) 285–2862.

Bank Barns and Bosky Fields

A bank barn was built into the side of a hill. Sometimes the lower area contained a spring and could therefore be used to cool milk and other foods. A "bosky" field was no farmer's dream, since it was filled with trees and bushes that had to be removed.

The area just west of Philadelphia is rich in colonial history. If you want to see where George Washington really did sleep, go to the **Valley Forge National Historic Park;** his canvas tent, 53 feet in circumference, was used as both office and bedroom. A good place to begin is the Visitors Center, on Route 23 and Outer Line Drive, where you can get an overview and begin self-guided driving tours to many sites in the encampment during the winter of 1777–78. There are also many reenactments and special events during the year, including the Marching of the Continental Army in December and French Alliance Day in May. Call (215) 783–1077 for more information and schedules.

If Washington had his way, the troops would have spent that winter of 1777–78 in Wilmington, Delaware, where equipment and supplies could be brought by water and the men could be housed comfortably. The Pennsylvania legislature, however, demanded that the troops remain out in the country to prevent British foraging parties from ransacking homes and villages. Washington knew from his own experience what their misery would be. Accounts written by men on the march describe the snow and cold, the lack of food, and their fatigue and utter despair. The winter encampment was supposed to rest the troops, encourage them to stay the winter, and then train them. As the winter progressed, many men died and many more deserted and returned home. Yet the men who did stay learned military discipline and gained confidence from their new skills, which raised their morale.

The **Isaac Potts House** was Washington's headquarters through much of that miserable winter. The **Dewees House,** the lodging of another officer, and adjacent huts for his lifeguards are also in this particular group of buildings. Visitors can explore the sites of earthworks where cannons were centrally placed, with men behind to load and fire them. **Artillery Park** contains a concentration of cannon; artillery was stored here, ready for use.

Washington Memorial Chapel contains stained-glass windows that depict the history of the founding of the United States. The bell tower features a fifty-eight-bell carillon. The chapel is open daily from 9:00 A.M. to 5:00 P.M. To find out more call (610) 783–0120.

The **Museum of the Valley Forge Historical Society,** which is located adjacent to the chapel, contains a collection of articles saved from the terrible winter of 1777–78. William Trego's famous painting *The March to Valley Forge* is here. Call (215) 783–0535 for more information.

There are many historic places for overnight stays and meals in the Valley Forge region. The **Kennedy-Supplee Mansion Restaurant,** on Route 23, is a restored mansion owned by Valley Forge National Historic Park (215–337–3777). To the east in **Gwynedd** is the **William Penn Inn,** on Route 202 and Sumneytown Pike, a 1714 structure that has been expanded several times to provide a variety of dining facilities. It has a limited number of suites and many dining rooms; Penn's Tavern is the oldest continuously operated tavern in Pennsylvania (215-699-9272). To the west **Fox Meadow Farm** (215–827–9731), at 1439 Clover Mill Road in **Chester Springs,** is a winery on a farm originally owned by Zachariah Reis, who arrived in 1751. This farm and others nearby housed and fed Anthony Wayne's two divisions after the Battle of the Clouds during the Revolution. The **General Warren Inne** is an eighteenth-century inn to the south of Valley Forge on Old Lancaster Highway West in **Malvern;** call (215) 296–3637 or fax (215) 296–8084. In the same region you may want to drive along Yellow Springs Road between Chester Springs and Malvern, to the **Yellow Springs Inn** (215–827–7477) for a meal. Formerly a health resort in the colonial era, this bulding also served as a hospital during the Revolution.

If you associate colonial history only with battlefields and old houses, there's a chance to add a look at early industry nearby in the **Hopewell Furnace National Park.** Mark Bird developed the furnace in 1771 on French Creek to meet the immediate needs of the Continental army during the Revolution; the furnace produced cannon, shot, and shells. Bird was an important backer of American efforts in a number of ways: He commanded the second battalion of Berks County Militia and also bought uniforms, tents, and provisions for 300 men; in 1778 he sent 1,000 barrels of flour down the Schuylkill River to Valley Forge to feed Washington's starving men.

The visitor center offers an audiovisual presentation and exhibits of tools and original iron castings made here. The Big House was the center of activity for the village; sometimes thirty people lived here, along with the ironmaster and his family. Because the village was so remote, visitors were always invited to stay overnight.

As you walk around the village, you will see a demonstration of the charcoal-making process, which shows all the layers added to a conical pile. Walk into the furnace building, look at the giant waterwheel, and listen to its slap-slap-slap as it turns. You can also visit tenant houses, barns, the blacksmith shop, and the office store. Open daily from 9:00 A.M. to 5:00 P.M. Closed January 1, Thanksgiving, and Christmas. Call (215) 582–8773 for further details.

THE SUSQUEHANNA RIVER VALLEY

The Pennsylvania Dutch region in Lancaster County contains a pocket of living history that does not need to be re-created because it has never disappeared in rural areas. Beginning in 1727 the Amish, also known as the "plain people," emigrated from Europe to find freedom from persecution. They are well known for their superior farming techniques. The typical farmer tills about sixty acres of grain, alfalfa, corn, and tobacco, using horse-drawn equipment. Because frugality is a virtue in this culture, any profits are put right back into the farm.

At the **Lancaster Visitors' Information Center,** located just off the Route 30 bypass east of Lancaster, you can see *The Lancaster Experience,* a film about the Amish people and their way of life (717–299–8901). The visitors center is open daily 8:00 A.M.–6:00 P.M., May to August; 8:30 A.M.–5:00 P.M. Sunday through Thursday, 8:30 A.M.–6:00 P.M. Friday and Saturday, September and October; daily 9:00 A.M.–3:00 P.M. November to April. Also in town, interpreters in colonial costume will take you on a **Historic Lancaster Walking Tour** to see homes, courtyards, and churches, as well as hear about inhabitants during the colonial era. A ninety-minute film precedes each tour (717–392–1776).

Lancaster Central Market, located in Penn Square, is a wonderful place to browse, buy, and people-watch. It is the oldest operating market in the country. Andrew Hamilton plotted the land for this market in 1730, and in 1743 King George II proclaimed the site as the Central Market. Now you'll find fruits, vegetables, cheese, poultry, meat, seafood, and flowers here.

If you want a fascinating glimpse into Amish rural life, visit the **Amish Homestead,** at 2034 Lincoln Highway East, which was built in 1744 by Thomas and Richard Penn, sons of William Penn. An Amish farmer and his family now live in the house and actively farm the property, so what you see represents daily life in the past and present. Visitors can go inside the house for a tour and also into the barns, where buggies are on display. The homestead is open daily 8:30 A.M.–6:00 P.M., June to August, 8:30 A.M.–5:00 P.M., April, May, September, and October; 8:30 A.M.–4:00 P.M. during the rest of the year. Call (717) 291–0832 for more information.

The **Landis Valley Museum,** at 2451 Kissel Hill Road, has a section that depicts a settler's farmstead as it would have looked between 1750 and 1800. Visitors will see implements, tools, and furnishings of that era; costumed interpreters are engaged in weaving or some other task. City dwellers will find it a rare treat to stroll into this peaceful setting on a sunny day when the animals are out.

The museum also offers seminars and workshops. Landis Valley Fair is held in early June; activities include life on the farm beginning in the 1760s, an eighteenth-century military encampment, and open-hearth cooking and craft demonstrations. The museum also has an unusual Heirloom Seed Project, using vegetable and flower seeds similar to those grown by the colonists. Gardeners learn how to harvest seeds from their own gardens as a "restoration" project. Some families have passed down seeds for generations. The museum is open Tuesday through Saturday 9:00 A.M.–5:00 P.M., Sunday noon–5:00 P.M. Closed holidays except Memorial Day, July 4, and Labor Day. To find out more call (717) 569–0401.

The Iron Indian

If you happen to see a house with an iron representation of an Indian on it, that tells everyone that the owner paid the Indians for the land.

The **Hans Herr House,** at 1849 Hans Herr Drive south of town, dates from 1719. It is the oldest building in Lancaster County and also the oldest Mennonite meetinghouse in America. The artist Andrew Wyeth is a descendant of Hans Herr, and you may have seen this medieval-style stone house depicted in some of his paintings. The house has been restored and furnished. Costumed interpreters will be working at their tasks on Heritage

Day, a colonial festival in August. Open 9:00 A.M.–4:00 P.M. Monday through Saturday, April to December. Closed Thanksgiving and Christmas. Call (717) 464–4438 for more information.

Accommodations in the area include the **Revere Tavern and Inn,** on Route 30 in **Paradise,** a 1740 stone building at one time owned by President James Buchanan; dining is located next to one of five original fireplaces; for reservations call (717) 687–7683 or 687–8601. Try **Haydn Zug's,** at 1987 State Street in **East Petersburg,** for a meal in an 1852 building (717–569–5746). Nearby **Strasburg** offers lodging in the **Historic Strasburg Inn** (717–687–7691), on Route 896, with colonial ambience, and the **Strasburg Village Inn,** at One West Main Street, which dates from 1788 (717–687–0900).

In **Mount Joy** the **Cameron Estate Inn,** at 1895 Donegal Springs Road, is an early nineteenth-century rural manor house built by Dr. John Watson; it later became the home of Simon Cameron, Lincoln's first secretary of war (717–653–1773). **Groff's Farm,** at 650 Pinkerton Road, serves meals in a 1756 farm house (717–653–2048).

Lititz was settled in 1743 by Moravians, who named it for their home town in Bohemia. Take a walk along Main Street to see eighteenth-century homes still lived in today. At the **Lititz Historical Foundation** in the **Johannes Mueller House,** there's a brochure available that describes a walking tour. Call (717) 626–7958 for more information.

The **Brothers House** (1759), at Church Square and Main Street, was a hospital after the Battle of Brandywine and now contains a collection of

Fractured Writing

"Fraktur" is an art form used in German printing that has a thin shape, pointed ends, and bristling serifs, that is, the ends of the strokes. This term describes colorfully painted or printed watercolor documents common in the German community during the eighteenth and nineteenth centuries. The letters in these documents look "fractured." You can see this writing on some baptismal certificates, documents, and song books.

church archives. For food and lodging nearby, stop at the **General Sutter Inn,** at 14 East Main Street, which was founded in 1764 by the Moravian church (717–626–2115).

The **Ephrata Cloister** was one of America's first communal societies. Conrad Beissel, a German Seventh-Day Baptist, gathered a group of celibate recluses, both male and female. With remarkable foresight somewhat unusual in strict religious communal sects, he anticipated the need for progeny. Besides separate male and female orders, he established a third order for "householders." These married men and women lived in the community, worshiped there, and supported the work of the Cloister.

The Ephrata Cloister cultivated dramatic choral-music presentations known as *Vorspiel.* Present-day performances of these musical dramas give visitors an idea of the way of life in this communal settlement. Residents were also well known for their calligraphy, called *Fraktur.*

William Penn Heritage Day is held at Ephrata Cloister in October, and the Ephrata Cloister Chorus performs on a number of occasions. Call (717) 733–6600 for more information and schedules.

Historic Smithton Bed & Breakfast Country Inn, at 900 West Main Street, offers bedrooms with fireplaces in this 1763 stagecoach inn. For reservations call (717) 733–6094.

Across the Susquehanna, York County became the refuge for besieged colonial politicians. During the fall of 1777, British troops were on the march to Philadelphia, forcing members of the Continental Congress to flee toward the west to a more secure place for conducting their affairs. They crossed the Susquehanna River and took lodgings in **York.** From September 30, 1777, to June 27, 1778, York was the national capital. Here the Continental Congress adopted the Articles of Confederation that first provided a legal national government.

In York the **Golden Plough Tavern,** at 157 West Market Street, was built in the 1740s and retains a German style of architecture with William and Mary period furniture. It has now been combined with the **General Gates House,** so you can walk from one into the other. General and Mrs. Gates lived here in 1778, and the house is remembered as the place where Lafayette prevented the ousting of George Washington as chief of the army. The nearby **Barnett Bobb House** is a log house typical of the colonial period. Look for the furniture decorated with a quill dipped in paint and the chest that looks as if it were painted with a corncob. The houses are open

10:00 A.M.–4:00 P.M. Monday through Saturday, 1:00 P.M.–4:00 P.M. Sunday. Closed holidays. Call (717) 845–2951 for more information.

Carlisle Barracks, on U.S. 11 (1 mile north of the city), was once a Revolutionary War forge. In 1777 Hessian soldiers built the magazine there; Gen. J.E.B. Stuart's troops burned it just before the Battle of Gettysburg. It was reconstructed and served as the first Indian school in the United States located off a reservation. Today it houses the **Hessian Powder Magazine Museum.** For more details call (717) 245–3152.

Mercenaries to Fear

Hessians were highly disciplined German mercenaries who fought for the Crown, and they were much feared by the colonists. They wore blue uniforms, had helmets with brass decoration, and often sported mustaches.

Accommodations are available at **Jacob's Resting Place** (1790), at 1007 Harrisburg Pike. At one time a colonial tavern and inn, this B&B is located right next to the Carlisle Barracks; call (717) 243–1766 for reservations. In nearby **Boiling Springs, Highland House** (717–258–3744), at 108 Bucher Hill, dates from 1776. The house was built for Michael Ege, who was ironmaster and owner of the Carlisle Iron Works.

Old Bedford Village, located on Business Route 220, is the reproduction of a village as it would have evolved from 1750 to 1850. Original log cabins, one-room schools, and other structures were moved from their sites and brought here to establish the village. Visitors may smell freshly baked cookies from the oven and watch a weaver, blacksmith, broom maker, or carpenter at work. Special programs are held throughout the year, including Militia Days in early June. The village is open daily from 9:00 A.M. to 5:00 P.M. from early May to late October. Call (800) 622–8055 for more information and schedules.

Stop in the **Jean Bonnet Tavern,** located 4 miles west of Bedford on Route 30, for a meal or overnight to enjoy its fieldstone walls and large fireplaces. This inn dates back to the 1760s; Jean Bonnet was the licensee, beginning in 1780. Call (814) 623–2250 for reservations.

The Hazards of Cooking

Early settlers used "lug bars" in fireplace cooking. They were made of wood, and pots hung on them over the fire. Colonial women were always at risk for serious burns because eventually a lug bar would dry out and break unexpectedly. The problem disappeared with the advent of hearth cooking. Women pulled hot coals out onto the hearth, placed trivets on the coals, and put their pots on the trivets. (Information from Old Bedford Village)

Recipe for **Indian Pumpkin Griddle Cakes** (from *Old Bedford Village Hearth Cooking* by Vi Laws)

1 cup yellow cornmeal	1 tablespoon light brown sugar
1/2 teaspoon salt	1/2 teaspoon baking soda
1/2 cup pumpkin	1/3 cup water
1 beaten egg	2 tablespoons browned butter

Mix the cornmeal, sugar, soda, and salt in large bowl. Add the pumpkin, water, and egg and mix well. Stir in the melted butter. Drop by heaping tablespoons onto a greased, hot griddle and fry, turning once. Serve with maple syrup.

WESTERN PENNSYLVANIA

Just as battles swirled around the Philadelphia area during the Revolution, so western Pennsylvania, which lay between French possessions in Canada and Louisiana, was the focus of conflict during the French and Indian War. Britain declared war on France in 1756, and the Crown encouraged the involvement of colonial militias to lessen the cost of the American campaign. Four battalions of Pennsylvania men were formed and called the Royal Americans. In 1758 Prime Minister William Pitt sent Brig. Gen. John Forbes to plan an attack on the key strategic point in western Pennylvania, Fort Duquesne, where the Ohio, Allegheny, and Monongahela Rivers meet.

Forbes took the fort from the French, but they blew it up during their retreat. He began reconstruction again and renamed it Fort Pitt to honor the Prime Minister, who was respected by the colonists.

The **Fort Pitt Blockhouse** was built in 1764 by Col. Henry Bouquet to curtail the destructive raids on settlements that the Indians had begun the year before. Along the walls of the blockhouse, you can see two rows of holes, through which the defenders could fire on attackers. There were two underground tunnels: one led to the fort and the other to the Monongahela River. The blockhouse is the only remaining structure of Fort Pitt, in **Point State Park.** Walk around the park to see some of the bastions and earthworks of the old fort. For more information call (412) 471–1764.

The **Fort Pitt Museum,** located near the blockhouse, contains a variety of exhibits, including scale models of the three French and Indian War forts at The Point, a reconstructed trader's cabin, displays of frontier life, and materials on early Pittsburgh. William Pitt Memorial Hall has a circular display at its center, with a large model of Fort Pitt. Pick up a telephone to hear the history of the fort. In 1772, when Fort Pitt was abandoned by the British, one of them remarked that "the Americans will not submit to British Parliament and they may now defend themselves." Call (412) 281–9284 for details.

Historic accommodations are available across the Allegheny at **The Priory,** at 614 Pressley Street, which once was home to Benedictine priests. Call (412) 231–3338 for reservations.

The struggle to control The Point led to many subsidiary battles throughout the French and Indian War. The area around **Uniontown**, southeast of Pittsburgh, was the scene of George Washington's first military actions in the spring and summer of 1754, also the beginning of the war in America.

In April of 1754 Washington marched from Alexandria and by May he had arrived at Great Meadows, the name at that time of **Fort Necessity,** located 12 miles southeast of Uniontown on Route 40. After leading his men in a successful attack against the French Washington returned to Fort Necessity and strengthened it, but the French attacked with greater numbers and defeated Washington's force, which then surrendered and withdrew from the fort. Visitors can tour a reconstructed stockade that encloses a storehouse. There is a slide presentation for orientation, as well as exhibits of photographs, maps, and artifacts. The fort is open daily from 10:00 A.M. to 5:00 P.M., mid-spring to late fall. For more information call (412) 329–5512.

In his campaign to dislodge the French from western Pennsylvania, Gen.

John Forbes built **Fort Ligonier** to stand as a base in the attack against Fort Duquesne. Today's full reconstruction of the 1758–1766 fort is located southeast of Pittsburgh at Ligonier, on Route 30. It contains barracks and a museum; there are mannequins in the Officer's Mess Building, the Officers' Quarters, and the Supply Room. In the Officers' Quarters, General Forbes is lying mortally wounded; he is talking with Col. Henry Bouquet and Col. Archibald Montgomery about military matters. The fort sponsors reenactments, encampments, craft demonstrations, and archaeological digs. Call (412) 238–9701 for more information and schedules.

For lunch or dinner try the **Ligonier Country Inn,** to the east on Route 30 in **Laughlintown** (412–238–3561) or the **Mountain View Inn,** also providing accommodation, to the west in Greensburg (412–836–1123 or 836–1138).

The Treaty of Paris was signed in 1763 to end the war between England and France, but troubles growing out of that conflict were not over in Pennsylvania. The Proclamation of 1763 forbade settlers to live west of the Allegheny mountains. This enraged the people who had chosen to live there, especially when they realized that the Indians they had been fighting were to have the land.

Fort Ligonier provides visual interpretation, such as the display in the Officer's Mess Building.

By 1763 Chief Pontiac of the Ottawas had decided to get rid of the British on his tribal land on both sides of the Alleghenies. In surprise attacks he captured all the western forts except Pitt, Ligonier, and Bedford. In retaliation a group of Scotch-Irish called the Paxton Boys attacked a group of Conestoga Indians, killing some in their village. The rest of the Conestogas asked for protection, but the Paxton Boys broke into the jail and killed them, too.

The **Battle of Bushy Run** in 1763 halted the Indian plan to capture the forts that remained in British hands and reclaim full control of their ancestral land. Bushy Run Battlefield, located north of **Jeannette** on Route 963, was the site of a double ambush between the Indians and the British, led by Col. Henry Bouquet. On August 5 Bouquet was surprised by the Indians and suffered heavy losses; on the next morning, through careful strategy, Bouquet returned the compliment by diverting and surprising the Indians, who had stronger forces than he did. This victory allowed Bouquet to reinforce Fort Pitt. It marked the turning point in Pontiac's war by reopening the line of communication and supplies. Ultimately it decided the territorial fate of the frontier. By 1768 a new Indian treaty established a boundary line that kept the existing villages within the colony.

The battlefield museum contains exhibits that fill out the details of the Battle of Bushy Run. The **Edge Hill Trail** is a walking path around the battlefield that allows you to visualize the scene in 1763. Look at the trail markers as you make your way around. You also may picnic on 183 acres. Call (412) 527–5584 to find out more.

Punxsutawney Phil

German immigrants brought with them a superstition, or "weather forecasting" technique, that takes place on February 2, known as Groundhog Day. If the groundhog comes out of his den and sees his shadow, there will be six more weeks of winter. "Punxsutawney Phil" is the designated groundhog who surfaces in Punxsutawney every year.

FOR MORE INFORMATION

Bureau of Travel Marketing
Pennsylvania Department of Commerce
453 Forum Building
Harrisburg, PA 17120
(800) 847–4872

The South

Virginia

Historical Introduction to the
VIRGINIA COLONY

hree English ships—the *Susan Constant,* the *Godspeed,* and the *Discovery*—left Blackwall docks on the Thames in December of 1606 and headed out to sea. After a four-month voyage via the Canary Islands and the West Indies, they coasted into Chesapeake Bay in April of 1607. Capt. Christopher Newport and 143 men had arrived to settle in the New World. The ships were heavily laden with food, ale, wine, muskets, gunpowder, farm equipment, and tools for building their houses.

The First English Settlement
in the New World

After exploring the lower bay they chose to continue up the James River, named for their king, and settle on a peninsula. They built a stockade and added fifteen houses, a church, and a storehouse inside. Jamestown was born. When they were safely established within the fort two months later, Captain Newport sailed for England.

Jametown's success was in question for some time. The colonists suffered from lack of drinking water, sickness, and worms in their grain. One of them, George Percy, wrote, "There were never Englishmen left in a foreigne countrey in such miserie as wee were in this new discovered Virginia." Luckily the Indians saved the colonists from starvation with supplies of corn, bread, meat, and fish.

Capt. John Smith was not reticent in using his strong will to turn any malingerers into productive workers. Despite his efforts, however, the winter of 1609–10 decimated the colony, killing all but 50 of the 500 settlers. Smith was wounded and returned to England, causing one of the company to write, "Now we all found the losse of Captaine Smith, yea his greatest maligners could now curse his losse."

Enter Tobacco and Indian Troubles

By 1612 John Rolfe had become the first American entrepreneur by planting seeds from a tobacco plant grown in the West Indies as a cash crop. When a shipment of his Orinoco leaf tobacco was sent to England, a labor-intensive industry that would both sustain and plague Virginia was born. In 1614 John Rolfe married an Indian princess, Pocahontas, with the blessing of her father, Powhatan. She died in England after they had been presented at court.

After Powhatan's death his successor, Chief Opechancanough, became a menace to the colonists. A fatal massacre by the Indians in 1622 killed 400 settlers. Living in constant fear of attack by Indians, the settlers did not have time to plant adequate tobacco crops. Then, to add to their troubles, the charter of the Virginia Company was revoked in 1624. Nevertheless, Virginia attracted more immigrants, who increased the population, and the land eventually produced more tobacco.

Jamestown remained uneasy throughout much of the seventeenth century. In 1676 Nathaniel Bacon and his men tried to get rid of Governor William Berkeley, who was accused of not punishing marauding Indians. Bacon's rebels ended up by burning Jamestown because they wanted to show King Charles II that they would not tolerate despotic rule. Ironically this turmoil and destruction put the town into decline, and the capital was removed from Jamestown to Williamsburg after the statehouse burned in 1698.

The Spirit of Rebellion Grows

Virginia continued to have difficulties with Indian raids, while low tobacco prices and growing efforts by the Crown to contain the independent spirit of the Virginia General Assembly created discontent among the colonists. That discontent, mostly directed against royal governors, rarely reached troubling proportions during the first half of the eighteenth century as long as the plantation economy prospered, the population grew, and land became available for new settlements in the Piedmont and Shenandoah Valley.

At the midpoint of the century, Virginians made their first moves westward of the Alleghenies into what is now West Virginia and Ohio, but the French and Indian War from 1754 to 1763 played havoc with the colony's westward expansion. From Washington's first unsuccessful attempt to protect the frontier through Pontiac's war in 1763, no settlements beyond the Alleghenies were secure.

Back in Williamsburg, the political accommodation that had kept relationships between the governor and assembly stable began to unravel through a series of acts by both the Crown and Parliament. Among them King George III closed settlement in the west in 1763, and Parliament imposed the Stamp Tax in 1765. Patrick Henry took action after the 1765 decision of Parliament to foist taxes on the colonists. His speech in the House of Burgesses was interrupted with shouts of "Treason!" after the words "Caesar had his Brutus, Charles the First, his Cromwell, and George III . . ." but Henry resumed, "George III may profit by their example."

Two years later, when the Townshend Acts imposed new taxes on a variety of articles, Williamsburg became a hotbed of revolt. The General Assembly declared that taxation without representation was unconstitutional and began an unofficial boycott of English goods. In the years immediately preceding hostilities, Virginians continued to take the initiative in organizing the colonies against what they regarded as unwarranted British intrusions in American affairs. They formed a Committee of Correspondence with other colonies in 1772 and urged the convening of the first Continental Congress in 1774. In June of 1776 a revolutionary convention adopted a constitution and chose Patrick Henry as the first governor of the Commonwealth of Virginia.

Regions to Explore

T he Virginia Colony has been divided into three geographical regions that represent different faces of its culture and its evolution during the colonial era. We begin where the colony itself began, in Tidewater Virginia, then move upstream along the Potomac shore, and finally into the central region around Jefferson's Charlottesville.

TIDEWATER VIRGINIA

Colonial National Historical Park encompasses the land on the penin-sula between the James and York rivers. Nowhere else in the country is so much colonial heritage and activity packed into such small space. The beau-tiful **Colonial Parkway** links Jamestown Island and Yorktown Battlefield, both within the park; just outside, between them, lies Colonial Williamsburg. Call (804) 898–3400 for more information on the park and its special events.

Although much of the original site of **Jamestown** has been washed away by the James River, some ruins remain, including a 1608 glasshouse used for making glass and the 1639 brick church tower. Inside the re-created fort interpreters dressed in colonial costume go about their daily tasks cooking, working on their houses, repairing weapons, and participating in military drills. The site, located at one end of the Colonial Parkway on **Jamestown Island,** is part of the Colonial National Historical Park.

Jamestown Settlement, located next to Jamestown Island, is a re-cre-ation of the original settlement under the auspices of the Jamestown-Yorktown Foundation. Here you can visit replicas of the three ships that brought the colonists to Jamestown. The ship replicas are usually moored at the dock and open to visitors daily from 9:00 A.M. to 5:00 P.M. Climb on board and see the space allotted to passengers and to cargo. Can you imagine what it must have been like to spend months in such cramped quarters during a voyage to the New World? Demonstrations include unfurling sails, changing the watch, posting colors, and steering the ship. A sailor will tell you about his life on board. Ask about the navigational instruments, like the astrolabe, which mea-sures latitude, and other sailing techniques used on that voyage.

Inside the **James Fort** you will find thatched houses and important pub-lic buildings like the church and the storehouse. Many of the settlers had lit-tle knowledge of farming, and after their wounded leader, Capt. John Smith, sailed back to England in 1609, a "starving time" took many lives. The sur-vivors had almost given up hope of relief when more settlers arrived from England with supplies, drawn by the urge to become wealthy by growing the tobacco that England insatiably desired. By 1619 a government structure was in place, and Jamestown remained its center until destruction from the Bacon Rebellion of 1676, combined with the burning of the statehouse in 1698, removed it to Williamsburg.

A re-created **Powhatan Village** offers you the chance to see how the Native Americans lived, prepared food, made tools and weapons, and prepared for war. Some of their Tidewater Indian pipes and arrowheads are on display in the museum.

Be sure to see the twenty-minute orientation film before strolling through the museum. The museum contains three sections: the English Gallery, the Powhatan Indian Gallery, and the Jamestown Gallery. Remnants of the settlement include weapons such as a sixteenth-century Iberian gunlock, a helmet, Spanish coins, a "bleeding bowl," mortar and pestle, coffin handles, wine bottles, and Capt. John Smith's original map of Jamestown. The King and Queen of England sent a ceramic jug to Pocahontas, and it, too, is on display.

There's a full slate of special events in Jamestown Settlement. If you're here in March, you can catch a reenactment of military life through the ages. Jamestown Landing Day, in May, is also a highlight, as men and women celebrate the anniversary of the founding of the first permanent English colony in the New World. The Virginia Indian Heritage Festival takes place in June to celebrate the role and way of life of the Powhatans. During fall interpreters focus on seventeenth-century foods and feasts in Virginia, and Christmas festivities take place in December. For specific dates and details of the programs call (804) 229–1607.

You can also drive around 3- or 5-mile loops on Jamestown Island to get a feeling for the type of terrain and environment the first settlers found. Audiotapes for the driving tour and the walking tour are available for rent in the gift shop.

Carving a Canoe

From the early 1600s in coastal Virginia, Powhatan Indians made canoes, some as long as 40 to 50 feet. Capt. John Smith described the method they used: "These [boats] they make of one tree by burning and scratching away the coles [coals] with stons and shels till they have made it in forme of a Trough." You may be in the Jamestown Settlement when interpreters are making a canoe, using Indian techniques and tools. You can watch them as they painstakingly hollow out an 18-foot tulip-poplar log.

Visit **Yorktown,** at the other end of Colonial Parkway, to follow the sequence of events that led up to American victory in the Revolution. The **Yorktown Victory Center** is the place to start for an orientation to the area. A chronological time line takes visitors through four phases of the struggle: treaty, taxes, tea, and troops. You'll find out more about the 1763 Treaty of Paris, which increased British holdings in our country, the odious tax acts, the Boston Tea Party, the First Continental Congress, and the culminating Battle of Yorktown, which led to British surrender in 1781. A film *The Road to Yorktown* graphically portrays these and other key events.

Exhibits change, so new ones may be in place by the time you visit. The following have been permanent for years: "At the Water's Edge: The Towns of York and Gloucester" draws a social and economic portrait of the towns most involved in the last important battle of the Revolution. Learn about life on board a ship in the "Yorktown's Sunken Fleet" display, based on artifacts taken from the *Betsy,* a British merchant ship sunk during the Siege of Yorktown.

"Witnesses to Revolution" shows how the conflict affected six persons: an African American patriot named Jehu Grant; a loyalist, Jacob Ellegood; a Quaker pacifist, Elizabeth Drinker; two Continental Army soldiers; and the wife of a Virginia plantation owner, Frances Bland Tucker. Information was gathered from their personal diaries and correspondence.

Outside in a Continental army camp, interpreters help you imagine the daily life of those in the camp. Soldiers' tents, two officers' tents, a weapons tent, and a cooking center have been re-created. You may be there for a military drill, a demonstration of musket loading and firing, or camp cooking. A typical farm is represented by the outline of a house and a separate kitchen. Herbs and vegetables grow in the garden, as well as corn and tobacco in a nearby field.

The calendar of special events includes a Yorktown Sampler in May, a Children's Colonial Days Fair in July, a military encampment to celebrate the victory in October, and Christmas programs in December. For specific dates and schedules of each event call the Yorktown Victory Center at (804) 887–1776.

You can take two driving tours around the battlefield and the encampment area to reconstruct the events of October 19, 1781, in your own imagination. The 7-mile Battlefield Tour includes the British Inner Defense Line and Hornwork, the Grand French Battery, the Second Allied Siege Line,

Redoubts 9 and 10, the Moore House (where surrender terms were negotiated), and the Surrender Field. The 9-mile Allied Encampment Tour begins at the American Artillery Park, then goes to Washington's Headquarters, the French Cemetery, the French Artillery Park, through the French Encampment Loop, and ends at the British Redoubt. Both of these tours are well worth taking.

Wandering around the **City of Yorktown** takes you by a spate of interesting historic houses. On Main Street the **Dudley Digges House** was home for a lawyer who served as council member for Virginia during the Revolution. The 1692 **Thomas Sessions House** is the oldest house in Yorktown. On Nelson Street stands the **Captain John Ballard House** and the **Edmund Smith House.** Back on Main Street is the **"Scotch Tom" Nelson House,** a Georgian mansion, which was also home to his grandson, Thomas Nelson, Jr., who signed the Declaration of Independence. This house, with cannonballs still in its side, is occasionally opened by the Park Service. In the next block you'll pass the **Pate House, Customhouse, Somerwell House,** a reconstructed **Medical Shop,** and the **Swan Tavern,** which is now an antique shop. **Grace Church,** on Church Street, is noted for the grave of Thomas Nelson, Jr., in the churchyard. For more information on which houses are open, and when, call (804) 898–3400.

If you would like a glimpse of the more peaceful pursuits of this maritime town, visit the **Watermen's Museum,** at 309 Water Street. Here you can get an overview of the work on the bay that helped sustain the tidewater region through the colonial era and far beyond. The museum has a variety of displays inside, including models of ships, dioramas, shipwright's tools, rigging, and a "tong" for oysters, and offers hands-on activities outside. Hours vary; call (804) 887–2641 for information.

When you have finished looking at Jamestown and Yorktown, head back to the middle of the peninsula, on Colonial Parkway, for a visit to the most extensive re-creation of colonial life in America. You'll want to spend at least a day at **Colonial Williamsburg** if you can. The city began inauspiciously as a branch of the Jamestown settlement in 1633, then called Middle Plantation. By the time the capital of the Virginia colony moved to Middle Plantation from Jamestown in 1699, its name had been changed to Williamsburg to honor King William III. It remained the capital for the next eighty-one years, passing the honor to Richmond in 1780.

Step back in time two centuries as you walk through the streets of colonial days in the footsteps of those who helped develop our nation. We suggest that you first head for the **Visitor Center,** which is well marked as you come into town. A film, *Williiamsburg—The Story of a Patriot,* provides orientation for your visit. Leave your car in the parking lot and take a shuttle bus to the Historic Area. Duke of Gloucester Street is the main street of Williamsburg, running for a mile between the Capitol and the College of William and Mary. You can immerse yourself in the eighteenth century by simply wandering into buildings along this street and adjoining streets. You'll have more fun—and learn more—if you start a conversation with anyone in costume.

Across the street in the **King's Arms Tavern,** everyone is encouraged to exchange eighteenth-century news and views with the proprietress, the widow Jane Vobe. This was the place to keep up to date on what was happening in the colonial world. Jane assured us that she doesn't gossip but just tells what she hears—after all, one has to watch one's tongue or be put in the pillory! She told the male half of this writing team that he should really shave off his beard when he has time because men with hair on their faces either have something to hide or are pirates. Men who want to stay in her four-teen-room inn pay 7 1/2 pence for two-to-a-bed comfort. Meal costs can't exceed 1 shilling—dinner is served at two of the clock, supper at nine of the clock, with the same food brought back redecorated. It pays to appear the first time food is served.

Continue by heading for the **Capitol** building. As you stand by the green seats in the House of Burgesses, a guide explains a bill George Washington proposed that had to do with hogs. It seems that hogs had been bathing in the drinking water, and Washington thought they should be fenced in so that people could drink clean water. Legislation had to be sent

Max the Milliner

Stop to chat with costumed interpreters, who are eager to talk with you about their crafts. Max, in the Milliner's Shop, told us about the fans that George Washington ordered there. The milliner had the latest styles in clothing and was considered a fashion consultant as she stitched new gowns for balls, changed the trim with the times, and suggested wearing "heart breakers" (corkscrew curls).

to the king in England, so an answer could be expected in a few years. More seriously, Washington explained the Virginia Resolves against the Townshend Acts, passed in this chamber in 1769. Four years earlier Patrick Henry had delivered his notorious "Caesar-Brutus" speech here and proposed a response to the Stamp Act.

The Council Chamber, housing the smaller and more powerful group that advised the governor, has a turkey-work carpet on the table. The portrait of Queen Anne that hangs here reminds us of her personal tragedy; she had seventeen children, all of whom died in infancy except the Prince of Gloucester, and he died at age eleven. The General Court was the place where pirates were sentenced to be "turned off" or hanged and where other malefactors were punished. People could be pardoned the first time, but a T (theft) or M (murder) was burned into the palm of the hand near the thumb to make a second offense unmistakable—no plea bargaining here!

One of our favorite buildings is the **Governor's Palace,** which housed seven royal governors and also the first two governors of the Commonwealth of Virginia, Patrick Henry and Thomas Jefferson. In 1780 the residence of the governor was moved to Richmond. The building was used as a hospital after the battle of Yorktown, but later in 1781 it burned completely. Today visitors see a carefully researched replica of the original building.

You will enter through the hall—decorated with guns, swords, pistols, and muskets arranged in patterns—but it wasn't so easy in colonial days. Then the butler managed the visits of those who wished to see the governor from his office to the left of the door. By their clothing and posture, he was able to screen the less important visitors, who had to wait in the hall; the more important, who were escorted into the parlor on the right; and the most important, who were allowed to walk upstairs. When you go upstairs, you'll walk through several bedrooms with period furnishings. Don't miss the set of fashion prints—one for each month of the year. In the Ball Room, the governor sat at the "preferred" end, decorated with portraits of King George III and Queen Charlotte; when visitors bowed to him, they were also bowing to the King and Queen.

The **Public Hospital,** at the southeast corner of Francis and Henry streets, was in operation from 1773 to 1885. Rooms display conditions for the mentally ill, including a 1773 cell—with a pallet on the floor over a lump of straw, a blanket, and a chamber pot—similar to a prison cell. The window was barred, and patients were chained to the wall. By 1845 conditions had improved, and each patient lived in a small apartment with plastered walls, furnished with a bed, a table, and a chair. During this age of "moral management," patients were encouraged to spend time doing something—playing the violin, spinning, or playing cards, for example. The "custodial care" era lasted from 1862 to 1885: Patients were subjected to physical restraints but were entertained with picnics and tea parties.

The **DeWitt Wallace Decorative Arts Gallery** is accessible by walking through the hospital and downstairs. Collections include musical instruments, silver, pewter, ceramics, clocks, globes, furniture, paintings, costumes, and textiles. Our favorites from the colonial era are an Aesop's fable candlestick, "The Tiger and the Fox" from 1765, a Greybeard face jug from 1645, a turquoise tea urn from 1770, brass pipe tampers from 1650, and crewel wool needlework from 1750. Some holdings go beyond the decorative, like the Charles Willson Peale portraits of Washington and George III and a copy of the 1755 map that was used in establishing the territories of the United States at the end of the Revolution.

The **Abby Aldrich Rockefeller Folk Art Center** opened after renovation and expansion in May 1992. Abby Aldrich Rockefeller began collecting folk art in the 1920s. Today the collection includes shop signs, weather vanes, carousel figures, portraits, furniture, chests, quilts, sewing implements, mariner's tools, and toys. We enjoyed the clown tobacconist sign from 1868, a group of weather vanes, a lion carousel figure, a monkey inkwell, a calico cat from the period 1900–1920, a 1907–15 mechanical pump on three levels, and a 1795 Pennsylvania Dutch Easter rabbit, to name a few. Contact Colonial Williamsburg (800) HISTORY (800–447–8679) for more information about programs in the center.

At the opposite end of Duke of Gloucester Street from the Capitol stands the **Wren Building** of William and Mary. It is so called not because it can be attributed to Christopher Wren himself but because it resembles his work in elegant simplicity, balanced proportions, and other elements of his style. The restored building, the oldest college building in the colonies, looks as it did in 1716. The college was founded in 1693 to train clergymen on this side of the Atlantic, and it played a key role in educating distinguished Virginians throughout the eighteenth century. Phi Beta Kappa, then a secret society for intellectual discussion and fellowship, was founded in 1776 in the **Raleigh Tavern**—a favorite retreat of students, politicians, and gamblers.

There are many places scattered throughout the properties of Colonial Williamsburg to have lunch or dinner in colonial ambience. On their menus you will find many authentic colonial favorites like soup, stew, seafood, or syllabubs (see recipe). As you wander through the historic district, look at the day's menus at the Williamsburg Inn, the King's Arms Tavern, Chowning's Tavern, Mrs. Campbell's Tavern, Shields Tavern, and the Williamsburg Lodge. If you would rather use your fingers than your feet for the same information, call (804) 229–2141.

To complete your immersion in the eighteenth century, there's a rare opportunity to spend the night in authentic colonial lodgings in Williamsburg—rare because almost everywhere else they have been burned, wrecked, or altered almost beyond recognition during centuries of growth and change. If you'd like to stay in authentic digs, contact Colonial Williamsburg Hotels and ask what's available. Colonial Williamsburg properties include a wide variety of lodgings, ranging from the spartan and simple to the luxurious and elegant. Some are in historic buildings; others are not. The properties include the Williamsburg Inn, Providence Hall, Colonial Houses & Taverns, Williamsburg Lodge, Williamsburg Woodlands, and the Governor's Inn. All are within the Historic Area, or just outside it, and some are right on Duke of Gloucester Street. For detailed information and reservations call (800) HISTORY (800–447–8679).

If you prefer to stay in a modern resort setting, you may want to try **Kingsmill Resort,** 1010 Kingsmill Road, located south of town on 3,000 acres along the James River. Kingsmill is a residential community within itself, built on land owned by Richard Kingsmill in 1736. Now it also has a full-blown luxury resort with golf course, tennis and racquetball courts, pools, restaurants—in short, the works—while maintaining a semirural ambience. Deer wander through the woods, almost undisturbed by walkers and golfers. Call (800) 832–5665 or (804) 253–1703 for reservations.

At **Carter's Grove,** located 8 miles southeast of Williamsburg on the James River, you'll have a chance to visit a plantation home that contains period furnishings, an eighteenth-century slave quarter, and a seventeenth-century settlement—all at once within a peaceful country setting that overlooks the river. Surprisingly, the archaeological museum on the grounds is located entirely underground in order to leave the original landscape undisturbed.

King Carter, the eighteenth-century magnate of the Virginia Colony, purchased the land for his daughter Elizabeth. He could well afford it, since before he died in 1732 he owned hundreds of plantations covering 300,000 acres of land, as well as 1,000 slaves. The original house was completed by

To whet your appetite for dishes from the colonial period, you can try this recipe at home:

Syllabubs

1 ½ cups whipping cream	rind and juice of 2 lemons
½ cup sugar	½ cup white wine
¼ cup sherry	whipping cream (optional)

Whip together the following ingredients in this order: whipping cream, lemon rind, sugar, lemon juice, white wine, and sherry. Whisk the mixture for 3–5 minutes, keeping in mind that too much whipping will turn it to butter. Pour into parfait glasses and refrigerate overnight. If desired, pile whipped cream on top of each glass before serving. Makes 6–8 syllabubs.

(Recipe from Colonial Williamsburg)

Docents describe what life was like in the slave quarters at Carter's Grove.

1755, and two wings were added in 1930 to connect the house with a kitchen on one end and a laundry on the other. The McCrea family purchased the house in 1928, and Mrs. McCrea lived here until her death in 1960. It is now owned by the Colonial Williamsburg Foundation.

Inside the mansion you can almost see colonial ladies seated on the window seats, doing their needlework. Portraits of the McCrea family hang on the dining-room wall, including one of seventeen-year-old Molly McCrea, in a yellow dress with flowers on the bodice. The kitchen contains a churn and a spinning wheel. A number of black iron pots stand in the large fireplace (mixing the centuries a bit, an early Hotpoint electric stove hovers nearby). The drawing room is also called the "refusal" room, because both Washington and Jefferson made marriage proposals here—and both were refused! Cigars in the ashtray of the library leave you with the feeling that someone has just left.

An archaeological team searched the grounds to discover signs of the early seventeenth-century settlement called Martin's Hundred, and they found it. The **Winthrop Rockefeller Archaeology Museum,** located underground, displays artifacts from the dig. Mockleyware cooking pots from A.D. 200–900 are here, also lead from casement windows with the words "John . . . 1625," a 1613 farthing coin, a seventeenth-century helmet, and the story of a woman, "Granny," who was partly scalped, with photos of her bones.

On the surface **Wolstenholme Towne** was once part of Martin's Hundred, and some houses, a store, and the fort are now marked. An eighteenth-century slave quarter has been reconstructed on the site. Interpreters tell a balanced story of the African Americans who lived and worked here as slaves, including tales of their singing and dancing after work was done.

ALONG THE POTOMAC

Mount Vernon rises from an emerald-green lawn above the Potomac River, symbolizing a perfect melding of gracious living and political responsibility in our first presidency, but it was built here for economic rather than aesthetic reasons. The Potomac, like the Hudson and the Delaware, was a great river leading inland, and as such its value for shipping produce and for general commerce was inestimable. John Washington, George's great-grandfather, patented the Mount Vernon homesite in 1674. Augustine Washington,

George's father, inherited the tobacco plantation of 2,300 acres in 1726, and in 1732 George was born here. When Augustine Washington died in 1743, George's elder half-brother, Lawrence, inherited Mount Vernon.

George Washington eventually inherited the plantation from Lawrence in 1761 and then wrote, "No estate in United America is more pleasantly situated than this. It lies in a high, dry and healthy Country 300 miles by water from the Sea . . . on one of the finest Rivers in the world. . . . " In spite of this admiration for his own estate, he was not able to live here for years at a time during the French and Indian War, the Revolution, and an eight-year presidency. Nevertheless when he was in residence at Mount Vernon, he studied the newest crop technology assiduously and was successful as a planter.

After George's marriage to Martha Dandridge Custis, widow of Daniel Parke Custis, he wrote, "I am now, I believe, fixed at this Seat with an agreeable Consort for Life and hope to find more happiness in retirement than I ever experienced amidst a wide and bustling World." No such luck. While visiting colonial inns and houses along the Eastern seaboard doing research for this book, we were astounded at the number he had actually slept in—rather than the home he loved—and the jocular phrase "Washington slept here" took on new poignancy. Luckily, Martha Washington spent eight winters with him during his northern encampments. Washington resigned his commission in 1783 and hoped to spend his remaining life at Mount Vernon. In 1789 he became President for the next eight years, which kept him away from home much of the time. When he finally did retire, he had only two and one-half years left at his beloved Mount Vernon before he died.

The mansion is a familiar sight to most Americans because photographs of its facade, enlarged by Washington with a long columned piazza and other features in Palladian style, have appeared incessantly. He first added onto the smaller house he had inherited before his marriage to Martha and, in later years, made other additions. When he was at home, Washington was personally involved in designing, supervising construction, and decorating and furnishing the additions.

The Banquet Hall is striking, with a Palladian window, green decor, and an ornate fireplace. The West Parlor also has an elaborate fireplace and mantel, with the Washington coat of arms on the top; James Sharples painted the portraits of George and Martha Washington that hang here. The Dining Room has a gallery of prints and a decorated ceiling. Upstairs George

Washington's bedroom contains his unusually wide bed, in which he died in 1799; the Windsor armchair next to the bed was in that position when he died. Don't miss important memorabilia in the house, especially the Keys to

Music at the Mount

B ecause music played such an important role in the social life at Mount Vernon, you will see a number of musical instruments in the "little parlor." George Washington gave "one very good Spinit" to his stepdaughter, Patsy Custis, and her brother received a violin and "a fine German flute"; Nelly Custis was given a harpsichord in 1793, straight from London.

the Bastille, given to Washington by Lafayette.

Outside on the grounds you can explore the "dependencies." The kitchen, where a staff of two cooks and two waiters produced sumptuous meals, now houses a collection of utensils and cooking gear. According to one writer of the time, "The dinner was very good, a small roasted pigg, boiled leg of lamb, roasted fowls, beef, peas, lettuce, cucumbers, artichokes, puddings, tarts. We were desired to call for what drinks we chose." Other buildings include the smokehouse, greenhouse, icehouse, storehouse, coach house, and slave quarters. A museum has been added to house the large collection of Washington artifacts.

George and Martha Washington are buried in the family vault. He directed that "the family Vault at Mount Vernon requiring repairs, and being improperly situated besides, I desire that a new one of Brick and upon a larger Scale, may be built at the foot of what is commonly called the Vineyard Inclosure—on the ground which is marked out—in which my remains, with those of my deceased relatives (now in the old Vault) and such others of my family as may chuse to be entombed there, may be deposited."

Because of the popularity of Mount Vernon with tourists, we suggest that you arrive early in the morning to avoid waiting in line, tour the mansion, and then stroll around the grounds in uncrowded leisure. Hours: 9:00 A.M. to 5:00 P.M. daily except during the winter when the closing time is 4:00 P.M. Call (703) 780–2000 for the changeover dates and more information.

Sixteen miles upstream from Mount Vernon, Scottish merchants founded **Alexandria** in 1749 and named it after John Alexander, who had bought the land in 1669 for "six thousand punds of Tobacco and Cask." George Washington (along with John West, Jr.) surveyed the land when he was seventeen years old. Later he kept a residence in town, but his original home at 508 Cameron Street, built in 1765, no longer stands. The building on the site now is a privately owned replica. Washington was heavily involved in the communal affairs of Alexandria. He had a pew in Christ Church, organized the Friendship Fire Company, and served as Master of the Masonic Lodge.

The city had become one of the main seaports and trading centers of Virginia by the time of the Revolution. Slaves were sold in the market, yet there were also several free black communities in Alexandria. Blacks were known and valued as skilled artisans.

Today, in spite of the suburban development around the center of the city, visitors can still soak up the ambience of colonial days as they walk through the streets of Old Town Alexandria. (Parking is tight in the center of the Old Town, so the best plan is to stash your car in a parking lot or find one of the specially marked "tourist" meters that allow you to stay all day.) Begin your tour at **Ramsay House,** 221 King Street (703–838–4200), which also serves as the Visitor Center. Here you can watch a video on colonial Alexandria, pick up brochures to help plan sightseeing, and begin guided walking tours, which are excellent.

Before you begin a walking tour, though, take a few minutes to look around Ramsey House. William Ramsay and his wife, Anne, had eight children in this original house, which has been moved from another location. The gambrel roof is similar to those used on other colonial homes between 1675 and 1725. Ramsey was a good friend of George Washington, who walked in Ramsey's funeral procession.

Carlyle House, 121 North Fairfax Street (703–549–2997), dates from 1752. John Carlyle journeyed from Scotland in 1741 and became a successful tobacco merchant in Alexandria. During the French and Indian War, Gen. Edward Braddock had his headquarters in the Carlyle House, where he held a crucial conference. He invited five colonial governors to meet with him, ostensibly to coerce them into raising money for their own defense in the war. They refused, and he sent a letter to London demanding that the colonists be taxed, setting in motion a long train of parliamentary measures that eventually led to the Revolution. Market Square, in front of City Hall, was a parade ground for colonial troops under Braddock's command. Braddock was later defeated at Fort Duquesne and died in that battle.

Turn left on Cameron Street, then onto Royal Street, and you'll come to the 1770 **Gadsby's Tavern Museum,** where you can have an authentic colonial meal and tour the museum. George Washington was a frequent visitor, and the annual Birthnight Ball took place in an elegant ballroom upstairs every year while he lived; it is reenacted to this day on the weekend of George Washington's birthday. The museum is open 10:00 A.M.–4:00 P.M. Tuesday through Saturday, 1:00 P.M.–5:00 P.M. Sunday; closed holidays. Call (703) 838–4242 for more information, and (703) 548–1288 for lunch or dinner reservations.

The museum features a taproom where the main meal of the day was served. Men met here to talk politics, smoke clay pipes, and play board games, such as backgammon. Upstairs you'll find a variety of inn bedrooms, some communal and sparse, others private and comfortably furnished. One sleeping room contains linen sacks filled with straw and a bedstead with a rope frame. Only men slept up here; no lady of quality would think of sleeping elsewhere than with friends or the local clergyman. Any man arriving after the beds were filled had to sleep on the floor.

Continue along Cameron Street to **Christ Church,** on the corner of Cameron and North Washington streets. Begun in 1767 and finished in 1773, the church had galleries added in 1787 and a tower in 1820. George Washington's pew is marked with a silver tablet, also that of Robert E. Lee. Washington's pew, number 60, cost 36 pounds and 10 shillings. Don't miss the cut-glass chandelier. Open 9:00 A.M.–4:00 P.M. Monday through Friday, 9:00 A.M.–noon Saturday, 2:00 P.M.–4:30 P.M. Sunday. Call (703) 549–1450 for the weekly schedule and further information.

Turn right onto Washington Street to the **Lee-Fendall House,** at 614 Oronoco Street. Philip Fendall built his mansion in 1785. Here Lighthorse Harry Lee worked on his farewell address from Alexandrians to George Washington as the latter left to become our first President. About thirty-five members of the Lee family lived in this house from 1785 to 1903, and many Lee possessions remain here. The house is open Monday through Friday from 9:00 A.M. to 6:00 P.M. and Saturday from 9:00 A.M. to 5:00 P.M. For details call (703) 548–1789.

Take Prince Street to Fairfax to see the **Stabler-Leadbeater Museum and Apothecary Shop,** 105–107 South Fairfax Street. George Washington and Robert E. Lee were among the patrons of this store. One record states: "Mrs. Washington desires Mr. Stabler will send by the bearer a quart bottle of his best Castor Oil and the bill for it." Open 10:00 A.M. to 4:00 P.M. except Sundays and some holidays (703–836–3713).

Alexandria's pride in its history is reflected in a busy schedule of festivals and celebrations. Special Christmas celebrations begin with a tree-lighting ceremony on the Friday after Thanksgiving, when Santa arrives. Then on the first Saturday in December, the Scottish Christmas Walk features kilted bagpipers, Highland dancers, and Scottish clans. As one might expect, February is loaded with celebrations related to Washington, including a ball, banquet, parade, and special tours. Historic ships come for the Waterfront Festival in June, and there are Scottish games in July. An eighteenth-century fair is held each September in Gadsby's Tavern Museum and Market Square. Call (703) 838–4200 for the exact dates and program of each event.

For a good meal try one of the fine restaurants in Alexandria. **Bilbo Baggins,** at 208 Queen Street (703–683–0300), is a cafe/restaurant with wine bar and Sunday brunch; breads and desserts baked on the premises are a specialty; **Gadsby's Tavern,** at 138 North Royal Street (703–548–1288), serves meals in a colonial dining room, with waiters and waitresses in eighteenth-century costume, and there's entertainment at night. **The Seaport Inn,** at 6 King Street (703–549–2341), dating from 1765, is a stone building that formerly housed a sail loft; you can choose river views or dining by the fireplace.

For overnight accommodations try the **Morrison House,** at 116 South Alfred Street (call 800–367–0800 or 703–838–8000, or fax 703–684–6283), a manor house in eighteenth-century style that features four-poster beds and afternoon tea.

The town of **Leesburg** played an interesting role in American history. Located near the upper reaches of the Potomac, it led both southwestward down the Shenandoah Valley and northwestward into Pennsylvania and Ohio. It was an outfitting post for Virginia troops during the French and Indian War, and George Washington had a headquarters there. After the Revolution it served as an emergency archive for the precious documents of the new nation. During the War of 1812 the Declaration of Independence, the United States Constitution, and other important papers were stored in the cellar vault of a nearby mansion when the city of Washington went up in flames under British attack.

Many historic buildings still stand in this attractive and hospitable town, with no artificial trappings designed to attract tourists. The surrounding countryside in Loudon County is beautiful, with rolling hills, old mills, plantation mansions, restaurants, and B&Bs from the colonial era. There has been so little change in the county that many of the secondary roads are still gravel—all within an hour of Washington's Beltway.

The **Loudoun County Museum,** at 16 Loudoun Street SW (703–777–7427), has a video, which provides orientation for a visit to Leesburg and the area. Powhatan Indians, who liked river valleys, lived here for many years and left behind arrowheads and pottery now on display in the museum. King Charles I granted the land to seven of his faithful followers in 1649, but when the monarchy ended and Cromwell took over, they were not able to claim their land. By 1660, when Charles II had reclaimed the throne, new grants were issued, but the land was slow to settle, perhaps because of fears raised by raiding Iroquois from the north and west. Then the Treaty of Albany in 1722 ordained that the Indians would not come east of the Blue Ridge or south of the Potomac without permission.

By 1757 Thomas, Lord Fairfax had surveyed Leesburg, and seventy half-acre lots were plotted. Silversmiths, blacksmiths, and traders kept the town's tavern busy. Stephen Donaldson, the first silversmith in Leesburg, built a log building in 1763 that is now the gift shop next to the Loudoun Museum. By 1760 the town that had been Georgetown was renamed Leesburg for Thomas Lee.

Local farmers provided food for George Washington's Continental army. Citizens gave clothing and wagons as well as contributing manpower to the war. Two generations later, during the Civil War, Gen. Robert E. Lee's men were fed and housed in Leesburg after the Battle of Manassas.

The best way to get a sense of Leesburg's heritage is on foot. "A Walk Around Leesburg" is available for purchase in the museum shop; visitors can stroll around a six-block area to get a feeling for the rich historical background of the city. At 29 West Market Street is a Federal-style stone house that at one point served as a girls' school; when the Marquis de Lafayette visited Leesburg in 1825, the girls performed a dance for him on the Courthouse lawn.

The **Laurel Brigade Inn,** at 20 West Market Street (703–777–1010), is the site of an "ordinary," now both an inn and a restaurant. The long section at the rear of the building was probably built as a ballroom to entertain Lafayette in 1825. Dr. Jacob Coutsman, the first physician to reside in Leesburg, lived next door, at 19 East Market Street; the deed for the house was filed in 1758. His office was located at 23 East Market Street, a building that has interesting Flemish bond brickwork, with arches over the openings.

The **Patterson House,** a 1759 Georgian house with a Colonial Revival porch at 4 East Loudoun Street, is one of the oldest in Leesburg. John and Fleming Patterson came from Scotland to build the house and settle here. Hessian soldiers, imprisoned in the house, drew caricatures of Washington, Patrick Henry, and other Revolutionary War leaders on the walls. It became Capt. Henry McCabe's Ordinary in the late 1770s. George Washington enjoyed a dinner of jowls and greens here, prepared by a Mrs. McGill, and Lafayette was toasted by the mayor of the town in 1825 on the front steps.

The Courthouse, dating from 1757, is located on the corner of King and Market streets. The bell in the cupola tolled the news of the Boston Tea Party with its very first peals. In 1774 Loudoun freeholders created the Loudoun Resolves, which protested the Stamp Act, and then sent them to Philadelphia for the Continental Congress in September 1774.

There are a number of interesting houses on Cornwall Street. The **Gray-Benedict-Harrison** home dates from 1759. The Flemish bond front combines Georgian and Federal styles. John Janney lived at 10 East Cornwall Street in a 1780 house. Reverend John Littlejohn lived at 11 West Cornwall Street. During the War of 1812, the Declaration of Independence and the Constitution were taken by wagon to this home just before the British burned Washington. Then they were transferred to a cellar vault in Rokeby House in the nearby countryside.

Sir Peter Halkett had his headquarters in the **Stone House,** at 24 West Loudoun Street, before the 1755 Battle of Monongahela, and this is the probable site of Washington's headquarters during the French and Indian War. The Stone House is now a great place to have an elegant afternoon tea in the garden. Call (703) 777–1806 for days and hours.

All of Leesburg turns out for its annual August Court Days. During the mid-1700s circuit judges traveled from town to town, and by the late 1700s they held "court days" on specific days in each county. Local people looked upon these days as a time to "make merrie" and enjoy the gossip about various court cases. Visitors will see Thomas Jefferson, George Washington, and the town crier strolling the streets. Colonial-dressed interpreters walk through the crowds, getting everyone involved in conversations of the day. There are colonial dances, musketry practice, and reenactments of that era. The Bluemont Concert Series presents wonderful music, and craftspeople come from all over the Mid-Atlantic region to display and sell their wares. For details call the Loudoun Visitor Bureau at (703) 777–0519 or (800) 752–6118.

Middleburg was established in 1781 by Col. Leven Powell and received its name because it is halfway between Alexandria and Winchester. For more than two hundred years the town has been a popular place for travelers to stop for a meal and overnight. The **Red Fox Inn & Mosby's Tavern,** at 2 East Washington Street in Middleburg (800–223–1728 [outside VA] or 703–687–6301, fax 703–687–6187), is said to be the oldest original inn in America. The buildings date from 1728 and retain the charm of that era. George Washington stopped here around 1748 when he was surveying for Lord Fairfax. Also in Middleburg is the **Tuscany Inn,** at 101 South Madison Street (703–687–6456). It's located in the Wright House, the second oldest building in Middleburg. You can stay overnight or have a meal in one of four dining rooms.

The Leesburg area has a number of great places to stay. Try **Fleetwood Farm B&B** on Route 1, Leesburg (703–327–4325, fax 703–777–8236). This manor house was built in 1745 by the Reverend Doctor Charles Green, who was doctor to George and Martha Washington. It's a working sheep farm, and there is a colonial herb garden. Mentioned earlier, the **Laurel Brigade Inn,** 20 West Market Street, Leesburg (703–777–1010), was a pop-ular "ordinary" (a pub that served food) during colonial days, and the Marquis de Lafayette was entertained there in 1825. There are six guest rooms and a dining room. The **Norris House Inn B&B & Stone House Tea Room,** at 108 Loudoun Street S.W., Leesburg (800–644–1806 or 703–777–1806, fax 703–771–8051), is located in the historical district and features antiques and canopy beds. The garden blooms to entice guests to relax a while. Tea is served in the Stone House next door. **Oakland Green Farm B&B** is nearby in Lincoln (703–338–7628). This house is in two sec-tions; the older log house dates from the 1730s. Family antiques fill the rooms, enhanced by hand-braided rugs.

JEFFERSON'S CHARLOTTESVILLE

The term "Renaissance man" suggests an almost inconceivable intellectual power and multiplicity of talents that we associate with Michelangelo and Leonardo da Vinci. Although we sometimes pay lip service to the ideal of being able to do many things well, the explosion of knowledge and hyperspecialization of our world make the possibility hard to believe in, whether we're talking about what it takes to be a nuclear physicist or a professional tennis star. Yet just two centuries ago the plantation owners and merchants who played the central role in founding our government were indeed men for all seasons, not only soldiers and statesmen but simultaneously farmers, businessmen, architects, scientists, and scholars. Thomas Jefferson represents a whole class of Virginians who demonstrated their capacities and vigor by playing many roles well, and the best way to appreciate this is to visit **Monticello,** the remarkable house he built on a hill above Charlottesville, overlooking the university he designed and founded.

Things may not make the man, but in Jefferson's case they often tell the tale of his taste, his accomplishments, and his amazing intellectual versatility.

Thomas Jefferson's beloved Monticello

They include his famous revolving Windsor chair; the mahogany lap desk on which he wrote the Declaration of Independence; and many portraits, including those of George Washington, the Marquis de Lafayette, and John Adams. Also a footed silver goblet made by a Parisian silversmith based on Jefferson's drawing; a bronze bell given to Sally Hemings, a household slave, by Martha Jefferson; and Windsor chairs, based on his specifications. After a tour of his amazing house, which anticipates many of the innovations in recent home architecture, you'll think of him as the Frank Lloyd Wright of the eighteenth century—and it's all done in rooms of modest proportions.

Jefferson inherited 500 acres and many slaves when he was just twenty-one years old. He started to build Monticello at the age of twenty-six and, after making detailed drawings, supervised its construction. Jefferson chose a formal classical design based on the work of the sixteenth-century Italian architect Andrea Palladio, whose influence pervaded the building of plantation mansions in Virginia. The house had a purpose beyond architectural elegance. Everything was designed to make daily living easier and more efficient. Jefferson married Martha Skelton three years later; she lived for ten years after their marriage and bore six children.

Jefferson attended the College of William and Mary, practiced law, and entered public life at an early age. In 1776 he was chosen to draft the Declaration of Independence. He served as governor of Virginia from 1779 to 1781 and in 1784 went to France, where he succeeded Benjamin Franklin as minister. In 1790 he became secretary of state under George Washington. Jefferson was elected president of the United States in 1800, after a tie with Aaron Burr was resolved, and held the office from 1801 to 1809. Jefferson authorized the crucial purchase of the Louisiana Territory in 1803 and supported exploration of the West by the Lewis and Clark expedition. In 1815 he sold his personal library to the Library of Congress to replace the national library, which had been burned by the British during the War of 1812. After a life of incredible accomplishment, Jefferson died at the age of eighty-three in 1826.

The best place to start comprehending Jefferson's accomplishments is the **Thomas Jefferson Visitor Center,** on Route 20 off Interstate 64. Here you can view several fine films, including *Thomas Jefferson at Monticello* and *Thomas Jefferson: The Pursuit of Liberty,* as well as collect sightseeing and lodging information. The center also sells a discounted combination ticket for Monticello, Michie Tavern, and Ash Lawn-Highland. (See below for details of sites.) All three historic sites are open daily, apart from a few major holidays, but times vary seasonally. Call (804) 293–6789 for further information.

Today visitors to Monticello can view the home in small groups. The Entrance Hall was the "museum of civilization," which contained his collection of Native American and natural history pieces. Visitors used to wait in this room, where they could view his collections. Pieces from his Indian Hall collection include a buffalo robe that depicts a battle, a tobacco pouch of otter skin from the Sauk-Fox, a Crow cradle, and an eagle bone whistle. The seven-day calendar clock has markers on the wall for the days of the week; to record them cannonballs move up and down on a rope, disappearing into a hole in the floor.

The South Square Room was an extension of his library. The Book Room at one time contained his 7,000 volumes. Books on the shelves now exhibit the same titles. His study contains a revolving chair, a Windsor bench, a table with a revolving-top, a telescope, and globes.

An alcove containing Jefferson's bed connects the South Square Room with his Two-story Bedroom, a marvelous anticipation of lofts. A skylight provides light, and several oval openings provide air into his closet, which is really on the second floor but accessible from the ground level. A black-marble obelisk clock is mounted at the foot of his bed. Jefferson was always up at first light, and the first thing he did was wash his feet in cold water, which he said kept him from getting sick.

The family gathered most of the time in the Parlor to talk, engage in games, play the harpsichord, and entertain friends. Portraits on the walls include those of Magellan, Columbus, Walter Raleigh, and Lafayette. The Dining Room, stretching up two stories with a skylight, also contains dumbwaiters, designed to bring up wine from the cellar. Because the din-

An Eighteenth-Century Xerox

Have you heard of an eighteenth-century polygraph? Jefferson anticipated carbon paper and photocopiers by two centuries. Most unusual is the two-pen letter-duplicating device, with which Jefferson duplicated his correspondence. A wooden frame holds two pens, which write in tandem on two sheets of paper.

ing room is located in the coldest corner of the house, both windows and doors have double glass. Look for a revolving serving door with shelves. Servants on the outside put food on the shelves while those on the inside removed it to serve the table.

Outside there is an entrance to an all-weather passageway under the house to access the kitchen, smokehouse, cook's quarters, stables, and ice house. Just beyond is **Mulberry Row,** which has buildings for weaving, nail making, a utility shed, and dwellings for slaves and carpentry. The flower gardens contain twenty oval-shaped beds, planted with a variety of flowers. Some of the species came from Europe, some bloom with woodland flowers, others were curiosities. A "roundabout" flower border winds around a curving walk that Jefferson planned in 1807.

Ash Lawn–Highland, the home of President James Monroe, is located 2¹/₂ miles beyond Monticello on Route 795. Monroe and Jefferson were friends, and Jefferson chose the house site for Monroe, later sending his gardeners over to begin planting orchards. By November of 1799 James Monroe and his wife, Elizabeth, moved into their new plantation home. Unfortunately, Monroe ran into debt and had to sell Ash Lawn–Highland instead of retiring there. He had held more major offices than any other President, including being a U.S. senator, minister to England, as well as minister to Spain and to France, governor of Virginia, secretary of state, secretary of war, and president of the United States from 1817–1825.

Jay Winston Johns, the last owner of Ash Lawn–Highland, gave it to the College of William and Mary, Monroe's alma mater. The college is completing a major restoration to coincide with the 200th anniversary of James Monroe's purchase of the house as well as the 300th anniversary of the founding of William and Mary. The house is open daily, but hours vary by season; to find out more call (804) 293–9539.

On the other side of Monticello, on the way to Charlottesville, stands **Michie Tavern,** one of the oldest homesteads in Virginia. William Michie, a Scotsman whose father had come to Virginia as an indentured servant, opened his home as an "ordinary" to travelers on the stagecoach route in 1784; it was moved to its present location in 1927. The Tavern Museum offers a glimpse into life of that era with a ballroom, keeping hall, parlors, and a wine cellar. Visitors can have lunch in the ordinary, which offers typical eighteenth-century Virginia cuisine daily. A general store carries

Virginia wines, specialty foods, and gifts. Hours (for museum): daily from 9:00 A.M. to 5:00 P.M.; call (804) 977–1234 for more information.

Years after designing his own house and completing his eminent political career, Jefferson laid out an elaborate plan for the **University of Virginia.** Its Rotunda is a half-scale model of the Roman Pantheon, and, in the early years of the university, it served as library and classroom together. Pavilions extend from the Rotunda; professors lived on the top floors and taught on the lower floors. Students lived in fifty-four lawn rooms on intermediate floors. This Jeffersonian "academical village" has been considerably expanded over the years, but its design influenced most of the major universites on the East Coast, so it is not inappropriate that a statue of Thomas Jefferson, by Karl Bitter, stands on the grounds. Perhaps we should remember the architect as much as the politician.

The **Pavilion Gardens** are divided into East Pavilion and West Pavilion. Each garden is numbered and has a different design. They are pleasant as a place to study and also designed to be an object of study. Jefferson felt that "such a plan would afford the quiet retirement so friendly to study." Professors planned and cared for some of the gardens; others contained buildings that served utilitarian functions, such as quarters for servants and sheds for animals. Thus the liberal and practical arts existed in cooperative union—an ideal at least a century ahead of its time. For more information about tours of the university campus call, (804) 924–3239.

There is no doubt that Jefferson was a remarkable man, as his house, gardens, inventions, books, scientific instruments, and the University of Virginia campus visibly demonstrate. Yet we must remind ourselves that he was not so much one of a kind as preeminent in a whole class of individuals whose houses and libraries represent a comparable range of interests. Through a combination of circumstances—classical education, leisure, opportunities for political leadership, and genuine interest in agriculture—a class of American Renaissance men was born who could, and did, do it all.

For lunch or dinner head for the **Boar's Head Inn & Sports Club,** on Route 250 West (800–476–1988 or 804–296–2181). The historic old section of the inn still stands, enhanced by extensive additions designed to complement nineteenth-century settings. Luncheon and dinner in the Old Mill Room is pleasant, with views of the lake and mountains. You can also spend the night here.

A good place for lodging is the **Silver Thatch Inn,** 3001 Hollymead Drive (804–978–4686 or fax 804–973–6156). The inn, which dates back to 1780, offers seven rooms. You can also find accommodations at **The Inn at Monticello,** on Route 19 (call 804–979–3593 or fax (804–296–1344). This historic B&B dates from 1850, when it began life as a farmhouse. A nearby lake offers swimming and fishing.

FOR MORE INFORMATION

Virginia Division of Tourism
1021 East Cary Street
Richmond, VA 23219
(804) 644–1607 or (800) VISIT VA (800–84748–81)

Georgia

Historical Introduction to
GEORGIA

*S*pain had founded Franciscan missions on St. Simons and Jekyll islands as well as the adjacent mainland by 1566. This made the British to the north nervous, and they were determined to create a buffer between themselves and the Spanish.

Fort King George rose in 1721 as a palisaded earthen fort, with blockhouse, near present-day Darien on the Altamaha. This fort was the southern outpost for the British in the New World. Col. John "Tuscarora Jack" Barnwell and his men lived here for seven years, enduring deprivation, disease, and stormy winters. In 1726 a fire wiped out the barracks and damaged the blockhouse. The next year the troops abandoned the fort and moved to Port Royal, South Carolina.

The First Settlement in Georgia

James Oglethorpe hatched a plan to bring imprisoned debtors from England to Georgia, where they could work and make a profit for the colony's proprietors. In October 1732 the group assembled on the galley *Anne* and went down below into crowded conditions. All the adult males were required to assemble on deck every day and learn how to be good soldiers, for part of their obligation on land would be to protect the settlement. As it turned out, of the 5,000 people who sailed for Georgia by 1750, only 2,000 were imprisoned debtors, and many of them may have been tossed in prison by their creditors—they weren't such a bad lot after all.

The newcomers were surprised at the warm welcome provided by a nearby Yamacraw Indian tribe, who came in procession bearing gifts of friendship. Chief Tomochichi gave Oglethorpe a buffalo skin, painted with the head of an eagle. The eagle symbolized swiftness and the buffalo strength, but, in addition, the soft feathers of the eagle signified love and the skin of the buffalo meant warmth and protection. John Musgrove and his half-Indian wife, Mary, also arrived, and she interpreted for the English. The settlers went right to work: They cleared land for a town, built a fort and palisade, and made the ground ready for planting; each freeholder had his own tract of land.

A Novel Approach

When people on board the *Anne* didn't get along, Oglethorpe gave each a pint of rum and told them to drink and be friends.

St. Simons Island and Fort Frederica

In 1736 Oglethorpe settled a group of families on St. Simons, where they built the town of Frederick. First they built the fort, then replaced their temporary palmetto huts with houses. The War of Jenkins' Ear took place in 1739 after Robert Jenkins, a British smuggler, had lost an ear in a fracas with the Spanish off the Florida coast. Parliament construed this as an insult to British honor and used it as an excuse to recruit the colonists against the Spanish.

By 1742 the Spanish were again on the move, but their attack ended in victory for the English, removing the last threat from the South. In 1752 Oglethorpe and the trustees surrendered their charter to the Crown, and a new Royal Governor, Capt. John Reynolds, arrived in 1754. He was very unpopular at the outset, and the dislike of two successors deepened as Parliament created the Stamp Act and other taxes for them to enforce. Yet Georgians had divided sympathies in the years that preceded the Revolution, a split that lasted until the Second Continental Congress in 1775.

Regions to Explore

T he Colony of Georgia has been divided into four regions that were important in the colonial era: the first settlement at Fort King George, near Darien; the Savannah area; Fort Frederica on St. Simons Island; and Jekyll Island.

FORT KING GEORGE

Fort King George, located near Darien east of Highway 17, has been rebuilt on its original foundation. Researchers found old records and drawings, which enabled them to reconstruct the blockhouse to original specifications, using the same building material, cypress wood. Visitors can view a slide presentation to orient themselves and then walk through the exhibits in the museum. Interpreters wear hand-sewn clothing that looks like the garments people wore in the 1700s.

The men who lived here had to put up with heat, insects, Indians, and the Spanish. During the eighteenth century this part of the country was not healthful because it was impossible to keep food fresh in the heat. Salt meat rotted, and they did not know the wisdom of eating fresh fruit, so many of them died of scurvy. Remains of British soldiers still lie in graves in one of the oldest British military cemeteries in the country.

Tabby in the Walls

T abby is an early building material made with lime that was produced from burning oyster shells. The lime was then mixed with sand and shells to produce the concrete you will see in many seventeenth- and eighteenth-century foundations in Georgia and South Carolina.

On the grounds you'll also see the tabby-and-brick (see box above) sawmill ruins from a later era, after the turn of the century; timber floated down the Oconee, Ocmulgee, Ohoopee, and Altamaha Rivers from the interior of the country to the sawmill.

SAVANNAH

In 1744 Francis Moore, in his *Voyage to Georgia Begun in the Year 1735,* wrote about Savannah's squares: "The use of this is, in case a War should happen, that the Villages without may have Places in the Town, to bring their Cattle and Families into for Refuge, and to that Purpose there is a Square left in every Ward, big enough for the Out-wards to encamp in." Today Savannah has twenty-two squares, and all are lush with greenery, blooming flowers, and live oaks. Some of them have statues, with ironwork scrolled around them, and fountains; others have benches and paths for a quiet rest.

Another feature that marks Savannah is the use of ironwork. Scrolled patterns enliven balconies, stair railings, doors, and the front of buildings. Visitors continue to look for iron griffins as foot scrapers, iron dolphins as waterspouts, and iron storks as newel posts. Much of the first ironwork in the city arrived from England after the fire of 1796, when people were rebuilding their homes. Again, after the fire of 1820, William Jay encouraged builders to use iron for floor joists, rafters, shutters, and sash frames. Decorative ironwork was very much in vogue at that time; later it dwindled in popularity, and now it is highly prized.

You can choose to look around Savannah on your own, take a Gray Line tour for an overall view, or do both. In any case plan your day so that you can have lunch at **Mrs. Wilkes' Boarding House,** 107 West James Street. She serves home-style cooking, family style, with delicious dishes, such as fried chicken, sweet potatoes, green vegetables, cole slaw, and pies, going round and round the tables. Call (912) 232–5997 for information.

The **Colonial Park Cemetery,** on the east side of Abercorn Street, opened around 1750. A tabby sidewalk runs through the cemetery under lovely old trees, which provide shade on hot days. Some inscriptions on tombstones are almost illegible, but plaques are provided so that visitors can read about those buried on the grounds. Some famous Georgians interred here include Button Gwinnett, a signer of the Declaration of Independence, Archibald Bulloch, James Habersham, Hugh McCall, and Edward Green Malbone.

The **Savannah Historical Museum** houses a wide variety of artifacts and collections, featuring pieces from the earliest inhabitants: a spear point from 1500 B.C. and one from 8000 B.C. as well as Indian poker chips that date from A.D. 1450. Uniformed models include a private from the 71st Highlander Regiment. A 1760 Hessian flintlock pistol is here. The museum is open daily from 8:30 A.M. to 5:00 P.M. Call (912) 238–1779 for information.

The **Ships of the Sea Museum** has a fine collection of scrimshaw (etching and carving on whalebone), including an ostrich egg with the ship the *Prince of Wales* on it. A pirate figurehead is unusual; he looks both handsome and fearsome. Models are housed on each floor, including those of a sixteenth-century Mediterranean galley, the *Charles Morgan,* the *Endeavor,* the *Eagle, Flying Cloud,* H.M.S. *Victory,* the *Anne* (which brought colonists

The Colonial Cemetery is dotted with plaques describing many colonial leaders from Georgia.

to Georgia), the S.S. *Juliette Low,* the S.S. *Savannah,* and a trireme that dates from the sixth century B.C. The shell collection includes a green turban snail, which was decorated and given to Queen Victoria and Prince Albert for the opening of the Crystal Palace in 1851. The museum is open daily 10:00 A.M.–5:00 P.M. Closed January 1, St. Patrick's Day, Thanksgiving, and Christmas. Call (912) 232–1511 for more details.

Savannah offers some special festivals, such as the Tour of Homes and Gardens in late March, the Hidden Gardens in April, the War of Jenkins' Ear in May, Tools and Skills That Built a Colony in September, Labor Day Weekend Encampment of Troops, Christmas at Colonial Wormsloe, and the Holiday Tour of Homes in December. For information call (800) 444–2427 or (912) 944–0456.

Accommodations in Savannah include the following. **Ballastone Inn,** at 14 East Oglethorpe Avenue (call 800–822–4553 or 912–236–1484; fax 912–236–4626), is a restored 1835 townhouse in the historic district. **East Bay Inn,** at 225 East Bay Street (800–500–1225 or 912–238–1225; fax 912–232–2709), is located in a restored 1853 warehouse with Georgian decor.

The **Gastonian,** at 220 East Gaston Street (call 912–232–2869 or fax 912–234–0006), is in connected 1868 houses, and there's a landscaped garden. **Liberty Inn,** at 128 West Liberty Street (800–637–1007 or 912–233–1007), is in a restored 1834 building. **Olde Harbour Inn,** at 508 East Factors Walk (call 800–553–6533 or 912–232–5678; fax 912–233–5979), offers suites with living room and kitchen, most overlooking the water so that you can watch the moving parade of boats. **Presidents' Quarters,** at 225 East President Street (call 800–233–1776 or 912–233–1600; fax 912–238–0849), dates from 1855 and the rooms are named for Presidents of the United States.

Restaurants include **The Chart House,** at 202 West Bay Street (912–234–6686), a nautical restored warehouse.

FORT FREDERICA ON ST. SIMONS ISLAND

Not far away from Savannah, there are more islands to explore: St. Simons and Sea Island. Head north to **Brunswick,** where you can see the shrimp fleet at the foot of Gloucester Street. Victorian houses line some of the streets near the Court House. Drive over Glynn Avenue to Overlook Park for a fine view of the "Marshes of Glynn," immortalized during the 1870s by Georgia's poet Sidney Lanier.

St. Simons Island has lush green foliage, vivid blooming plants, and live oaks. **Retreat Plantation**, now the Sea Island Golf Course, houses the ruins of a slave hospital, as well as a fishing pier, on its grounds. The **Bloody Marsh Battle** site is on Demere Road. On July 7, 1742, the Spanish, on their way to invade Fort Frederica, were defeated here by British troops. One account, told by British survivors in later years, said that the Spanish thought the fighting had stopped, put their arms in a pile, and sat down to have some refreshment. At this point a Highland bonnet emerged from the woods, which was the signal for the British to open fire into the Spanish contingent. The Spanish were routed and fled in all directions. This was the turning point of Spanish aggression into Georgia as the Spanish army left St. Simons and headed back to Florida.

Another important site is **Christ Church,** on Frederica Road. John and Charles Wesley held services here under oak trees in 1736. The church was built in 1884; one of the windows, depicting the Confession of Christ by St. Peter at Caesarea Philippi, was designed in Germany in 1899. Families of early settlers are buried in the churchyard.

Fort Frederica was developed by General Oglethorpe in 1736 and named after Frederick, the only son of King George II. It was the most expensive fort the British built in North America. Ruins of the magazine still stand on the waterfront. Its guns were trained on the water, and few enemy ships could pass without notice. Oglethorpe had a wall built around the entire fort to protect its citizens. Broad Street divided the town in halves. The first settlers included forty-four men, who were mostly craftsmen, and seventy-two women and children. Each family had a lot for building and fifty acres in the country for crops.

Walk out on the grounds to read the informative plaques that are placed beside the foundations of some of the buildings. The first houses were palmetto huts, replaced by structures of wood, tabby, and brick. The house on the left side of Broad Street, directly behind the magazine, was a double house, shared on one side by Dr. Thomas Hawkins and his wife, Beatre. He was the regimental surgeon, town physician, and apothecary, as well as an officer of the court. Samuel and Susanna Davison lived on the other side. He was a tavern keeper, a town constable, and a ship inspector.

The demise of Fort Frederica came with peace. Oglethorpe left for England in 1743, and the regiment was disbanded in 1749. Shopkeepers could not continue with few customers, and soon the town was one of "houses without inhabitants, barracks without soldiers, guns without carriages, and streets overgrown with weeds."

The Untamed Shrew

Documented gossip tells that Mrs. Hawkins was a veritable shrew, a mean and neurotic troublemaker, whose temperament may be deduced from the fact that she beat her servant, broke a bottle over a constable's head, and threatened John Wesley with a pistol, biting him in the wrist when he attempted to disarm her.

A cannon stands sentinel at Fort Frederica.

If you're looking for a nice vacation spot, try the **Cloister at Sea Island;** for reservations call (800) SEA ISLA (800–732–4752) or (912) 638–3611. Sea Island was almost uninhabited until 1924, when a causeway was built from Brunswick to St. Simons. Four years later The Cloister opened; it's great for families, for honeymooners, or for anyone who wants to get away.

JEKYLL ISLAND

Jekyll Island is one of the barrier islands that protect the southeast coast of Georgia. Located 6 miles from the mainland it is accessible by causeway. Early residents included the Guale Indians. During the fifteenth century European explorers came, seeking gold. Spanish missionaries arrived in the sixteenth and seventeenth centuries and founded Santiago de Ocone, a mission. Gen. James Edward Oglethorpe settled Savannah in 1733 and in 1734 sailed by the island, which he named for his friend Sir Joseph Jekyll.

William Horton, one of Oglethorpe's officers, created a plantation on the island; it was destroyed by the Spanish after the Battle of Bloody Marsh in 1742. Horton built another home and rebuilt his plantation by 1746.

For information about the island, call the Jekyll Island Convention and Visitors Bureau at (800) 841–6586. Wonderful accommodations are available at the **Jekyll Island Club Hotel** (800–333–3333), part of the orginial complex from a century ago, on the land formerly occupied by early settlers. Guests live as the founders of the club did years ago, with oriental rugs, stained-glass windows, lovely furnishings—and croquet on the lawn!

FOR MORE INFORMATION

Georgia Department of Industry, Trade, and Tourism
Box 1776
Atlanta, GA 30301
(800) VISIT–GA (800–84748–42)
(404) 656–3590

North Carolina

Historical Introduction to the

NORTH CAROLINA COLONY

*W*e sometimes think of North Carolina as a state on a tilt, rising into the Great Smoky Mountains at its western edge and dipping into the great sounds of Albemarle and Pamlico along its eastern fringe. There is more water than land behind the big bulge of barrier beach that forms Cape Hatteras, but the fertile land that surrounds sheltered sounds and their tributary rivers invited early settlement in plantations. So it is not surprising that the first British attempt to establish a permanent colony occurred here.

What happened to this British colony is another question. If you like unsolved mysteries, think about the "Lost Colony" on Roanoke Island, tucked behind the barrier beach along one of the most fearsome stretches of coastline in North America. Eighty-nine men, seventeen women, and eleven children were last seen there on August 27, 1587. Two of the women were pregnant when the company of colonists left England, and on August 18, 1587, Virginia Dare was the first baby born on the island. Nine days later Governor John White sailed for England to bring back supplies needed for the survival of the colony.

A Mysterious Message

When Governor White returned more than two years later, in 1590, he "saw a great smoke rise in the Ile Roanoke neere the place where I left our Colony in the yeere 1587, which smoake put us in good hope that some of the Colony were there expecting my returne out of England." The smoke may have been an Indian fire, but the place was empty, and there were no traces of the settlers he had brought to the new land. White's party found the letters CRO carved on a tree, which seemed to be a sign left for them. Before White's departure the settlers had agreed to carve a cross to indicate a sign of distress; none was found.

White and his men walked inland and found the remnants of the settlement, with chests broken open, books lying under the shrubs, and a message carved on a post: CROATOAN. (*Croatoan* is the Indian word for Hatteras). Perhaps remnants of the colony would be found on Croatoan, the land where their Indian friend, Manteo, had been born; however, the fierce gales that batter the Cape Hatteras region kept them from landing there, and they eventually gave up, assuming that further search would yield nothing about the fate of the colonists.

Earlier Attempts at Settlement

Ironically, this colonizing venture had set forth with the strongest and most influential backing. In 1584 Sir Walter Raleigh had received a charter from Queen Elizabeth I "to inhabit and possess . . . all remote and heathen lands not in actual possession of any Christian Prince." A colony led by Sir Richard Grenville, with Ralph Lane as governor, spent a year on Roanoke Island and then sailed back to England in 1586. The next contingent to arrive was the group led by John White in 1587.

Navigation along the uncharted coast of a "new" continent known only for its major features was uncertain at best—and especially so nearly two centuries before there was an accurate method of determining longitude. The original plan had called for settling in tidewater Virginia at the lower end of Chesapeake Bay after a brief stop on Roanoke Island. Unfortunately the pilot, Simon Fernandez, chose to drop all of the colonists and leave them on the island—and no one knows what happened to them between 1587 and 1590.

More Settlers and More Troubles

By the 1650s colonists from Virginia settled on Albemarle Sound. Nathaniel Batts built a two-room house at the western end of the sound in 1653. He traded with the Indians, and gradually more settlers came to join him. In 1663 King Charles II named a group of men Lords Proprietors of Carolina and granted them land from the southern shore of Albemarle Sound to the (now) Georgia-Florida state line. The proprietors, however, also wanted the "Southern Plantation," located on the northern side of the sound and in 1665 received that additional territory.

Nevertheless troubles were brewing. Cary's Rebellion occurred early in the eighteenth century after Governor Thomas Cary tried to coerce Quakers into swearing an oath to the Anglican church, which they refused to do—not without cause, since many of them had left prosperous farms in England and Wales for that very reason. Edward Hyde became the next governor in 1712, but he had to displace Cary with a contingent of soldiers from Virginia.

With all of this disagreement among the settlers, the Tuscarora Indians took the opportunity to annihilate the whites, and in September 1711 they ravaged the colony. In the face of a common enemy during the Tuscarora War, the squabbling colonists came to their senses and joined forces, Quakers and Anglicans alike. The war, however, devastated their territory, leaving them with burned houses and barns, slaughtered cattle, and no crops.

At the same time the next disaster was brewing, this time from the sea. The pirates who had been tossed out of the West Indies by the British invaded the North Carolina coast. The Outer Banks and mouth of the Cape Fear River were ideal for their purposes, but, in the summer and fall of 1718, forces from neighboring colonies made a concerted effort to rid the coast of pirates. After a tough battle, even the infamous Stede Bonnet was captured by a South Carolinian, tried, and hanged in Charles Towne. Crews from Virginia found Blackbeard near Ocracoke Inlet on the Outer Banks, killed him, and placed his head in the rigging of his ship for a triumphant return home.

After this scourge had been removed, things calmed down a bit. Edenton was incorporated in 1722 and soon became the center of government. More settlers arrived from other colonies, and some settled along the Cape Fear River, a deep-water port. In 1732 a group arrived from the Scottish Highlands. After the Battle of Culloden in 1746, Parliament made life very difficult for the Scots, so even more fled to North Carolina, where they were welcomed.

Regions to Explore

T he North Carolina Colony has been divided into three geographical
regions: the Outer Banks, the Great Sounds, and the Piedmont.

North Carolina

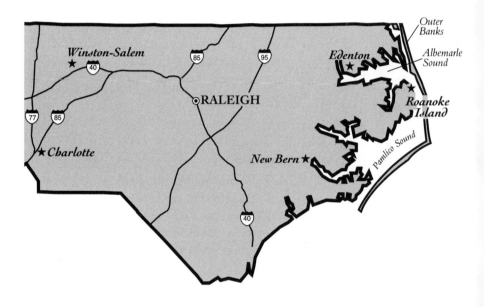

THE OUTER BANKS

Every summer *The Lost Colony* is presented on stage in **Manteo,** on Roanoke Island. This drama of men, women, and children ready to begin a new life who then vanished mysteriously has fascinated theatergoers for more than fifty years. Pulitzer Prize–winning playwright Paul Green wrote the script, and Porter Van Zandt directed and produced the play. Call (800) 488–5012 or (919) 473–3414 for performance schedules and tickets.

Once desolate and deserted, **Roanoke Island** is now chock-full of interest for visitors. In addition to the play, there are replicas of a ship, a fort, and elaborate gardens to visit.

The *Elizabeth II* was built to commemorate the 400th anniversary of colonizing activity in America. This 69-foot, square-rigged vessel is similar to those used in Sir Walter Raleigh's day. You'll get strong visual impressions of life on board from the film *A Roanoke Voyage* and interpreters dressed in period costume. Open daily from 10:00 A.M. to 6:00 P.M., April to October; 10:00 A.M.–4:00 P.M. Tuesday through Sunday during the rest of the year. For details call (919) 473–1144.

The **Fort Raleigh National Historic Site,** with displays, a film, and interpretive programs, stands on the north end of Roanoke Island. It includes a reconstruction of the small earthen fort and sites of some houses from the settlement. Archaeologists found artifacts to establish the location of the fort, built in the shape of a square, with pointed bastions on two sides and an octagonal bastion on another. The site is open daily 9:00 A.M.–5:00 P.M., June through August; 9:00 A.M.–dusk during the rest of the year. Call ahead (919–473–5772) for a schedule of special events.

The **Elizabethan Gardens,** created by the Garden Club of North Carolina in 1951, adjoin Fort Raleigh National Park. Luckily club members heard about some statuary that was being removed from the Greenwood Estate of The Honorable John Hay Whitney, Ambassador to The Court of St. James. Although Mr. Whitney was thinking of giving it to the Metropolitan Museum in New York, he changed its destination to the Garden Club. The set of statuary includes an Italian fountain and a pool with balustrade, wellhead, sundial, birdbaths, stone steps, and benches. The gardens opened on August 18, 1960, the 373rd anniversary of the birth of Virginia Dare.

Massive iron gates (from the French Embassy in Washington) open through a wall of old handmade bricks. The Gate House is patterned after a sixteenth-century orangery. The walls are hung with an oil portrait of Queen Elizabeth I, a 1663 map of Devonshire, the coats-of-arms of Queen Elizabeth I and Sir Walter Raleigh, and a roster of the men and women from the Lost Colony.

As you walk through gardens, heady with the scent of herbs and flowers, you'll come upon marble statues, like the one of Virginia Dare. Sculpted in 1859, the statue was shipwrecked off the coast of Spain and spent two years on the ocean floor. Today she stands in a beautiful garden, holding a fishnet draped around her waist, with a heron by her side. Indian legends tell that she grew up with Indians and that her spirit now bounds around Roanoke Island in the shape of a white doe. For more information call (919) 473–3234.

THE GREAT SOUNDS

More than 400 years of American history play a slow waltz in the bucolic region that surrounds historic Albemarle Sound. **Edenton** is a good place to begin a leisurely survey of this beautiful country—a place the colonists claimed as their choice, as the name suggests. Fronting the sound and filled with clapboard colonial houses, Edenton is still a lovely spot to call home, and local inhabitants are so comfortable they don't bother to lock their doors. Begin your exploration of town at the **Historic Edenton Visitor Center** (919–482–2637), 108 North Broad Street, where docents lead a walking tour. Tour hours are 9:30 A.M., 11:00 A.M., 1:00 P.M., 2:30 P.M., April to November; 10:00 A.M., 11:30 A.M., and 2:00 P.M. the rest of the year.

Your first stop is **St. Paul's Church,** on West Church Street, where colonists came with conflict in their hearts between loyalty to the Crown and desire for freedom. After being raised in the Church of England, the settlers found this dichotomy disturbing. The parish was organized under the first Vestry Act in 1701, making it the oldest charter in North Carolina, and its building, begun in 1736, is the second oldest in the state. Narrow pews were designed to keep parishioners "aware and awake." The ladies used foot warmers, and the doors on the pews kept some of the heat inside. The solid brass Flemish chandelier is 500 years old.

The oldest house in town, **Cupola House** was constructed in 1725 by shipbuilders and is thought to be the finest wooden Jacobean-type house south of Connecticut. Francis Corbin, an agent for Lord Granville, the last of the Lords Proprietors, probably added Georgian interior woodwork between 1756 and 1758. In 1777 Dr. Samuel Dickinson bought the house. His wife, then Elizabeth P. Ormond, was one of the signers of the famous "Tea Party" resolutions, proving that politics was not entirely a male domain even in colonial times. A group of women in town felt strongly enough to meet and sign this resolution on October 25, 1774:

> *The Provincial Deputies of North Carolina having resolved not to drink any more tea, nor wear any more British cloth, &c. many ladies of this Province have determined to give a memorable proof of their patriotism, and have accordingly entered into the following honourable and spirited association. I send it to you to shew your fair countrywomen, how zealously and faithfully American Ladies follow the laudable example of their husbands, and what opposition your Ministers may expect to receive from a people thus firmly united against them.*

Inside the Cupola House visitors will see fireplace mantles made of wood, painted to look like marble. A portrait of Penelope Barker hangs in the dining room. This sharp marriage entrepreneur had several husbands; she cleverly sold the house to each successive husband and banked the money. Upstairs there is a dress that belonged to her, a three-sided baby crib pushed up against the parents' bed, a French potty chair, and a daybed used for naps. The guest room shows signs of a ghost, who apparently sits on the bed after it has been made and creates a depression. We also enjoyed seeing a collection of toys including a tea set, dolls, cradles, and valentines.

Walk down to the water's edge for a view of the **Barker House**, which was probably built for Penelope and Thomas Barker around 1782. Penelope was the spokesperson for the Edenton Tea Party ladies. You'll see a teapot, sitting on a post on the Green, and a tablet on the 1767 Court House as reminders of this event. News of the Edenton Tea Party was sent to England and published, generating a spate of not entirely complimentary cartoons. London, of course, was outraged at this effrontery, and the *London Times* printed a caricature that depicted meddlesome women.

Benjamin Franklin, Silas Deane, and Charles Lee, American commissioners in Paris, purchased the cannons on the **Green** in 1777. Forty more

Cupola House is furnished with period pieces and memorabilia.

were also brought to Edenton in 1778. All of them were eventually pushed into the bay so that the British would not capture them.

The **Court House** dates from 1718. Restorers from Colonial Williamsburg came here to measure it as a model for one of their buildings that lacked documentation, and archaeological digs still continue on its grounds. In early colonial days a circuit judge came here to represent the Crown every few weeks, bringing with him a scarce item—news. During his attendance people wandered in and out, fighting, shouting "He's guilty!" and transforming court day into one of public amusement.

The **Iredell House** dates from 1773, when Joseph Whedbee, a silversmith, built the older section of the present structure. He sold it to James Iredell, Deputy Collector for the Port of Roanoke. Iredell married Hannah Johnston, the sister of the future Governor Samuel Johnston. The parlor contains his portrait, and this was the room where dances were held, followed by midnight dinners. Portraits of James and Frances Iredell hang in the breakfast room, and the dining room has displays of china and silver. Upstairs, the master bedroom is decorated with a kitten's-ear spread, a lock box for private papers, quill pens, a horsehide bucket filled with sand for fireplace sparks, a bed warmer, and a foot warmer to take to church.

Every other year Historic Edenton organizes a Pilgrimage of Edenton and the countryside. Visitors have the chance to tour private homes during two days in April. During the same month every year, the Historic Edenton Antique Show & Sale is held in the National Guard Armory. Other annual events include the Fourth of July Celebration on the waterfront and a Christmas Candlelight tour during the second weekend in December. Call (919) 482–2637 for more information.

For lodging try the **Governor Eden Inn B&B,** at 304 North Broad Street (919–482–2072). Governor Eden was a Proprietor from 1714 to 1722; the inn has Ionic columns and a large wraparound porch. Another good choice is the **Granville Queen Inn B&B,** at 108 South Granville Street (call 919–482–5296 or fax 919–482–4319). Each of the guest rooms is furnished with pieces from a different location in the world. The **Lords Proprietors' Inn,** at 300 North Broad Street (800–348–8933 or 919–482–3641), is a complex of three restored homes in the Historic District. Each has a parlor with a fireplace; breakfasts are served in the Whedbee House, overlooking a patio filled with dogwood trees. The **Trestle House Inn,** on Soundside Road (Route 4), is structurally interesting; large redwood beams were milled from railroad trestle timbers to support the house, hence the name. Guests may fish for bass and bream in a private lake. Call (919) 482–2282 for reservations.

A number of eighteenth- and nineteenth-century plantations survive in the region around Albemarle Sound. These houses and plantations in the land around the great sounds of North Carolina are not as large or architecturally pretentious as some in Virginia, South Carolina, and Louisiana, but they are off the beaten track and fun to visit. Perhaps they give Northerners a better feel for lives tied in various ways to land rather than cities and commerce. Not far west of Edenton, near Windsor, stands the **Hope Plantation** and adjoining **Bazemore House.** The latter was moved to its present location in 1979 to form a historic complex. Hours vary seasonally; call (919) 794–3140 for more information.

William and Elizabeth King built the Bazemore House in 1763, and their initials are carved with the date on a brick outside. The bricks are laid in Flemish bond style, and most of the window glass is original. The house is one of two left in North Carolina with brick ends and a gambrel roof. The gambrel roof was constructed to gain space and outwit the king's tax collector; the large room below it was classified as an attic and thereby taxed at a lower rate.

Inside, furniture was arranged around the walls and pulled out for use when needed. The cupboards contain pewter, blue-and-white china, and finger vases to hold flowers. Upstairs the bedrooms housed seven children. The girls' room has a picture of the last King daughter born in the house. The washroom up here is equipped with a little pan for washing. One young visitor recently asked the guide, "How did they get the water up here? How did the girls get their bodies into that little pan?" The master bedroom contains the second oldest known bedstead of its kind east of the Mississippi, dating from 1710.

The adjoining **Hope Plantation House,** built just forty years later for Governor David Stone, represents a far more prosperous era in tidewater North Carolina. Stone was an early proponent of Jeffersonian Republicans, and his home is reminiscent of Jefferson's Monticello. Like Jefferson, Governor Stone was a wealthy man, yet he died at forty-eight without a will; consequently, his house and goods were sold at public auction. Fortunately an inventory was kept so that the restored house could be furnished with similar pieces.

The parlor, where Mrs. Stone entertained guests and served tea, is furnished as it would have been in the Federal era. A portrait of Governor Stone hangs in this room. Striking cobalt-blue crystal graces the dining-room table. The little girls' room contains a dolls' bed and dolls; the children ate here until they were old enough for more formal meals in the dining room. The master bedroom contains an apothecary chest, a chess set, a red Wedgwood vase, and some of Mrs. Stone's handwork. The library, with 1,400 books, is said to house the largest private collection in North Carolina at that time. Governor Stone was a precocious scholar; he attended Princeton at age fourteen and graduated at sixteen in the 1780s.

Not far east of Edenton, on Route 1336 in **Hertford,** stands the 1685 **Newbold–White House,** the oldest house in North Carolina. It is thought that Joseph Scott, a magistrate, legislator, and Quaker, built the house. Between 1689 and 1704 it was used for public meetings. The house is made of brick, using Flemish bond design on the upper part of the house and English bond on the lower; the leaded casement windows have diamond-shaped glass panes.

Inside, the original fireplace has niches in the ends to keep food warm. Closets were a sign of wealth in the 1600s because they were taxed as rooms, and this house has many of them. The "hall" was the room where the family lived—cooking, eating, weaving, spinning, and playing. Because there were no public meetinghouses, the same room served as a meeting hall for the General Assembly and court sessions. The house is open Monday through Saturday 10:00 A.M.–4:30 P.M., March 1 to Decmeber 22. Call (919) 426–7567 for more information.

On the Neuse River, which leads into Pamlico Sound, **New Bern** (named after Bern, Switzerland) was settled in 1710 by Swiss and German colonists. Queen Anne had granted land to their leader, Baron Christopher de Graffenried. Originally the town was laid out in the shape of a cross, but the Tuscarora Indian raids destroyed that plan and demoralized the colonists, many of whom returned to Europe.

At one time the colonial capitol of North Carolina, **Tryon Palace** was also the home of Governor William Tryon. Built in 1770, part of the building burned in a fire in 1798 but has been reconstructed on its original foundation. Local people thought the palace was too luxurious, so they organized as "regulators" for a protest. These men were tough: They had fought at Culloden for Bonnie Prince Charlie before they came to the New World to make a new life in North Carolina. They were nevertheless subdued by Tryon's militia at the Battle of Alamance in 1771.

Although the furnishings are not original with the house, they are antiques from the period. Upstairs, servants quarters are extensive to house the large number the mansion required. The gardens, which overlook the Trent River, are lovely. Hours from 9:30 A.M. to 4 P.M. and from 1:30 P.M. to 4 P.M. Sundays, except some holidays. Call (919) 638–1560 for more information on Tryon Palace and the John Wright Stanly House.

The **John Wright Stanly House,** at 307 George Street, dates from 1783. President George Washington spent two nights in this house and proclaimed it to be "exceeding good lodgings." Stanly was a merchant and ship owner. His ships were active seizing British ships to help the patriots during the Revolution.

If you're in New Bern in October, don't miss the Ghost Walk to see Cedar Grove Cemetery and a number of private homes while hearing about the lives of past inhabitants. There's also a Spring Homes Tour that will get you into a number of lovely colonial homes. Call the Chamber of Commerce at (919) 637–3111 for exact dates. If you'd like to get some real exercise on your journey into the past, you can take a historical bicycle tour to colonial sites in several cities in the region, including New Bern. Call **Paradise Pedallers** at (800) 992–3966 or (704) 335–8687, or fax (704) 335–8686 for more information and schedules.

New Bern has a number of historic inns including **Harmony House Inn,** 215 Pollock Street (919–636–3810). This Greek Revival 1850 home is located in the historic district. At one point the house was sawed in half, one end moved over nine feet, and a new hall and stairs added to increase its size. **King's Arms,** 212 Pollock Street (800–872–9306 or 919–638–4409), dates from 1847 and is located on the gardens of the original Haslet House. All rooms have fireplaces. **New Berne House,** 709 Broad Street (800–842–7688 or 919–636–2250), is located in a Colonial Revival home with lovely gardens shaded by magnolias, pecans, and camellias. Mystery weekends are offered every month, sometimes twice a month.

THE PIEDMONT

Visitors to **Charlotte** now will be struck by the forest of huge spires—that is, bank buildings—each one vying to be taller than the rest, just as cathedrals did in the Middle Ages. At night their lights brighten the whole area, but Charlotte is not all modern and glossy. At a lower level some remnants of the city's interesting past have been preserved.

As explorer John Lawson wandered through the Piedmont region during the early 1700s, he remarked that the Catawba Indians lived in the "finest part of Carolina," whereas the English had settled in the less desirable coastal sections. By 1740 settlers were traveling by covered wagon along the Great Wagon Road from Philadelphia and Maryland to the Piedmont. Thomas Spratt and his wife stopped where the center of Charlotte is now, worn out from the trip, and claimed it was "a gude place" to settle. Thomas Polk chose to build his home along the Indian Trading Path, now Tryon Street.

In 1768 the county was named Mecklenburg to honor King George III's young bride, a princess of Mecklenburg-Strelitz in Germany. The village of Charlotte, named for the same young woman, was incorporated in 1768. By 1774 Hezekiah Alexander had completed his house on the hill, along with a number of Scotch-Irish, French Huguenot, and German Lutheran immigrants.

As the Revolution approached, the citizens of Charlotte raised the cry of freedom and on May 20, 1775, signed their own Mecklenburg Declaration of Independence. (The original document was lost in a fire, and there is some question about its authenticity, but there is no doubt about the patriotic sentiments of the residents.) In 1780 about 150 local militiamen in buckskin, led by Col. William Davie, fought and won "The Battle of the Bees" against Tarlton's Dragoons, who outnumbered them with 2,000 men, at the **McIntyre Farm,** on McIntyre Road (704–336–3854); eventually, however, they had to retreat before superior force. Cornwallis occupied Charlotte but found he was constantly badgered by the feisty militiamen; he left, saying that Charlotte was "a veritable nest of hornets."

The **Hezekiah Alexander Homesite** is the oldest building still standing in Mecklenburg County. Dating from 1774, it is called the Rock House. Hezekiah Alexander was one of the signers of the 1775 Mecklenburg Declaration of Independence. He was a delegate to the Fifth Provincial Congress and helped draft the North Carolina State Constitution and Bill of Rights.

A blacksmith by trade, he lived with his wife and ten children in the house, which is furnished with period pieces. Behind the house is a cabin with a large fireplace, herbs drying overhead, a "curfew" (a pottery piece used to cover coals at night), candle molds, and, behind the door, a set of stilts for children. The family stored their dairy products and food in a spring-house on the property to keep them from spoiling—some say that it

343

also held arms for patriots. The house is open Tuesday through Friday from 10:00 A.M. to 5:00 P.M., Saturday and Sunday from 2:00 P.M. to 5:00 P.M. Call (704) 568–1774 for more information.

When you're ready to stop for the night, try the **Dunhill Hotel,** at 237 North Tryon (800–354–4141 or 704–332–4141), by no means colonial but nevertheless a more recent historic hotel, dating from 1929. Renovated in 1987, the hotel creates colonial ambience with eighteenth-century period furnishings. The Monticello Restaurant offers candlelit dinners.

Winston-Salem was founded in 1753 after some Moravians from Pennsylvania bought land in the Piedmont. They built **Bethabara,** which means House of Passage, and became a trading and crafts center. Old Salem, the residential town, was consolidated with a newer and expanding Winston in 1913.

Historic Bethabara Park, on Bethabara Road, has a wealth of properties, including the 1788 Gemeinhaus (church), the 1782 Krause-Butner Potter's House, a reconstructed 1756 fort, God's Acre cemetery—with more than 4,000 graves dating from 1771—gardens, and foundations of the original settlement. Interpreters in costume explain the history of the place. Special events include a Revolutionary War encampment on Memorial Day weekend. The park is open daily, but hours for the buildings vary: call (919) 924–8191 for details.

Old Salem, located on old Salem Road, is a restoration of the town as it stood in 1766. Originally the Moravians came from the Czech Republic, but when they were persecuted there to the extent that their leader, Jan Hus, was burned at the stake in 1415, they left for Saxon Germany. Some of them settled in Bethlehem, Pennsylvania, and then another group continued the journey to North Carolina.

Begin your tour at the **Old Salem Visitor Center,** at 600 South Main Street, to get a map and learn more about the town. Nearby the Single Brother's House, a half-timbered brick building, dates from 1769. Men and boys lived and worked here; today artisans are at work in craft rooms. You'll probably see the cooper's shop, with tools of the era, stock for barrels, and a supply of hoops. The tailor's shop made clothing under the eye of the church; it had to conform to modest norms rather than be frivolous. The tinsmiths made kitchen utensils from tinned iron and also "black iron," which was sheet iron without the tinned surface. Weavers primarily produced linen and cotton fabrics. Thread was spun in the homes, dyed, and then brought to the weaver.

Interpreters wear the modest attire prescribed by the Moravian church at the restored eighteenth-century town of Old Salem.

The **Museum of Early Southern Decorative Arts,** at 924 South Main Street (919–721–7360), has collected furnishings that date from 1640 to 1820. Visitors can now see nineteen period rooms; don't miss the 1640 cupboard from Tidewater, Virginia, or the 1711 silver pieces.

George Washington stayed in the **Salem Tavern** in 1791 and remarked that he enjoyed the music played for him that night. Today visitors can have lunch or dinner here; call (919) 748–8585 for reservations.

The oldest tobacco shop in the country dates to 1771 and is the **Miksch House,** on South Main Street. Wares inside include twists of chewing tobacco that have been sweetened with honey. As you wander around you may see a woman adding dye—made from nuts, onion skins, or flowers—to a boiling kettle. Perhaps someone will be dipping candles or roasting a pig when you visit.

If you can visit Old Salem on July 4, you're in for a treat. Approximately 130 costumed citizens walk in the Torchlight Procession that night. Another special event is Old Salem Christmas, an interpretation of Moravian traditions, which takes place in mid-December. Hours are from 9:30 A.M. to 4:30 P.M. Monday through Saturday and from 1:30 to 4:30 P.M. Sunday, except some holidays; call (919) 721–7300 for more information and a schedule of special events.

FOR MORE INFORMATION

Travel & Tourism Division
430 North Salisbury Street
Raleigh, NC 27611
(800) VISIT-NC (800–84748–62) outside Raleigh
(919) 733–4171 in Raleigh

South Carolina

Historical Introduction to
SOUTH CAROLINA

Before the founding of Charles Towne in 1670, a number of explorers had ventured into the region that was to become South Carolina. In 1520 Spanish explorer Lucas Vasquez de Ayllon landed on the coast, then left with a number of Indians to use as slaves. He returned again in 1526 to found a settlement near Georgetown, but the colony was abandoned after nine months of bad weather, disease, and Ayllon's death.

Giovanni da Verrazano explored the coast in 1524, and Hernando de Soto passed through in 1540, as did Angel de Villafane in 1561. Jean Ribaut settled near Beaufort, South Carolina, in 1562, naming the spot Port Royal as he claimed it for France. He built a four-bastioned fort and called it Charlesfort, then departed for more supplies and colonists, leaving twenty-eight men, but as their food ran out, they abandoned the site. Pedro Menendez de Aviles arrived in 1566, settling a group of Spaniards in Port Royal. Indians decimated this settlement ten years later, but the Spaniards returned, only to leave again to reinforce St. Augustine after Sir Francis Drake burned that settlement.

First Settlement at Charles Towne

All these comings and goings set the stage for the first successful settlement in Charles Towne. Britain had already founded Jamestown, Virginia, in 1607 and more colonies farther north along the coast. By 1663 Capt. William Hilton, on Barbados, realized the need for more land and religious freedom than was available there and so sailed for the Carolina coast. In 1666 Robert Sandford also explored a coast filled with rivers and islands that must have been attractive to mariners, and both men reported their enthusiastic reactions back to England. Hilton wrote, "The ayr is clear and sweet, the countrey very pleasant and delightful. And we could wish that all they that want a happy settlement of our English nation were well transported thither."

In 1663 Charles II granted Carolina to the eight men who were known as the Lords and Proprietors. By 1669 Lord Ashley had taken charge of the project. A fleet of three ships left England in August 1669; only one, the *Carolina*, survived and made her way to Albemarle Point on the Ashley River. Lord Ashley informed the colonists that "the Towne you are now planted on we have named and you are to call Charles Towne."

Dealing with Spaniards and Indians

Times were hard as the colonists worried about attacks from the Spaniards; they needed to keep watch and also build more defenses, which left them little time to plant crops. Although they had set out with plenty of food, two ships had foundered, so most provisions were lost. Governor Sayle wrote, "Wee have been put to purchase our maintenance from the Indians, and that in such small parcels as we could hardly get another supply before the former was gone."

Henry Woodward, a doctor, an adventurer, and a pioneer of English expansion in the lower South, traded with the Indians and developed friendship and loyalty to them. They returned his friendship with current news, so he heard about an impending attack by Spaniards and Indians in 1670. The colony was able to raise a successful defense of Charles Towne, and the Spanish returned to St. Augustine. The first year was tough because ice nipped the crops and supplies ran low, but the second year found the colony prospering with the sale of lumber and more crops. Capt. Joseph West became governor in 1674 and was tireless in developing the early colony— clearing land, building houses, and establishing defense palisades.

By 1671 relationships with the Indians had deteriorated, and Henry Woodward changed allegiance from the coastal Indians to the Westo Indians, who conducted raids against the Spanish missions in Georgia. These Indians provided the settlement with a buffer zone against both Spanish and French invaders. In 1672 the Spaniards sent a soldier from St. Augustine to spy on Charles Towne. His report to the Spanish Governor provides the best early description of the settlement:

> The place where they have the village built is a wooded village consisting of dwelling houses without having any formal streets although he could count about ninety houses, some higher than others apparently according to the means of each individual. And in this same tract they have their fields of maize, pumpkins, cow-peas, peas and in each house their trellises for grape vines of different sorts. And also a great quantity of sweet potatoes and some fig trees. . . . Inside of this fortification there are some lodgings and others of the same sort outside of it which, as he was informed, were built at first when they began to settle for fear of the Indians . . . ships and frigates of good burden could enter [the harbor] because he saw an outrigger with yards which was about to sail for the island of Barbados whence they receive what they need in the way of food and other necessities.

A New Charles Towne

By 1680 the colony had moved the town across the Ashley River to Oyster Point, where a second Charles Towne developed. In 1682 Thomas Ash, special agent to the king, wrote, "The town is regularly laid out into large and capacious streets, which to Buildings is a great Ornament and Beauty. In it they have reserved convenient places for Building of a Church, town House, and other publick Structures, an Artillery Ground for the Exercise of their Militia, and Wharfs for the Convenience of their Trade and Shipping."

Religious tolerance was evident as non-Anglican sects developed during the 1680s and 1690s. French Huguenots arrived in 1680 and gave a boost to the colony with their skills as artisans and farmers. In 1692 Thomas Newe complained of inflation, reporting high prices—such as milk at 2 cents a quart and beef at 4 cents a pound—but the settlement prospered. Colonists continued to trade with the Indians and export skins, barrel staves, pitch, tar, beef, and lumber. By the 1690s rice production had become a profitable cash crop. Later waves of immigration increased both the population and the prosperity of the colony. Immigrants arrived to settle nine townships inland from Charles Towne during the 1730s. Germans, Swiss, Scots, French, and Welsh joined the original English, Barbadians, and Huguenots.

Further Afflictions

St. Augustine continued to harass Charles Towne, smallpox killed a large number of colonists between 1697 and 1699, and a plague and an earthquake added their toll. Yellow fever killed 160 persons in 1699 and was followed by a hurricane that flooded the town. By 1718 pirates loomed as serious threats to the economy as they snatched valuable cargoes going in and out of the harbor. They also nabbed some of the most prominent citizens in town and held them for ransom.

In June of 1718 "Blackbeard," or Edward Thatch (or Teach) came into Charles Towne with four ships and 400 men. Also on board was Stede Bonnet, a retired British Army major who had a penchant for pirating. Bonnet eventually commanded a ship, changed his name to Thomas, and engaged in battle with Col. William Rhett on the vessel *Henry;* he surrendered, escaped, and then was recaptured. The colony took a stand and hanged forty-nine pirates during the month of November in 1718; Bonnet was tried and hanged a month later. Thereafter an armed vessel hovered in the harbor and another cruised off the coast, putting an end to buccaneering in and around Charles Towne.

Regions to Explore

S outh Carolina was not a separate colony until 1729, when Carolina was first divided into northern and southern sections. The boundary between the two was not ratified until long after the colonial era, in 1815. The history of settlement crawled along the seacoast, so we follow suit and examine four major towns: Charles Towne was the first to be settled, then Charleston, followed by Beaufort and Georgetown.

South Carolina

CHARLES TOWNE

Today you can visit **Charles Towne Landing** on the west bank of the Ashley River, a state park with 663 acres of hands-on history. A thirty-minute movie sets the stage for understanding life in this patch of South Carolina low country. Tram tours, with narration, provide an overview of each area within the park. The Settlers' Life area is a reconstructed seventeenth-century village, complete with carpenter shop, print shop, and smithy. You can dip your own candles from a pot of wax or print colonial documents in the print shop. The crop garden grows rice, indigo, cotton, sugar cane, and other crops in season. Students who visit are encouraged to help in the planting or harvesting, depending on the season.

The Indians of Coastal Carolina area displays tools and other items used by Indians in their daily lives. One of the most popular attractions is the Pirate Program, in which students read the pirate's rules for life on board ship during the sixteenth and seventeenth centuries. You can also watch a "black powder" demonstration of a swivel gun, blunderbuss, pistol, and musket. On the riverfront the *Adventure,* a 53-foot replica of a seventeenth-century trading vessel, is available for visitors to board. Inland the English Park gardens contain eighty-five acres of azaleas, camellias and many other shrubs and trees. Open daily from 9:00 A.M. to 5:00 or 6:00 P.M., depending on the season. For more information call Charles Towne Landing at (803) 556–4450.

CHARLESTON

One of the nicest things about **Charleston**—the "new" city on the peninsula between the Ashley and Cooper rivers—is its low profile. Church steeples are still taller than surrounding buildings, and it is a lot easier to imagine oneself living during colonial times without skyscrapers around to break the illusion. Beyond this, the city fairly reeks with Old World ambience that is not contrived, just a pattern of living and building that has not changed much in centuries. It even reemerges after disasters like the hurricane of 1989. To appreciate it, you must wander through the streets aimlessly and peek into piazzas and gardens behind iron fences and gates. Among other things you'll see marvelous flowers in full bloom, fountains, statues, and perhaps a small barking dog to scare off intruders.

Earthquake Bolts

As you walk around Charleston, you will notice "earthquake bolts," iron circles with a bolt and nut protruding from the center. An iron rod extends through the building to give it strength and stability. They were first installed in buildings after the 1886 earthquake.

In spite of its tranquil appearance, Charleston has suffered not only hurricanes, but fires and earthquakes as well. The 1752 hurricane took out 500 houses, and it was followed by equally destructive hurricanes in 1885, 1893, and 1989. The fire of 1698 destroyed 50 houses, and 300 houses were lost in the conflagraton of 1740. The town has also been shaken by earthquakes and by enemy shelling during wars. Nevertheless, Charleston has survived all these disasters and still retains an extraordinary atmosphere of grace and beauty.

If you haven't visited Charleston before, you might want to start at the **Charleston Visitor Center,** at 375 Meeting Street (803–724–7474). Here you can see "Forever Charleston"—a multimedia show that encapsulates the history of the city—and pick up scads of current information on special events throughout the city and surrounding countryside. This stop will be especially helpful if you are interested in arranging boat tours, architectural walking tours, or attending performances at the remodeled **Dock Street Theatre,** at Church and Queen streets (803–723–5648), first built in 1736. The **Festival of Houses and Gardens** also arranges tours of some private homes, gardens, and plantations, as well as special events. Call the Historic Charleston Foundation, at 51 Meeting Street, for more information and schedules (803–722–3405 or 723–1623).

Many of the fine historic houses are of antebellum vintage, but one with a particularly interesting heritage belongs to the colonial era. Col. Daniel Heyward bought the **Heyward-Washington House** at auction in 1770 after submitting the highest bid of £5,500. He took down the existing structure and built a three-story house from Charleston gray brick. As a wealthy entrepreneur, Heyward owned many plantations, where he grew rice and cotton. Since it was not easy to import cloth during the Revolution, he also developed a cotton factory to make fabric for his slaves' clothing.

His son, Thomas Heyward, Jr., read law at the Middle Temple of the Inns of Court in London. He helped defend Dr. John Haley, accused of having murdered Peter DeLancey. The two men had fought a duel, and DeLancey, a royalist, was killed. By the time he was not quite thirty years of age, Heyward was a signer of the Declaration of Independence. In 1780 Charleston surrendered to the British, and Heyward was sent into exile in St. Augustine with twenty-eight other revolutionary leaders.

Inside, the house is filled with eighteenth-century furniture made in Charleston. A "library case," which looks like a very long china cabinet, measures about 15 feet. A "triple chest" unique to the area has handles on each end for ease of transport. The dining room has a collection of china, an English mirror, seventeenth-century Dutch landscapes, portraits of Mr. and Mrs. Daniel Heyward, a mahogany cellarette for wine, a sugar box for a cone-shaped lump of sugar, and a fly catcher baited with honey. Upstairs, Heyward's own bed is in the green bedchamber. Most of the beds had movable headboards that could be raised during the summer to hold up mosquito netting.

George Washington entertained his guests in the drawing room. Today it contains a 1686 French spinet, a marble-topped table, a settee and side chair that belonged to Drayton Hall, and an English mirror with a gold peacock on it. Thomas Elfe, a cabinetmaker, made the mantel, and the fretwork resembles the style of Thomas Chippendale. Open from 10:00 A.M.–5:00 P.M. weekdays and from 1:00 to 5:00 P.M. Sundays, except holidays. Call (803) 722–2996 for further details.

The **Charleston Museum,** at 360 Meeting Street, founded in 1773, may be the oldest museum in the country. Here you will find a fine collection of furniture made in the city, including the "rice" bed, which represents an important early industry in Charleston. Much of the furniture can be seen in the three properties owned by the museum: the Heyward-Washington House, the Aiken-Rhett House, and the Joseph Manigault House. Open from 9:00 A.M. to 5:00 P.M. weekdays and from 1:00 to 5:00 P.M. Sundays, except holidays. For more information call (803) 722–2996.

The **Battery,** lined with beautiful homes, is the best place for a pleasant stroll along the waterfront. Cannons stand in the park, not really ready to do battle but as reminders of some of the devastating bombardments of the past. **White Point Garden** got its name from the white oyster shells that were tossed all over the point. The Ashley and Cooper rivers meet here, and you can look out at Fort Sumter straight ahead. While you're in this vicinity, don't miss a stop at the **Old Exchange and Provost Dungeon,** 122 East Bay at Broad, the site of much Revolutionary War history, including the election of delegates to the First Continental Congress in 1774 and the imprisonment of signers of the Declaration of Independence and other patriots during the British occupation of 1780. Open from 9:00 A.M. to 5:00 P.M. daily, except major holidays. Call (803) 792–5020 for further details.

Even if you are focused on the colonial era, it's almost impossible to ignore Civil War history in Charleston. **Fort Johnson** is on James Island, at the entrance to the harbor; the first shot of the War Between the States was shot onto **Fort Sumter** by Confederate forces. **Fort Moultrie** stands on Sullivans Island, across from James Island. Edgar Allan Poe wrote "The Gold Bug" when he was stationed here. **Castle Pinckney** was built on another island in the harbor; it once housed Union prisoners of war during the Battle of Bull Run, and it is now a national monument.

Three historic properties lie just outside of Charleston on Highway 61; Drayton Hall, Magnolia Plantation and Gardens, and Middleton Place.

Drayton Hall, built from 1738 to 1742, is an outstanding example of colonial architecture. Seven generations of the Drayton family lived in the house after John Drayton bought the land next to his family home, Magnolia Gardens. Its Georgian-Palladian style is symmetrical and beautiful, now restored and open without furnishings. It may be easier to focus on the patterns in friezes and on the ceilings without the distraction of furniture. The great hall has a shell-and-fruit swag over the fireplace, and the handsome ceiling has a medallion in the center, decorated with stars, flowers, and leaves. The drawing room has a seventeenth-century free-hand sculpted ceiling; a sham door was placed on the wall for symmetry. Look for the frame of the doorjamb in the bedchamber, where the family still comes to mark the heights of their children and dogs. A sign warns DON'T PAINT THIS PANEL. Open daily from 10:00 A.M. to 4:00 P.M. or 3:00 P.M., depending on the season. Call (803) 766–0188 to find out more.

Nearby **Magnolia Plantation and Gardens** were originally planned in the 1680s by the Drayton family. J. Drayton Hastie is the current owner of the oldest major garden in the country. You can wander through fifty wonderful acres, including a horticultural maze. John Grimke Drayton brought 250 varieties of azalea to the area, and the garden features 900 varieties of camellia. There's also a waterfowl refuge and the Audubon Swamp Boardwalk.

The first Drayton came from Barbados about 1671 and settled in a home called Magnolia. After its destruction a second plantation house was built a few yards away, on the site of the present house. This one was burned also, by General Sherman's men. The Rev. John Grimke Drayton, rector of St. Andrew's Episcopal Church, had his summer house taken apart, brought to Magnolia on the river, and placed on the existing ground-floor walls. The home was occupied by Draytons until 1976. Visitors can tour the upper floor, which houses a gallery of works by local artists, plus an outstanding collection of ornithological paintings collected by the owner. You can have lunch at the restaurant on the first floor. Open daily from 8:30 A.M. to 5:30 P.M. Call (803) 571–1266 for more information.

Middleton Place was home to Henry Middleton, President of the First Continental Congress. His son, Arthur Middleton, was a signer of the Declaration of Independence. One wing survives of the original 1755 house; Federal troops burned the rest. Inside, the portraits of family members hang on the walls. The dining room contains a graceful 1771 silver epergne for fruit, nuts, and candy; Lafayette and Andrew Jackson had dinner here. Upstairs there is a cowhide-and-brass trunk, lined in camphor wood, that was buried during the Civil War to keep precious things safe. The Nursery contains a domino game, dolls, a desk, and a toy Noah's ark.

Extensive terraced gardens bloom with azaleas, camellias, magnolias, crape myrtle, and roses at various times during the year. The plantation stableyards offer docents in costume who work as blacksmiths, potters, carpenters, and weavers. Horses, mules, hogs, cows, sheep, goats, and guinea hens are there too. Hours: Gardens open daily from 9:00 A.M. to 5:00 P.M.; house hours vary. For more details call (803) 556–6020.

If you can visit Charleston from mid-March to mid-April, you'll be in time for the Festival of Houses and Gardens tour. A Candlelight Tour of Homes and Gardens takes place in September. Middleton Place holds its annual Plantation Days in November, when craftspersons demonstrate eighteenth- and nineteenth-century crafts. For more information and the dates of special events, call the **Charleston Visitor Center** (803–720–5678) or the **Charleston Trident Convention and Visitors Bureau** (803–853–8000).

For overnight accommodations you'll have lots of historic places to consider. **Ansonborough Inn,** at 21 Hasell Street (call 803–723–1655 or fax 803–577–6888), in 1900 a stationer's warehouse, is now an all-suite B&B. **Barksdale House Inn,** at 27 George Street (803–577–4800), is in a 1778

The Gardens at Middleton Place have statues and peaceful vistas.

building, filled with period and reproduction antiques. The **1837 B&B and Tea Room,** at 126 Wentworth Street (803–723–7166), is a renovated planter's home and carriage house. **Elliott House,** at 78 Queen Street (803–723–1855 or 800–729–1855), dating from the early 1800s, stands in the Historic District and has a garden courtyard. The **John Rutledge House Inn,** at 116 Broad Street (803–723–7999 or 800–476–9741), was built by a signer of the United States Constitution in 1763 and is filled with antiques. The **King's Courtyard Inn,** at 198 King Street (803–723–7000 or 800–845–6119), is an 1853 building in the Historic District. **Maison Dupre,** at 317 East Bay Street (803–723–8691 or 800–662–INNS), consists of three houses and two carriage houses, filled with antiques. The **Middleton Inn,** at Middleton Place, Route 61 (803–556–0500), is a modernistic inn on the river, right next to Middleton Gardens; all rooms have fireplaces and Nordic decor. **Planters Inn,** at 112 North Market Street (803–722–2345 or 800–845–7082), dating from 1844, also contains **Robert's Restaurant.**

Charleston, like New Orleans, is noted for its stock of fine restaurants to keep you sampling various cuisines during your visit, especially if you like seafood or plantation specialties. One terrific choice for colonial buffs is

Magnolia's, at 185 East Bay Street (803–577–7771). The building dates from 1783 and was once the Customs House; now it serves gourmet meals and also features some Southern low-country dishes on the menu, such as Magnolia's Veal Meatloaf, smoked double pork loin chops, spice shrimp and sausage over creamy white grits, and "Down South" eggroll.

BEAUFORT

The first inhabitants in **Beaufort,** more than 4,000 years ago, were the Archaic Native Americans. The sixteenth and seventeenth centuries saw a succession of explorers and settlers. By 1514 a Spanish sea captain, Pedro de Salaza landed, to be followed by French Huguenots in 1562, then English privateers and pirates. In 1566 the Spanish founded the town of Santa Elena on Parris Island; it was the Spanish capital of America until 1573. Archaeological excavation is in process there now. In 1670 an English colony was begun on Port Royal Island and then moved to Charleston. Stuart Town, settled by a group of Scots in 1685, was annihilated by Spaniards in 1686. Finally in 1711 the British proclaimed that the town of Beaufort be "established," and a new batch of settlers put up homes of tabby and clapboard.

Later houses built in the "Beaufort style" combined elements from Georgian, colonial, Greek Revival, and semitropical Spanish styles. The typical Beaufort house was erected on a large lot, sometimes with a formal garden, and placed to take advantage of the prevailing southwesterly breeze. None of them, unlike Savannah and Charleston homes, were built next to each other on small lots.

Beaufort houses sit high on brick or tabby foundations and offer cool comfort from their two-story piazzas. The houses are usually T-shaped, with inset chimneys and central hallways that lead to an elegant stairway at the rear. Sometimes there is a Palladian window on the landing. Ornamental woodwork includes paneling, wainscoting, mantels, and cornices. Mantels ranged from marble to delft tile to decoration in the style of Adam. Plaster ceiling medallions and cornices were added at a later date; ceiling heights were generous, from 14 to 18 feet. Ask the Chamber of Commerce (803 524 3163) for a Historic District Tour Map to set you going on a pleasurable walk through a town loaded with wonderful houses. Also inquire about the annual spring tour of private homes and gardens (803–524–0363).

If you're in town during October, you may be lucky enough to catch the tour of private historic homes (803–524–6334).

The **George Elliott House,** at 1001 Bay Street, dates from 1840; visitors pass through an iron gate and up the stairs to a fanlit doorway. Mr. Elliott, like many of his contemporaries, was both a planter and a politician. His elegant home, in Beaufort style, is oriented toward the south, with a veranda open to prevailing breezes. Inside, furnishings date from the mid-nineteenth century.

The **John Mark Verdier House,** at 801 Bay Street, was built by a prominent merchant in 1790. This Federal-style house stands on a raised tabby foundation and is five bays wide, with a double portico. The fanlight over the door is semielliptical. Inside, each room reflects Adam-style decoration. The reception parlor and the dining room each have beautifully carved mantels.

On March 18, 1825, the Marquis de Lafayette arrived for a visit in Beaufort. Because he had been delayed during festivities on Edisto Island, the people of Beaufort had gone home to bed. Word of his arrival spread, and the citizens sprinted to welcome him as he entered Verdier House. After this high point of hospitality for an elegant house, its fortunes declined. During the Civil War Union forces occupied it as headquarters. Then it became a fish market, an ice house, a law office, a telephone office, and a barber shop. After further deterioration precipitated by the Depression, the house was condemned, then saved by local citizens for dedication as a memorial to soldiers who had died in World War II. Restoration began in 1955 and recurred in 1975. The office of the Historic Beaufort Foundation is on the ground floor. The house is open Tuesday through Saturday from 11:00 A.M. to 4:00 P.M. from February 1 to mid-December. Call (803) 524–6334 for more information and dates; hours for touring the Verdier House vary seasonally.

The 1717 **Thomas Hepworth House,** at 214 New Street, is the oldest house in Beaufort, built by Thomas Hepworth, Chief Justice of the Colony. Because of threat from the Yemassee Indians, the house has a row of rifle slots on the north side. Local historian Dr. John A. Johnson wrote: "The only remaining memorials of that war [the Revolution] within our present view are the two redoubts in the northwestern suburbs and the little Dutch house on the corner of Port Republic and New Streets." Apart from special tours, this house is not open to the public. To arrange for a tour call (803) 524–6334.

The **Arsenal,** at 713 Craven Street, was built in 1795 on the site of the first courthouse in Beaufort and was rebuilt in 1852. The building, which looks like a fortress, has Gothic windows. In April 1775 the Beaufort Volunteer Artillery was organized here. Two brass trophy guns taken from the British in 1779 were later removed by Union solders in 1861 but were finally returned to Beaufort after 1880. Inside the arsenal visitors can see a collection of local memorabilia, including Indian pottery, swords, guns, and plantation crafts. The arsenal is open 10:00 A.M.–noon and 2:00 P.M.–5:00 P.M. Monday through Friday, 10:00 A.M.–noon Saturday.

St. Helena's Episcopal Church, at 501 Church Street, one of the oldest functioning churches in the United States, was built in 1724 with ballast bricks brought from England; the church has a small steeple, which replaced the old one that stretched up 118 feet. The altar silver was given by Capt. John Bull in 1734 to memorialize his wife, who was massacred by the Yemassee Indians.

During the Civil War graveyard slabs were removed and used as operating tables by the Federal troops stationed there. Col. John Barnwell, who died in 1724 after becoming famous as the leader of raids against the Tuscarora Indians, is buried here; so is a local physician, Dr. Perry, who asked his friends to bury him along with a loaf of bread, a jug of water, and an axe—just in case he awoke and decided to storm his way out. Open weekdays from 10:00 A.M. to 4:00 P.M. Call (803) 524–7595 for details.

The **Old Point** area contains many fine homes and gardens that are privately owned. Movies, including *The Great Santini* and *The Big Chill,* were filmed here. One of the homes, Tidalholm was built by Edgar Fripp in 1856 as a summer home. During the Civil War his brother, James Fripp, owned the house. He returned after the war to find that the house was being sold for taxes by the U.S. Tax Commission. Tears rolled down his face when he realized that he could not bid on the house; a Frenchman bought the house, walked over to Fripp, kissed him on both cheeks, gave him the deed, and returned to France. Apart from special tours, Tidalholm is not open to the public. Call (803) 524–0363 or (800) 524–3163 for more information.

For overnight accommodations try **The Rhett House,** at 1009 Craven Street (803–524–9030). This antebellum mansion (1820) offers candlelit dinners and live classical music. The **Bay Street Inn B&B,** at 601 Bay Street (803–522–0050 or 524–7720), dates from 1852 and has a view of the Beaufort River. The **Whitehall Plantation Inn,** on Whitehall Drive in South Beaufort (803–521–1700), is a good place for dinner with a river view. Another good dining place is **Gullah House,** at 761 Sea Island Parkway on St. Helena Island (803–838–2402), especially for fresh okra, collard greens, and other low-country cuisine.

GEORGETOWN

Spaniards tried to settle where Georgetown now stands in 1526 but abandoned the site after they became disease-ridden. John and Edward Perrie received the land from the Lords Proprietors of the Carolinas in 1705. They made an arrangement with John Mott to take his goods on the brigantine *Success.* The ship arrived and Mott settled a plantation for Perrie on the land. By 1737 the area that is now the Georgetown Historic District was filled with more than fifty homes.

Prince George Winyah Church, at 300 Broad Street at Highmarket Street, dates from 1735. The first church in the parish was located at Brown's Ferry, then located here after merging with another church. Pews were sold in 1753 to raise money, and import duties collected in Georgetown helped finance the building. A number of colonial residents and Revolutionary War men are buried here. Hours are seasonal; call (803) 546–4358 for more information.

Rice was a major crop in Georgetown from its earliest days. Visitors can explore the **Rice Museum,** at Front and Screven streets, to learn the history of rice culture from 1700 onward. Maps, dioramas, and artifacts provide the story. Take the time to stroll in **Lafayette Park,** which winds around the Rice Museum. Open 9:30 A.M. to 4:30 P.M. daily except Sundays and holidays. Call (803) 546–7423 for information.

The **Harold Kaminski House,** at 600 Front Street, overlooks the Sampit River. This 1760 town house contains antiques, including a magnificent mahogany Chippendale-design banquet table that extends across the room. Many of the pieces were passed down through the Kaminski family; look in the library for the walnut slope-lid desk made by Thomas Elfe, a Charleston cabinetmaker. Open 10:00 A.M. to 5:00 P.M. Monday through Friday except holidays; call (803) 546–7706 for more information.

South of Georgetown stands **Hopsewee Plantation,** on Route 17. Thomas Lynch, Sr., built the house in 1740, and his son, Thomas Jr., followed him in politics. Because Thomas Lynch, Jr., had suffered a stroke and could not sign the Declaration of Independence, there was a space left for his name; he was well enough to sign it in July. This typical low-country rice plantation house has four rooms around a center hall on each floor. The foundation is tabby, and the walls are sturdy black cypress. Hours are seasonal; call (803) 546–7891 for information.

FOR MORE INFORMATION

Division of Parks, Recreation and Tourism
Inquiry Division, Box 71
Columbia, SC 29202
(803) 734–0235

Florida

Historical Introduction to
FLORIDA

*P*once de León arrived on the site of St. Augustine in April 1513 and named it *Pascua florida;* statues of this Spanish explorer stand tall in several parts of the city. He had in fact first reached America with Columbus, on his second voyage in 1493. Ponce de León had been governor of Puerto Rico in 1510 but was deposed; he then sailed north in 1513. Some historians say that he was looking for the fountain of youth and thought he found it in St. Augustine. In any case his claim for Spain set the stage for conflict with the English, who also wanted the New World, for years to come, and St. Augustine was in a good position to provide defense against pirates for Spanish galleons.

FIRST PERMANENT CITY IN THE NEW WORLD

St. Augustine was the first permanent city in the New World. Captain-General Pedro Menéndez de Avilés established St. Augustine in September 1565. A mission, *Nombre de Dios* (Name of God), was founded on the site of his landing; it was the first in a group of missions established on the southeastern coast. In 1586 Sir Francis Drake came in with twenty-five ships and 2,300 men to invade and burn St. Augustine.

By 1672 the fort we can see today, Castillo de San Marcos, was in the process of construction; it was completed in 1695. Foundations were set below high-tide level of the ocean. Rafts brought hand-hewn blocks of coquina from quarries on Anastasia Island.

Alternating Control by England and Spain

In 1702 the British governor of Carolina, James Moore, invaded the town, took it, and then surrounded the fort. When Spanish warships arrived to blockade the harbor, Moore burned his eight ships and left for the North while St. Augustine burned. After this incident the settlers built walls and redoubts around the entire village so that all of St. Augustine was guarded, with the fort as the keystone of defense. Another Carolina English commander, Col. William Palmer, set forth and arrived at the gates of St. Augustine. He could not get in but did steal cattle and made friends with Indians who formerly had supported the Spanish. The British gradually became stronger and more of a threat.

Amalgam from the Sea

Coquina is an amalgam of millions of years' collection of seashells with their lime content, sand, and water; it is like sedimentary rock.

In 1740 Gen. James Oglethorpe attacked St. Augustine for twenty-seven days until Spanish seamen got through the blockade with provisions from Havana. Shallow-draft Spanish vessels sailed behind Anastasia Island, emerged from Matanzas Inlet, slid down the coast, and reached the harbor with their welcome provisions. When they returned to the fort, Oglethorpe and his men had departed.

The British finally received Florida by treaty because they were holding Havana as the ace card in negotiations. Spain ceded Florida to Great Britain after the Seven Years' (French and Indian) War, and the British held Castillo de San Marcos during the American Revolution. Their rule lasted for twenty years, and they turned the city into a commercial seaport. After the Revolution, in 1783, Britain gave Florida back to Spain in the Treaty of Paris. Spain controlled Florida until 1821, against the wishes of many early settlers, then ceded it to the United States.

Regions to Explore

S t. Augustine is the principal destination for those interested in colonial sites in Florida, both for its long history and its strategic location at the border between British and Spanish North America.

ST. AUGUSTINE

St. Augustine Historical Tours, Inc., at 167 San Marco Avenue (904–829–3800) offer on-and-off trolleys so that visitors can stop and look at a site in detail, then climb aboard again to continue the tour. Our host advised us to ride completely around the trolley route once to catch a glimpse of sites we might want to visit later; we did and then returned to learn more. The tour starts outside the **Visitor Information Center,** at 10 Castille Drive, near the zero marker on the old Spanish Trail; call (904) 824–3334 for information.

The trolley passes the 1808 city gates and the **Oldest Wooden Schoolhouse,** at 14 St. George Street (904–824–0192), which is more than 200 years old. Inside, models depict the members of the last class (1864) with their teacher. Look on the wall for a 1931 photograph of the same members attending a reunion. Displays include 1872 Rules for Teachers (they couldn't do much and still remain in their posts), a letter beginning "Dear Teacher," slate and chalk, a *Sixth Reader,* and a book of farm ballads.

The tour continues along Avenida Menéndez to the **Bridge of Lions** and then turns right at a statue of Ponce de Leon. The **Basilica-Cathedral of St. Augustine** is next, and across the street stands **Government House,** where an archaeological dig is going on. Visitors can see the section under excavation and walk inside the museum to see a collection of incised pots from A.D. 1000, bullets, buckles, pipe stems, stoneware, and more.

A hands-on History Puzzle allows visitors to match what people used with the items by moving the artifacts around. There's a rack of clothes from the 1700s to try on. One room displays a wall that contains objects found in a trash pit from 1580, a well shaft that contains trash from 1760, oyster-shell footing from 1720, and a 1720 coquina wall. To learn more call (904) 825–5033.

The **Gonzalez-Alvarez House,** at 14 St. Francis Street, is known as the Oldest House, and someone has lived on the site since the early 1600s. The house is mentioned in Eugenia Price's *Maria,* which refers to Maria Peavett, who once lived there. Her husband was both a gambler and a spendthrift, so they lost the house at auction in 1790. Visitors will find the living room on the second story, a typical Spanish custom. Call (904) 824–2872 for more details.

The **Castillo de San Marcos** is a hollow-center square, with bombproof storerooms around the edge and diamond-shaped bastions at each corner. There is only one way into the fort, through the triangular-shaped ravelin, complete with a portcullis (a grating lowered across the

Castillo de San Marcos

entrance). Pirates and Indians still harassed the settlers, and in times of dan-
ger everyone huddled together inside the fort even before it was completed.
Inside, a diorama explains the Battle of 1740, when Gen. James Oglethorpe's
British troops arrived from Fort Frederica in Georgia to attack St. Augustine.
The fort stood strong during the subsequent twenty-seven-day seige.

You can visit soldiers' quarters, set up for guard duty, as well as a chapel
for Indians and a prison. Walk up the stairs to the bastions for a view of
Matanzas Bay; a garrison of Spanish soldiers guarded St. Augustine during
the colonial era from here. The fort is open daily 8:45 A.M.–4:45 P.M. Closed
December 25. Call (904) 829–6506 for more information.

Nombre de Dios is the site where Pedro Menéndez de Avilés landed
in 1565 and the site of the mission called Our Lady of La Leche. Walk by
the statue of Father López, which is larger than life size; the Great Cross,
which is 208 feet tall; the Shrine of St. Francis; the Mission Chapel; and
Shrine of Our Lady of La Leche.

The **Fountain of Youth,** at 155 Magnolia Avenue, is said to be the one,
according to legend, found by Ponce de León in 1513. Today visitors are

invited to have a drink from the spring. A diorama depicts Ponce de León being welcomed by the Indians. Walk around the grounds to see artifacts from daily life in those days. Open daily 9:00 A.M.–5:00 P.M. Closed December 25. For details call (904) 829–3168.

The **Spanish Quarter,** in Old St. Augustine, is a colonial village brought alive by docents in costume, who demonstrate their skills at weaving, blacksmithing, carpentry, cooking, and gardening. They will take visitors back to the 1740s, when Spanish soldiers, settlers, and their families lived here.

Begin your walk around the Spanish Quarter beginning with the **Maria Triay House,** which dates from the late eighteenth century, when Minorcan families came to the New World. Inside, visitors can explore the orientation center and look at artifacts found on the property. Next door you'll find the small **Lorenzo Gomez House,** which formerly belonged to a foot soldier. Take a look at the shop inside, which was the place to buy goods or to barter for work. Artillery Sgt. Martín Martínez Gallégos lived in the next house with his family. The house is larger than the Gomez house because Martínez was an officer and therefore earned more.

Mike Wells, who stands in the blacksmith shop, is the third-generation blacksmith in a family that has practiced the occupation for 200 years. He explained that blacksmith guilds required an apprentice to work for five years, then four as a journeyman. To become a master blacksmith, he needed to produce a product judged worthy by those who certify blacksmiths and to have worked in the trade for twenty years. Most master blacksmiths were forty or fifty years old before achieving this honor.

A docent in the **Bernardo Gonzáles House** explains the process of spinning, dyeing yarn from native plants, and finally weaving the yarn into garments and household fabrics. Geronimo de Hita y Salazar lived with his family in the next house. All children were expected to work for the family in the house, and today school groups can become involved in hands-on craft activities.

Antonio de Mesa built part of the next house around 1763; later Juan Sanchez added to the house to make it a two-story building. The home is furnished as it would have been for a St. Augustine family in comfortable circumstances during the period from 1821 to 1845. The next house is a duplex, built by José Peso de Burgo, from Corsica, and Francisco Pellicer, from Minorca. De Burgo was a merchant and Pellicer a carpenter. Call (904) 825–6830 for more information about the Spanish Quarter.

You can take a scenic cruise on *Victory II,* a 64-foot vessel that was built for the owner's grandfather in 1917. You'll enjoy seeing landmarks from a new perspective, as well as the salt marshes, filled with dipping and soaring birds. For further details call (800) 542–8316 or (904) 824–1806.

You can plan to be in St. Augustine for many festivals and special events, including the popular *Cross & Sword,* a symphonic drama that depicts the settlement of St. Augustine by Spanish colonists; it is performed from mid-July through the third week in August. Greek Landing Day festival takes place in June to celebrate Greek settlers, who first arrived in 1777. Also in June the Spanish Night Watch is staged in the Spanish Quarter by reenactors, dressed in eighteenth-century costume. September is the time to gather at the Mission of Nombre de Dios to commemorate the landing of the Spanish in 1565. The Grand Illumination takes place in early December, with a torch-light parade that features British colonial customs. Carolers, dressed in eighteenth-century costume, sing as they walk from the plaza to the fort. For more information write to the **St. Augustine/St. Johns County Chamber of Commerce,** One Riberia Street, St. Augustine, FL 32084, or call (904) 829–5681.

When you're ready to stop for the night, try the **Kenwood Inn,** at 28 Marine Street (904–824–2116), a Victorian inn with swimming pool and courtyard, or the **Old City House Inn & Restaurant,** at 115 Cordova Street (904–826–0113) in the historic city; the restaurant offers a generous variety of dishes that are nicely presented by the chef, and guests may borrow bicycles. The **Southern Wind,** at 18 Cordova Street (904–825–3623), is a B&B in a home; it also offers accommodations on the *Southern Wind,* a 76-foot sailing yacht.

Good restaurants in St. Augustine include **Barnacle Bill's Seafood House,** at 14 Castilla Drive (904–824–3663); the **Creekside Dinery,** at 160 Nix Boatyard Road (904–829–6113); **La Parisienne,** at 60 Hypolita Street (904–829–0055); and **Le Pavillon,** at 45 San Marco Avenue (904–824–6292) offers German and Swiss cuisine.

FOR MORE INFORMATION

Florida Division of Tourism
126 West Van Buren Street
Tallahassee, FL 32399
(904) 487–1462

For Further Reading

GENERAL

Boorstin, Daniel J. *The Americans, The Colonial Experience.* New York: Random House, 1958.

Fischer, David Hackett. *Albion's Seed, Four British Folkways in America.* Oxford, UK: Oxford University Press, 1989.

Greene, Jack P. *Pursuits of Happiness: The Social Development of Early Modern British Colonies and the Formation of American Culture.* Chapel Hill, London: University of North Carolina Press, 1988.

Hawke, David. *The Colonial Experience.* Indianapolis, New York, Kansas City: Bobbs-Merrill, 1966.

Kennedy, Roger G. *Rediscovering America: Journeys Through Our Forgotten Past.* A National Trust for Historic Preservation Book. Boston: Houghton Mifflin, 1990.

Middleton, Richard. *Colonial America: A History, 1607–1760.* Cambridge, Mass. & Oxford, UK: Blackwell, 1992.

Reich, Jerome R. *Colonial America.* Englewood Cliffs, N.J.: Prentice Hall, 1989.

SERIES

The American Heritage History of the Thirteen Colonies. New York: American Heritage Publishing Co., 1967.

Morris, Richard B. and the Editors of *LIFE. The Life History of the United States: The New World. Volume I: Prehistory to 1774.* New York: Time Incorporated, 1963.

Visiting Our Past: America's Historylands. Washington, D.C.: National Geographic Society, 1977.

AMERICAN REVOLUTIONARY WAR

Commager, Henry Steele and Morris, Richard B. *The Spirit of Seventy-Six: The Story of the American Revolution as told by Participants, Vols. 1 and 2.* Indianapolis, New York: Bobbs-Merrill, 1958.

Lancaster, Bruce. *The American Heritage History of The American Revolution.* New York: American Heritage/Bonanza Books, 1984.

Stember, Sol. *The Bicentennial Guide to the American Revolution. Volume I: The War in the North; Volume II: The Middle Colonies, Volume III: The War in the South.* Saturday Review Press. New York: E.P. Dutton, 1974.

REGIONS

Albion, Robert G., Baker, William A. and Labaree, Benjamin W. *New England and the Sea.* Mystic, CT: Mystic Seaport Museum, 1972.

Cronon, William. *Changes in the Land: Indians, Colonists, and the Ecology of New England.* New York: Hill and Wang, 1983.

Tree, Christina. *How New England Happened: a Guide to New England Through Its History.* Boston, Toronto: Little, Brown and Co., 1976.

Vila, Bob. *Guide to Historic Homes of New England.* New York: William Morrow, 1993.

————*Guide to Historic Homes of the Mid-Atlantic.* New York: William Morrow, 1993.

———— *Guide to Historic Homes of the South.* New York: William Morrow, 1993.

INDIVIDUAL STATES

Each state has a Bicentennial History in the States and Nation Series. New York: W. W. Norton & Co, Inc.

Also, some of them have guides in the American Guide Series. Boston: Houghton Mifflin.

Index

Abby Aldrich Rockefeller Folk Art
  Center, 303
Abigail Adams Birthplace, 80–81
Abijah Rowe House, 20
Adair, New Hampshire, 127
Adams Mansion, 81–82
Adams National Historic Site, 81
Adamsville, Rhode Island, 148
Albany, New York, 244–45
Alexander Grant House, 216
Alexandria, Virginia, 309–11
Allen House, 104
American Independence Museum,
  125
American River Fortifications, 246
Amish Homestead, 281
Amstel House, 188
Annapolis, 200–205
Appalachian Gap, 171
Apthorpe House, 90
Aptucxet Trading Post, 107
Aquidneck, Rhode Island, 133–34,
  148–49
Arnold Trail, 55
Arsenal, 360

Artillery Park, 278
Ash Lawn-Highland, 318
Ashley Falls, Massachusetts, 107
Ashley House, 105
Augusta, Maine, 53
Axel de Fersen House, 140

Bainbridge House, 220
Balcarres Redoubt, 246
Bannister's Wharf, 153–54
Barbers Wheatfield, 246
Barker House, 337
Barker Tavern, 78
Barnett Bobb House, 283–84
Basilica-Cathedral of St. Augustine,
  366
Basin Harbor, 171
Bassett House, 238
Batsto Furnace, 217
Battle of Bushy Run, 288
Battle of Great Plains, 27
Battle of Monmouth, 222
Battle Monument, 219

Bazemore House, 340
Beaufort, South Carolina, 358–61
Benefit Street, 135–36
Benjamin Franklin's Statue, 86
Benjamin Nye House, 111
Bennington, Vermont, 175–77
Bennington Battle Monument,
  175–76
Bernardo Gonzales House, 368
Bethabara Park, 344
Bethlehem, Pennsylvania, 276–77
Black Rock Fort, 32
Block Island, Rhode Island, 161–62
Bloody Marsh Battle, 327
Bloody Pond, 251
Bloomfield, Connecticut, 19
Boston, Massachusetts, 83–93
Boston Common, 85
Boston Latin School, 85–86
Boston Tea Party Ship and
  Museum, 87–88
Bourne, Massachusetts, 107
Bradley Monument, 126
Brandywine Battlefield, 273–74
Brandywine River, 273
Brattle House, 90
Brewster Home, 75
Breymann's Redoubt, 246
Brick School House, 136
Bridge of Lions, 366
Bridgeton, New Jersey, 215
Bristol Historical and Preservation
  Society Museum and Library, 145

Bristol, Rhode Island, 143–47
Brome-Howard House, 198
Bronck Museum, 244
Brooklyn, New York, 234
Brothers House, 282–83
Brown University, 136–37
Brunswick, Georgia, 327
Buckingham House, 25
Buckman Tavern, 92–93
Bunker Hill Monument, 88–89
Burgess-Lippincott House, 274
Burgoyne's Headquarters, 246
Burial Hill, 72
Burlington, Vermont, 169–70
Burnham Tavern Museum, 59
Burr's Hill Park, 142
Burying Ground Point, 168
Bush-Holley House, 35–36
Butler-McCook Homestead, 13
Buttolph-Williams House, 15

C

Cambridge, Maryland, 208
Cambridge, Massachusetts, 89–90
Cambridge Common, 89
Cambridge Creek, 208
Camden, Maine, 57–58
Camden, New Jersey, 216–17
Canterbury Shaker Village, 126
Cape Ann Historical Museum, 102
Cape Cod, 107–11

Caprilands Herb Farm, 29
Captain John Ballard House, 300
Captain John Smith Monument, 79
Captain's Nook Hill, 75
Captain Tom Lawrence House, 108
Carlisle Barracks, 284
Carlyle House, 309
Carter's Grove, Virginia, 304, 306
Casey Farm, 159–60
Castillo de San Marcos, 366–67
Castine, Maine, 58
Castle Pickney, 355
Cazenovia, New York, 261
Center Church, 14
Chadds Ford, 273
Chapman-Hall House, 55
Charles Carroll House, 204
Charleston Museum, 354
Charleston, South Carolina, 352–58
Charles Towne Landing, 352
Charles Whipple Green Museum, 142
Charlotte, North Carolina, 342–44
Charlottesville, Virginia, 314–19
Charter Oak, 13
Chase Cory House, 147
Chase House, 120
Chase-Lloyd House, 203
Chatfield Farm, 246
Chatham, Massachusetts, 108–9
Cherry Hill, 244–45
Chesapeake Bay Maritime Museum, 207

Chestertown, Maryland, 209
Chimney Point, 173
Christ Church, Georgia, 327
Christ Church, Massachusetts, 89
Christ Church, Virginia, 310
Clarke Cooke House, 154
Cliff House, 49
Clinton Academy, 237
Cochegan Rock, 23
Coffin House, 103
Coggeshall Farm, 146
Coles Hill, 72
Colonial National Historic Park, 297
Colonial Park Cemetery, 325
Colonial Pemaquid Historic Site, 55–56
Colonial Williamsburg, 300–306
Commons Burial Ground, 147–48
Concord, New Hampshire, 126–28
Connecticut Historical Society, 14
Connecticut River Foundation, 30
Conway Homestead, 57
Copp's Hill Burying Ground, 88
Corbit-Sharp House, 187
Cotting-Smith Assembly House, 97
Courthouse, Leesburg, Va., 313
Court House, Edenton, N.C., 339
Covenhoven, 223
Coventry, Connecticut, 28–29
Coxsackie, New York, 244
Craig House, 223

Croton-on-Hudson, New York, 241

Crowninshield-Bentley House, 97

Cudworth House, 76–77

Cupola House, 336–37

Custom House, Sag Harbor, N.Y., 237

Custom House Maritime Museum, 103

Customs House, Chestertown, Md., 209

Cutchogue, New York, 236

D

Damariscotta, Maine, 55

Damm Garrison House, 124

Daniel Nunez House, 185

Day-Lewis Museum, 16

deVries Monument and Fort Site, 183

Deane House, 16

Deerfield, Massachusetts, 103–5

Denison Homestead, 24

Derby House, 95–96

Derby Wharf, 95

DeWitt Wallace Decorative Arts Gallery, 303

Dexter Mill, 110

Dinsmore Shop, 120

Dr. William Beaumont House, 28

Dover, Delaware, 186

Dover, New Hampshire, 123–24

Drayton Hall, 355

Dudley Digges House, 300

Dutch House, 188

Duxbury, Massachusetts, 75

Dwight-Barnard House, 105

Dyckman House, 231

E

Eastham, Massachusetts, 109–10

East Hampton, New York, 237–38

East Hartford, Connecticut, 15

Easton, Maryland, 206

Edenton, North Carolina, 336–41

Edgartown, Massachusetts, 112

Edmund Smith House, 300

Elizabethan Gardens, 335–36

Elizabeth Perkins House, 48–49

Emerson-Wilcox House, 48

Enfield, Connecticut, 19

Ensign John Thaxter House, 80

Ephrata Cloister, 283

Essex, Connecticut, 30

Essex Institute, 96

Ethan Allen Homestead, 170–71

Exeter, New Hampshire, 124–26

$\mathcal{F}$

Falmouth, Massachusetts, 108

Falmouth Historical Society
  Museum, 108

Falsington, Pennsylvania, 274

Faneuil Hall, 87

Farmington, Connecticut, 16

Farthing's Ordinary, 198

Federal Hall National Memorial, 231

Ferry House, 241

Fifer's Folly, 273

First Baptist Church, Providence,
  R.I., 136

First Congregational Church,
  Newport, R.I., 152

First Parish Church, Plymouth,
  Mass., 71–72

First Parish Congregational Church,
  York, Me., 47

First Parish Meeting House,
  Provincetown, Mass., 110–11

Fisher-Martin House, 185

Fisher-Richardson House, 83

Flower Farm, 273

Fogelsville, Pennsylvania, 277

Ford Mansion, 221

Fort Barton, 147

Fort Christina Monument, 189

Fort Crailo, 244

Fort Edward, 247–48

Fort Frederica, 328

Fort George, 58

Fort Getty State Park, 156

Fort Griswold Battlefield State Park,
  24

Fort Johnson, 355

Fort King George, 324

Fort Ligonier, 287

Fort McClary State Historical Site,
  46

Fort Mercer, 216

Fort Moultrie, 355

Fort Nathan Hale, 32

Fort Necessity, 286

Fort Nonsense, 221–22

Fort Pitt Blockhouse, 286

Fort Pitt Museum, 286

Fort Popham State Historic Site, 55

Fort Raleigh National Historic Site,
  335

Fort Sainte-Anne, 168

Fort Stanwix, 259–60

Fort Sumter, 355

Fort Ticonderoga, 254–57

Fort Wetherill State Park, 156

Fort William Henry, Maine, 56

Fort William Henry, New York, 251

Founder's Monument, 17

Fountain of Youth, 367–68

Frary House, 104

Fraunces Tavern Museum, 232

Freeman Farm, 246

Freeport, Maine, 59–60

Friends Burying Ground, 216

Fuss House, 19

Gadsby's Tavern Museum, 310

Gay Head, 111

Gemein Haus, 276–77

General Gates House, 283

General Henry Knox's
Headquarters, 242

General William Hart House, 29

George Elliott House, 359

Georgetown, South Carolina,
361–62

Gilbert Stuart Birthplace, 158–59

Gilman Garrison House, 125

Glastonbury, Connecticut, 16–17

Glebe House, 39

Glen Sanders Mansion, 259

Gloucester, Massachusetts, 101–2

Godiah Spray Plantation, 198–99

Golden Plough Tavern, 283

Gonzalez-Alvarez House, 366

Government House, St. Augustine,
Fla., 366

Governor John Langdon House, 122

Governor's Palace, Williamsburg,
Va., 302

Governor Stephen Hopkins House,
137

Grace Church, 300

Granary Burying Ground, 85

Granby, Connecticut, 20

Grand Isle, 169

Gray's Store, 148

Great Barrington, Massachusetts, 106

Green, 186, 187–89

Green End Fort, 149

Greenwich, Connecticut, 35–36

Greenwich, New Jersey, 215

Groton, Connecticut, 24

Gunn Historical Museum, 39

Gwynedd, Pennsylvania, 279

Haffenreffer Museum of
Anthropology, 147

Hagley Museum, 191

Hallowell, Maine, 55

Hall Tavern, 104

Hamilton House, 50

Hancock Cemetery, 83

Hancock-Clark House, 91

Hancock House, 216

Hancock Shaker Village, 105

Hannah Robinson's Rock, 160

Hanover, New Hampshire, 129

Hans Herr House, 281

Harlow Old Fort House, 73–74

Harmond-Harwood House, 204

Harold Kaminski House, 361

Harrington Meeting House, 56–57

Hartford, Connecticut, 13–16

Harvard College, 89

Hathaway House, 97

Havens House Museum, 236

Hawthorne's Birthplace, 97, 98

Hendrickson House, 190

Henry Whitfield State Historical Museum, 33–35

Hertford, North Carolina, 341

Hessian Powder Magazine Museum, 284

Heyward-Washington House, 353–54

Hezekia Chaffee House, 17

Hezekiah Alexander Homesite, 343

Hicks House, 90

High Street, 103

Hingham, Massachusetts, 79–80

Historic Deerfield, Massachusetts, 104–5

Historic Richmond Town, 234

Holmes Shipyard, 75

Holy Trinity (Old Swedes) Church, 189–90

Hooper-Lee-Nichols House, 90

Hope Plantation, 340

Hopewell Furnace National Park, 279

Hopsewee Plantation, 361–62

House of the Seven Gables, 97–98

Howland House, 73

Hoxie House, 110

Hubbardton, Vermont, 173–74

Hubbardton Battlefield, 174

Huguenot House, 15

Hunter House, 154–55

Hurd House, 39–40

Hyde Log Cabin, 169

Hyland House, 35

Hynson-Ringgold House, 209

I

Ill and Millrace Pond, 222

Immanuel Episcopal Church, 188

Independence Hall, 270–72

Independence National Historic Park, 270

Indian Leap, 27

Institute for American Indian Studies, 38–39

Ipswich, Massachusetts, 102

Iredell House, 339

Ironmaster's House, 217–18

Isaac Potts House, 278

Isaiah B. Hall House, 108

Isle La Motte, 168–69

J

James Fort, 297

Jamestown, Rhode Island, 156

Jamestown, Virginia, 297–98

Jamestown Settlement, 297

Jamestown Windmill, 156

Jean Hasbrouck House, 243

Jekyll Island, 330

Jeremiah Lee Mansion, 100

Jesse Baker House, 143

Jockey Hollow, 222

Johannes Mueller House, 282

John Adams Birthplace, 82

John Alden House, 75

John Baldwin House, 26

John Brown House, 138–40

John Carter Brown Library, 137–39

John Dickinson Plantation, 186

John Hancock Warehouse, 48

John Mark Verdier House, 359

John Mason Monument, 24

John Paul Jones House, 122

John Perkins House, 58

John Quincy Adams Birthplace, 82

John Updike House, 159

John Ward House, 96–97

John Waterman Arnold House, 141–42

John Whipple House, 102

John Write Stanly House, 342

Jonathan Hasbrouck House, 242

Jonathan Trumbull House, 27–28

Jones House, 120

Joseph Brown House, 140

Joseph Reynolds House, 145–46

Joseph Tillinghast House, 140

Joshua Hempstead House, 22

Joshua Jackson House, 120

Josiah Quincy House, 82

Judges' Cave, 32

K

Kennedy-Supplee Mansion Restaurant, 279

Kennett Square, 273

Kent, Connecticut, 38

Kinderhook, New York, 244

King Hooper Mansion, 101

King's Arms Tavern, 301

King's Chapel, 85

King's Fort, 258

Kintersville, Pennsylvania, 277

Kittery Historical and Naval Museum, 46

Kittery, Maine, 46–47

Knox Trail, 106

L

Lake Champlain, 168–73

Lake Champlain Maritime Museum, 171

Lake George Battlefield Park, 249–50

Lake George, New York, 249–54

Lakeville, Connecticut, 38

Lancaster Central Market, 280–81

Lancaster County, Pennsylvania, 280–84

Landis Valley Museum, 281

Laughlintown, Pennsylvania, 287

Lebanon, Connecticut, 27–28
Lee-Fendall House, 310
Leesburg, Virginia, 311–13
Lefferts Homestead, 234
Leffingwell Inn, 26
Lewes, Delaware, 183–85
Lewes Historical Society Complex,
  185
Lewes Presbyterian Church, 185
Lexington and Concord,
  Massachusetts, 91–93
Liberty Bell Pavilion, 270
Liberty Tree, 203
Lincklaen House, 261
Litchfield, Connecticut, 36–37
Litchfield Historical Society, 36–37
Lititz, Pennsylvania, 282
Lititz Historical Foundation, 282
Little Compton, Rhode Island,
  147–48
Liverpool, New York, 260–61
Longfellow National Historic Site,
  89–90
Long Island, New York, 234–38
Longwood Gardens, 191
Lorenzo Gomez House, 368
Loudon County Museum, 312

M

McConkey Ferry Inn, 275
Machias, Maine, 58–59
McIntyre Farm, 343
Magnolia Plantation and Gardens,
  355–56
Maine State Museum, 53
Major John Bradford House, 74–75
Manchester, Vermont, 175
Mann Farmhouse and Historical
  Museum, 77
Marblehead, Massachusetts, 99–101
Marden House, 120
Maria Triay House, 368
Maritime Museum, 79
Market Square Historic District, 103
Marshfield, Massachusetts, 75–79
Martha's Vineyard, 111–12
Marvil House, 185
Maryland State House, 202
Mary Meeker Cramer Museum,
  57–58
Mashpee, Massachusetts, 108
Massachusetts State House, 85
Massacoh Plantation, 19
Maxwell House, 142
Mayflower II, 70–71
Mayflower Society, 72
Metcalf House, 185
Middleburg, Virginia, 313–14
Middlebury, Vermont, 172–73

Middlebury College, 173
Middleton Place, 356
Middletown, Rhode Island, 149
Miksch House, 345
Military Academy Museum, 242
Military Museum, 152
Milton, New Hampshire, 124
Minute Man National Historic
  Park, 93
Minute Man Statue, 92
Mission House, 106
Moffatt-Ladd House, 121
Mohawk Trail, 105
Molly Stark Trail, 176–77
Monmouth Battlefield, 222
Montauk, New York, 237
Monticello, 315–18
Moon-Williamson House, 274
Morris-Jumel Mansion, 230–31
Morristown, New Jersey, 221–22
Morristown National Historic Park,
  221
Morrisville, Pennsylvania, 274
Morven, 220
Mount Hope, 146
Mount Independence, 173
Mount Vernon, Virginia, 306–8
Mulford Farm, 237–38
Museum of the City of New York,
  230
Museum of Early Southern
  Decorative Arts, 345

Museum on the Green,
  Glastonbury, Ct., 17
Museum of the Valley Forge
  Historical Society, 279
Mystic, Connecticut, 24–25
Mystic Seaport Museum, 25

N

Nantucket, 112–14
Nantucket Whaling Museum, 113
Nathan Hale Homestead, 28
Nathan Hale Schoolhouse, 23
Nathaniel Hampstead House, 22
Nathaniel Porter House, 143
National Monument to the
  Forefathers, 74
Nemours Mansion and Gardens,
  191
New Bern, North Carolina, 341–42
Newbold-White House, 341
Newburgh, New York, 242
Newburyport, Massachusetts, 102–3
New Castle, Delaware, 187–88
New Gloucester, Maine, 53
New Hampshire Farm Museum,
  124
New Haven Colony, 31-35
New Haven Colony Historical
  Society, 32
New Hope, Pennsylvania, 274–76

New London, Connecticut, 21–23
New Paltz, New York, 242–43
Newport, Rhode Island, 149–57
New Windsor Cantonment, 242
New York City, 230–34
New York Historical Society, 230
Nightingale-Brown House, 139
Noah Webster House, 14
Nombre De Dios, 367
North Weymouth Cemetery, 80
Norwich, Connecticut, 26–27

Odessa, Delaware, 187
Old Atwood House, 109
Old Barracks Museum, 219
Old Bedford Village, 284
Old Burial Hill, 101
Old Burying Ground,
  Massachusetts, 75
Old Burying Ground, Connecticut,
  17
Old Chapel, 277
Old Chatham, New York, 244
Old Colony House, 151
Old Corner Bookstore, 87
Old Court House, 188
Old Cove Cemetery, 110
Old Dutch Church of Sleepy
  Hollow, 240

Oldest House, 113
Oldest Wooden Schoolhouse, 366
Old Exchange and Provost
  Dungeon, 355
Old Fort House Museum, 248
Old Fort No. 4, 128
Old Fort Western, 53
Old Gaol, 48
Old Halsey, 238
Old House, 236
Old Lyme, Connecticut, 29–30
Old Narragansett Church, 158
Old New Gate Prison and Copper
  Mine, 20–21
Old North Church, 88, 91
Old Ordinary, 79–80
Old Presbyterian Church, 188
Old Salem, North Carolina, 344–46
Old Saybrook, Connecticut, 29
Old Schoolhouse, York, Me., 47
Old School House, Portsmouth,
  R.I., 148
Old Ship Meeting House, 79
Old South Meeting House, Boston,
  Mass., 86
Old State House, Connecticut, 14
Old State House, Delaware, 186
Old State House, Massachusetts, 87
Old State House, Rhode Island, 136
Old Stone Mill, 152
Old Treasury Building, 201
Old Windmill, 109–10
Old York Cemetery, 49

Old York Historical Society, 47
Oliver Ellsworth Homestead, 18
Oriskany Battlefield, 260
Orwell, Vermont, 173
Osborn-Jackson House, 237
Oxford-Bellevue Ferry, 208
Oxford, Maryland, 208
Oyster Bay, New York, 235

Packet Alley, 188–89
Palatine Graves, 162
Paradise, Pennsylvania, 282
Pardee-Morris House, 32
Parry Mansion, 275
Parson Capon House, 102
Parsons House, 19
Pate House, 300
Patterson House, 312–13
Paul Revere House, 88
Pavilion Gardens, 319
Peabody Museum, 96
Peirce-Nichols House, 97
Pennsbury Manor, 274
Permaquid beach, Maine, 56
Philadelphia, 171
Philadelphia, Pennsylvania, 269–72
Philipsburg Manor, 240–41
Pierce-Hichborn House, 88
Pieter Clasesen Wyckoff House, 234

Pilgrim Hall Museum, 71
Pilgrim Monument, 110
Pine Barrens, New Jersey, 217–18
Pioneer Village, 99
Plimhimmon, 208
Plimouth Plantation, 67–70
Plymouth, Massachusetts, 67–74
Plymouth National Wax Museum,
    74
Plymouth Rock, 70
Point State Park, 286
Pollock Rip Passage, 108–9
Pomona Hall, 216
Portland, Maine, 50–52
Portland Observatory, 52
Portsmouth, New Hampshire,
    119–24
Portsmouth, Rhode Island, 148–49
Portsmouth Historical Society,
    148–49
Portsmouth Trail, 121–23
Powhatan Village, 298
Prentis House, 171
Prescott Farm, 149
Prince George Winyah Church,
    361
Princeton, New Jersey, 219–21
Princeton Battlefield Monument,
    220
Princeton University, 220
Priory, The, 286
Providence, Rhode Island, 135–42

Provincetown, Massachusetts, 110
Public Hospital, 302–3
Putnam Cottage, 35

Quaker Cemetery, 236
Quincy, Massachusetts, 81–83
Quincy Historical Society Museum, 81
Quincy Historic Trail, 81
Quincy Homestead, 82
Quincy Market, 87

Raleigh Tavern, 303–4
Ramsay House, 309
Randall's Ordinary, 26
Raymond E. Baldwin Museum of Connecticut History, 13
Raynham Hall, 235
Red Bank Battlefield Park, 216
Redwood Library, 152–53
Regina Laudis Abbey, 39
Rensselaer, 244–45
Retire Beckett House, 97
Revolutionary War Office, 28
Rhinebeck, New York, 243–44

Rice Museum, 361
Richard Sparrow House, 72
River House, 209
Roanoke Island, 331–32, 335–36
Rockwood Museum, 191
Rogers-Hicks House, 142–43
Roger Williams National Memorial, 136
Rome, New York, 259–60
Ropes Mansion, 97
Royal Mohegan Burial Ground, 27

Sag Harbor, New York, 236–37
Sag Harbor Whaling Museum, 236–37
St. Andrew's Church, 19
St. Augustine, Florida, 366–69
Sainte Marie among the Iroquois, 260–61
St. Helena's Episcopal Church, 360
St. John's College, 202–3
St. Mary's City, Maryland, 197–99
St. Michael's, 206
St. Michael's Church, 101
St. Paul's Chapel, 232–33
St. Paul's Church, 336
St. Simons Island, 322, 327–29
Salem, Massachusetts, 93–99

Salem, New Jersey, 216
Salem Heritage Trail, 94–95
Salem Maritime National Historic Site, 95
Salmon Brook Settlement, 20
Salisbury, Connecticut, 37–38
Sandwich, Massachusetts, 110–11
Sarah Orne Jewett House, 50
Sarah Whitman Hooker House, 14
Saratoga National Historical Park, 246
Saratoga Springs, New York, 247–49
Saunderstown, Rhode Island, 158–60
Savannah, Georgia, 324–27
Savannah Historical Museum, 325
Sayward-Wheeler House, 49
Schenectady, New York, 257–59
Schenectady County Historical Society, 258
Schoolmaster's House, 274
Schuyerville, New York, 246–47
Schuyler House, 246–47
Schuyler Mansion, 245
"Scotch Tom" Nelson House, 300
Scotia, New York, 259
Second Congregational Church, 151–52
Second House Museum, 237
Shaker Museum, 53
Shaker Museum and Library, 244

Shaw-Perkins Mansion, 22
Sheafe Warehouse, 120
Shelburne, Vermont, 171
Shelburne Museum, 171
Sheldon-Hawks House, 105
Shelter Island, New York, 236
Sherburne House, 120
Ships of the Sea Museum, 325–26
Shrine of Saint Anne, 168
Skaneateles, New York, 261
Sleepy Hollow Cemetery, 240
Sloane-Stanley Museum, 38
Smith's Castle, 157–58
Society Hill, 272
Somerwell House, 300
Sotterley, 199–200
South Berwick, Maine, 50
South Duxbury, Massachusetts, 75
Southampton, New York, 238
South Kingston, Rhode Island, 160
South Street Seaport Museum, 233
Spanish Quarter, 368
Spooner House, 72–73
Stabler-Leadbeater Museum, 310
Stanley-Whitman House, 16
State House, 198
Staten Island, New York, 234
Statue of Liberty Museum, 233
Stephen Daniels House, 99
Stockbridge, Massachusetts, 105–6
Stockbridge Mill, 77–78
Stone House, 313

Stonington, Connecticut, 25–26
Strawbery Banke, 119–21
Strong-Porter House Museum,
  28–29
Sunnyside, 240
Swedish Granary, 215–16
Sydney L. Wright Museum, 156–57

T

Tantaquidgeon Indian Museum, 23
Tapping Reeve Houe and Law
  School, 37
Tarrytown, New York, 240
Tate House, 51–52
Tea Burners Monument, 215
Tennent Church, 223
Third Haven Meeting House, 206
Thomas Clark House, 220
Thomas Cooke House, 112
Thomas Griswold House Museum,
  35
Thomas Hepworth House, 359
Thomas Sessions House, 300
Thompson-Neely House, 275
Tiverton, Rhode Island, 147
Touro Park, 152
Touro Synagogue, 153
Tower Hill, 160
Transit Street, 139–40
Trenton, New Jersey, 219

Trinity Church, Maryland, 198
Trinity Church, Newport, 152
Trinity Church, New York, 232

U

Uniontown, Pennsylvania, 286
United First Parish Church,
  Quincy, Mass., 82
United States Military Academy,
  242
University of Virginia, 318–19

V

Vails Gate, 242
Valley Forge National Historic Park,
  278
Valley Railroad, 31
Van Alen House, 244
Van Cortland Manor, 241
Van Cortland Mansion, 233–34
Van Sant House, 275
Vincent House, 112
Vineyard Haven, 112

W

Wadsworth Atheneum, 13–14

Wadsworth-Longfellow House, 52

Wadsworth Stable, 28

Waitsfield, Vermont, 171–72

Walter Fyler House, 17

Wanton-Lyman-Hazard House, 151

Warner House, 123

Warren, Rhode Island, 142

Warwick Historical Society, 141

Washington College, 20

Washington Crossing Historic Park, 274

Washington Crossing Memorial Building, 275

Washington Headquarters Museum, 221

Washington Memorial Chapel, 279

Watermen's Museum, 300

Water Mill Museum, 238

Webb-Deane-Stevens Museum, 15–16

Webster Cottage, 129

Wells-Shipman-Ward House, 16–17

Wells-Thorn House, 104

Wentworth Gardner House, 122–23

West Hartford, Connecticut, 14–15

West Point, 241–42

Wethersfield, Connecticut, 16–17

Wethersfield Historical Society, 15

Weymouth, Massachusetts, 80–83

Wheelwright House, 120

Whitehall Mansion, 24–25

Whitehall Museum House, 149

White Horse Tavern, 153

White Point Garden, 354

Wickford, Rhode Island, 157–58

Wickham Farmhouse, 236

Wick House, 222

Wide Hall, 209

Wilbur House, 148

William Paca House, 204

William Pitt Tavern, 120

William Pratt House, 30–31

Williamsburg, Virginia, 300–306

Wilmington, Delaware, 189–91

Wilson Museum, Connecticut, 17

Wilson Museum, Maine, 58

Wilson-Warner House, 187

Windsor, Connecticut, 17–19

Windsor Locks, 18

Wing Fort House, 110

Winn House, 120

Winslow Cemetery, 76

Winslow-Crocker House, 108

Winslow House, 76

Winston-Salem, North Carolina, 344

Winterthur Museum and Gardens, 190–91

Winthrop Rockefeller Archaeology Museum, 306

Witch House, 98

Wolstenholme Towne, 306

Woodbury, New Jersey, 216
Woodman Institute, 124
Wren Building, 303
Wye Mill, 206
Wye Oak State Park, 206
Wyman Tavern, 128

York, Maine, 47–48
Yorktown Victory Center, 299
Yorktown, Virginia, 299–300

Zwaanendael Museum, 183

Yale University, 31–32
Yarmouth, Massachusetts, 108–9

ABOUT THE AUTHORS

Veteran travel writers PATRICIA AND ROBERT FOULKE have traveled the world together for more than forty years. Their 175 newspaper articles and 15 magazine articles have appeared in the *Christian Science Monitor*, the *Boston Globe*, the *San Francisco Examiner*, the *St. Petersburg Times*, *Walking*, *Sea History*, *Vista U.S.A.*, *Rotarian*, *Oceans* magazine, and other publications. They have also written 6 travel guides, among them *Daytrips, Getaway Weekends and Vacations in the Mid-Atlantic States*; *Daytrips, Getaway Weekends and Vacations in New England*; and *Exploring Europe by Car* (all published by Globe Pequot); and *Fielding's The Great Sights of Europe*. Robert is a professor emeritus of English at Skidmore College in Saratoga Springs, New York, and Patricia is a retired teacher.